The Paris Diary
and
The New York Diary

1951–1961

The Paris Diary
and
The New York Diary
1951–1961

Ned Rorem

New introduction by
Richard Howard

Preface to *The Paris Diary* by
Robert Phelps

DA CAPO PRESS • NEW YORK

Library of Congress Cataloging-in-Publication Data

Rorem, Ned, 1923–
  [Paris and New York diaries of Ned Rorem, 1951–1961]
  The Paris diary and the New York diary, 1951–1961 / Ned Rorem; new intro-
duction by Richard Howard.—1st Da Capo Press ed.
      p.   cm.
  Originally published: Paris and New York diaries of Ned Rorem, 1951–1961.
San Francisco: North Point Press, 1983.
  ISBN 0-306-80838-2 (alk. paper)
  1. Rorem, Ned, 1923– —Diaries. 2. Composers—United States—Diaries. I. Ti-
tle.
ML410.R693A3   1998
780′.92—dc21
  [B]   97-46200
                                                                         CIP
                                                                          MN

First Da Capo Press edition 1998

This Da Capo Press paperback edition of *The Paris Diary and The New York Diary*
is an unabridged republication of the edition published under the title *The Paris and
New York Diaries of Ned Rorem* in San Francisco in 1983, here supplemented with a new
introduction by Richard Howard and the 1966 preface to *The Paris Diary* by
Robert Phelps. It is reprinted by arrangement with the author. (*The Paris Diary*
was first published in New York in 1966 and *The New York Diary* was first
published in New York in 1967.)

Published by Da Capo Press, Inc.
A Subsidiary of Plenum Publishing Corporation
233 Spring Street, New York, N.Y. 10013

Introduction

"I am a composer who also writes." That settles our hash or, in the nature of the case, clarifies our ragout: the music comes first and—Rorem feels obliged to remind us, indeed sometimes rather sternly—need not concern us further as *readers.* *

With regard to "also writing," Rorem's finest, or let me say his most lapidary, prose is to be found in certain essays (occasionally masquerading as journalism) in his six volumes of music criticism and chiefly in his memoir *Knowing When to Stop.* Diaries are something else, something much more gritty than lapidary, and of course it is Rorem who identifies the difference:

> The distinguishing feature of a diary as opposed to a memoir is on-the-spot reaction, the writer's truth as he feels it, not as he felt it. If that truth is no more "truthful" for being in the first person, it does contain the defining character of immediacy.

These first diaries of Ned Rorem, published thirty years ago and written during the previous decade, inaugurate a series which continue with *The Later Diaries, The Nantucket Diary,* and end-

---

*I shall disobey my old friend in order to make two (perforce writerly) observations. First, that it is heartening to note how continuously and copiously the music, since it does come first, *has come*: there is no question of this composer's palaver serving as a sort of *pis aller* for drying up—as devil's work for hands compositionally idle; and second, that Rorem's taste (perhaps a corollary of his skill as a writer?) is more than judicious in his choice of the texts he so characteristically sets. Not even Benjamin Britten exceeds Rorem in the vitality and power of his literary inspirations.

lessly herald, in the manner of such things, *the last diaries* to which we are perhaps not entitled, but must, of course, covet. So intense, so distinct, and so reader-friendly have Rorem's diaries proved to be that they have not escaped the homage of parody; the late Howard Moss (whose fastidious lyric poems Rorem often—and quite as fastidiously—set) published an "Ultimate Diary" in *The New Yorker* and even reprinted in his *Instant Lives & More* this hilarious excruciation of Rorem's diaries while they were still coming out, as it were. My favorite entry from Moss's loving and lovable spoof, just in case you are a rolling stone, reads thus:

> Thursday. Half the Opéra-Comique seems to have fallen in love with me. I cannot stand any more importuning. Will go to Africa. How to break with C? Simone de Beauvoir, Simone Signoret, Simone Weil, and Simone Simon for drinks. They didn't get it!

The diarist proper, if that is the word, begins in 1951, quite oblivious of even the possibilities of parody; he is the classical—and classically profiled—Young Man from the Provinces in pursuit of his art and his identity. He releases a cascade of great names and self-lacerations that sets the tone—the temperament, to speak more musically—of the world he will aspire to and (eventually) inhabit, blessed by the fortunes of talent, brains, reading, wit, and exceptional good looks. Exceptional for the comic consciousness of his narcissism as well; in 1951, the same year he reads Genet (he must be one of the first Americans to do so) and fails to discern the art of *Our Lady of the Flowers* (*"au fond,* I am really a middle-class American"), he also puts himself in the arriviste's pillory:

> Famous last words of Ned Rorem, crushed by a truck, gnawed by the pox, stung by wasps, in dire pain: "How do I look?" It's harder to maintain a reputation for being pretty than for being a great artist.

Apparently within the first five years of diary-keeping, Rorem had arrived at Mae West's Law, that a diary, properly kept, would in the dreaded long run *keep him.* By 1955, aboard the S. S. *United States,* he articulated the formal truth of his second *métier*:

> A diary has impact only through the accumulation of unlimited observations (of which many are obsessive and recurring), never through the development of themes (for then it would no longer be a diary). . . . A diary necessarily has no form beyond the accidental one of improvisation; hence, though it cannot be a work of art (improvisation precludes this), perhaps it can be a masterpiece.

And if it can be, Rorem will work damn hard to make it so. *Behind him,* carefully studied, assimilated, and as often regurgitated, are the great examples of Henry James and Henry Miller—those icons of expatriation and alienated consciousness—and of his acknowledged Virgil through the inferno of *le tout* *Paris,* Virgil Thomson, with whom the diaries engage in a continuous agon from which Rorem is released only by a generous tribute he obliges himself to write for the dead master in 1989:

THE whole OF PARIS

> During the decades of our friendship (sometimes warm, sometimes cool) I never thought of him as less than this century's most articulate musicologist and most persuasive opera-maker. . . . Through his prose he convincingly evoked the sound of new musical pieces, and through his musical pieces he continues to evoke the visual spectacle of all our pasts.

Ahead of him, though, extends a darker prospect of ageing, dying, and what he calls "the horror of the carnal hunt, as though the cultural hunt weren't sufficiently atrocious." Sometimes the notations are grotesque in their self-engagement: "Dior died. I'm thirty-four"; sometimes they are flavored by a perfectly crystallized Gallic salt: "Claustrophobia is my fever and liquor my reward"; and at all times there is the spontaneous concentration of a realized self, which will make these books so much more than the decorative (though hardly decorous) *traces* we may have been beguiled into supposing them.

Indeed, the real reason I want to introduce these reappearing diaries—which certainly "need no introduction"—is precisely their fierce focus upon what Baudelaire called the evaporation and concentration of the self, by which he meant, I believe, that systole and diastole of expressive being that enables us to achieve transformation. Rorem is the one American diarist of our century who achieves something of that cognitive sharpness, that linguistic energy and inventive power that we recognize in the soliloquies and asides of the great Shakespearean characters: like Falstaff and Iago, he overhears himself and thereby changes himself, so much so that sometimes he no longer recognizes himself (how harshly the later diaries will deride the young man who here tells us "my philosophy was entirely based on the Quaker Church and American cinema"). All of us nowadays proceed, as Harold Bloom puts it, endlessly talking to ourselves, endlessly overhearing what we say, then brooding and acting upon what we have learned. In Rorem's often horrifying diaries, as in the Elizabethan dramatist, what we read is not so much the colloquy of the mind with itself as it is *literature's reaction to what life has become*. Of course there are felicities of local color to be found here ("the worst surprise was discovering that grownups had all the weaknesses of children, and none of the strengths"), and there are the entertainments of professional deformation ("opera should be seen and not heard"); but it is the respiring life of an overheard identity that is most grandly and graciously afforded in these diaries, the discourse of a man (that particularly symbolic man, *a maker*) changing and by his own words made aware that he is changing:

> Today it's June and I've no summer plans, no money, nothing to work on, no love; too much liquor and leisure, too much sleep, and too much worried humidity all over the whole world's sky. I'm thirty-four and waiting: it isn't easy. ..

Silly? occasionally; stupid? never; sagacious, more often than not, and assiduously attentive to that severest of suzerains, the overheard self. Rorem's is the truth of the most sapiently cultivated gardens: weed 'em and reap.

RICHARD HOWARD
New York City
October 1997

CONTENTS

Illustrations follow pg. 150.

Preface to
THE PARIS DIARY

A Portrait of the Diarist

*Je n'entre pas en ligne de compte que les
oeuvres plaisent ou déplaisent Elles
doivent "être."*   —JEAN COCTEAU

*. . . and there are always those to whom
all self-revelation is contemptible.*
          —F. SCOTT FITZGERALD

Here in lonesome, wistful, Puritan America, we are shy about
diaries. We have a few good ones—Alice James's, for instance—
but we make little of them. The ones we tend to read are im-
ports (other people's indiscretions)—Nijinsky's, Virginia Woolf's,
Katherine Mansfield's, Gide's—and we assure ourselves that we
are trespassing only because the diarist is important for some
prior achievement. His book is not an end in itself, never; and
even so, it is only when the text is unintimate and generalized,
as in the case of Dag Hammarskjöld's, that we read without guilt.

At the same time, the *idea* of diaries has haunted us. From
almost the beginning, and in our best writers, we can trace a
literary ideal which, whatever you call it, would look and read
like a diary if it were incarnated. Listen to Poe:

> If any ambitious man have a fancy to revolutionize, at one effort, the uni-
> versal world of human thought, human opinion, and human sentiment, the
> opportunity is his own—the road to immortal renown lies straight, open,
> unencumbered before him. All that he has to do is write and publish a very
> little book. Its title should be simple—a few plain words—"My Heart Laid

Bare." But—this little book must be *true to its title*. No man dare write it.
No man *could* write it, even if he dared. The paper would shrivel and blaze
at every touch of the fiery pen.

Or Thoreau:

> I desire to speak somewhere without bounds, like a man in a waking mo-
> ment to men in their waking moments.

Or Emerson:

> These novels will give way, by and by, to diaries or autobiographies—cap-
> tivating books, if only a man knew how to choose among what he calls his
> experiences that which is really his experience, and how to record truth
> truly.

Listen to Walt Whitman:

> No man can understand any greatness or goodness but his own, or the
> indication of his own. . . .

Or Howells (writing to Mark Twain):

> Even you won't tell the black heart's truth. The man who could do it would
> be famed to the last day the sun shown upon.

Or even Henry James (writing to a young poet):

> I am also envious—envious of the lyric mood, the lyric *leak*. You can say
> the egotistical thing—*I never!*

And then think of all those maverick books that keep turning
up in American literature, and which sound, more than anything
else, like audacious asides to the audience—the novelist or poet
appropriating a tone and a form which his official, public art does
not quite allow: *Eureka, The Enormous Room, The Crack-Up,
Death in the Afternoon* (or the late, as-yet-uncollected memoir
The Dangerous Summer), *The American Scene, The Tropic of
Cancer, Let Us Now Praise Famous Men, Images of Truth, Life
on the Mississippi*. . . . It is as though the whole tradition of
American writing, underneath its acquiescence to the properties
of the novel, the short story, the poem, the autobiography, were
yearning to give us some less indirect form of the writer's vision
and presence—something closer to himself.

I do not mean to sound dogmatic. I have no theory to advance. I simply sense, in much contemporary writing, an instinct

(unconscious in some writers, very self-conscious, even precious, in others) to invent, or subpoena, a form in which they can speak more intimately, more precisely, in terms of the authority which their own experience has conferred upon them. And this, in turn, always makes me wonder whether, as readers, we shall ever be able to help these writers to the extent of admitting to the literary canon the convention of the published diary. In other words, I wonder if, sooner or later, we may not allow a man with Poe's ideal to offer us his results directly, in the diary form he himself used, rather than oblige him to translate it all, so to speak, into what we then agree to call a piece of "fiction" (*Herzog*, for instance) and which, inevitably, we later ask biographers to translate back into his original terms. . . .

But this can be a dangerous train of speculation. It can make many people impatient and angry. Merely by asking if a diary could not be read for its own sake—as a novel is—I could be charged with unseemly curiosity, or, more gravely, with obscuring the difference between Art and Life, Imagination and Fact, Making Images and Bearing Witness. "We have art," said Nietzsche, "in order that we may not perish from life. . . ." And some of the time, certainly, he is right. We *do* need stories and songs and plays which seem impersonal, detached from their creators and uncluttered by a first person. But sometimes we also need something closer to one man's untidy essence. Oftener than I'd like to admit, I read a novel or a poem and am conscious—Nietzsche to the contrary—that we use art chiefly in order *to hide out* from life. At worst, this stifles me. At best, it leaves me hungering. Parable, fable, fiction are all fine. I want them. But whether I can gracefully justify it or not, I also want diaries, letters, marginalia, table-talk, all the nonofficial literary forms by which men have also revealed their mystery, disguises, wishes, feints.

All of which, I hope not irrelevantly, brings us to the present book, which amounts to selections from a diary kept between 1951 and 1955 by a young American composer who was living in France and North Africa. It differs from most diaries I have read chiefly in that it is better written, more aptly observed, less fearfully self-guarding. Insofar as there is any plot, it is self-portraiture and self-reckoning; but the elements that compose this particular Self are very exceptional.

At the time he is writing, the author is in his late twenties (he was born on October 23, 1923) and midwestern by way of Norwegian ancestors. He is gifted, good-looking, and in the circles in which he moves, celebrated for both. Besides being a composer, he is an imaginative social climber, a Quaker (though he sounds more like a Calvinist at times), an earnest narcissist. He is also an intellectual, a hero-worshiper, an excessive drinker of alcohol, and a lover—or more exactly, the sort of sensual man Montherlant must have had in mind when he said *"le corps fait trop l'âme pour qu'on doive s'excuser quand on parle de lui."*

At the same time (otherwise he could not have been so good a diarist) he is a born watcher, with a shrewd sense of theater, and rarest of all, the gift of recollection. It is one thing—luck, or connivance—to encounter Poulenc, Alice B. Toklas, Cocteau, Paul Eluard or the Vicomtesse de Noailles; it is another to be able to remember and record something they actually said, or did, or how they looked. Ned Rorem gives us specific *choses vues*, and so among other things his diary becomes a small but valid documentary on Paris in the early Fifties. By the time he arrived, Valéry had already said *"l'Europe est finie,"* and in some sense, perhaps it was. But part of Valéry's own Paris still flourished, and the last of a generation of its ringleaders—Cocteau, Poulenc, Auric—were still calling the tune. There was silliness and phoniness and pretention. There was also cultivation and appetite and enterprise. The arts were not necessarily better understood in Paris. But they did enjoy the prestige accorded elsewhere only to politics and sports and the weather. Moreover, it was not unknown for a great lady to offer a young composer the use of her salon for a concert and to invite a hundred people who had once heard Stravinsky and Ravel play their own music in the same precincts. Other gifted young Americans were living in Paris at the same time—William Styron, James Baldwin, George Plimpton. But they lived among themselves, on the Left Bank. Ned Rorem lived with the French, in the *16^e arrondissement*, and this is an important part of his self-portrait.

But it is his own personality that is principally embodied here, and which, at least for me, has made his diary such resonant and nutritious reading. In the decade since it was written, Ned has become, relatively speaking, well-known, even famous. He has been called "the world's best composer of art songs," and in the past season (1965–66) his first full-length opera, *Miss Julie*, had its New York premiere. But still, for many of his potential readers, he is probably not famous enough to enable his diary to offer itself as an adjunct to his career, as, say, Leonard Bernstein's might be, or Stravinsky's conversation books are. It must therefore be offered, and read, for its own sake—as a book of personal history, anecdote (gossip), glimpses, questionings—as a soliloquy, one man talking, originally perhaps to himself only, but now for anyone to eavesdrop upon.

Could anything be more vulnerable? More presuming, self-conscious, arrogant? And at the same time, more humble, courageous, generous? Even if the author were not someone I esteem as a composer and love as a friend, I would be moved and respectful. I might flinch at the egotism, or frown at the assumption. But I would want to remember that some of this reaction is my own doing. "To have great poets," said Whitman, "there must be great audiences too." The same is true of vulnerable diaries.

But let me not seem to exaggerate. No—this diary is not at all the "total" book that Poe dreamed of—"My Heart Laid Bare." Nor does it sustain anything like Thoreau's "waking" tone of voice. But here and there it comes closer to those peculiar and dangerous ideals than—well, than any other book published in America during the past year. Is this fatuous talk? Am I doing Ned Rorem the disservice of staking untoward claims for what, after all, is only part of one man's very ego-prone diary? If so, I am eager to implicate myself in whatever impertinence or bad taste may be involved. For as truly and needfully as I trust in any kind of literature, or in any use of our language, I believe in this genre of book—unconditionally; and for this particular instance of that genre, I am, at the very least, grateful.

Let me put it this way. In the secular, pulverized world we live in today, some of us have little or no sense of community, of

communion left. The forms may still be observable, in varying
stages of atrophy or mimicry. But community itself is hard to
come by. Yet whenever a writer, any writer, uses some semblance
of his own first person and tells me something about himself or
the world around him which only he could have known, then a
viable community of two is formed as I read. It can be a friend
or a stranger. It can be my son writing a letter from his prep
school, or it can be Marcel Jouhandeau writing a diary from a
Paris suburb. Someone speaks and I listen. For a time we make
a whole greater than our separate parts. I may not like what he
tells me, I may not understand him. I may suspect him of being
a liar, or self-deceived. But there he is—one unanonymous, unsure, all-too-human *semblable.* If I am not too prudent, I can
hear him, join him, as Thoreau wanted to be joined. But more
than the literary art is involved, and I must bring more than my
safe aesthetic responses. The encounter may be joyous. It may
also be maculate, messy, perturbing, as human relations so often
are. And if I am merely afraid of perishing, and quote Nietzsche's
half-truth, is it fair to blame only the other party, in this case,
Ned Rorem? Won't I myself be at fault, too, in my timidity, or
"good taste," or tenuous pride?

ROBERT PHELPS
1966

The Paris Diary

PART 1
May–July, 1951

Paris

No artist needs criticism, he only needs appreciation.
If he needs criticism he is no artist.

GERTRUDE STEIN

A stranger asks, "Are you Ned Rorem?" I answer, "No," adding, however, that I've heard of and would like to meet him.

Have been back in Paris over a week now. I'm never really happy here: not only because I drink too much and don't work very well, but also because I have no *chez moi* and am envious of all friends who do. It is spring with warm nights beautiful and sad. Most of the time I spend endlessly walking from quarter to quarter ("looking for love where it can't be found — waiting for love where it will not come"), and have memorized the entire city, knowing also where love *can* be found.

　　Lunch yesterday with Nora Auric and Guy de Lesseps. We talked of nothing but masturbation. Guy maintains that, yes, it *does* cause circles under your eyes, being an unshared act, an unbroken circle of sensations given to oneself with no true release.

Two years ago tonight (May 20th) I left New York for Le Havre, where the S.S. *Washington* arrived very early on a morning of screaming sea gulls and silver fog. France. And I looked toward the land knowing that deeper into it, behind those gutted buildings, lay the place where I would not have to bring myself. (Dr. Kraft had warned against the danger of displacement. He was wrong: displacement has made me new.) Very early, as on the morning of Christ's ascension, in a drizzle of gray toward a miniature country seemingly made of berets and real, live French stevedores, I descended from the boat, and my first long home has since become always the farthest away of dreams. The two months I'd planned to stay became two years, and may become two hundred.

The other day in Galignani's Julien Green bought me a beautiful Bible with gold-edge pages. Robert Kanters, browsing, saw us, and whispered to me: *"Quel puritain!"*

BUT NO   YOU WOULD BE SURPRISED   THE INSANITY OF THE BIBLE

"Mais non," I replied, *"Tu serais étonné. C'est fou comme la Bible peut faire bander, elle aussi!"*

CAN BE A WONDERFUL COMFORT, REALLY

Youth is beautiful, age ugly. But is the wisdom of age beautiful? We know nothing old we did not know as children; we merely submit essentially unchanged reactions to a wearier refinement. I detest subtlety; I like strength. Strength is never subtle in art or in life.

This afternoon I met Picasso. . . . Valentine Hugo had come to lunch, after which Marie Laure de Noailles sat me at the keys like a wise student to play my little pieces. Then Valentine (she who costumed Dryer's *Joan of Arc*) with her blond Anna May Wong bangs, bewitched by new blood, danced for me (at her age) *Le Sacre du Printemps* as she recalled it from that fatal day in 1913. . . . Later Marie Laure took me to a screening of *Los Olvidados* (Buñuel had, after all, been her *poulin*). We arrived late in darkness. The somber finish unprepared me for the coquettish tap on Marie Laure's shoulder when the lights went up. We turned: it was Picasso. Those jet bullet eyes both burned into my brain and absorbed me into his forever. I was so carbonized I forgot their glib exchange. . . . Later, with Jacques Fath, we went to dine in the country *chez les Hersent*, and I returned in time to meet Guy Ferrand's midnight train at the Gare d'Austerlitz.

Jennie Tourel, never better, sang *Schéhérazade* at the Empire. At *"ou bien mourir"* she threw her whole weight into the audience! . . . Tea with Ciccolini. *Souper chez* Fulco Verdura, Quai Voltaire.

I know I *can* compose and I know *how*; but I don't know *why* I came to this instead of to sculpture or poetry, or perhaps even dance. (Couldn't one kind of creator have been any other kind?) After ten years of chattering every known musical speech, of imitating now one and then another school, of wanting to become famous by writing like the famous, I've decided now to write again the way I did at eleven when I knew no one: *my* music from *my* heart with *my* own influences. It's important to be "better than," not "different from," and everyone has forgotten how to write nice tunes.

I guess this music is really *French* at the core (though I steal from Monteverdi occasionally, and pretty much from Bach naturally— not to mention what I hear at the movies, what I hear all around).

In New York I had already heard of Marie Laure de Noailles; I was aware of both the lady and her attributes, and on leaving for France in the spring of 1949 I was determined to know her. I arrived like any other francophile tourist with intentions of spending one summer. But from the outset that insular nation contradictorily greeted me with open arms: within a month I knew and—so much more important! —was known by most of the musical milieu.

My first meeting with Marie Laure took place that fall at the opera. Eager Henri Hell presented us. I said: "How do you do?" She turned her back. . . . Second encounter: the Méditéranée restaurant. She, to Sauguet: *"Je ne le trouve pas si beau que ça."* Sauguet: *"Ah, non? Mais vous lui ressemblez beaucoup, chère amie."* . . . Third time, *chez* Mme. Bousquet. Me: "I'm writing a ballet on your *Mélos* scenario for the Biarritz contest." She: "We'll see that you win it." And again turned her back.

After interludes in Morocco and Italy I returned to Paris for another siege. Then occurred my first contacts with Cocteau, Julien Green, Marie Blanche de Polignac, etc. But the Vicomtesse de Noailles remained *insaisissable*. One afternoon I learned she was to attend, that evening, a performance of *Yes Is for a Very Young Man*. I went, too, alone, in a black turtle-neck sweater. I approached her and her companion Charles Lovett and we adjourned to the latter's apartment. Marie Laure was simultaneously cool, coy, and cultured; I, playing the ingenuous American. She invited me to lunch next day, to various events the following week, painted my two portraits (one pale blue as a *voyou*, the other dark green as a Satie student), and I felt I was *in*. . . . A fortnight later we were to leave at dawn with Labisse for a month at Hyères. When I arrived for the departure at her house, 11 Place des États-Unis, they'd already left. This was the first of her endless "tests." So I got drunk with Boris Kochno (who was also to have gone) and we telegraphed to Hyères. (Such abject persistence has, hopefully, quit me: it's the prerogative of *le jeune arriviste*.) Marie Laure answered cordially that we should come down the following week, and we did.

There began our bizarre and fruitful friendship, our love affair. The fact that we were both born under the sign of Scorpio is what finally converted her.

At first I behaved as I felt she wanted me to. She encouraged gaudy and exhibitionistic comportment, partly in defiance of her formal background, partly to give herself an identity with the post-surrealist gang she hung out with. For instance: a few months after we met she gave me a party. It was to celebrate the première of my *Six Irish Poems* by the radio orchestra with soloist Nell Tangeman (whom Marie Laure hated: my soprano friends frustrated her because *she* couldn't sing). A buffet, groaning with champagne and smoked salmon and apricot tarts, voraciously stripped to a skeleton by rich old dukes and pompous movie queens elbowing their best friends as though they'd been starving for weeks, while Marie Laure, with a Gioconda smile, looked on. I arrived brash, open-necked and, above all, young. By 3 A.M. I'd downed who knows how many magnums. Whereupon, in front of everyone, I approached the Vicomtesse, and with no conscious provocation gave her a whack that sent her reeling to the floor. *"Mais il est fou!"* they all screamed, as I was restrained by the *maître d'hôtel* and Guy Ferrand. But the noble hostess motioned for them to release me, then rose with a bemused stare of utter satisfaction: she had triumphed before her friends: somebody new *cared.*

LE TOUT PARIS. It is easy to become intimately acquainted with the unapproachable innermost snob-life of Paris. You need only know one member, and in twenty-four hours (which includes the attendance of a single party) you will know them all, because each individual of this group knows no one outside. There are only about seventy-five members (of which the musicians are the classiest), and of course it is simple getting intimate with seventy-five people in twenty-four hours. . . . At a dinner offered by the delectable Mme. Hersent there was a discussion on new "motifs" for next season's Balls. Jacques Fath suggested that everyone come so completely disguised as to be unrecognizable. What inexhaustible boredom! I suggest that sixty-nine refugees from *la Place Blanche* be introduced into the grand salon and that *le Tout Paris* be told that these are other members incognito. Marie Laure proposes costumes so arranged that only a toe, a nipple, or a tongue be allowed to show. . . . Such is their conversation.

At fifteen I used to sit in school, scared at not knowing the answers (at being "dumb," hence conspicuous). For the night before, instead of doing my homework, I had been discovering love as thoroughly as I ever will. Were my classmates aware?

Each time I go to Henri Hell's we hear again Ravel's *Poèmes de Mallarmé*. This is delicious music, music that can be eaten. Is it because my first association with Mallarmé was the word *marmelade*? André Fraigneau once wrote: *"Les oevres de Mr. Ned Rorem . . . ont la candeur éblouissante du plumage du cygne de Mallarmé. Très personnelles, elles sont pourtant autant d'oiseaux qui se souviennent de la France. . . . "*

I bite away my fingernails and cuticle, realizing I'm practicing a sort of autocannibalism. We shed our skin completely every seven years; and I'm sure that without knowing it, we eat our own weight of ourselves during our lifetime.

One New York evening long ago, at Virgil Thomson's with Maurice Grosser and Lou Harrison, the four of us planned to dine in, and, as the maid was absent, we proposed preparing the meal ourselves. So everyone bustled about. Everyone but me. I stood around inefficiently not knowing how to behave. (I've always disliked domestic cooperation.) Maurice, peeved by my usual vagueness, handed me knives and forks, saying, "Here, make yourself useful!" But Virgil piped, "Leave Ned alone! Ned doesn't have to work. Ned's a beauty!"

Since birth I had lived by this slogan. I'll always be a spoiled child, but will never lose track of to what extent. Nor, I presume, will Virgil. I was working for him then as copyist, in exchange for orchestration lessons (every lucid word of which I'll always remember) and twenty bucks a week—of which I banked five! Such thrift impressed him, just as I was impressed by *his* thrift with notes. And so I composed my first songs, with an instinctive formal economy which I've since tried vainly to recapture.

All great [artists] have robbed the hives of diligent bees and, paradoxically, genius might be said to be the faculty for clever theft.
                                                              ENID STARKIE, Rimbaud

My song "The Lordly Hudson" (1947) is dedicated to Janet Fairbank, a kind and needed lady who died the day it was published.

Everett Helm gave a Christmas party in 1946. But it was John Edmunds who got all of us to write songs, and in their presentation as an "affectionate garland" to Janet, it was he who presided. After everyone had played his piece and Janet's initial thrill was calmed, the performers each sang. We did my "Alleluia"; then Romolo DiSpirito sang Poulenc. I had never heard "C" before, and at the final words "*Oh ma délaissée*" when Eva Gauthier began to weep, I began to compose as I often do when my brain is befuddled (this time on hot punch). . . . I went to meet George Perle and played for him what I could remember of "C." He retched! My guilt began. We drank a lot of beer and went through a lot of music (mostly twelve-tone, and Machault, on whom he was writing a thesis). But always "C" kept running through my head, getting increasingly distorted— more distant, changed. I'd heard it only once. . . . When I woke up it must have been Sunday. I wanted to write a song. The two sections of "C" that I liked were the same that everyone likes: "*De la prairie* . . . " and "*Et les larmes.*" . . . I recalled that Poulenc had skipped the voice a fifth to the ninth of a ninth-chord. Naturally this had to be changed a little. But I'd forgotten the tune, the rhythm. I looked around for a poem onto which I could force my vague ideas, and though I was sick of using Paul Goodman, I decided to borrow "The Lordly Hudson" (which was called simply "Poem" at that time). I'd already once made some not very successful notes for these verses but had thrown them out.

In one sitting I wrote the song. The composing, though accompanied by a hangover, was not the *result* of a hangover.

Here's how I did it: deciding on 6/8 because that means "water" I suppose, I first wrote the vocal phrases "home, home" and "no, no" —skipping a seventh and rising in the sequence, because Poulenc had skipped a fifth and dropped. Then I decided on the accompaniment pattern, and for the rest of the words I simply used taste and a melodic stream of consciousness. This can't be explained, but it's called "filling in" and sometimes by accident it works. What I mean is that after the precipitating inspiration of "home, home," all the rest was devised, often in variation form (it goes without saying that "this is our lordly Hudson" is merely an elaboration on "home, home").

Without any changes I gave it to Janet Fairbank who sang it under the title of "Poem," then "Driver, What Stream is it"—until Richard Dana said he would print it, and then Paul said "call it 'The Lordly Hudson.' " We all think now it's his best poem.

Any good song must be of greater magnitude than either the words or music alone. I wouldn't mind if this piece were played in concert on the violin; or, omitting the vocal line, as a piano solo.

I was always embarrassed when I played this song over for myself. It seemed too obvious, too schmaltzy. Like most composers I can't sing well, but I *can* be moved to tears when I sing. And so I used to write for the voice everything I couldn't do, until I realized that singing is the most natural of all expression. Anything a composer can't sing well enough to please himself, he shouldn't write. Of course when I had to sing it for others the embarrassment began. But nobody said it was horrible, so I began to like it (one can't continue to create well without being complimented). Then it won a citation for being the best song of 1948 and so I have practically no more guilt. No one dreams of the rapport with "C." (Is making a piece of art perhaps an act of shy but aggressive guilt?)

In finishing, I must say there's a misprint in the tempo mark. It reads: "Flowing but Steady—($\downarrow$. = 114)." Of course it should be $\downarrow$ = 114, for as it stands now it wouldn't be flowing but a whirlpool —nor steady, but jittery.

It is a *conscious* plagiarism that demonstrates invention: we are so taken with what someone else did that we set out to do likewise. Yet prospects of shameful exposure are such that we disguise to a point of opposition; then the song becomes ours. No one suspects. It's *unconscious* stealing that's dangerous.

Yesterday I met Man Ray. I'd always mistakenly thought he was French. For twelve years I've admired his pictures of the French Great, of sadness or sadism (women chained in a courtyard living among their own excrement), pictures of people. These things nourished the legend we Americans are raised on, that celebrities are of different flesh than others. Yet Man Ray himself is a meek little man, not particularly interesting despite his myriad contacts. In fact all the great I've met have disappointed me: they are too concerned with their work to be personally fabulous. They are like anyone, they are like me. Well, then where *are* the myths that, as an American, I craved in my youth? They must, of course, be the movie stars (I have never known one). Gloria Swanson is great through her person and not through her work. It is she, then, whose clothes we rip off in the street to see if she exists (would we do the same for Gide, for Einstein?). Therefore I must know a movie star: Lana Turner or Dietrich. (The men don't count, they don't wear make-up.)

I'd rather have known Nijinsky, whom I've venerated since childhood, for he was what we all would like to have been: a flying man. But I did actually meet Barbara Hutton Troubetzkoy in flesh and blood.

She's a legend to all Americans of my generation because the inimitable Miriam Hopkins fifteen years ago made a movie about her called *The Richest Girl in the World*, and the movies are our history book. With my poet friends at twelve, lovers of immortal women, we would discuss for hours the sumptuousness of Miss Hutton's scandals, her jade screen. . . . Later, in Tangier, I saw the house she'd built there, though I was told she never visited it.

Then one early evening recently, Marie Laure (because it is part of her profession, attending parties) took me to a "Cocktail" (as the French say) at the apartment of a Mr. Straus and wife who spend their life looking out onto the Place Vendôme. I was already high from a "Cocktail" at Mme. Bousquet's and one for Aix at the Véfour (joyously leading the Parisian life I despise in others), so that the apartment struck me as atrociously dreamy. Decorated only in purple (and its offshoots) the spacious place resembled a dignified funeral parlor: mauve bathroom and bedroom with mauve curtains (which were drawn), mauve light bulbs, sheets of lavender satin, and a dressing table with violet-tinted mirrors into which Louise de Vilmorin observed herself comb her hair. There was a flood of rosy-mauve champagne flowing from room to purple room, and in this flood floated dozens of beautiful thirty-seven-year-old pink gigolos in which *le Tout Paris* abounds. We stood dizzily at the window watching a pretty purple sunset disappear behind the gray stone of the Ritz Hotel. Then we drank more sparkling burgundy as the guests began to thin out. Pretty soon I realized through a haze that I had been left alone on a red velvet couch beside the liquor table where a white butler kept pouring and pouring with an elegant sneer. All was hushed. From a room I had not yet seen came the languorous strains of the *Rosenkavalier* waltzes. Suddenly people began running in and out, nervously looking for smelling salts and crystal-mauve cologne bottles, tearing their hair and exclaiming, "Oh, this time it's surely the end!" etc., while the waltzes played sadly on. Finally Marie Laure came up to me saying something like, "It's Barbara Hutton. She had a stroke and is dying of stomach cancer in the next room." I was now allowed to go in too, as long as I promised not to stare, to "act natural." . . . There she was, dancing moodily with one of the forgotten gigolos, the two of them trembling slowly in the middle of the floor. She can't have weighed sixty pounds and her moronic eyes oozed like black wounds from beneath an enormous hat. She fell upon the couch in a daze and asked to be alone with me for a moment, and though nobody liked that idea since I was not famous and they would rather have worried about being natural in front of Miss Hutton with smelling salts, etc., they acquiesced and went away to discuss her death. We talked about America and how nice we both were. Then everyone came back and I was forced to leave.

Afterwards, at about eleven, Marie Laure and I, each quite depressed, went to the Catalan for dinner during which there was a thunderstorm.

What is music? Why, it's what musicians do! It's whatever a given listener feels it to be. It's any series of sounds and silences capable of moving at least one heart. It may move us, but won't change us. The experience of exposure to music may change us (though one may be exposed for years with immunity), but not the music itself; it can only awaken and make us more what we already are. Art has no ethical purpose and does not instruct. The same "message" can be reiterated by different artists but is most educational when least artistic (i.e., most literal).

What is *good* music? The music that is good for you, that disturbs involuntarily like an erection. Longevity is no prerequisite since "good" is not an artistic but a moral ingredient. . . . But *great* music doubtless does deal with Time, though not with decisions of the greatest number. The mass does not decide. If Michelangelo did create for a mass (debatable) his subject matter was the same as that of lesser artists. He was great not because of his material or mass appeal, but because he was Michelangelo. The masses don't know the difference. Ask them!

Until yesterday music's very nature was such that explanation was unimportant to appreciation (proof of the pudding was in the eating); today music's very nature is such that explanation is all-important to appreciation (like certain political polemicism which theorizes beyond proportion to reality). I say *appreciation* advisedly: *enjoyment* is now a niggardly, if not an obscene, consideration. That composition should need such verbal spokesmen indicates that, for the first time ever, the very essence of the art has changed. There's no more room for the *petit maître*, that "second-rater" (if you will) whose talent is to delight or, even sadly, to move his hearer to dance and sing. There is room for only masterpieces, for only masterpieces have the right to require the intellectual (as opposed to sensual) concentration and investigation needed for today's "in" music. Masterpieces are made by the few geniuses born each century. Yet hundreds now compose *in the genius style* while denigrating those who compose *what they hear*. Certain painting now is healthy if only because it's witty. Music, as always, trails humorlessly behind the other mediums.

The fact that music is scandalously received seems automatically to validate it for those afraid of ultimately being proved wrong.

Since we all must live in a cage (also the artist: without restraint he is not one), I prefer my own design. If I've not joined the avant-garde (henceforth called the Academy) it's not that I don't approve of — or even agree with — them; it's because of a terror of losing my identity. Still, I'm capable of arguing any view or its opposite, depending on who I'm trying to persuade what to.

I have just finished *Notre Dame des Fleurs*. It's upsetting. Nobody reads Genet without suffering attacks of sexuality, and sincere, gross depression. But daily news reports of domestic crimes have the same effect on me (the wonderful Heirens trial in Chicago six years ago), and I cannot believe that Genet will be remembered.

For art is form, and also disguise. With him it is neither. How much more troubling is Jane Austen's torturous *lack* of orgasm, exquisitely wound in an air-tight tube, envied by the better detective-story novelists (*they* who are the writers of today).

Lesser French geniuses will last longer: Cocteau, because he knows where are Beginnings and Ends (art needs these); or Gide, because he knew that one does not write of love and crime in sexual description. Art is *greater* than being natural. It's concentration and suggestion.

But, oh, while it lasts, I quiver from the stimulus! (Though afterward I can do nothing with it.) I am told that in his film there is no *jouissance* — that it is touching.

In Washington, D.C., Glenn Dillard Gunn writes: "Rorem is the first successful modern romanticist."

If I am a significant American composer it is because I've never tried to be New. To reiterate: it's more pertinent to be Better than to be Different. American composers have the most dazzling techniques today; but they all have "masterpiece complexes" and write only symphonies. I believe I shall be ever more tempted to write just songs (the forgotten art) with as few notes as possible.

At Jacob's Pillow years ago a Mrs. Derby told my fortune. The cards said I had wasted myself since very early; that I'd never exerted my full potentialities because of another equally strong blocking force.

But it was not too late to choose between good and evil: growth of music, or ethical deterioration.

Picasso says *"que l'artiste qui se répète n'a été qu'une fois artiste."* He is wrong, and for himself as well. We all have but one obsession, though it can show itself in different ways. . . .

Eyes askew and wild hair! The only time I ever met Wanda Landowska was long ago when I went to show her my harpsichord concertino. No sooner had I entered than she took the pins from her hair, which fell in waves to her waist. "Take it," she said, "take it in handfuls and pull it, pull it *hard!* and never go tell people I wear a wig!"

    Her first words to D. P. had been: "You look so *sympathique*, young man! Are you a pederast?" *"Oui, Madame."* "Good. Now let's talk about music!"

Every day I find myself wondering in what manner I'll finally die. Of course, I am convinced that it will be violent, unpleasant, and soon, either by the hand of a friend near the Boulevard Clichy (though, unfortunately, I never take chances unless drunk, and drunks are never murdered)—or in a concentration camp for vaguer reasons, and by tortures of which one does not speak (this I wouldn't be able to avoid by will). . . . Perhaps I write this from fear, knowing that what is written does not occur. I feel that I shall die in "a certain way" before I grow old; I'm not sure of it and don't want it but I feel it. I have no idea if this will be by trade or war for the two things are equal in my soul. . . . Some people just *do* die in certain ways: Julien Green will die in a certain way, as did Maurice Sachs and Jean Desbordes; Henri Hell will not, nor Xénia, nor did Dino Lipatti (though he was very young, like Mozart, like Janet Fairbank). Bérard died in what I call a certain way. Boris Kochno wants to but probably won't. Other people just die, whether they are young or old. It's hard to explain why. Sometimes we are quite surprised.

Death is a private affair, and the secret of its duration (when we learn it) should never be divulged. A friend said (rather ingenuously, I feel) that far from fearing death he hoped for total lucidity at the end so as to savor that supreme moment. . . . Really there's no relation between life and the death which so illogically concludes it. Lucidity? What difference if we are in a coma?—comas are part of life. The pearly gates won't be appreciable through a state which in life we name *lucid*.

And that friend continued: "You too are dying already from birth, and any stranger passing in the street carries off a shred of you in his memory." . . . *I* feel we live when we live and die when we die and those facts are unrelated. If strangers steal my shreds, don't I steal theirs? Who gives without taking? Sometimes I even feel quite swollen (though the earth, I believe, keeps its own weight). Is a *chef d'oeuvre* the less beautiful, the more old, for the million pairs of eyes that have converged upon it?

Socrate of Satie. Yesterday I sang it through to myself for the first time since I bought it along the *quais*. (I later stole an old copy from Marie Laure, dedicated to Valentine Hugo in Satie's remarkable hand; this is one of my treasures.) I first heard it around eight years ago when Virgil Thomson sang it for me at a piano in the New Jersey countryside. All the 1920-Paris-New Yorkers had a copy, sacred as the Bible but infinitely rarer, just as Falla's Harpsichord Concerto is the golden calf of young South Americans. But I wasn't able to really know Satie's *Socrate* (Plato's I'd forgotten and known and reforgotten) until last fall. As I had no piano, Michel Girard let me come to work at his house every afternoon (that is where I wrote *Mélos*). The first day I arrived alone into this most beautiful home in Paris, 56 rue de Varenne, with the best piano in France, high ceilings, and three nervous incestuous Dachshunds with Wagnerian names. I had on my famous Kelly-green sweater. A servant gave me a Coca-Cola, then left me with the dogs beneath the high ceilings and my new score of *Socrate* with which I sat down on a velvet piano stool and began to sight-read. . . . I seldom come across more than one new work a year which upsets me, for masterpieces are quickly known if one is starved, and my adolescence was an impatient one. I think that every musical and literary work that I love most today, I knew and loved at seventeen. Because a receptive person discovers early what he seeks, and his inclinations rarely change. . . . Being Norwegian, I don't often cry. But when Michel came home that Monday night he saw me at the piano, a green stain smeared with tears at Socrates' death. Julien and Robert de Saint Jean (who live next door at 52 *bis*) then showed up to dine that night and we talked of nothing else. I remember I got very drunk on *marc*. It's hard to know at the instant who is the more moving: Plato or Satie. Hugues Cuénod, though he sings this work marvelously (so "whitely"), feels that much of it is arbitrarily, not inevitably, monotonous. . . . Yes, *Socrate* is a piece for composers: we all know it by heart and sing it to each other but it never has a public performance.

I permit people to think they're "communicating" with me, but they aren't really. I need their love, not their complicity. Yet whatever happens to me — that I *allow* to happen to me — is my life. Tomorrow, in six weeks, in ten years will I be reconciled to dying? Do we never change? Are we indeed *alive?* or is that word an invention?

Nadia Boulanger, to everyone in the musical world and to thousands out of it, is the most remarkable pedagogue of our century, and perhaps (who knows) of all time. I've just come from a necrophilic representation at *l'eglise de la Trinité*. Lili's funeral is more or less restaged there annually, to an accompaniment of her compositions performed with taste. Each guest is greeted with a tear-stained smile by Nadia Boulanger. Now I know why she is as she is.

Had Lili (surely far from greatness) not died thirty years ago, her acutely Roman sister might today be unknown. Certainly in those early days Nadia's *soeur cadette* was her dearest thing, so that young death was a canonization. Nadia has since profitably devoted her maiden life to a shadow with substance. Her sister having been her final treasure, she's ever after shunned all others of that sex (all but those stooges who *solfège* like machine guns but have the talent of octopi), and symbolically espoused each gentle youth in her vicinity. This she accomplishes as only a strong and pious woman could: by fortifying the myth of technique. Only a female (and uncreative) could have built within herself the most spectacular musical métier in the world today. Hers is the search for a true spark among those crackling in her synthetic electricity, a shimmer attacking others who fear to make love.

This shimmer exploded into flame just before the war, in Boston, where she was the chief guide for any composer anywhere (a prejudiced guide, of course: all great spirits are). Though I'm told she'd already begun to long again for countesses at her command.

The flame's extinction (if such it may be called) came in the late forties when the new young Americans emigrated to Paris like good shepherds bearing dubious gifts. But they found (with the change of air) they didn't now need her. Does she know she's been cheating herself for thirty years? Nothing's more tragic than a teacher. She was a grand one.

Now, at her "Wednesdays," she moves like an automaton with still enough oil in its unreal veins to provide transfusions for certain human ladies. But the boys? Who was her prize? Jean Françaix? How can she help but resent the creative male too, the robber who, with her help, stole her sister's genius?

Realizing her notable lack of gift she has herself become a countess. She *receives*, and in a manner unrivaled for quaintness. Along with her yearly memorial for Lili she offers a weekly wake for her own virginity. She has been generous in her masochism and it has often been fruitful. One observes the fruits each Wednesday at the wake. "No, it's worse than a wake," says Xénia, "for at wakes they feed you!"

My visit to Cocteau—to "the inspired Jean," as Paul Goodman calls him—was paid Friday at eleven in the morning. A perfect, sunny day. I was in a state of terror which wouldn't have taken hold if I had just been going to see him cold. But I'd written him a warning of my approach in two flirtatious letters (snapshots of myself enclosed), and received eloquent and equally flirtatious replies.

He lives at 35 rue Montpensier in a smallish and very low-ceilinged apartment overlooking the Palais-Royal garden, the hordes of playing children, and the Véfour restaurant. (He can wave to Colette who lives on the same courtyard, but he spends most of his days now with his friend—Paul, from the film of *Les Enfants Terribles*—in the country at Milly; he can work nowhere else.)

He opened the door himself, and immediately showed me into a tiny room at the right where he followed, locking the door, after telling the maid not to bother us for two hours. This tiny room had a tiny bed with a scarlet spread piled high with books, prints, current art and literary magazines, none of the pages of which was cut, a desk and a drafting table (each also piled high with books), a telegraph set (out of order), and a blackboard reaching to the ceiling, on which was a chalk drawing by Jean of a boy's profile, a Siamese cat (female). . . . Cocteau himself wore a floor-length sky-blue dressing gown cut like a medieval priest's; the sleeves completely covered his hands, though his gestures were so violent that I caught frequent glimpses of the longest fingers I have ever seen. His voice had no relation to the one we've heard at the movies: it sounded rather higher; he talked incessantly. He didn't sit down once, but continually paced the little room, occasionally petting the cat in passing. His favorite words are *con* and *emmerder,* and he scarcely makes a sentence without one or the other. Yet everything about the congested atmosphere was elegance itself: none of those crumbling corners one finds in even the grandest French homes.

At no time did I feel the hot, lazy, demoralizing magic which proved so fatal for Maurice Sachs during his friendship with Cocteau twenty years ago. Nor did I find him beautiful. He did strike me as more "sincere" than I would have guessed, and *au fond* has the tone of a real artist. From his social style (that of an actor) I have no reason to believe that the identical conversation was not repeated with the next admiring young American who came to call. . . . Nevertheless I tried to talk as much as I could, and as he ends every phrase with a brutal *quoi* or *hein*, it's impossible not to answer. Each time I said something with which he agreed, he would role it up into a "cliché" (a *formule*, the French say) and throw it back to me. Though we seemed almost always in accord (far from passively) I can think of no one who might fatigue me more, so stereotyped has he become, as though he were before one of his own mirrors! He had the graciousness to ask if I'd learned French as a child along with English. On learning I'd been speaking it just a year, he feigned astonishment.

We spoke *en somme* of three things: how, why and where the creator does or should create; how a possible war should effect a creative person; sex and crime in American cities (other than New York). . . . Creating is like shitting; indeed, this was the image he used. *"Quand j'ai chié mon Orphée,"* though he might have said, "when such an idea fell from heaven," which for me would be more expedient. The artist must grow ever more selfish, must never seek to rearrange the world. *"Il doit s'en foutre des guerres. . . . "* Like all the French, Cocteau is more amused than fascinated by Dr. Kinsey (and by psychoanalysts).

I forgot to ask if his star came off an alchemist's hat, and if he used it when signing checks.

Is a fugue the pointless conversation of persons in too-perfect agreement? Or someone insane talking to himself?

PART 2
July, 1951

Hyères

We arrived here at three this morning, Marie Laure and I, hideously out of sorts. Fifteen hours by car during which the only interesting sights are when passing through Lyon, the one French city that intrigues me. It's closed and cold and terrible, and despite its lack of art, the black mass is still celebrated here if one knows how to find it. Seemingly endless miles of *quais* bordered with seven-story buildings (without elevators), all identical in the evening sunlight. And wasn't it in Lyon where George Perle, once during the war, entered a *pissotière* and, looking down, saw there in the urine a decapitated human head?

The night before leaving Paris it seemed as if I had already gone. This was Friday. As always before quitting the great city I took a long walk, this time going far up by *l'Observatoire*. Of course I knew something would happen, since Experiences on the eve of a departure are inevitable (and become more meaningful than similar occurrences at other times, when one can reject or postpone them. Love is Resignation, which means an incident one does not know how to postpone). So, almost to Boulevard Montparnasse, I hear feet and then a bespectacled young man stops me. Would I like to visit his home and *"bavarder un peu"*? He lives on the third story of a house on the darkest street in Paris. I find myself in a huge room lined with books, at least ten thousand books, and all in Russian. My host is a professor of that language, and I eat two small oranges and drink a cup of very good coffee (as I have walked a great deal). It is midnight. Then the guessing game begins; it is always the same. "You have a slight accent; may I ask if you are of foreign origin?" (This question inevitably followed by: "You must be a student *aux Beaux Arts!*") I hate these interrogations which give me a personality when I would prefer to remain anonymous; anonymity and lack of profession make the game more exciting (not to mention getting it over quicker, which is convenient if one has things to do early next day. In strictly anonymous encounters I generally play a role as far removed from my

"natural" one as I can manage: this stimulates me). I almost say I am
Dutch (that is what I'm most often taken for), then decide this is too
revolting, and admit to being American, his Russian books not-
withstanding. He says that although he's an accomplished linguist,
English is the one language he could never learn — which gives me a
feeling of superiority. I decide to tell him I have read *Stavrogin's
Confession* and also Gogol, and that Prokofiev made an opera out of
The Nose (though it may have been Shostakovich who made it a
ballet, but in any case my host wouldn't have known). He falls out of
his seat, since until then I have said almost nothing and he has taken
me for the anonymous nonprofessional. . . . I tell him I am deeply
fond of Russian literature; that I feel I have a French soul; that, although I read much less now than when I was fourteen, my taste has
not changed and probably never will; that I feel that people whose
taste changes have no taste; that I am twenty-seven (he had obviously taken me for younger).

Now he no longer finds me a stray cat ("stray cat" is what he
said) and I feel he is drawn to me, and as I consider this a weakness,
I become bored. Therefore I use his phone to call Marie Laure and
speak in English to increase the mystery. Marie Laure advises me to
go to bed soon as we're leaving early. On hanging up I tell the Russian
teacher that the woman with whom I've spoken has told me to retire
early and that I must therefore leave. This is dangerous, since there
is nothing sadder than the parting of a brand new friend, and had he
been a maniac or something (they never are) he would have killed
me on the spot. I say I am a composer, and he gives me a green leather
edition of *Anna Karenina* as I have never read it (on reaching home
I inscribe it myself). I leave, but to my aggravation he decides to
accompany me as far as Boulevard St. Germain. There we say goodby.
. . . It is a beautiful summer night of the kind that only happen in big
cities. . . .

On the rue de Rennes I come across Bel-Amich, who says where
did I get that book at such an hour, as he had seen me walking by
earlier and I wasn't carrying any book. We go for hot milk on a café
terrace and, as I am telling him where I got the book, a man at the
next table asks me for a light, and while I am giving it to him he
strokes my hand and whispers can he see me tomorrow. His face is
pleasing, but I answer that alas I cannot as I'm leaving town (forgetting

the danger once again, that the parting of a brand new friend, etc.).
He says he has never seen eyes like mine, gives me an address, asks
me to write. Marie Laure thinks I should.

It's during the mornings that I try to do my composing here, but I'm
finding it difficult to get back into the habit; to write something that
is more than "well made" and which ignores the surroundings. . . .
Every day at eleven Thérèse, *la bonne*, comes into the music room
where I am attempting to work, and brings me a tray of coffee. She
doesn't say a word and steals out quickly, for she thinks I am a genius and is respectful (not wishing to disturb my inspiration with her
worldly presence). This amuses, but at the same time worries me, as
Thérèse knows less than I how feeble are my efforts at this moment.
And if I cannot work well, then I have not the right to eat.

Alcohol, like sex, is an end in itself. But art is not. For artists art
unfortunately isn't enough. Our gifts aren't necessities, they're luxu-
ries we're chained to.

I have allowed Marie Laure to read this book and she says I have a
childlike quality. This delights me, for in my heart my outlook has
never advanced beyond that of a seven-year-old. *Et tant mieux!* I
know no artist who thinks with the realistic disillusionment of adults.
I met Picasso once and then for an instant: he was very old, but his
presence dazzled with the enthusiasm and naïveté of an infant.
     The quiet of the Midi is exhilarating, and Marie Laure an al-
most ideal companion (I would not have believed it). We have been
just the two of us now for days, and we work like insects. *Mélos* is
finished. At night we read (I Gogol, she detective novels) or we talk
about wars, and the martyr Jean Desbordes whose eyes were ripped
out and beetles put in. . . . I play *Socrate* three times daily, and I
orchestrate. Also I'm posing for the third picture of my life. Still, there
are dramas: either the dog Diego has trembling fits, or Boris Kochno,
being drunk, frightens us, as we are all alone on a country estate. . . .
The other day they asked me why I did not like the English and I

said because one cannot tell the men from the women: the race has
so crumbled that the sexes have merged and there is no further relationship between the modern Englishman and Shakespeare, between
the modern Englishwoman and Jane Austen.

What is more loathsome than a totally educated man? I think no genius (at least in our day) is really well acquainted with arts other than
his own. Kafka hated music. Painters know nothing besides painting.
An artist does not *need* the other arts. A visit to a gallery sterilizes
me, but even a bad concert is my inspiration.

Marie Laure took my measurements (lying on my back, arms outstretched) and found them to be according to the classic golden law.

In my new canary-yellow shirt (from Chez Vachon in St. Tropez), my
golden legs in khaki shorts, my tan sandals, and orange hair, I look
like a jar of honey.
    Paul Eluard and his wife Dominique have come over from St.
Tropez to spend the evening and the night. In expectation I panicked,
as I always do when I must meet somebody new, even the janitor's
daughter. As always happens, it passed more easily than I would have
thought. For Eluard is all ease and quiet beauty. He is deeply sun-
tanned (they had spent the afternoon on Ile du Levant, the land of
nudists), has white hair, a black sweater, and an elegant voice. To
him the Word is All—only the human voice has real meaning. Therefore Poulenc's rendering of his poetry into song leaves him cold, as
he does not recognize the music he had heard when writing the verses,
nor can he understand the word when sung (at least if it's Bernac, he
says). He likes declamation; he likes *Socrate* and *Pelléas*. . . . But a
musician must never speak too long with a poet since they are both
making the same thing (all art is the singing of old songs with new
words) in unrelated ways; to each his own device is the more important, though he may admit the other's is more moving. . . . After dining we sat on the terrace and he read us Baudelaire ("La Madonne")
and a half-hour's worth of his own poems in that magnificent slow

speech of tragedians. I am still not sure that poetry should be read aloud. But how the French love their language! They will say, for instance, of Racine, "He writes beautiful French"; whereas *we* say, "Shakespeare writes beautifully." . . . Eluard feels that all creators are women in men's bodies, that he himself has a woman's instincts: *"Je me sens femme pénétrée"*: that it is therefore natural that they seek to sleep with men, or with the various substitutions of men found in real women. Artists like himself or like Picasso who prefer women, he considers abnormal: *"Picasso et moi, on est des vieilles gousses!"* He thinks it better to be drunk than sober; maybe he's right. I have always felt it unimaginative to want the head clear in order "to see things as they are."

Cocteau says all creators are half man and half woman, and that the woman is insupportable.

Coincidence: Mme. Eluard lived from 1941 to '44 in Fez at the Hôpital Cocard where Guy worked for years and where I visited daily. . . . She has now gone to the tower studio and is asleep. I am alone up in my room. The night is stifling (this fourteenth of July without firecrackers) so my windows are wide open and I can hear Marie Laure and Eluard still down on the terrace drinking cognac. It's very sad. They are talking about *me*.

This evening I told Marie Laure innocently (though I realized it was the malicious result of strange and logical images passing before me since morning) of a letter to my mother in which I explained that our relationship was "strictly platonic." She was thunderstruck; and I, nonplussed by her reaction. After a half-an-hour of restraint she fell into spasms of tears, and I grew aware of my crime. Can one have his mother and another woman at the same time without unhappiness? If the woman is happy, the mother is not, and vice versa. My ignorance had wounded, and the scene which followed shook me. . . . Later we had a long whimsical talk on the nature of family structure, with the kind of fresh and precipitating inspiration that comes after vomiting.

The Eluards (of which he the wife, she husband) left us this morning; tomorrow the whole Auric clan arrives. And the peace of Hyères becomes like the nervous last scene in *Petrouchka* where bear overlaps nursemaid in the snow and everybody dances.

Why must we know so many people? Because any single person has his limits. One will begin to repeat himself after ten minutes, another after ten days, a third after three months, and a very sly one after a year. Sooner or later we know them all, and all their secrets. Each goes in his orbit, a cycle of subtleties which are our own and which we have known since the age of two. Each of our *clichés* becomes new insofar as we expose it to a new person. But *we* stay the same. Therefore no two people on earth are sufficient unto themselves.

Julien Green is obsessed by statues. Not just in his novels; but also, from one standpoint, his conversation and life may be said to consist of little else (like myself, he is essentially Protestant—despite his Catholicism—and therefore suspicious of the slightest motion of his little finger). . . . One day, while walking together through the Tuileries, on our way home from one of the innumerable Paris teashops of which only Julien knows the whereabouts, he told me that once he had a plaster cast made of one of the half-life-sized Apollos from the Louvre. But he had toyed with it so much that it had finally collapsed. . . . He then told me he used to have a friend—a fifteen-year-old Swedish writer of bad verse—who fell in love with one of the statues in this very garden (by the fountain near rue Cambon). One evening during the war he arranged to get locked in the garden, whereupon he raped the statue all night long, and then fell out of love. . . . Julien says that his idea of Paradise is to be alone in a room full of nothing but beautiful statues. And I, being American, quite understand the fear of all that is flesh.

Love implies a soldering anonymity which repels me. Or did. . . . I am never *with* anyone, *anyone*—but nobody knows, because my barriers are made of glass. . . . Quarrels in France strengthen a love affair, in America they end it.

Once we've defined a thing, the thing is frozen, breathes no longer. To "know" is to be steile. To "look for" is to be young. All artists are by definition children, and vice versa.

"When I was a little boy we spent summers on a farm where I had a passion for physical cruelty, in spite of attempts at self-control. Hating myself, I used to go mornings toward the roost and kick the chickens from their sleep, leaving them helpless on the floor to squawk and flop. I then went smiling for breakfast, my young father blaming the crime onto foxes or snakes. . . . As a farm boy I experienced a constant turning turmoil as I carved spears from hard birchwood, for I never enjoyed inflicting pain; I simply could not help it. Yet the desire enlarged for acts against animals. I'd just destroyed barnyard birds, but wished now to injure mammalian creatures. A strong decision — but I had strength of character! . . . I meditated. I was going to maim the horse. A perfect horse he was, with a sleek black back, thick-legged and masculine, and gentle intelligence. Day after day I dreamed in my hayloft which afforded a view over this horse's stall, a small manger where it was impossible to turn completely around. Day after sunny day in the dark of the barn I took my six sharp birch spears; my precocious intention was to thrust these into six parts of the horse: the two eyes, the nose, the spine, the genitals, the mouth. . . . And I looked down onto the horse, watching his elegant male motion. An hour passed. I looked down, and two more hours went by, and my nervous perspiration dampened the hay with a smell of sick terror. And I tensed, and took one of my spears and sunk it deeply between the animal's shoulders. (I wanted, you see, I *wanted* this horse to *pay attention* to me!) Fright. He reared foaming and bellowed and shook and couldn't escape, quivering as he was with hurt. And I, fearful, slid from the loft and began running from the barn, but at the door stopped to look back. The horse was upright, shaking, his hooves crossed upon the gate of his stall, and large tears flowed on his face. And he said: 'Little boy, don't run away or be afraid. If I reared up it was only because the pain of your weapon shocked me so. I was not going to hurt you. O, come back.' . . . But I walked from the barn, and went slowly into the hills that surrounded my young father's farm. Here I sat beneath a pine and felt absolutely nothing and breathed the odor of needles and cones. Far below I could see the barn and still hear howling as the horse tried to extract the spear from his back. Then the noise became more and more feeble until it died away all together. . . . But like unexpected thunder an insane shriek occurred and I knew the horse had forced himself through the wooden doorway. I waited for his revenge. But he went free, escaped to die, whinnying off through the trees in the *opposite* direction instead of galloping over to stamp out *my* small life."

The Aurics are daily visitors since they live next door. Nora has given me a marvelous Mexican shirt (cream and lavender brocade), and Georges took me to visit his mother, age eighty, to whom he recounted the first time he ever saw me: in June, 1949, I had just arrived in France, and was sitting late on a bar stool at La Reine Blanche, ordering innumerable cognacs with innumerable admirers and singing themes from *Le Sang d'un Poète* to Auric who spoke no English. Two years later such behavior would seem undignified, to my great, great sorrow.

Last night we had a *bouillabaisse* which I couldn't touch because of the terror in its preparation. The secret is to throw live sea creatures into a boiling pot. And we saw a lobster who, while turning red in his death, reached out a claw to snatch and gobble a dying crab. Thus in this hot stew of the near-dead and burning, one expiring fish swallows another expiring fish while the cook sprinkles saffron onto the squirming.

How old was I? ten? eleven? when I wrote Jean Harlow requesting her autograph. She answered: "To Ned Rorem with sincere best wishes—cordially, Jean Harlow." For years afterwards I signed my letters "Cordially."

Late last night, on returning from an adventureless evening in Toulon with Raffaello, I found this note from Marie Laure slipped under my door:

> *My own beloved Ned,*
> *I think I must explain why I love you so much. You are the total expression of what I have loved or still love in fragments. My whole*

life seems to have been a drive with pitchfalls [sic] towards you: marriage, children, lovers, friends and that everlasting quest of beauty and refusal of ugliness: my only conception of God or the universe. You are a little more than sex, a little more than childhood, much more than nature, and more than death; for if I died, my ghost would still haunt you, more living than any other alive female. Whatever you do, whatever I do, whatever happens I will always love you because I have loved you and you are also more than time and space. For the space in which you move is beauty and the time music. And what is at the moment of beauty will always be. So sleep well my love.

(signed with her famous "leaf" insignia)

Evenings here we play four-hand music, the *Epigraphs antiques* —or I play the phonograph: my skillful string quartet, or old Ella Fitzgerald records which remind me of Olga and the summer iciness of Lake Michigan where I first learned what an orgasm was. We also drink cider (I've had not a drop of liquor for nine days). . . . And in the morning I begin to read alone with my (famous Noailles-type nearly American) breakfast, so that I can't smartly realize the difference between my book and my dream.

Being myself a coward, a cheat, a weak-kneed opportunist, stingy and dishonest—I despise these things. Yet I have scant respect for courage and find that nine times out of ten it's the result of dullness or vanity. Not to cheat is to ignore love. I must admit that strong legs are exciting to behold, but I always walk swiftly, and besides I could strangle you if I so desired (still I've always been afraid, nearly ashamed of my strength. I know why). . . . Creative men have always known where to look; this is what makes them seem selfish on the first level, but on the second (and on all the following rungs as far as the sky) they are the most generous of all. Sincerity is the virtue of tiny folk; I prefer a many-faceted personality. . . . Yet how long can this go on, since I continue to detest myself because my motives are irreconcilable.

In finishing *Opium* I wondered first, and especially, how Cocteau could have corrected the proofs of a book that flows with such improvisatory swiftness. But he did. Today he speaks with as equal intimacy of Proust, Debussy and Diaghilev, as he does of flying saucers; he wants it to be said in one hundred years that he embraced all. He would like also that there be a confusion of epochs about him, that people say, "But when exactly *did* he live, anyway? His life span seems to have been gigantic." At the same time, today, he receives countless young fans since he feels he's beginning to be forgotten as a person. Like Chaplin, he's beginning to be forgotten as a person. Like Chaplin, he's exceeded the permitted glory (*"il a dépassé la gloire permise,"* as he himself said of Picasso) and become immortal during his lifetime. He therefore quite naturally never listens to anyone else, as there's no one else to listen to.

Oscar Dominguez maintains he's seen three flying saucers, but of course this is impossible, since not only is he nearsighted (I myself have known what glasses are since thirteen), a Surrealist, and an alcoholic but he has no religion. I like to think of flying saucers as holy stars announcing the Rebirth. Today is the first moment in the world's billion-yeared history that we have had a universal poem. And it is a beautiful one.

Lunch at Charles de Noailles's in Grasse. Cocteau is the only other guest. He speaks of Garbo. "Because she has carte blanche she only goes where she's not invited. Last week in Paris she knocked unexpectedly at my door. I was busy, *mais que voulez-vous?* there's only one Greta. I took her to eat at Véfour. In her baby French and my baby English we talked of how sad, how sad that she was afraid to mime the Phèdre that Auric and I created for her last year. After coffee she vanished into the afternoon. Next day I lunched alone, again at Véfour. The headwaiter asks: 'Monsieur Cocteau, that lady yesterday—was it Madeleine Sologne?' I explain it was Garbo. 'Well,' he replies, 'I knew it was *someone* like that!' "

Garbo today might be hailed with—*cheers of disappointment.*

Julien, in his agitation, persists in referring to Marie Laure as Marie Blanche, and then blushes. *"Tu rougis,"* I say to him. And Marie Laure adds, *"Et moi, il me blanchit."*

And there was the alcoholic who, two hours before he was to be burned at the stake, began drinking (from a bottle bribed from the jailer — to lessen pain — though just a little) to such an extent that memories of all the other sad and happy liquor debauches teemed up around him. So in his execution he was consumed in a sparkle of nostalgia, not to mention burning quicker because of the brandy in his stomach.

What disappoints in Sade is his lack of obsession (I've just thumbed through *Les 120 journées de Sodome*); as a matter of fact he's rather gay. He's too general; whereas it's precision, singularity, choice, which makes a pervert. When I have finished the sexual act (as I see it), I say silently to the other: thank you for having allowed me — without anger — to think my very special thoughts. . . . When I was little I thought that "intellectuals" never made love — that they could never be troubled by what troubled me. (They played the harpsichord, so how could they hear dirty jokes?) I do not know, and am afraid of what's often called Life; I avoid experience, which nevertheless hurls itself at me. Yet I have memories. Unfortunately nostalgia cannot be manufactured consciously, or I would go have a picnic at the suburban zoo with a close friend just to remember this pleasant day years hence.

What have I done in my weeks of Hyères? I read fourteen books; went to a mediocre Aix performance of *Figaro* with Marie Blanche de Polignac, Robert Veyron-Lacroix, and Jacques Février (the first and third of whom stagger to a point where it's sure they'll each live fifty more years: their habits are strong as statues'); saw, and was saddened by (as always with great men, knowing their pain to be as ordinary as mine) Eluard again, this time in the distasteful town of St. Tropez; became a lush yellow-tan so that Robert said as I ate my fruit, *"Tu as l'air d'être une pêche qui en mange une autre"* (but I ate raw carrots too, for, like an alcoholic, I care for my health); orchestrated, orchestrated, and orchestrated; almost finished my *Five Eclogues*; wrote stacks of letters; became even closer to my dear Marie Laure; lunched with Poulenc who, with Auric, becomes less and less sure of himself and manifests this by speaking of the inadequacies of others: they both want to change, whereas if they stayed the same they might become great. (I am sure that each of *"Les Six"* dreads the day when one of them will die: the others will say, "Ah! at least it wasn't me this time; nevertheless it's beginning!" Moral: If death worries you, don't associate yourself with others. . . . Unfortunately Margaret Truman is the same age as I, and I must go through life being the same age as she; even if she dies first, nothing can stop the awful fact that I'll die second.)

Famous last words of Ned Rorem, crushed by a truck, gnawed by the pox, stung by wasps, in dire pain: "How do I look?" It's harder to maintain a reputation for being pretty than for being a great artist.

Fez, Morocco

Yesterday Guy Ferrand and I passed the day swimming with Henri Lhébrard (and friend) on the wild beach of Safi. The only other bathers were a group of native whores taking Sunday off from the town brothel. While their boy friends played a sort of baseball with a tin can, the whores (naked) dressed up in seaweed to attract our attention. But the baseball was also to attract our attention: that is how Morocco is made.

On the road to Safi are more camels than anywhere in the world. A camel has terrific strength; he can take off your arm with one bite. The leg bones are of unshatterable steel built to combat outrages rampant before history. . . . A car — a "baby Simca" — can smash into a camel and be reduced to smoking crumbs; a few moments after, the camel, unscratched, stands off to consider the wreckage, chewing calmly, and smiling his bovine smile of stupid disdain. . . .

Jean-Claude is also here in Fez. Yesterday he took me and Robert Levesque up the mountain far behind our house to see a dead horse he'd found there some days ago. Lodged in a sort of stone pit, this exquisite sight was in a state of shocking putrefaction and smelled like nothing on earth. White worms and newly-hatched flies crawled from all directions toward the cadaver from which perforated intestines emerged. The horse (a mare, we concluded) seemed to have fallen from a height of twelve feet and broken its neck. The unexpected descent had deposited her quite prettily (meaning quite naturally) on the ground. Her legs — slim and now practically bone, making the hooves look enormous — were dainty as a dancer's, and the head was wonderfully twisted, eyes to the soil, in an attitude of modesty. This scene was the sole rupture in a fifty-mile desert of pebbles. So I recalled my first knowledge of death: that disemboweled cow in the vacant lot on our way to school in Chevy Chase's second grade; we kids then all dressed up as cows to counterfeit our wonder, our terror.

Levesque, without further ado, began reciting Baudelaire's "Une

Charogne," but before he had finished we noticed coming over the
hill an Arab funeral procession. This is the truth. The unelaborate
group of three male mourners carried their dead friend (dead for a
matter of hours) hoisted high on a board, uncovered, the head facing
Mecca. With careful haste, paying us no heed, they dug a deep hole
into which they placed the body, upright, as is the custom, and left.
. . . We left too, returning to the house to play the Fauré *Requiem*. It
was early evening and drizzling slightly, though the sun still shown.
Then there appeared the most perfect rainbow we had ever seen:
one of its feet was a thousand miles south in the Congo somewhere —
but the other foot was firmly planted in glimmering glory among the
green roofs of Moulay Abdallah, which is the location of all the whorehouses in Fez.

In a flurry of *arrivisme* one year ago — during my initial enthusiasm
with this continent of Africa — I mailed to Gide (whom I'd never met)
an envelope containing birthday greetings, a song, and an equivocal
snapshot of myself. He immediately answered from Paris as follows:

André Gide
I bis, rue Vaneau
Paris — 7   *Le 24 Décembre 49.*

Mon cher Ned Rorem,
    Combien je vous envie: j'ai gardé si bon souvenir de Fez! Un
des séjours les plus agréables que j'y ai fait, c'était avec un jeune ami,
Robert Levesque, lequel vient d'être nommé professeur au lycée de
Fez; cela doit suffire comme adresse. Je pense que vous auriez prob-
ablement, vous et lui, un certain plaisir à vous recontrer.
    Merci pour le Alleluia. *Trop fatigué pour vous en écrire plus*
long. Je n'ai de force que pour vous serrer la main en pensée, bien
cordialement.

                                    André Gide

    Naturally I looked up Levesque, whom I didn't take to at first:
he may have been *jeune* to Gide, but to me he was forty, and his
sexual obsession was embarrassing. Moreover, he talked even to his
peers as to illiterate children, illiterate children being his sole preoc-

cupation both professionally (at the *lycée*) and socially (when, as always, on the make). But he was, and is, the best Fez had to offer intellectually, and we ultimately became friends. (North Africa, let it be said, is more "cultured" than France: the tackiest *colon*, being out of the swim, feels duty-bound to attend all artistic functions — and there are many, mostly high class, which come touring from Brussels to these provinces. But I've also seen Wilde's *Salomé* performed by natives in Arabic.) Contrary to most here, Levesque's clean intelligence stems from inside; when he can be diverted from *his* subject, he can be diverting indeed. It is clear that his relationship to Gide (as described in the latter's journal, as well as by himself) was less one of literary colleague than of companion in crime, even of *maquereau*. But his honest satyr's grin permits us to forgive him everything.

The knuckles of my hand and my arm up to the elbow are shot with pains from working so much in the composer's cramped position. But never have I been so pleased with my own music: I have a recognizable style. At the moment I am polishing and copying the choral pieces I wrote last month at Marie Laure's. Am also writing three "medieval" songs to be sung by Gordon Heath; they are in the manner of Folksong. Folksong (that is to say, Art "in the rough") has never interested me; I have always thought it a medium for unmusical Communists. I remember as an adolescent in Chicago I was vaguely acquainted with some now-vanished members of the YCL. They would sit around for hours listening to records of Burl Ives or Richard Dyer Bennett, expiring in joy at what they thought was the "true expression." This is because folk music has appeal through association: by way of the words. Real music has no fixed associations. The artist *cannot* be concerned with politics, for a regime may change each year, but a work of art remains. I prefer folk music as rewritten by, say, Roy Harris than in its original form. Art is made by tricks played in memory, and our souvenir of an experience is never exact. Art is the artifice of recollection. . . .

    In Fez, just outside of the great purple gate of Bou-Jeloud, there is a slaughterhouse. At night one can crouch beside the low windows, and through the grating see the death of camels. These prehistoric monsters, chewing their cud with terror in the reddish gloom, wait in line for their individual massacre. And all around the soggy smell of death. An Arab workman fells the beast with a single blow on the temple, after which comes the astonishing echo of a shriek. . . . In Paris last winter it was my misfortune to witness a criminal master-piece in the form of a documentary called *Le Sang des bêtes*. It is a series of episodes taken in a French *abattoir*, showing how domestic animals are killed. The film was cruel because the animals are pre-sented as human (close-ups of frightened eyes, bleating, helplessness, mass hysteria, etc.), and because the background music was of a young girl's voice singing nursery tunes.

Three days ago Monsieur Bogeart, Guy's medical assistant here, ac-cidentally swallowed some leeches with a scoop of well-water. They have lodged at the back of his throat just out of reach, and are get-ting regularly larger. Bogeart, normally of flaming complexion, has grown quite white. Perhaps for the moment this is good for his health as he is a fat man. But he begins to have trouble breathing. The leeches may grow so big as to burst, which would be one solution (he spits blood already); or they may descend to his stomach and die of acid mixtures. But they may also remain where they are (unobtainable save by instruments most obscene), necessitating the continuation of nicotine injections in his throat. This puts the creatures to sleep with the hope they'll lose hold, but it also makes poor Monsieur Bogeart so drowsy that if the leeches don't soon expire he's likely to. Meanwhile he keeps on with his daily routine, which was always quite dull, the only change being that he no longer takes wine or salad oil.

There is a pastry shop in Tangier without equal in the world. It's on the hill across from the French Embassy, and instead of a door, it has a thousand threads of jangly beads to keep the flies out (or in). This makes it very like the movies, and the delights within are similarly fantastic. My favorite is the *tarte aux poires*, a wee individual pie all gushing with golden pears and slightly colored with random cherries; the flakey crust is even lovelier than *Good Housekeeping* advertise-ments. Guy likes better the devil's food cakelets stuffed with cream swirls, because whipped cream is more of a delicacy for the French than for us. Whereas Themistocles Hoetis prefers a sort of small mountain of wafers topped with a strewing of green coconut (a bit too dry for my taste) about which he makes the staggeringly original observation that it's like Coca-Cola: the more you partake the more you desire. Paul Bowles always chooses an almond paste with squirts of gray sugar. But there are all manner of alternate goodies stacked high on the chromium table; Flaubert would have turned pale at the extravagance of mixtures: every combination of fruit and dough known to man is arranged in a dump from which one selects, piling plates high, and heading for one of the lacy tables (probably already occupied by a Spanish family, dogs and grandparents included). Needless to say we accompany our confection with either a *glace pistache* or a *café liègeois* or both, and then careen into the sunlight feeling sick but full of praise. It was in this establishment that Truman Capote performed a dance last week, but the customers were all too glutted to change expression.

Peach Surprise. When I'm on the wagon (it's classical) I'm so hysterically fond of desserts I can't enjoy the first helping for thinking of the second.

The weather is ferociously hot (or rather, passively hot) which makes one feel a mist, though the sky is clear. This week is the height of Ramadon, the Mohammedan lent; everyone fasts by day, and rejoices by night; there is no sleep.

Last night there was an accident on the route to Taza. A passenger bus collided with a truck, and twenty Arabs were burned to death in the trap (*carbonisés* as the French papers say). We got there around nine-thirty. The car was on its side which increased its size. A desert road, deserted. Crickets chirped. There was still a thickish smoldering. Nothing recognizable: pieces of chest, steaming jawbones, a foot — all nearly powdered. On removing a burnt jacket the flesh too came off. The smoke still twists around the flashlights which move here and there.

Dream: Standing in a street I don't know in Tangier with Paul Bowles, we are aware that "bull-training" is going on over there in a field behind that building. A tree one hundred feet high looms above the building, and gradually we see a bull—a great black bull—moving slowly through the upper branches. He is, as it were, guided from the ground by radar, and (like some cats) can climb but not descend. Carefully he steps among the highest twigs, chooses a final one into space, treads it like a pirate's plank, and falls with a crash to the earth from which rises an ugly pink dust of dying. Loud cheers.

France, Edith Piaf is your great lady. She knows the secret of popular song (the secret Bernhardt knew so well) which is expressivity through banality, the secret of knowing what must be added where. This formula can apply only to "popular" artists: they interpret mediocre works by completing them. Jennie Tourel, on the other hand, is a great lady because she adds nothing. One does not add to art.

Edith Piaf who—with the now-immortal Cerdan—is France's idol, has for me too almost replaced Billie Holiday. I cannot forget how, rue de la Harpe and later at the Hôtel du Bon La Fontaine, we would sit for hours on end drinking wine and listening again and again to those two records ("Un homme comme les Autres," "Je m'en fous pas mal") sung by this brave unnoticeable, tiny, rigid woman, tears streaming down our faces, knowing that we ourselves were in her mouth, a mouth howling the most brazen clichés.

Two years ago I wrote my parents who were worried about how much money to send: "You have given birth to an exceptional child; you must therefore expect exceptional behavior from him." I, in turn, was given an exceptional family who have always made every effort to understand and help.

Morocco is no land of monuments like Italy, it *is* a monument—like America. Nevertheless Rabat contains a museum (clean, free, silent,

neat) with many Roman statues and a few living customers. Among
the latter I saw a Berber boy with a face handsome enough to complete the torso he gazed upon. (Or rather, the torso deserved his breathing head.) Beauty shocks, hurts, and forces; the beautifully living
countenance (of stupidity even) surpasses those ages of art it inspires.

The paper today tells us that Louis Jouvet and Arthur Schnabel are
dead. With Gide, Koussevitzky, and Schoenberg, that makes five who
have died these past months. As an adolescent it seemed it was only
my young friends who were constantly dying, but that the old people
lived on and on, ever more fixed and legendary. This impression is
rather true, as I was an adolescent during the war years. I was too
young to remember when most of my old relatives died, but between
my seventeenth and twenty-first year a series of my dearest contem-
poraries died; Georg Redlich (23), of an auto accident which deformed
him beyond recognition; Don Dalton (24), instantly decapitated by
walking into a propeller; Myra Itkonen (24 and a beautiful girl) of a
broken back; Lorin Smith (33), his head crushed by a chain as he
walked along a California dock; Janet Fairbank (44), finally suc-
cumbed to Hodgkin's disease (her arms always black and yellow from
injections); unhappy Allela Cornell (30), of suicide by swallowing
sulphuric acid. . . . Who remembers them? It is to them that I dedi-
cate my series of choral songs *From an Unknown Past.* . . .

In Chaucer's day the verb "to die" was synonymous with the verb
"to come" ("to have an orgasm").

I have been reading Guy's medical books again, this time a chapter
called "De la Mort Apparente." I liked the story of Cardinal Donnet
about a young Bordeaux priest in 1826. During his sermon the priest
had an attack and fell upon the floor. Pronounced dead by a doctor,
his funeral preparations were begun. He was in his coffin, the *De
Profundis* was sounding, the earth was falling upon him, when all of
the sudden a loud knocking was heard coming from inside the wooden

box. The box was opened and the young priest rose up. He had not been dead, but had, in fact, been perfectly conscious and heard the funeral arrangements around him from the voices of friends. He had simply been unable to move or speak. At the end, by a superhuman effort, he managed to make himself audible from the coffin and was liberated.

This is a true medical story to show that death must be certified before burial. For it seems that the human body — hardly breathing in the unconscious state — can live underground for extended periods.

And Guy tells me that at the war's end, when certain of his French friends were freed from Dachau, they strung up their guard by the feet, head down, cut open his neck like a pig, caught the blood in a pail and threw it into his face.

Murder. These two hard syllables have always held a fascination. For several years I have kept a scrapbook of clippings of criminals, or at least people who look criminally interesting (for a criminal is a creator gone wrong, unless perhaps the converse is true): Proust on his deathbed; Edith Sitwell on hers (as seen by Cecil Beaton); the young killer Heirens of Chicago; Paul Klee; Ernst Bloch; the English boy who can't stop hiccuping; Kokoschka; the faces of anonymous athletes; pictures, in other words, of people who attract and revolt me as in the Xondi test. When I was younger I was scared by my loss of conversation at a party; that is still why I drink; though I find that if I begin discussing crime everyone becomes interested. Perhaps I am wrong, but I do not feel this is affectation simply by the fact that when reading of Damien's death (in the book on Sade) I vomited. I can't like the reality of violent cruelty.

I loathe every sort of competition (Quaker?).

The newsreels have shown a new endeavor of a boy going over Niagara Falls in a barrel. He, also, failed. At the news of his death his brother stated that he (the brother) planned to renew the attempt and felt convinced that *he* would succeed. I think this could only have happened in America. For us, any form of failure is a disgrace whether it is concerned with defying Niagara Falls in a barrel, or an indifferent public reaction to a new symphony. We seldom take leisure with a clear conscience; we must try and try again until success comes. If it doesn't come, at least we can say we have died trying. The French have three times as many holidays as Americans, a three-day weekend and a two-hour lunch period. They take their religion seriously (and seldom think about it). The average American works hard at a job he detests and thereby feels that his period of *fun* has been honestly earned. But look at all the weird and useless things we have built. Why? Is it to show our European cousins that we too know how? I believe that we are living to enjoy ourselves and not to be strained and unhappy like Hitler (who nevertheless seems to have been the model leader toward which every young boy is striving). Yet America has the greatest culture of today: our manner is our style and blood.

On the beach earlier this month, discussing certain friends who are addicted to drugs, Jacques Février said, "Oh, to think what they could have done if they hadn't started taking dope; how the talent deteriorates!" But is it not just *because* they were the kind of people who desired to take drugs that they were able to do the wonderful things they've done? We are what we are and because of it we do what we do.

Finished *La Porte étroite* which I read without pleasure, interest, or emotion. Was I afraid of it? of finding myself in it (as we do in all strong works) as a Protestant? I want so to be pagan, yet I know I never shall be. Nevertheless, the last twenty pages moved me despite myself, especially these words on the funeral of Alissa in the letter from Juliette to Jérôme: "They were not the only ones to follow the bier. Some patients from the sanatorium had wanted to attend the ceremony, and to accompany the corpse to the cemetery. . . . " I am always touched by this generous boredom in the old, who, deep down, are glad it's not *they* who died.

Also, in Alissa's journal: "Sadness is a state of sin. . . . Sadness is a complication. I never tried to analyze my happiness." And: "All of a sudden, he asked me if I believed in an afterlife. 'But, Jérôme,' I cried out immediately, 'for me, it's more than a hope: it's a certainty. . . .'

"And suddenly it seemed that all my faith had poured itself into that cry." ("*Et brusquement il m'a semblé que toute ma foi s'était comme vidée dans ce cri.*")

Did Gide mean her faith had left her? Then: "The path which you teach us, Lord, is a narrow path, too narrow to walk two abreast."

Three minutes after putting down this book, I made love with abandon. Now I am sorry, as it seems an insult to everybody.

The heat is relentless and I have never felt so constantly exhausted. Yesterday, finally, Guy decided to give me again some of the horse-blood capsules I took last spring. The result was a frightful attack of sneezing and itching and a paralyzing stomach-ache which lasted for hours. In analyzing this, it appears that I have always been allergic to everything concerning horses. The only time I ever rode (summer 1935 at Yellowstone Park) my eyes became swollen slits, I sneezed incessantly, my hands bled. As a child my inoculations for diphtheria (a horse serum) put me to bed with fever. Later in Paris, on rue de la Harpe, when Xénia and Jean-Claude in their luxuriant poverty used to have feasts of horse steak, the very smell of the meat cooking would give me fainting fits. . . . It's amusing to think that this allergy might be psychosomatic, and yet I feel so friendly towards horses, especially when reading Swift's "Voyage to the Country of the Houyhnhyms."

One thing that amused me about Rome last summer was the intense sexuality everywhere. It seems the Italians (who love it any old time or place) wait especially for the Holy Year to come around every quarter of a century. This spells special fun. For instance, before going into St. Peter's for the first time, we stopped to get our pilgrims' tickets stamped in a classy kiosk just made for that purpose. The agent of information took me for French as I was with Guy. "*Tenez! Je vais vous donner cette médaille gratuitement (bénie par le pape, bien entendu!) parce que je sais que vous êtes croyant. Vous en avez l'air,*" said he, pinning the token onto my shirt with clumsy leisure, tickling my chest the while with his little finger. *"Et vous pouvez revenir n'importe quand; j'y serai toujours à votre disposition! Aimez-vous Rome?"* he rippled in his Italian accent, which makes it hard to understand (the Spanish speak better French, I don't know why). .... *Le bedeau de la cathédrale de Sienne nous a chatouillé les fesses,* and winked deliciously as he uncovered the wonderful parquet, but he took a tip all the same. .... They are far from vicarious, so the onanism rate is doubtless low; they've lost none of Nero's giddy abandon. The brothels were closed for Holy Year. *Quel coup!* On every corner are such inexpensive temptations (not to mention the pettiest trickeries) that the year seems holy only to the pope and some of his foreign friends. For the others it's a quarter-century carnival. Sam Barber likes the story of a friend, who, seeking an uncontaminated native, went far away to a mountain village near the Swiss border. For reasons unnecessary to relate, he found himself in a sleeping bag with the blacksmith's child. "Oh, I don't mind," said the blacksmith's child, "as long as you give me two hundred lira."

The Jews here paint their houses blue. That color repels flies. The Moslems cut off their nose to spite their face, and refuse to paint *their* houses blue.

Three Beautiful Birds of Paradise. Why do I retch reading Falla's interview on advice to young composers (or any other master's council, for that matter)? They all say the same thing: don't hurry to publish, work slowly, reflect. Then they all cite Ravel, who would pause a year between completion and presentation; and they all mention their "private" discovery which is inevitably that most priceless of priceless things, *Trois Beaux Oiseaux du paradis.* I first heard it at age sixteen. Looking for a practice room (one of Northwestern's gray, brothel-like cubicles), I became aware of magic from behind a door. I had to go in. There sat a soprano, deciphering at the keyboard, squeaking prettily. "But what *is* it?" "Why it's from Ravel's *Trois Chansons* and all the mezzos in school are auditioning tomorrow for the solo in the second one." So we went through it together—and I was floored! This lady, pale and plain, a Public School Music Major on the verge of donating uninspired instruction to untalented children (the desire to teach is itself vain, destructive, indicative of uncreation)—what right *she* to this wonder! I later stole a library copy and have been on my knees ever since (take that as you will); it was mine. Such moments that break the heart also open the ears; how could I not have dreamed of France! People don't think like this anymore; or if they try, they don't succeed. I won't believe that Ravel toiled to make *that* one come out: it just was, born from the words. Perhaps I shall make my new song "Philomel" into a chorus with *soli* —it could be done in one *coup* (and if I do, it will be better work than a slave's). He alone could make any noise he wished, and at the same time worth listening to, rehearing indefinitely. Now we're going swimming.

At 4 A.M. we all went to swim at Sidi Hrasem. Yesterday's unprecedented rain made the *piscine* overflow with warmth reflecting the post-card violet of the palm leaves. It's not easy to bribe the guardian to let you enter: a week ago a woman was murdered in the pool and parts of her are still floating around. It's cheaper and quicker than divorce which, however, is not difficult with Moslems.

There is a new insane-asylum in Fez; the old one's abolished. The old one was more savage than Hogarth, with the moaning Arabs, already centuries away from our world, lying year after year in their iron collars and chains, in horse stalls crusty with excrement and pails brimming with abominations. The asylum of Tangier is still like this. . . . Guy tells me that the new institutions are built just for outer show but the patients still bang their heads against the wall. To approach the asylum of Marrakech by car, is to approach a motionless wind: a deadly wail comes from that building for twenty-four hours at a stretch, then fades sickeningly as the car recedes. . . . As a child I remember the kitchen of the "violent ward" in Yankton, South Dakota: grayish mashed potatoes in iron vats like those filled with boiling lead in medieval torture chambers. . . . The grammar-school language for mental hospital: booby hatch, loony bin, nuthouse,

bughouse, laughing factory, etc. How far from the troubling poetry
of Yeats about the insane ("Sweet Dancer," for instance).

To get to the Mérinèdes roadhouse from Fez proper you take the road
that leads out of the new town past Avenue de France, but instead of
going into the civil prison (across from which we live) you turn right
on the road which surrounds the town and also leads to the Palais
Jamai. You pass the graveyard—which is white and decorative, but
foul-smelling (because Moslems are buried upright, and at night hy-
enas come to gnaw their skulls)—and pass also a little annex city
where people live like cave dwellers. In five minutes you arrive at
the highest point of the foothills by which Fez is tightly closed in.
There, someone has built a café and called it Les Mérinèdes; you
could recognize it with your eyes closed by the smell of mint tea and
kif. The latter is indistinguishable from marijuana and its odor makes
me slightly sick. Guy drinks *Oulmès* and I drink *Jus d'or*, local soft
drinks from which we never switch. The view is of course frightfully
exciting—especially at night—and not unlike the approach to Mexico
City via the mountains south. Every house in old Fez is visible as in a
child's garden or the *hameau* at Versailles (or Florence, except that
in Florence all the roofs are reddish, while those here are of a dull
religious jade). Lights and noises from afar are, I suppose, about the
most pregnant impetus which exists to sentimental situations. And
one can see over the glittering valley to the mountain on a level with
you. But it has no cozy den for drinking *Jus d'or*. Here in our Café
des Mérinèdes we sit in deckchairs poised like rabbits above a sheer
drop of a thistley hundred feet (best stick to *Jus d'or*). There are no
other European clients, only the Arab *patron* and his friends, all high
as kites on their hashish that is always consumed with mint tea (which,
on the other hand, smells divine). There's said to be an art to its
making, though I can't see why: It's tea in a pot with chunks of raw
sugar and clear mint in dewy broken bunches stuffed to the brim.
Drunk in steaming glasses—which makes it as irritating as *café-filtre*
—it is as characteristic as the *kif* which always accompanies it. (Is
that why our slang for marijuana is "tea"? Personally I prefer alcohol,
not liking to be consecutively aware of my follies as they occur.) This

is no place for rendezvous; they take place along the dark river which dissects the town: a hotbed of hot people who have no beds. I have cut all my hair off and look like a fool or a chicken. My head is velvety with nothing but glinty traces of the *eau oxygenée* put there months ago.

Admitting to be a fool doesn't keep one from being a fool. The public is lazy, likes only lies. From the minute they sense the truth they lose interest.

A few moments ago, as I was sitting on the toilet reading Giraudoux, a big insect flew in the window. It looked like a winged scorpion with a Frankenstein head. It hovered hypnotized, stared at me, quivered a full minute, and then flew off again. But I could do nothing more.

PART 4
September–December, 1951

Paris

Back in Paris for four days. . . . Rain. . . . And an atrocious welcome: we had drunk a lot of brandy on the airplane from Marseilles and landed tired in Paris at midnight. Then of course I stayed out most of the night drinking with forgotten friends. Returning home, I was attacked on the Place St. Michel by a Senegalese—who blackened my lovely left eye, stole my passport, boat ticket to America, two hundred dollars in traveler's checks, and a pair of glasses. A gratuitous crime, since none of these objects can be of use to the robber; yet *I* am left without a country. I'm broken by this, especially since I have always felt invulnerable, yet calamity befalls me every third week. I have been spending my first days here then, looking in the mirror at the black eye on this face which, Julien says, in a few years no one will notice any longer in the street, and by that signal I shall know that I have gotten old.

My hotel—the Bisson—is between the Pont Neuf and Pont St. Michel. For the moment I have an expensive room which looks onto the Seine, and across the river is the police station, Quai des Orfèvres, where two years ago I was held for a night after a raid on a St. Germain bar. Upon the river, between the police and my window, there is nothing but rain and rain and rain. Leaves are turning color, and today is the first of fall.

At the beginning of the month, after my return from Morocco, Marie Laure took me to Venice for Charles Bestigui's ball, and for the première of *The Rake's Progress* (interchangeable functions, you might say). The housing shortage was so crucial that we shared a room at the Danieli with Christian Mégret sleeping in the bathtub. I was the youngest and worst-dressed at the Palazzo Labia, from where I returned at eleven next morning to find this letter on my pillow:

> *Darling,*
>   *I was feeling so tired that I thought it better to go home: inferring that you were all right with Tony or Christian. I am frantic with*

anxiety — got into your bed all morning. Bless you. I love you truly.
                                                              Marie Laure

Am I wrong? Do I "use" people? Was Venice cursed? Has Marie Laure (with tears and coiffure trailing over her evening gown in the noon of St. Mark's, before her own daughter and all of society) simply a taste for scandal? Is it too soon to know?

It is more difficult to write words on one's family than on any other subject. Probably if I were able to elucidate certain acts and sensations performed and experienced as regards my parents and sister (which I shall never have the courage to do, even after their deaths), then I would no longer feel the crushing necessity to be an artist.

The only reason I don't commit suicide is because I'm afraid to be alone. And yet, being among people, I am distant from them all. Really I should be done away with, being a two-headed monster.

Talked for an hour with Dora Maar who, for four years, did not drink a drop, even of wine. Four months is as big an oath as *I* can take, and I swear here not to drink at all until February (at which time some of the habit will be lost).

I'm not working well either: the desire is terribly there, but my imagination simply cannot focus on the ballet I'm supposed to be writing. This imagination vanished with the robbery in the solitude of Paris. Besides, I cannot think except for the human voice.

My room has been changed. Now I am high up, looking onto a court and Latin Quarter roofs. A piano and a bathtub. Everyone is so very good to me (but where is the *difference* between any two people?). I miss Guy.

Yet when I go through periods of abstinence — although I am smug in my buoyancy — I feel always in a state of *not being drunk*. This is an artificial state, but it can hardly be said to be harmful.

Belles journées, souris du temps,
Vous rongez peu à peu ma vie,
Dieu! Je vais avoir vingt-huit ans
Et mal vécus à mon avis.

APOLLINAIRE, La Souris

Today is my birthday. (This is not true; I will not be twenty-eight until after tomorrow. But today I have birthday thoughts, and anyway have been feeling twenty-eight for some time.) October 23rd was also Franz Liszt's birthday, and Sarah Bernhardt's. And 1923 when I was born, was the year of Sarah's death. Also Fauré's. Did a wand touch me at birth, instilling me with the living souls of these people? Certainly all my music is slow like Fauré's (his fast music is really slow music played fast). Certainly I constantly play-act like Sarah; except that this "acting," being a part of me, is no longer acting. . . . Twenty-eight years! But I stopped learning at twenty-five. And I shall spend from now till fifty either trying to forget what I have found out, or attempting to adapt it all into something nice and selfish and profitable. For nothing seems new anymore. If I went to China I would feel I had seen it before. . . . But like any child I know the world was made for me; I am incapable of foreseeing a gloomy future.

Her husband Charles being away, Marie Laure took me and Jerry Robbins to his house for the weekend, the former Palais de Pompadour in Fontainebleau. Leaves had fallen and rotted, the corridors were icy, every gorgeous room had fires like the one shining from Googie Withers' mirror in *Dead of Night*. By Saturday Jerry and I were so uneasy from Dominguez' habitual pranks, from our hostess' weird indulgence, from the atmosphere in general, that we decided to play a joke. As we dressed in our wing for the evening meal we invented this romance to relate while dining: "We were dressing when there was a knock. At the door stood a woman in filmy black, coiffed in eighteenth-century style, and with tears on her cheeks. She beckoned, and as we approached she turned, floated down the hall, entered a guest room, and closed the door. We followed—but found only an empty parlor except for a pool of tears on the rug." . . . While dining I began to relate: "We were dressing, when a woman in tears appeared at the door—" Marie Laure interrupted: "Was she coiffed in eighteenth-century style and dressed in filmy black?" We babbled: "Yes." "Well, of course! She's the ghost of Charles' ancestor, la Comtesse de _____, who used to inhabit your wing."

My dream life being of considerably more interest than my real one, I see no reason for not staying in bed twenty-four hours a day. Especially during this thick French bleak gray drunk season one feels like crawling back toward the *"bon grand fond malampia"*! Anyhow, who's to say that our waking life might not be the one of dreams, and contrariwise?

Last night I walked alone all over Paris searching and searching for miles on end. Toward two in the morning, tumbling with fatigue down one of those empty lanes between the Luxembourg and the boulevard St. Germain, I suddenly heard the hollow tones of wooden-heeled footsteps approaching from far behind. I smiled to myself, slowed my pace, the feet came nearer, growing louder, swifter. When they were nearly upon me I shivered and was thrilled. Then the steps passed me—but I saw no one. The regular clack of the feet walking before me grew fainter, farther away, turned a corner and disappeared. But I hadn't seen a soul. . . . I went to bed and had this dream. I was escaping in a canoe down a deep jungle river, but the travel was slow as trees hung low at every point. Surly savages emerged and disappeared on the night land. While paddling I looked down and saw far below the surface two dismembered feet, dead and luminous, walking with a terrifying slowness, like floating plants. I was to be likewise cut apart if my flight were unsuccessful.

Today lunch with Balthus at the Catalan and afterwards a visit to his very messy studio (it resembles what must have been the interior of the Collier brothers' home) in the adorable Cour de Rohan just off the rue Jardinier. Balthus is working on a most frightening oil. The canvas is enormous, four yards wide, and high as the ceiling.

On this are nothing but two curious girls: one, a naked dead doll in
false light stretched on a couch awaiting love; the other, a vital little
idiot sister in a green sweater opening the curtain and exposing her
rival to the real light of the sun. There is also a vase and cat. All this
in colors hitherto uninvented. . . . I had to shiver! Poor great Balthus:
so Jewish and sorry for himself; so rich, so poor.

Later in the day I went to see Bernac. Who could be more contrary to Balthus? Which doesn't keep him from being just about as
sad. Overly neat, overly tolerant (to me tolerance means getting old).
He feels nobody loves him, and this may be true, though he is one of
our master singers.

But I loathe more and more discussing music in any form or
shape. We spend most of our lives repeating ourselves. To say I want
to stay home doesn't prevent me from going out and repeating myself.
I loathe concerts, but this didn't prevent me from going tonight to be
bored by Igor Markevitch. What is sadder than a half-filled concert
hall? Nothing. Backstage Igor is sad and cold (*bien qu'il m'ait tutoyé
pour la première fois*), Boulanger is icy, Marcelle de Manziarley frigid,
Poulenc chilled in a box with his peculiar niece, everyone is glacial
and lacking in glamor. Concerts need glamor.

This was my Thursday, omitting important things like street-
walking.

Paris today is a city asleep. And snoring loudly.

What I have longed for most during these awful days has not been
my forgotten music, but the snow in New York. I should like to sit
and drink rye in the Café Royale on Second Avenue once again and
watch the snow falling slowly outdoors onto that brightly lighted Jewish theater. And as I drink to think about how everybody loves me.

The more I think of my short but not short enough conversation with
Souvchinsky, the more my blood boils. He simply cannot be talked
to (a woman I would forgive, a man should know better). He always
chooses the wrong time to express himself, as at a party, where people

need only say things they don't care about. How am I to answer when he asks, "Don't you think that Boulez' is the only music today? That he is taking the only possible path?" Of course I don't think so; I am a composer too and Boulez' path isn't mine. What's more, Boulez will not attain the nonexpressive element he seeks because his "system" has as origin *le dodécaphonisme*, inherently the most expressive of musical devices. . . . Nevertheless I was disconcerted.

I am content with my work, the *Cycle of Holy Songs* and the ballet for Jerry. There is nothing on earth of which I'm not capable except experimentation. Because I am an American Protestant. How I love the French! And I love Americans too for their youthful sweetness in apologizing for every daily action.

1 A.M. Almost I am afraid to write here tonight for fear that clarifications may make me burst into tears, knowing my whole life has been only an expedition of waiting. Seven days of chaos began with my return from Denmark. How could I dare transfer my reactions to this trip? How dare look back upon these seven days since? the worst nightmare of any all interspersed and oozing with heavy sick and juicy dreams, more crazy and real than life.

Yesterday Marie Laure gave a lunch to which she had the bad sense (or unconscious cruelty) to invite me as spectator. Because—although I'd known each of the guests before—all of them were old friends from the last generation, and all were painters. And painters with musicians have nothing in common (as everyone knows: it's all been explained before). But let me describe them as freaks:

Léonor Fini has a mysterious round hat made from a pea-green furry substance, and a coat to match. This is how she is naked when coming out from behind her famous masks; with a laugh of masculine assurance she echoes all other sounds in the room which reach her, only to have them bounce off again from her green hat. She is like her own picture without enough power for real cruelty or pathos. I tell her, "You haven't the right to draw men who love, because you are a woman and if you go any farther you'll reach a dangerous land where you're not wanted and be pushed from a cliff breaking your

thick neck. Since a woman's hand that desires to depict a man's domain is, by nature, incapable of making the excitement it seeks, it
can only make embarrassment." She laughs again and says, "I'd like
to make you cry." She couldn't though; I just burn with anger. But of
course, being me, I say nothing.

We all know Dali. I'll mention that if he were of my métier and
generation I would spit in his face. It's hideous to see humanity leave
a man as he grows progressively more famous. Screaming on sex is
funny, but one cannot joke about war in parlor conversation. He had
said, "We need more wars, but shorter ones." Where will *he* be? It's *I*
who will die a painful death. What has he done that approaches
Guernica? I am ashamed to be in a room with Dali, his mustache,
his cane; I blush that my parents should discover I have known him;
my mother, who has devoted her life to peace.

Now I wish just for knowledge of the simplicity of lovemaking.
Just to drink every night with beloved Heddy de Ré (who knows how),
or write little operas with gentle Elliott Stein (who can be funny), or
to cry with bewitching Marie Laure (who has found out how to read
books). Yet I know that I will never know that love-making is a thing
of nature.

11:30 A.M. It's now been fourteen days since I've had a drop. This
period on the wagon has been more necessary than any of the others,
since finally my health seemed corroded. But I only emerge into the
raw light of great doctor bills, absence of love, incapacity for work. I
prefer the sensation of being drowned. More and more I appear to
be getting *insaisissable*, even to myself; when I stand apart I see my
body moving about the city like a self-denying marionette. To look
back on this two week orgy of sterile sobriety and realize that in any
case I was doing the same things as when I'm drunk (only less blurred),
for instance, being in that place full of semifemale impersonators,
rue de Bourgogne, where a wiry queen with incredible hair, who
looks like a cross between Jean Harlow and Harpo Marx, is weeping
on the bar; or the Club de Paris (there is a pianist in similar clubs all
over the world—in St. Louis or Hong Kong—who plays the same
tunes in the same way, without rhythm, without energy, like rubber
for the same pallid withering chromium clientele, which chatters

and never gets drunk): it's the not being alone — or, if I find myself alone, I become frightened and can think of nothing to say to myself. So I see hundreds of people, bad or indifferent, and can't tell one from another — and can't wish to work. Well, then what is the use of being in superlative physical condition if this wonderful instrument of the body can't profit thereby? So Heddy and I have made a date for next Friday to get conscientiously plastered, beginning in the Pont Royal bar. She'll be there before me (as I must come directly from the dentist) with a bottle of olive oil: it seems that if the stomach is lined then the liquor causes no suffering. What good is it to be aware, to see all real things closely or know every muscle of the beings which fly around you in space? It is not for nothing that God has made me nearsighted: I converse with deep-sea animals. *Et le bon Dieu me permet de déconner.*

Mid-afternoon was like night with a fog thick as London, through which came a hard hot red-silver sun absolutely round, looking as though it were the twilight of the world. In this cold soup I walked around to toy stores with Stephen Spender and Peggy Bernier buying gifts — pistols and glass sailors! — for their children (and *he* a pacifist! *We* were never allowed guns). Then we had coffee *aux Deux Maggots*, and Stephen is certainly better in Paris than England (like all the English away from their wives) but depressing all the same, since he would like to save the world, and this is something I generally try not to think about. Also all his tastes have a firm basis in the Germanic and therefore, of course, he doesn't feel for French art, which makes the two of use essentially different. I can't agree with his personal definition, but he says: German art constantly moves, comes toward you and passes like a train; but the whole French aesthetic is based on *cooking* in a series of additions (a pinch of garlic here, some to-mato sauce there); that it works fine in painting, but that the music seems to be seen and not heard. . . . Of course the curt preciousness of this kind of expression is basically French already, and therefore Stephen's opinion (as long as he uses these words) cannot, for the moment, mean anything.

Encore des séries de bonnes cuites! I thought I'd been able to stop. No, this time I've come home with a deep gash in the forehead and a deep depression. Last night was Cocteau's new *Bacchus*, during which I came close to dying: my green forehead a mass of sweat. I try — but can only remember a sequence of faces.

The *gaffe* I made at Marie Blanche's a few weeks ago was divine! Little François Valéry (son of the late Paul Valéry) was there. And the three of us were chatting about Leonard Bernstein, who had just married and settled in Cuernavaca. Marie Blanche said, "How lovely! What adorable and talented children they'll have!" upon which she reeled across the room, her face smiling and blank, and collapsed into a large armchair. But I replied, "Oh, I don't think so: children of the great are always *cons!*" . . . No sooner had this escaped my lips than I realized what I had said. What could I have added to expiate my crime? — that, after all, Paul Valéry was insignificant?

Maggy's marvelous breakfast of long ago: eggs in pepper rings poached in cider and served with Canadian bacon. . . .

Livid descriptions of my drunkenness reach me again from all sides: how, once, on a stormy morning in Cherry Grove, I crawled out of the sea and fell into the house of a strange blond girl, saying, "I want to die." This girl, it seems, is now in France and remembered me (like so many others) not as a composer but as a drunk. . . .

Lise Deharme's dinner was a catastrophe: Marie Laure, to impress Milhaud (tragic in his silver wheelchair), monopolized the conversation; my forehead began to bleed again and I also broke a vase; Sauguet was his nastiest to everyone; Jacques Perrin was drunk and cruel. The only coherent conversation was devoted to the Cocteau play, and it was sad to see the disappointment of old friends. . . . I'm beginning to prefer the eternal nightmares of my sleeping hours to those of waking.

Christmas night: In a state of complete exhaustion; am losing weight, becoming more and more fragile, frighteningly pale. These days leading toward Christ's rebirth have been scary and surrealistic, beginning with *Les Noces* which always leaves me feeling slight. Then a pointless dinner at Marie Blanche's where I played my *Sicilienne* at two pianos (with Robert V.-L.) and nobody said they liked it because Sauguet hates me on account of Jacques Dupont, and that is Paris society, more babyish and spiteful than in America. During these days Chapeauval committed suicide, and Tom Keogh slit the wrist of his right arm (he's left-handed) — his room was drenched in blood, even the windows. Every painter I've ever known has killed himself at Christmas. Because when there's no light the painter is lost (he doesn't know how to read), and in December there's little daylight. So he fills himself with alcohol and dies. . . .

Suicides which succeed are, in a sense, failures; one seldom does it to die: the implied blackmail would be worthless without the instigator's enjoyment. No one believes in his death: one attends one's own funeral — as guest, not corpse.

To sink so low that only rising is conceivable — and then to sink lower!

New Year's eve was pretty much like this: lunch with Claude Bénédick can be skipped as of no importance; then I changed money at Julius'; then I went to Milhaud's to finish a nervous dark afternoon of thaw, and to begin the end of a year. Milhaud for twenty-five years has lived in a barren apartment on the Boulevard Clichy looking down into the million wild lights of Pigalle's merry-go-rounds. He is enormously fat in all parts of his body (it is said that his sweat glands don't function), and literally does not walk: his life is spent in a chromium wheelchair. But his voice is music itself. Being the most significant of *"Les Six,"* he is less *maître* than any of them: has none of Poulenc's elegance, Tailleferre's *bêtise*, Auric's worldliness, Durey's nonexistence, or Honegger's weariness. He loves youth and lives for music, and when he tells me good things about my work I forget what anyone else ever said. As with all elderly composers, I felt a certain sadness come into Milhaud's expression when I entered; a feeling of disappearance before new growth as if he were saying to himself: "Soon this boy will be breathing my air."

Coming out onto the always exciting mystery of the Boulevard Clichy I had difficulty finding a taxi, so I arrived late at the *réveillon* of Marie Laure. There was lots of champagne, quarreling, and tears, but no sense of Christmas, though I kept screaming the child Christ was born. I recall that someone described a Chinese torture, consisting of a rat in a cage, the open side of which is placed against the buttocks; fire is applied to the other side of the cage, forcing the rat, in his terror and suffering, to gnaw his way into the victim's body by way of the rectum. We all became drunk, and at eleven the florist delivered a practical joke sent by the Lopez': a life-sized figure made of flowers, which looked like Frankenstein dressed as a woman. This took three hours to burn, and expired with hideous fiery twists.

After this, everything crumbles; I remember only Oscar, Balthus, Etienne P., and Dora, and have a hazy recollection of receiving the next day Juliet and Man Ray, with Heddy (naked) in bed beside me, eating sandwiches and saying to the beautiful Christian Mégret, about me, *"Ne vous en faites pas pour moi; je ne baise jamais mes soeurs!"*

A mouse has just died in my piano. I believe she entered there to give birth, but was killed instead by the hammer strokes.

Then my life is brightened just a bit by the good and delightful libretto that Elliott made for me. It was drawn from Hawthorne's "The Snow Image," but we call it *A Childhood Miracle*.

With reddish-gold brown hair and a wonderful nose, dressed in black shoes and socks, jet-black corduroy jacket and trousers, coal-black jersey shirt with a Byronic collar from Dominique Franz, the wide wine-colored tie of softest velvet (the birthday gift Julius Katchen found in Munich); and the spectacular little bandage on my forehead, which is beginning to bleed again. This is how I appeared at *Bacchus*; and now I blush.

I have a horror of sluggishness, moral or bodily. What have I done since May, 1949? I have composed and orchestrated and beautifully copied in India ink and had performed a symphony, a string quartet, a piano sonata, an opera, a fiddle sonata, a piano concerto, five song cycles, fifty songs, a suite of songs for voice and orchestra, a Design for orchestra, three ballets, and a great deal of choral music and short piano (and miscellaneous) pieces most of which are already published; I have also traveled; given concerts and broadcasts; written three volumes of this journal and three thousand letters; made and lost countless important friends and unimportant ones; written articles; fallen in love three times; exerted my charm and my ugliness to a maximum — not to mention having gotten dead drunk and recovered at least four hundred times. In other words I have maintained what I consider my duties on Earth, though I nevertheless have a constant guilty conscience for what I consider my laziness. . . .

After his little party last Thursday, Virgil tells me that since I am the only "star" representing America in Paris at the moment (that is, the only expatriate composer), it's my responsibility to be well-behaved, and if I can't pay the bills, then not misbehave, but smile politely and go home and work.

Let's develop our faults: they're our true nature.

The alcoholic can stop drinking, and when he does, he has milk, does exercises, sleeps well, goes to movies. He can stop drinking, but only for a while. His abstinence never lasts. There is always the image of a glass waiting; it's the glass that gets impatient, not the drinker. And there is always the startled expression at his new happy body. He says: Why get into good condition if not to break it down again? Is that not why countries arm?

    If you drink heavily you find yourself in strange places and never know how you get there (locomotion is not recalled since it's a constant shifting of place, and even a place where you've passed many hours can be obliterated from the memory next day); you find yourself in strange places and in search of something never quite found, since it's more likely to be in the next strange place where you will be drunker. I can remember looking all night for a face seen ten years ago while drunk. We can walk for miles without knowing it. Getting drunk the following day is like wanting to return to bed in order to recapture last night's dream where it left off. The remarkable romances I have had in a stupor, I cannot reduplicate until the next stupor; not because I am too shy, or have misjudged the beauty of a half-forgotten face, but because when I am sober I simply haven't the interest (which could be called a "lack of responsibility") to remain in bars until seven in the morning with other remarkable people who are in the same strange place at seven in the morning. No one has a *sense of order* like an alcoholic on the wagon. But no days are as difficult as those which immediately follow the oath of abstinence (always temporary). The variations are infinite. It is not the physical letdown, lack of ability to work, nor guilt at looking friends in the face, so much as knowing one has renounced a habitual dream of even the goriest myth, the possibility of finding eternal love (usually with some crazy butcher-boy who empties your pockets) — the scary but still magic possibility of waking up, your mouth in shreds and your head in crumbs, staring stupidly at the Tour Eiffel, which looks like a toad with an apothecary's hat.

Our gifts are not gifts, but paid for terribly.

Marrakech, Morocco

Back now in Morocco, wintertime, all feels blue and gold.

But my health all feels worse; if it isn't one thing it's another, and not a moment's peace. The whole side of my face seems paralyzed and my left ear is completely deaf, which makes me live more and more in my own world. I've had to see another doctor here (I left Paris in the middle of dental treatment, teeth still in rags), and he says I'm deaf because I haven't blown my nose in two years; that most creative personalities have ear trouble what's more!

Mother and Father — when Rosemary and I were twelve and eleven — took us to see Nazimova in *Ghosts*. Two women in the row behind whisper: "Shameful! to bring children to such a play" — at which Rosemary turns around and says, "It's people like you that make plays like this necessary!"

I live in Marrakech and do nothing but work. But strangers visit here only to make love, with such single-tracked viciousness that one would think they had no tomorrow. Part of me dies too, as I stand away and watch their insatiable and nervous dance through the square, like ants upon a stove.

If two people find each other in the street, they will be in bed together an hour later. But how? My desire is to turn and run. What have they said to each other between street and bed? That's a magic secret that I've kept myself from knowing. Or, if I find myself on the way to the bed, I think: it happened this time, but how will it happen next time? Then — there being no mystery, and knowing I *could* if I *wanted* — I invent an excuse and vanish. Because if I found myself in bed, I would want to reduce myself to that delicious idiocy which is true love. But even stronger is my fright of losing independence. As I walk I hate having my arm taken, for my step is my own and nobody else's.

In Latin countries men walk arm-in-arm; Arab men attach themselves together by crooking their little fingers. I always walk without physical touch on the left of anyone in order to defend myself with the right arm. Also I spit a lot to the annoyance of all friends.

What's weird is to be at home here late at night and all alone, submerged in work of this time, and then to go into the lanes of Marrakech and find a life of two thousand years ago. To walk alone at night among the coppersmiths and veiled women selling bread, the pimps and water-merchants and cobra-charmers, and the men who sell perfume and the trained pigeons and drums and flutes all under the shaking night light of tapers burning and the odor of sweet potatoes. To have left suddenly my quiet room where I was thinking about twentieth-century music. Then to dine alone high up on the terrace of the Café de France and look down upon this squirming square with the wind blowing through a hundred candles and Arab music. On the other side of me the restaurant's radio is playing American jazz, and I try to read *Le Poète assassiné* as I eat my *fraise melba*. The sound of the radio makes me remember the windy summers of Chicago fifteen years ago when we'd go swimming in the lake at midnight, our wet bodies illuminated by the changing colored lights of the nearby nightclub which sent the wail of saxophones out over the water. . . .

Marrakech — one of the three hottest cities on earth — is indeed cool this winter, and the pirate-city of Mogador last Sunday was like ice.

Mme. P. asked us all to dine with her *à la Maison Arabe, un restaurant chic (aux salons particuliers) blotti en pleine Médina.* She's the kind of woman who is only found in colonial towns: around forty-five, hair bleached pale pink, the withered face of a monkey, silly and talkative, wealthy (but forced to spend the winter in Morocco away from her elegant Paris friends because of her husband's work), crazy about good-looking boys and the "artistic personality" . . . We were six in a private dining room full of rose and silver cushions like a DeMille harem. I detest eating with my hands and see no reason for doing so if one is not the guest of an Arab. Yet this is how we proceeded, even with a greasy pigeon pie covered with cinnamon. And then Madame P. asks the question I despise the most (the question showing that people may love artists, but can't love art): "What magnificent inspiration you must find in Marrakech, you, a composer so attuned to beauty! Have you ever written better?" . . . If I *have* written better it's because I've turned my back to the view. It's hard for people to realize that the artist's inspiration is always present and all he needs to express it is concentration; beautiful surroundings are disconcerting. Casanova's marvelous book was inspired by a prison cell. Ravel pulled down the shade when he composed, and Wagner closed the palace door. We all know that the beauty of art is interior, but if the composer writes what he sees in nature, he'll cultivate nothing more than Cyril Scott's lotus or MacDowell's wild rose. I've come to this country to work, not to make love. If I allow myself to go astray to Tinerhir, which is the garden of Eden, then I am lost. For instance, Sunday we took a long ride — *dans le bled sur la route d'Amismiz* — and this is paradise. Returning at six the sun was setting, and the highway was covered with mad people whose eyes were turned toward the ramparts of Marrakech looking like the wall of China — a belt burning for miles like orange velvet in the dying sun and full of green blood. Nothing could be more silent, so silent I could hear my own circulation like a waterfall of blood in my skull, the noise of blood; and the sadness that always accompanies beauty as we entered the city gate and came to watch the death of the sun in the Place Jemâa-el-Fnâa. Then the lamps begin to go on, one by one, in the square; the fire-eater starts to swallow his torch; under a hundred tents supper is begun.

Because I found it amusing, I sent my parents one of the typical postcards bought in any Moroccan stationery store. It represents two prostitutes in one of the weird whorehouses of the Quartier Réservé. They are naked (except for turkish towels thrust between their legs), heavily made-up, impassive faces, smoking and drinking tea in a Baudelairian décor. Mother was "quite shocked," for, as she wrote, she is "getting older." Her reaction, in turn, shocked me.

Nothing can touch me more than lay-people's love for music. Not those who sit in concert halls, but those who play at home; not those who say, "If only my mother had forced me to practice!" but those who practice anyway. Sometimes in the evening I watch with wonder as Guy practices the piano. He plays badly, but with such devotion (he has a gigantic repertoire by heart) that I realize the greatest pianist in the world could not give him as much joy as his ability to make these sounds himself. So many medical men have a need (not to mention sacred awe) of music; it must be the strain of their profession. Though music in no sense should be a relaxation. (How wrong was Shakespeare's "concord of sweet sounds"! One might just as well say: Painting is a juxtaposition of pretty colors.) It makes me cry with tenderness to realize that Guy has sacrificed voyages to buy the piano with which he has spent months of his life *alone*. Just as a Jew can "spot" another Jew, so can a musician know in a minute whether the person with whom he is talking has a feigned or real love. I've always respected those who say, "Music means nothing to me! I've tried, but it just means nothing." Some are my best friends (perhaps because I'm not afraid of them?). On the other hand I am suspicious of compliments. But those who say, "What chance you have to be among the 'chosen few,' to be able to *create!*"—those are the ones who trouble me, and without knowing it, make me remorseful for the idiotic life I lead. Yet can any composer truthfully say he's at all times faithful to his work? Our lives are what they are, we live by our responses to other people, *et il n'y a rien à faire*. The true amateur moves the heart, because, for an inch of progress, he has the patience of an ant, yet has no jealousy for those able to travel with ease through the air like angels. I say that the true amateur is the more *complete* and sincere (though I've never thought sincerity a prime quality), whereas I've never known a professional who was not propelled by ambition (which I've never thought a particularly *base* quality). But the amateur has a blind faith in us, a respect for our natural responsibility that we deceive in ways he'll never be aware of. That is why I'm touched by the layman's love: he sees creation as a magic world, and *I* know that it's not.

Evening. Supper at the Ménara. And in all that elegance, what should appear: bedbugs! If there is a bedbug within twenty miles it will find me immediately. (It is like being *en panne* in the desert, far from anywhere, no vegetation, just a hot, empty lunar landscape. Yet a million flies buzz out of nowhere with a savage bite, and groups of Arabs arise like a mirage. Throughout North Africa there are nomads, lone wolves always a bit out of their minds, who, in the wilderness, will lift their *djellabahs* and show you their genitals with a dim smile.) The itching became so atrocious that I had to leave my marvelous soufflé and rush to the washroom, tear off my coat, and discover my arm in shreds. I looked frenetically through my shirtsleeve for the nasty little beast, but of course couldn't find it.

It is often in the chicquest places that bedbugs flourish: the last time for me was in the Parade bar at Tangier, and before that, on the Algerian border two and a half years ago in Oujda's best hotel. Don't tell me! There's nothing I don't know about bedbugs. How my heart leapt to see the delightful pages about this vermin in Casanova's *Histoire de ma Fuite des Prisons de Venise que l'on appelle les Plombs* (an admirable book in any case), which compares with the famous section in *Les Caves du Vatican*.

My first and most harrowing experience with bedbugs was in 1943 when I lived at Xénia's on Delancy Place in Philly. Bedbugs (except in Philadelphia) seldom practice their trade by daylight; and even at night (though you can be rolling in a mass of nervous sweat, a throbbing welt) they are difficult to find when you suddenly turn the light on and search for them in the sheets and woodwork. But those *chez nous* were monsters of shamelessness: all we had to do was sit with our back to the wall in the blaze of noon, and down they would crawl from the moldings, making a "V" like an army of airplanes heading straight for the back of our neck. Then we'd be interrupted in the reading of our Proust (or whatever) by abominable and almost bumpy itching, and realize the bedbugs were out again. But *our* bedbugs were so sluggish and huge, so glutted and thick from our blood, that they could not disappear as we turned around, and we were able to kill them against the wall with the heel of a shoe. *Try* to kill them, I should have said, for their crust is hard as a diamond. But if one of them managed to break, it gave off the sweet nauseating smell of almond extract. They are flat and mean and shiny. A plague: everywhere bedbugs, enormous, even eating each other — not only in the bed and walls, but in books, in the toilet paper, in the piano keys. Our faces were black from sleepless nights, so we called the exterminator. This meant that the apartments above and below had to be vacated for six hours while the exterminator did a spray-job of cyanide. (It turned out later that the people next door hadn't been notified, and their baby was killed by the fumes.) That night after the exterminator's visit, we went to bed with hearts relieved and gay. But two hours later in the black, oh God! the itching began anew, simultaneously with an air-raid siren which meant lights out. But we switched on the light — doped with fatigue and despair — to see the bed aswarm with escaping bedbugs like a hundred maddened crocodiles fighting frantically in a small pool of boiling water. We were consequently fined by the air-raid warden, but as he happened to be Roy, the alcoholic from upstairs, he forgot about it.

When I moved to my little apartment on New York's 285 West 12th Street in 1944, Noel Sokoloff (who, two years before had taken it from Norman Dello Joio, and now was giving it to me) said, "Just remember this: the fireplace doesn't work. It looks quite capable, but it's a 'front'; it would have cost six hundred dollars to make an opening flue into the chimney." That night I came home drunk, and the sodden bedbugs (for Noel had hitherto offered them nothing: they only like certain skin) were wild with joy at my young flesh, and began gnawing immediately. I couldn't stand it; I took my Christmas tree, thrust it into the fireplace and started it flaming, hoping thus (by the drunken reasoning I'd already been using five years) to suffocate the tiny cannibals. And the fire burned wonderfully. Now it seems my chimney let out directly into the apartment above, from which, ten minutes later, a young couple came flying down, their faces black from soot, screaming.

"The baby! Our baby is dying from the smoke!" (another baby!), and we threw a bucket of water onto the Christmas tree — which caused such an additional density of smoke that the fire department arrived. I explained that it was the bedbugs. (I had never lived alone before.) Everyone went back to bed, but I went out again into the night of Village bars (probably the San Remo) and when I finally returned I was not alone. I recall that my companion smelled most unpleasant—so unpleasant, in fact, as to have disgusted the bedbugs and sent them all away. Because the next day they seemed to be quite gone, and I never had contact with another one there, though I lived on in that room for five years.

Not a word from Jerry since the two long letters just after he left Paris in October. Perhaps because of this silence which I'm almost used to, he now seems the only person I'd like to hear from. It's now obvious that our ballet won't be done, at least not this season, and I can't help but think he's embarrassed to write because of his disappointment in the score. (Today, in looking over the music, I too find it forced and hasty and without great interest except for the Waltz already used in *Mélos*.) I believe, too, that Jerry feels my interest in him is "professional"—he being abnormally suspicious—and this hurts. (I'm the opposite: I feel that everyone likes me "for myself alone." Yet, strangely, those who have been the most helpful professionally are editors and performers who've never met me.) I could strongly wish Jerry didn't feel this way, for with few people have I so quickly built up a series of sentimental connections. How wrong to proudly go telling everyone about our ballet, and how blushful when it doesn't come off! *Tant pis!* Mostly it's order I want; I loathe things left hanging. I lose such order in drinking (maybe even in writing music) that in my conscious life have a phobia. No love note thrills me half so much as a musical fan letter from a stranger. But once the letter is read I sink back to where I was, because I've never been much interested in hearing my own music played: it embarrasses me, like standing naked before a crowd which suddenly sees that you have just one leg (if only they knew about my internal organs!). . . . I'm not sure what "happiness" means to me; I *do* know that unfortunately it's never a situation of the moment, but rather a condition of sensual perfection which I'll achieve when I "grow up"—that is to say, *never*. . . . I don't suppose he'll believe me, but I'd like Jerry to think in later years that I really loved him.

An army cannot be made from a group of people of which each one is different. And how we change every hour! I don't mean that yesterday my hair was peach-colored, tomorrow sea-green. It's a change interior, unrealizable because of Time; we all breathe the same molecules which metamorphose even as we do: we can't *see* them because we *are* them. For instance: two people sit and talk; the man leaves the room for twelve minutes; but, at the start of these twelve minutes, it's arranged that—for the woman in the room—Time stops: she is frozen, Time too. This arrangement ends at the man's return. Now the woman is twelve minutes behind him (as though she'd been born twelve minutes before the universe). She will literally not recognize the man. . . . Julius Caesar could never inhale our air. How much more complex is the ebb and flow of our relationships from lack of understanding! Can we recognize the stars from night to night, which change their sense as we approach? How can I know if the blue I see today is the blue of yesterday, unless yesterday's comes back to stand beside today's? Can we have two simultaneous Times? How can I know if my blue is yours? When may we be sure of what may turn false? Some words I pronounce in a curious way because my mother pronounced them thus when I was learning to speak. To me this is the right way, though it is called wrong by the world. And still the Arab and the Manhattanite are as knotted together as Siamese twins.

From the threads of so many methods the same desire for expression is woven. Who but researchers (those I hold most in contempt) care where a masterpiece comes from as long as it comes? Which doesn't keep me from writhing in envy at the methods of others—I want only what isn't mine. I, too, change, and remain the same. Why, yesterday, did I—the image of order—burn my hand six times, either in lighting the stove or in putting out my cigarettes? Today I haven't burned myself. *Passons.* . . .

Gide said that at twenty-five he knew already all he had to say; the remainder of his life would be dedicated to saying it. He got up early, saw beauty in everything, worked regularly, sought love at specific hours, didn't drink, wasn't bored. So he is accused of living out his era in ignoring "major issues." Cannot we have great men with happy natures, to whom the writing on major issues does not seem writing, since everything changes? For me, I like things to stay as they are; it is I who would move among the frozen landmarks. Yet I work by crisis and devote myself to garbage like so many now.

Ohana, not being *chez lui*, I left him a note and took a walk through the Mamounia gardens. It's almost indecent, this January weather. The paths are heavy with hot smells like living inside of an orange (Venice is like strolling through the veins of a dead woman). Personally I never just stroll (despite what I used to tell my parents after supper, with the excuse that I was a melancholy poet) though I do walk a lot, always in suspicious parks looking for encounters which haven't materialized since I was fifteen; my happiest love was then because I didn't know danger, and danger can't plunder innocence. Yet at that age I was much more the Corrupter than now. With that shyness, how could I have dispelled our high-school poetry club with just a lyric about lesbians? My passivity was always stronger than other people's aggression. . . . At that age too we all had special modes of expression, like saying "this" for "that" ("*This* is very interesting" instead of "*That* is very interesting"). After all these years then, I was nonplussed in Paris to come across an American intellectual of eighteen who exclaimed: "What! You live in Marrakech? But don't the nightingales drive you crazy?" I had forgotten how the hideous style of the young never changes from generation to generation.

On the way back from Tangier, I went into the monstrous church of Rabat. There were just four other people there, and I watched them. French Catholics cross themselves more slowly than Americans; they do it as I used to in imitating what to me was a mystery but what was just habit to others: the movement of the hand, from forehead to chest to left shoulder to right, traced a burning thread which stung itself into the flesh, then faded like a headache with aspirin, or the smoke of a forest fire. . . . The first time I was in a Catholic church I must have been nine: Mother took me (on Chicago's 55th Street) with my sister to witness the mass for our "education." How different it was from the hard chairs, the frigid silence of our Quakers! What surprised me most in this fog of gold incense, was a strange woman in rich blue wool, with wonderfully manicured hands joined in prayer. That beautiful person was A CATHOLIC (magic word, lucky person!). Until then I had imagined all Catholics wore rags, that only Jesus had a right to sparkling robes.

I don't know why, but Sex has always been the favorite topic of every intelligently cultured person I've known. The favorite topic for every *un*intelligently cultured person I've known is Books, or, what is worse, Music. Casablanca is the sexiest of towns: the air swims with it. I had to hurry home and resume work to forget all this. Only to find, in the middle of the sunny Place Jemâa-el-Fnâa, an ostrich which will swallow any coin smaller than a five-franc piece. Tomorrow morning his masters will search his excrement for their reward.

Last night I had a dream. Two small dogs fighting became two fighting boys. One ripped out the eye of the other. A voice said: "Then two bluish strings hung from the hole's edge, like remnants of a rotten egg flowing out of the broken shell."

Today's Maggy's birthday.

Ten years ago my favorite foods were sweet potatoes (with marshmallows), beer (Milwaukee's best "amber fluid," as Dick used to say), and cherry pie (with the crumbling, tan crust that only Olga could make). But not at the same time.

I like to fill ash trays just in order to empty them. . . . Am attracted by people who are attracted by Youth; in twenty-two years I'll be fifty; and then what.

I saw the spirit's fire once or twice, but only long ago during childhood's discoveries. With growth of technique and its cluttering of the mind I hear things differently; the wide-open door through which I once saw brilliantly has become a hairline. I work more and more toward the *clarity of youth* which proportionately recedes. Death is quick, life long. Our greatest discovery is in dying. How then will it benefit us? Learning is for living.

The same piece of music alters at each hearing. But oh, the need to repeat and repeat and repeat unchanged the sexual experience.

I loathe Marx's "Religion is the opiate of the people." Yet the statement is true and thank God! Marx meant this with shallow cruelty; but the Church, with all its bloody history, has given magic and poetry for two thousand years. I think if the Quakers had offered incense to my childhood I might not be a composer today.

Elliott Stein and I are writing a new libretto. Maybe we should call it *Father of the Sphinx Killer*. It's about Oedipus' father. In the legend, Laius was banished from his native Thebes for kidnapping a boy. He fled to Athens, and thereby introduced pederasty to that country for the first time.

I'd like to do a third opera in the form of a comedy on Saint-Germain-des-Près with a Negro contralto singing the blues with an oboe. Also perhaps a "Grand-Guignol" melodrama, ridiculously bloody. These operas will all have the same instrumentation, and should be performed by school children. The one on Oedipus will have only two men's voices; the sound of men is less tiring than women: the former sing more in their speaking tessitura. The son will be the bass and the father the tenor. Why not? The bass will sing high, the tenor low — the tension will petrify. The first words — "Father, tell me. . . . " As much suspense as in *Sorry, Wrong Number*. A keyboard orchestra (that Lou Harrison used to dream of): harmonium, organ, piano, celesta, glockenspiel, two harpsichords, three clavichords, plus four bass flutes in unison. . . . I want an aria on sexuality (description of touch) sufficient to "erect" the audience, an aria on cruelty (description of blood) sufficient to scare the audience, and an aria on nostalgia (description of past springs) sufficient to make the audience cry.

But I've heard nightingales sing and it's not so beautiful as all that.

Received today from Paul Bechert a subjective letter bawling me out (good-humoredly) for how I "make people suffer" — except for *him*. Then he adds: "I don't really need you, because the world is full of fascinating, capricious creatures like you. But I think you need me. No one else tells you the truth about yourself. I do, and always will." Jesus! How many people have told me *that* in my life? Fifty maybe? Seventy-five?

Guy recounts a disease (or rather a perversion) he has observed in certain Cheleuh tribes: the compulsive eating of soil. An otherwise normal citizen is attracted, not by food, but dirt. Desire for nourishment is as foreign to him as a lesbian's for a sailor. His family forces him to eat, as he has lost all instinct for self-preservation.

During the two years before puberty (simultaneously with my craze to become a Catholic) I collected birds. Live birds, in an array of cages I made myself: cages of wicker, or metal bars, cages of glass, all huge and containing miniature forests of ferns and twigs. . . . My passion for ornithology was ferocious; I knew all the Latin names (but wild birds didn't interest me, only domesticated). Now I just remember the standard names: Strawberry Finches, Cordon Blues, Red-billed Weavers, Gold-necked Weavers, Java Rice Sparrows, Gouldian Finches (these were the most sensational), Society Finches. When we were in Paris in 1936 I took many more home from the bird market on the Ile de la Cité; they cost nothing. I spent hours, months, spellbound before the great cages, watching the slightest movement of my multicolored parakeets, my dwarf parrots. (These were the hours, months, I later spent alone figuring what music was all about.) I was disdainful of canaries. . . . They would breed. We would let them fly loose in the living room among the sunny plants. Sometimes a surprised visitor's poised teacup would be spattered by droppings as a feathered friend whizzed by. I had names for them taken from my reading: Ichabod Crane, Edmond and Mercedes, Zeus and Hera. Cosette and Marius were a pair of Zebra Finches (the female is the more beautiful: about half the size of a canary, all pearl-gray plumage with a bright orange beak). We gave them vast amounts of cotton and they built a nest as elaborate as a beehive, high up behind a bust of Shakespeare on the bookshelf. Cosette laid one egg which never hatched. She later died. Marius committed suicide; that is, we brought him another mate soon after and they killed each other.

This was my first heartbreak. My life was birds: I belonged to bird clubs, went to bird shows, subscribed to bird magazines, wrote to the bird farms of California to send me live shipments of their rarest specimens (most of which originate in Australia). I sought avicultural references in all of life's variations the way a thrilled masochist looks for murder in the daily papers. I heard that Chinese emperors blinded nightingales to make them sing by day. I stole the sky-blue Robin's egg from the Vermont farm of our poet friends the Hendricks, who were also pacifist, and did not believe in theft. The smell of summer was the light of birds to me, and I hated people who didn't know the word "Bird". . . . Then, almost overnight, as my voice changed into adolescence, I lost interest. I put all these creatures into one cage, took them downtown to Vaughan's Seed Store (anyone named Vaughan was magic to me) on Chicago's Randolf Street, and sold the bunch for seventeen dollars. With this money I bought two record albums: *Skyscrapers* of Carpenter, and *Le Sacre du Printemps*.

I was thirteen.

Passed an almost perfect day in Mogador with Hélène Rémy. Two touching dramas took place.

We went to the sultan's castle, deserted in the seventeenth century, a few kilometers out of town, crumbled on an immense beach. No one is near, just sand and the sea. The whole palace is invaded by sand: the roof is gone, and you walk from room to room and in and out of the windows on hills of sand. The stone walls seem torn like paper, and half the building has disappeared beneath the sand streaked with tiny footprints. Then Hélène came running toward us with something cupped in her hands: a baby rabbit, numb with fright, his ears flat against his head, his nose bruised, and his little hind paws crushed and dry with blood. We examined the sand on the floor of a roofless room and found traces of what seemed a battle with an eagle who must have taken the rabbit in his claws, then dropped him from high. . . . What were *we* now to do with this dying thing? We considered a series of possibilities, then decided. A thousand yards away on the edge of the ocean was an old fort eroded from the center and slumping outward on every side like a cake that has failed. We crossed slowly to it on the long stretch of beach—a funeral procession in the stifling light, the quivering animal with just enough strength to make his eyes gleam. We climbed high onto the ramparts which literally hung lopsided into the waves. We paused a long sad time, reasoning, looking at the moss in the sun. And then, with all our force, we hurled the baby rabbit out to the air where he twirled for a moment in the brightness, then was flung by the wind into the ocean. He was certainly killed instantaneously by the blow. We were depressed. We came back past the sultan's forgotten castle filled now with wind as evening was approaching.

In the city proper we went again to the white-walled cemetery (filled mostly with Spanish and English children dead two hundred years ago) built right on the sea. But we were asked brutally to leave by the guard who discovered us standing on tombstones and peering over the wall onto the wild beach, which was littered with large rocks of orange, heavy blue and brown, like Braque. . . .

Tonight I am all alone. The lights down in the city are beginning to come on, and the dogs in the Médina are yelling. There's quite a wind. Mésäoud has fixed me a good supper (veal, watermelon, thé à-la-menthe) but he's now gone, though he offered to spend the night in case I were afraid. And I am a little afraid. Any indigène *who felt like it could come and cut my throat — no doubt with reason. . . .*

We've been listening ten times a day to Ralph Kirkpatrick's "long-playing" version of Falla's masterpiece. Years ago I had the composer's own recording, and it seemed more savage and raw, a kind of Spanish Kafka in music. Ralph is slicker, but the harpsichord doesn't make enough noise. . . . It's funny how one knows that certain masterpieces must have been totally conceived in a single day. These three movements overflow into each; it *had* to be written quickly so as not to spill on the floor and disappear. Think of the great works that have been forgotten in dreams — that have been known to just one person! My best works have burst from me like a lonely infection that finally splits the skin. Pieces I have slaved over have always been artificial failures. That's my way of working. Schubert's too. It has to do with poetry already written. I mistrust Poulenc when he says he sweats out every song: I'd like to know how *Figure humaine* was written

(I'll ask him, next time we meet *en promenade* between the two confessionals of the Luxembourg). . . . Beethoven was different. I'll never forget Xénia coming home wilted after her first hearing of the *Missa Solemnis*. "How could he write such a thing? He was just a man." Just a man, she said, with tears in her voice.

A letter from David Diamond who writes: "I want you always to remain a dedicated craftsman. . . . I hope Janey Bowles is continuing to write as she's immensely gifted!" *Dedicated craftsman, immensely gifted*, these phrases turn my stomach, the same as (years ago at school) the expressions: *Play the game!* or *sense of responsibility*. To whom would I be responsible, were I to know the sense of the word? *Je ne puis guère croire qu'il y aurait davantage de crimes si nous n'avions plus de lois*. And a craftsman is the last thing *this* composer wants to be. David's splendid technique is exactly the reason he may not go down in the history he's planning. I prefer Satie who had no technique, therefore no responsibility. Certainly technique and gift together don't make genius. The combination is inhibiting.

Composition is notation of distortion of what composers think they've heard before. Masterpieces are marvelous misquotations.

Tonight as I packed Guy said, deeply moved:
    "If anyone saw you packing your bags like that, he'd never suspect your self-satisfaction which is, *au fond*, quite superficial. It's feigned, and to protect yourself. You who have no home, who leave me in order to settle with others in any old hotel room! With only those disgusting pants, and that ugly briefcase which hides your latest *chef-d'oeuvre* on which you worked so hard! How many people, less important than you, enter a house like a whirlwind and leave it the same way, worrying about their clothes and their affairs of the moment! And I, who want to build a new house only so that you might live there, with your own piano! But it's clear that despite all your airs, you just live for music. You need so little luggage, you make so little noise in leaving, like birds who fly away."

Tomorrow I take the plane from Casa to Paris. I don't think it will crash. I must be back before the twentieth as my passport (I only have a temporary one since the theft last September) expires that day. And I must cash my Fulbright check and resume the classes with Honegger. I have exactly 2,080 francs. . . . I am nervous, excited, embarrassed at the pleasant thought of seeing Marie Laure and three hundred other friends, and the dentist and his drill and his bill. Though what is my uppermost idea? Shall I admit it? It is the wonder of how my first *fine-à-l'eau* will taste after seven weeks of abstinence.

It is warm and cloudless.

PARIS

For more than a week I've been back in Paris, and the horrors here are even worse than those of Casablanca where the streets were lined with rioting Moslems screaming *Indépendence!* Perhaps in ten years Casa will be deserted, crumbled, no more than the old sultan's sandy palace on the Mogador beach.

On the airplane were twins: frightful girls covered with lipstick and long hair and heavy bellies. With them was a third girl, shorter and older, but dressed and painted identical to the other two. The three were obviously part of a circus. Their absolutely similar ugliness was stultifying. (I thought of Karl Shapiro's "Mongolian Idiot," and of D. H. Lawrence's "Elephant.") And yet what envy, what solace, what total mutuality in their caresses, their breasts, their *tutoiement* lisped quietly.

... nothing is worse than death. And if one consoles oneself that death is the end of all, it's also certain that nothing is worse than life. Why work, why bother? For of that which was Nikolai Nikolaievitch nothing remains. (Tolstoy on his brother's death.)

My order and actions are conscious in spite of myself, and nearly all in defiance of death. With every street crossed I say, Well I wasn't hit *that* time; with every cigarette I say, Well I've managed to smoke one more before dying; with every letter written I say, Well at least it's in the mail and even if I die someone will exclaim: "To think I received a note from him the day after his death!" So I cross more and more streets, smoke more and more, write more and more letters — always trying to increase the number of living gestures between myself and my death. Whenever a work is finished death feels closer, which is why I must launch myself immediately into a new one. For the idea of dying in the middle of unfinished business seems not only indecent, but impossible. That I should die while others live is insupportable, but is nevertheless the force that blasts me for-

ward into actions monotonous and useless, into other actions performed even while saying: If I don't do this thing, then I'll have died
without having done it, and though it bores me and saps my strength,
my strength is still stronger than myself.

I suppose this is why I keep a diary (or let myself be painted,
fornicated, led into foreign countries). Fear of being forgotten is so
compulsive I'd like to be remembered for each time I go to the bathroom, and I'd even prefer not to go alone.

Lunch with George Bemberg and Raffaello de Banfield, the richest
boys in the world, who (after a penetrating conversation on the sorrows of our world) quibble about the division of the check to such a
degree that I paid for all three of us.

Patricia Neway tells me she sang three of my songs on B.B.C.
last month, but she can't remember the titles.

Work going well (*The Resurrection*). But of this one mustn't write
in a journal, or the music itself will never be realized.

Have just learned that I must leave this apartment (75, rue de
Vaugirard) as the building has been confiscated by priests.

Last night I read *Les Cenci*. It would make a wonderful movie-
opera. Stendahl himself speaks of Francesco Cenci as a ghastly Don
Juan character. There are pages of good form, terror and beauty and
detail, especially at the end. Beatrix' words are heart-rending:
"*Comment est-il possible, ah! Dieu! qu'ainsi à l'improviste je doive
mourir?*" . . . Perfect for singing. . . . The machine of execution called
a *mannaja* (is it a Spanish word?) sounds uglier than the electric chair.
A kind of guillotine, the footnote explains: "*La mannaja devait
ressembler à l'instrument de mort français.*" It's as though one said:
Like an octopus, only worse.

Before going to see Julien I had the weird pleasure of meeting Iris
Adrian in flesh and blood, at the St. James bar (drinking ginger ale,
which I haven't seen for three years). Said she, "I don't care *who* you
are, but I like you anyway. Sit down!" It was Margaret Bonds' friend
Muriel Landers who introduced us; they're singing together in Jack
Benny's show which is touring Europe. I was with Elliott, who

explained to me that I. A. had made three hundred movies, always
taking the part of a dumb blonde, notably in "Blondie" pictures, and
in *Lady of Burlesque* with Barbara Stanwyck. "And I hope to make
three hundred more," said Iris. "There's a lot of laughs in that racket.
And a lot of tears!" Her hair is so blonde it's silver; she must be forty.
She continues: "So you're writing an opera! Hope you make money.
In show biz there's only two kinds of audiences: the kind you got,
and the kind you don't. The kind you don't got don't pay off, and I
don't care *how* good you think your opera is. . . . You fellows live in
Paris? You must speak a little French by now? Why'd you leave the
States? Of course it's easier for a guy to live away than for a girl when
you've got a husband and children." . . . She says "children," not "kids,"
showing she takes marriage very seriously. Her voice is loud, sad
and steady. She drops her cigarette and speaks to it as it lies on the
floor: "Goddamn you! I'll get you back. Don't just lay there looking
back like that! You won't get away from me. . . . Write for television,
boys. *That's* what pays off." . . . I go away feeling touched, knowing
these girls live with their mothers. Why should I explain that our
paths and standards vary? . . . I relate all this to Julien who doesn't
think it's funny. He is too French for the American myth and magic
of the movies. Elliott is in seventh heaven.

On the Boulevard des Batignolles last Sunday night was a bicyclist
who (walking) turned three times to look at me, then vanished. For
my part this was a love I will never forget. Unhad love is sweeter.

Lunch today at Robert de Saint-Jean's. Cocteau arrives in dungarees —
the excuse being he's between rehearsals (*Oedipus Rex* at the Champs-
Elysées). Fine food, and a finer monologue by the guest of honor.
Julien finally manages to exclaim: "Really Jean, you should have a
Boswell!" Jean retorts: "Yes, but it's not all mine. For instance, did
you know? it wasn't I, but Péguy who said: *Il faut savoir jusqu'où on
peut aller trop loin.*" (We must know how to go too far.) Why has he
never admitted this in print? Then again, why *should* he?

To be in a police car taking you to prison, and by accident to drive past your own house where your mother is innocently sweeping, and expecting you home from school! To be in your father's car taking you to church, and by coincidence to drive past the place (a bar, a bench) where last night you fell in love!

Sauguet phones to ask if I'm free to write a ballet about *Dorian Gray* in collaboration with (of all people) Jean Marais. It seems Marais will control, Cocteau-fashion, all but the musical elements: write the scenario, supervise the choreography, design sets and costumes, and mime the decaying picture. The hour-long production will be premiered less than two months from now in Barcelona. I love pressure. I accept.

On my floor here at 75, rue de Vaugirard (which I must soon leave forever), there are five nationalities: to the left a German student learning his father's trade of manufacturing slate for roofs (and who, through the thin walls, hears me at love more often than I hear him); at the end of the hall, next to the *lavabos*, a Turk who is *en proces* with the landlady and who has a room full of kindling; at the other end a French couple (I have never seen them); across, a Chinese who has a French mistress; on my right, Henri; then myself, American. . . . My own room is large and rather *chichiteuse*, aglimmer with color and plants, a ladder and bedspread given me by Marie Laure, several portraits of myself, books, my own music conspicuously on display, and framed drawings Cocteau did for me. The contrast of Henri's room excites me; I go in there each noon (when I get up) for coffee and *croissants* if I don't have a hangover. There is nothing but the dull hotel furnishings which have always been there, and the drably marvelous and distant odor of dirty socks; a broken tube of shaving cream and an unmade bed that speaks. Across the room a clothesline hung with white shirts and shorts. Henri is away in Malakoff working since six-thirty in the morning, but I drink his coffee sitting in his armchair, smoking my Chesterfield in my red bathrobe with great monk's sleeves, and think about how Americans are clean and the French dirty, and go wild.

2 A.M. Heavy, moonless night. Even the rue de Vaugirard seems dead. Feeling alone, panicked at amorous responsibilities, awed at abilities to smash. Henri has long since gone to sleep next door.

Noon next day. Shortly after writing the above I went to bed and a few hours later awoke from the realest nightmare of my life. If I write it here (a thing I never did during psychoanalysis) it's because, still trembling, I must shake it from me. . . . I was alone here in my dark room, and walking to the window I looked down into the street instead of which I saw a black lake where nuns and priests were drowning in their effort to reach the door below. I knew I must leave before dawn and was waiting only for Henri to come. He lifted me in his arms and at the speed of a herd stampeding carried me down an endless road of poplars whose leaves hit my face in passing. A bleak day was breaking as we arrived into a huge room which resembled an empty theater, or rather an arena. Three or four ushers were cleaning up, and refused to speak to us, or in any way help us to escape. Henri had grown tall and blond. I had forgotten how to fly which generally I am able to do. The only road out was on the side of a mountain, but this was blocked by the hind legs of a beautiful and strong orange horse. I was told he would not kick, but after we had passed he began to kick ferociously. Once more in Henri's arms we descended a deep circular staircase with banisters of living eyes. And then, in my dream, I awoke. Total blackness. I ached horribly, especially in the mouth and on the right side of the abdomen as though I'd been kicked. On touching my face I realized I was drenched in blood. I also realized I'd fallen to the floor, but was relieved in knowing the pain came from the fall and not from an attack. Some very real accordion was playing a loud German waltz. I wanted it to stop. In spite of the wounds I managed to turn on the electricity — and this was the awful moment: my room had been transformed, transformed as only a dream could do. The two armchairs were nailed (or glued) to the ceiling, the floor was littered with thousands of blades and tacks which cut my feet, the walls were streaked with the painting of insanity, and the whole had been redecorated in shiny black and orange Chinese furnishings. I knew it was myself who had done it all while sleeping, who had risen and worked with a somnambulist's swiftness. The blood was

thick as velvet all over my body; staggering to the mirror I saw my
reflection white as paper with the eyes of a madman staring back. I
went down the hall to awaken Henri and show him my room, but
was too numb with fright to speak. So I wrote with my finger in the
dust on the Chinese screen these letters: S A N G. And Henri said:
"*Va te rinser la bouche, elle sent le sang.*" He then turned into a woman
and began to sing the waltz I'd heard earlier. His singing was so loud
that I gestured for him to hush, but he only smiled as if to say: I wasn't
singing, you only thought I was because you've gone crazy. He was
standing by the door. Blood began to flow into my eyes. When it cleared
away Henri had vanished as quickly as a bird. . . . Then I woke up in
a paralyzed sweat, turned on the light, looked at my watch: it was
ten to five (the hour in my dream which was scheduled for my flight).
The right side of my abdomen and my mouth ached horribly. Sum-
moning the courage to get out of bed I went down the hall to wake
Henri, so that he could come and sleep his remaining few hours with
me. He did, comforting me with his arms as I cried and cried and
cried and cried.

A cool and languid lobster lunch at Marie Laure's with Poulenc who
is witty and bright and religious and knows it and you know he knows
it and say so and it's a bit spoiled.

Lunch again *chez* Marie Laure who is so ill she couldn't come out.
We are worried but it is natural; she herself thinks she's dying which
of course means she isn't. . . . Later went to Julius' to hear him do my
sonata before he records it for Decca next week. I don't like the work
much anymore and would not have the nerve to write it today. But
Henri found it *"très bien, qu'elle coulait comme un chapelet entre
les doigts."* . . . A filthy dinner in Raffy's where some strangers recognized me and stood at our table to talk. As always, I was terribly
flattered, but affected a matter-of-factness, which, if I could see it
from afar, I would find despicable. . . .

Marie Laure says that my French is a cross between that of the Princesse de Clèves and Jean Genet; that my accent is Russian; that I write it nearly as fluently as English but with a quite different personality.

What does a boy soprano have that even a Tiena Lemnitz lacks? I think it is that hollow white French pure sound of Trust; all the more exciting as we would like to hear it defiled. The *Ave Verum* of Fauré. Nobody can say anything more beautiful than the Gregorian exists. But as I listen to it I cannot escape the blond notes of credulity answered by low sonorities with black beards around them. This is sufficient for me to expire. My entire libido is based on this image of the dark which envelops the light. And I never forget my Norwegian ancestry.

At Lise Deharme's the young editor, Jacques Damase, all but dies as I enter, for I am the ghost of René Crevel. He's not the first to have seen this.

It is above all her voice which makes Lise Deharme the great lady. The sound of a whore in a room where she doesn't belong. You hear a rusty flower. Her parlor contains an emerald-colored carpet and six thousand plants, an aviary, a stuffed owl, countless oriental trinkets. The heat is atrocious. In this room she talks and wins hearts.

Six o'clock coffee with Francis Rose. His voice is his loss. I also suspect him of being a liar (a tragic liar, not a jolly one). However, he tells long tales of his son in prison, and in the end you are more afraid for yourself than anyone else.

Auric is alone in Paris for the others have gone to Spain. And so we spent the evening together at the restaurant Albert, rue de Grenelle. The poor man has been suffering so from gout for two weeks that he must use a cane. With his hat on I almost didn't recognize him when we met *aux Deux Maggots*, and it took us half an hour to walk five blocks. We spoke of what all musicians speak of: how we are cheated;

the comparison of working habits; miserliness; public urinals; the excruciatingly hopeless trend the world is taking; who of our friends is bedding with whom and why; danger and love and the reasons for his own fame. But nothing private about him, and about me nothing personal. He talks well, and when he talks of the past he glows as though speaking to his son. But he is sad — in pain even — and his life is one of hinting. We drank a barrel of *muscadet* and then we stopped. I like Auric too well to say more, though I know this is a kind of cheating.

When I was fifteen, once after one of those trembling and tender adolescent disputes with my family, when the child has not yet enough logic for his heart's defense, I ran away from home (oh, just three blocks distance to Chicago's Century Hotel on 55th Street) and for forty-eight hours was *a bohemian.* And then I received a marvelous and comprehensive letter from Father telling me his understanding and why, and that the heart newly opened to freedom (which will *never* be) is ignorant. So I returned home, crumbled in tears, to my family's arms. I'll be always the prodigal son as long as I live away from America, and landmarks, any arms I find along the way, are just substitutes for Father's. Unfortunately arms are a comfort only when they are being a comfort (that is the *present*); one cannot go about daily chores handicapped by pairs of open arms.

Nadia Boulanger writes me: *"Vous êtes doué, merveilleusement. Puis-je me permettre de redire 'qui veut faire de grandes choses doit longuement songer aux details.' La citation n'est hélas exacte que dans l'esprit. . . . Tous mes profonds voeux pour que vous faissiez tout ce que nous sommes en droit d'attendre de vous. . . ."* The underlined *tout* is her scary method of censuring my whole collection of private relationships.

But I *do* care what others think, and there are those who see me only as a sop (a "human rag" the French say). Or, if they know I write music, they wonder (without interest) why I should have collapsed at the Pergola in a pile of broken glass at eight in the morning. Heddy de Ré takes me into the Discothèque, brings over Daniel Gélin so he can tell me how moved he was by what I'd done to his poems (which are mediocre, though the music is agreeable). I pretend not to recognize him . . . . To add to the horror, summer has really struck here, and the heat of a Paris dawn in August is intolerable when one is drunk. Not to mention its soonness: dawn hits the city towards four, illuminating the bloodshot eyes of friends, and their wrinkles filled with dirt.

Lise sits at the Flore; I go by; a stranger behind her says, *"Voilà Ned Rorem qui passe. Je l'ai vu l'autre soir, seul comme d'habitude, installé devant son demi. On aurait dit un ange déchu."* According to Lise, this is the prettiest compliment one could receive.

Lenny Bernstein once said (it must have been at least eight years ago), "The trouble with you and me, Ned, is that we want everyone in the world to personally love us, and of course that's impossible: you just don't *meet* everyone in the world."

Back from Barcelona where *Dorian Gray* flopped ignominiously. Nevertheless, after the performance, backstage at 2 A.M., a hundred adolescent girls storm me with programs to autograph. Complacent among these adoring gigglers, I begin to sign. Then Marais emerges from his dressing room. All heads turn. In a flash they desert me like rats from a ship, and fall upon the star. I remain alone. One of them returns furtively — to snatch her pencil from my hand.

Paris is brimming with signs (printed, or simply chalked on walls) saying: GO HOME AMERICANS. One sees also — though less often — LES STALINIENS A MOSCOU. For we who are not French, it is unpleasant to come across them. Even the wealthy French never travel, feeling their own country and language to be superior to others; they therefore misunderstand the voluntary displacement of foreign colonists. The Communist element here is disheartening in its force, though I can only look at it with a certain irritation, since I have always found Communists individually charmless and without humor; they are using an inhuman procedure to humanize the world.

What do I think about Modern Music? Gertrude Stein answered about painting: "I like to look at it." I say: "I hate to listen to it." The reply is a reaction, not a judgment. Now I find myself ever less able to judge, ever more moved by reactions. The public? This summer I saw Picasso, after a bullfight in Arles, accosted with the gifts of live infants. With a stroke of charcoal he designs on a baby's naked ass, and returns this art to the parents. What will they do, skin the child? Refuse it a bath for decades? The musical audience, for better or worse, cannot possess and so cannot brag; it is reduced to judgment and no longer reacts.

The biggest insult an American can receive is: "He isn't *natural*; he's always playing a role." But from the moment we learn to talk we start an existence of unnaturalness; a few years later we decide more or less what our particular role is and play it the rest of our life. . . .

At Julien's, we discuss "dirty words" and how we both prefer the slang to the "proper" term for sexual organs and primary acts. There are certain medical terms I would rather die than utter, whereas the familiar substitute appears naturally in my vocabulary of a child. The dirtiest words I know are J— D—. With shame I admit that while drunk recently I allowed this person to drive me alone all over Paris; he must have spent 200,000 francs on champagne, tips, private entertainment and such ostentation, not a sou of which he would have disposed of on me as a composer. He told me his personal detectives had informed him I was a "pale-pink Communist," which is the most idiotic accusation I have ever received.

Jacques Bourgeois, who was a paratrooper during the war, recounts for us the details of throwing oneself from an airplane. The fear is

basic, since even the insane have no desire to fall from high places.
My twin cousins in the Coast Guard used to tell of suicides off the
San Francisco bridge: how women, as they fell would moan slow and
loud, "Why did I do it . . . ?"

It has been seven years; seven years ago I began this diary in 1945,
the September after the war. "Seven" is a good number, holy, the
length of the Egyptian plague, and the itch; also the number of years
Hans Castorp spent up in that magic mountain; there are also the
seven deadly sins and the wonders of the world; it is the age of which
the priest says, "Too late. If you had given me your son at six I could
have made him a Catholic; now he is formed, and should he have a
vision it would not be one of ours." . . . Seven could doubtless be high
time for me to cease such writing, but Marie Laure just gave me this
little book, which she got in Holland, and said, "Write! For if you
feel hideous afterwards, it is nonetheless pleasant while the hand is
in motion."

Is this diary dishonest? Should I write here now? or go out and *do*
something that should be written about? Still, one shouldn't write
about what one does, but what one thinks about what one's done.
Or should have done. So I'll write here now.

Ethel Reiner maintains that, for us, there are only five thousand people
in the world, and sooner or later we meet them all. That's brutal.

Julius Katchen has read these diaries. "There are two conspicuous
absences," says he. "Your love affairs and your family." What could I
say of my family that would not be sacrilegious betrayal? This is for
novels. It is not the place of a journal to investigate cores, but to discuss the misery of effects. I have no courage to go deeper: I would
scare myself (as I used to, as a child, making weird faces in the mirror)
and I want to be happy: without that I can't work. . . . Love affairs,
that's different. If I spend more time alone with those with whom I

am in love than with even my dearest friends, it is nevertheless a different kind of time, like that of creation about which I never write. This is a period removed from Time and, like the act of love, has no limits, no beginning nor end.

The days are shorter, darker, already much colder: going-back-to-school weather. Bookstores display a sign *Rentrée des Classes* and windows full of rulers, erasers. The square of St. Sulpice steams with leaves and the Concorde is surrounded with rusty orange as I prepare with terror to leave this country. Had tea alone in Smith's today reading Bernanos. Next week I depart for America.

PART 7
1953

PARIS

Three months in New York were expensive. To save money, I've accepted Jacques Damase's invitation to stay *chez lui,* and ten years ago this bohemianism would have suited my fancy fine; but today my hands are too blue-cold to touch the keys; we hover around the stove, the floors are strewn with old magazines on top of which are plates caked with last week's eggs; the *bidet* is thick with slime; there are dead flowers and crumbling mannequins and dust and broken windows and lighted candles everywhere, and cold, cold, cold. I groan to feel my head so full of ideas and unable to notate them because of the squalor. If I don't notate them now, when will I? Life is passing. To escape the atmosphere I go out and drink (Monday, for the first time in twenty-three days!) only to return at 6 A.M. exhausted and too tired to care about the water's being turned off. The housing problem in Paris is beyond belief, and if I don't soon get a prize or commission or money of some kind, I'll be forced to suicide. In this frozen mess, Jacques plans to give me a cocktail party on Saturday, though I have no desire for that lost array of congealed faces I'd hoped to avoid by plunging into work far from New York. Marie Laure I see often (tomorrow we go to Desgobert's, the lithographer, to make some song covers), but she is concerned with a life far from mine without temperance to tolerate my lack of interest in the outer world. But this city is far from the South of France where eventually we'll find each other again. My one pleasure is Henri, but love is not so much the memory of shared pain as of happy days. Poverty destroys all, the heart included. Just in order to live Henri must rise daily at six, spend ten hours in Malakoff, then pass four hours of conscious liberty before retiring. This is mysterious to me: it does not permit alcohol.

Feeling low, and slightly high from fear of a war. Played my new *vocalises, chez* Marie Blanche on Sunday (long religious songs), and the French consensus is that I am a Protestant: no Roman would have set those words in that way (the *Holy Songs, Resurrection,* etc.).

Poulenc's comment: "I find she [Ethel Semser] sings better since she has taken out her contact lenses and put on her regular glasses." . . .

Rather drunk then, and feeling low, because I make no money and feel no appreciation and have reached a point of stagnancy with no ideas. Would like to be really drunken, but haven't even the force to combat the rain. Everywhere is talk of a war.

Heddy has become the barmaid at Agnès Capri's (not to mention having fallen in love with Jay Harrison, making a social cobweb of the earth once more). Heddy *mixes* drinks these days, and (with Jay) asks too many questions about why love is love: that domain's more evasive than the sky. For me, I eat radishes and drink myself into a trance (radishes are a favorite trance food).

Today I learn from Mother's letter that once more I have *not* been granted the Rome Prize nor an Arts and Letters Fellowship. Next month we'll know about the Guggenheim, though I am sure to fail a sixth time. Why keep trying? It's not the idiotic recognition I want but the money: in nine months I'll be thirty, and though I feel I have a great deal to say, it seems that no one wants to listen.

Paris for a week has become radiant in an early spring; we can walk out in shirtsleeves, buds seem to spurt shiny before our eyes, and we too in the vernal jerking feel we're being born again — a terrible urge to say the same old words of love, but to new people.

Arthur Laurents asks: "I wonder what would have happened to Romeo and Juliet if they had lived." . . . But it is *because* they died that we know their names. Great love *must* die young. Beauty is beautiful because it cannot endure. If love lives on, it leads to middle-class quarreling. The potion of Tristan and Isolde was brewed to last only three years. Even the slabs of gold wore away from the pyramids.

It's been three weeks since I moved here to Marie Laure's — 11, Place des États-Unis — by far my best residence in Paris. It's all that keeps me alive, the thrill of being alone in a comfortable bed. Of course I'm in love, but, as we know, that has nothing to do with happiness.

Philippe Erlanger says that love is bestowing. But *I* am sure anyone can give; force is in receiving: *n'est pas aimé qui veut.*

In France, if I am invited to lunch on Sunday at the home of a middle-class family, there is always a deaf and friendly grandmother, hard heavy streaks of sunlight landing on abominable furniture, and the eldest son (with a little mustache) who, for the first time, feels pangs of love (whether he knows it or not) because I am there. Someone will whisper to him that I'm often given to excesses, which is why I'm not drinking today, and for months afterward he will not be able to concentrate on his lessons at law school.

André Dubois troubles me when he says my work is too perfect, too serene, too refined, like Reynaldo Hahn; that in my music as in my (Quaker) life I have not said what I really desire — which is too bad since prettiness disappears at death. And André adds that Boulez has lost patience with the waste of such a talent. Honegger had faith in me, but he is not of my time. I am more intelligent than outsiders know, but less than friends think. *Pour moi, je ne suis pas assez fort pour savoir où doit aller ma génération. . . .*

I will not have the courage to say in this diary the things that should be said until I reach an age when the saying of such things will no longer be becoming.

Stella Adler, who pretends never to recognize me, explains that all "goyim" look alike to her.

Sam Barber is in town again, rather sad and unenthusiastic, though witty and sympathetic. He tells of Copland's interview with McCarthy. Copland, after a dignified explanation as to why he had lent his name to certain lists, suddenly realized that McCarthy didn't know who or what he was.

Bernac, too, seems sad and older, but showed interest in my new French cycle which he plans to sing in Fontainebleau. . . . Since coming to Europe I have not written more than three songs equal in expression to those of the New York years which I play now with a sense of time-passed and the notion that another person put those notes on paper.

With that poignance of retrospect, I have been going through the twenty-five or thirty letters received through the years from David Diamond and Paul Bowles. David's (obviously written for posterity) are those of someone *not* a writer: profound, self-conscious, poetic, full of advice, human and long. But Paul's (like Julien Green's) are of the dullest. Men of letters don't waste time writing letters.

The Paris weather, pale as death, continues as in January though July is nearly here. Everyone talks of the Rosenbergs.

Hot and cloudy. Yes, the Rosenbergs were electrocuted. Europe seems less sad than stunned. The Place de la Concorde is filled with police cars half-heartedly preventing crowds from throwing rotten eggs at the American Embassy. Every free wall bears a poster caricaturing Eisenhower's famous grin: each tooth is an electric chair. Martyrdom is unbecoming to those who impose it.

Henri Hell, who has already read the just-published Rosenberg letters, says they aren't those of guilty people. Yet who believes himself guilty who has acted through conviction? Naturally the letters are sincere, pathetic. Besides, guilt isn't guilt until discovered. How many think me always drunk because they only see me thus, ignoring my thousand silent sober days? A drunkard is only a drunkard when he's drunk. Is a murderer a murderer only when he's murdering?

A cruel joke is circulating: Mr. Rosenberg, examining the electric chair, expresses interest and asks questions about its mechanism. The guard answers: *"Ne vous en faites pas, mon ami — on va vous mettre au courant."*

Marriage resembles the involuntary union of snakes — and something always comes between. A boa can swallow a pig, though it takes hours. A second boa can start swallowing the same pig from the other end. But their mouths eventually join and the larger snake swallows the smaller, like it or not. There's no choice: being locked together by a doubly half-digested pig, the little boa must smother, all writhing inside his rival's body.

All endings are sad, even the end of pregnancy. I resent my friends' wives who rob me of my friends, who end the meaning of this friendship. And all change too is sad, even a change for the better. Stars' meanings alter as we come near, but *we* never change really — though nothing stays truth in a third person's mouth.

What's new for the old is old for the new, so how do we know where we are? I mean, the old are new yesterday, the young today. A child, not having been born, can't see this. Yet an old person feels newer today than yesterday when he was younger. So things get newer as they grow older, because today is younger than yesterday.

Old's the opposite of new, but also of young. Old people are more recently old than the unborn, more newly old, newer, constantly on the crest of the wave, advancing, nearer to that future from which the young are distant. Antiques grow ever newer — new hags, a new crone. Newborn babies are all wrinkled with age.

Last month is older than today. Is today younger, or only newer? The past, now old, was when the world was young. So we become

younger and younger as we continue on and away from that old time
when the world in flames was brand new, and so very agèd it now
seems. And we are newer, being more recent. . . . Memories of the
future, the ancient future.

Oceans are old and they don't wrinkle. Now Marie Laure cor-
rects me: "Darling, oceans are nothing *but* wrinkles!" Well, I could
wish forever to be nailed to those waves.

He is looking older and unchanged. (I am afraid of looking older
if not changed.) . . . But neither would I look changed and nobody
has ever been changed and nothing ever changes, which is why fairy
tales are about the turning of ducklings into beauties and pumpkins
into coaches, and why children now take drugs—to ignore what seems
to be an alteration in the world outside them.

I want so to notate these joys of the past, but hesitate, for fear
the very words may themselves become memories to break the heart
in later years. . . . I feel happy. Unhappy only that all must change.
Glad that nothing changes. I live so as not to be anonymous; how
many say this? are they more content? Why must I evolve? Books
don't—why must I? But books *do*, depending on the reader's age
and the time he lives in. They change too in rereading, generally for
the worse; when they change for the better it's not, unfortunately,
because the reader is smarter, but because the book is older.

Styles, like skin, change every seven years but with such overlapping that we notice nothing. If only we could shed like snakes! or,
like caterpillars, emerge from cocoons as butterflies into a new season of joy. Nothing again will ever be new, though every homecoming necessarily indicates a change. But the same voyage will always
be new. Nothing is waste that makes a memory.

The hand that wrote me the burning letter is dead. Old letters
die but we still remember. Finally we don't remember anymore. All
passes. Beauty too. Masterpieces last longer (longer than living)
though seen newly by new eyes, but they also disappear. Even
continents, which are here the longest, must finally be washed
away. The most exciting crotch won't stay that way, nor this paper,
nor this ink. Will it all be back like our flying saucers in a universal
circle?

Books have ends. But there's no denying the fact that the older I
get the more past I'll have. The speed of that past, like the speed of

the things of the earth, increases with the world's age, accumulates
with the hysteria of a falling boulder.

It's painful, occasionally dangerous, to share a tender experience,
for the future so quickly becomes the past where we find ourselves
alone again. But without this sharing, how live? By molding silently
that which the public will eventually snatch away to share among
themselves? These sentimental sharings nonetheless take place every
day despite us, and are accumulated in a nebulous attic from which
we withdraw them in our old age and laugh.

Irène Joachim invited me to meet Kabalevsky (and Aragon with Elsa
Triolet) at the *Maison de la Pensée Française*, and I went, taking Jay
Harrison. Life being short, I prefer to ignore the consequences of
fear; but it is much worse being bored to death, as we were. The
intellectual Communist never changes, regardless of geography or
generation. I reproach him most his lack of humor (not to mention
his addiction to folksongs).

And I got drunk again with Heddy and Julius, starting toward
midnight at the Steinway factory, in a room with twenty pianos, where
we drank two cases of beer and played Satie until dawn.

We've now all read Huxley's new book on devils. There are those who
get famous without caring for the publicity; others who care, but do
not get famous. There are those who could escape death at the stake
(Grandier) but do nothing to save themselves; others who would give
any number of denunciations to escape the fire, but are burnt anyway.

To become famous I would sign any paper.

Monday night (rue Monsieur le Prince) I dined on melon, salmon,
and apricot melba beneath a bouquet of orange gladiolas. This is a
"hangover-type" observation.

Virgil at a *vernissage*: "There're so many pictures you can't see the
people."

I am privileged to say *"The Moonlight Sonata,"* having passed from
when one says it and shouldn't, to when one knows it's inexact, to
the third convolution when one says it in jest without smiling because that's quicker than opus numbers. Similarly Ezra Pound says
"ain't."

When I left America I was still a little boy; now I am not any more —
except on certain days. It is hateful to recall long ago during an early
week in Paris, sitting with John Cage and others at a summery café
near the Sunday-night fountain of the Place St. Michel. We were
laughing sweetly and literarily, when a rosy-cheeked middle-aged
American gentleman sitting alone nearby came up to our table. "I
just wanted to tell you young folks that it does my ears good to hear the
English language," he said smiling, and went off. "How disgusting!"
I murmured, with the assured superiority a new tourist feels when
surrounded by friends in a strange land, himself already French,
though ignoring the tongue (an attitude I notice in many countrymen
who arrive in conquering hordes each June) and disdaining even
lonely old men for being a week younger. "Why?" answered John,
who had already read Henry James. And he was right.

There are two breeds of U.S. representative in Paris: those who look
too American (crew cuts and cameras) to be anything but American,
and those who look too French (berets and *Gauloises*) to be anything
but American. Expatriates from "back home," no matter what their
style (from besotted sexagenarians in Right Bank hotels, to youths
at the Flore who've "forgotten" English, yet say only *merde*), are identifiable by their eyes — their credulous gaze, both embarrassing and
wonderful. No Europeans have it, not even infants.

If, as I figure it, there are 531,460 hours in the life of a man who dies
at seventy, will I (at the average of one whole day a week for the past
twelve years) already, at twenty-nine, have been drunk during at
least 18,000 hours of my life?
    As a "serious" composer is this any more degrading than B.'s

spending his years in dressing as a fine lady and prancing about to
Nellie Lutcher records for our delight, or reading the letter-scene
from *Traviata* to Stravinsky's Psalm Symphony? He and I just have
different faces, different talents.

Once Stella Brooks took me to Julius Monk's on First Avenue, and I
threw a beer bottle at a white piano because at that moment I didn't
like white pianos on a summer night. The management locked me
in the basement as dangerously insane (really) until the police came,
and Stella pretended not to know me. . . .

Late into last night I read Boulez' brainy article on the rhythm of
Stravinsky. What opposites we are: he, pondering for months on the
analysis of another's work (as I did at twelve); I, passing days pasting
pictures into scrapbooks to glorify my own person. He makes me feel
cheap, yet I neither admire nor approve of him.

    As for my own work, I'm in a state of sterility. Not only have I no
ideas, but no desire for work; nor any interest in the fact that I have
no interest, desire, or ideas.

Spent the afternoon with Jay (who returns to New York tomorrow)
at Poulenc's in that sunny high apartment on the Luxembourg, with
chairs of orange plush and squeaking floors. Poulenc plays the role
of Great Master more than any French composer, and he passed a
witty hour giving details on his new opera to the Bernanos film
scenario, which he'll take two years to complete before its La Scala
production in Italian with Tebaldi, Duval, and others. I won't believe
that he works with the amount of declared precision he pretends.
His favorite interpreter in the whole world is Bob Shaw, whom he
says has divined the speed of the very blood in his (Poulenc's) arteries.
All the more surprising that Shaw is Protestant: *tendu*, and the *Stabat
Mater* is Catholic: *calme*. . . .

    But I listen too closely to everybody and become confused
(jealous) before such confidence. How difficult to follow one's own
heart.

We write in diaries mostly when feeling bittersweet, and leave a blank during periods of untroubled work. It's not always so bad when one can dine out-of-doors on summer nights near the French Theater, watching the fountain lights of the Palais-Royal go on.

Talking with Henri of the tribe of Mau Mau and their current behavior in Southern Africa, I say: "What *are* their tortures?" He invents: "They snip a varicose vein at its base and pull it slowly loose like a string the whole long length of the leg as the victim shrieks." Imagine a person crucified face to the wood and sodomized.

Here again my dishonesty is useless since the above devices are without meaning unless I mention names: I am very well aware who had veins, who was crucified.

"Aimer les femmes intelligentes est un plaisir de pédéraste."
                                                    BAUDELAIRE, Journaux Intimes

Marie Laure has come back too (so the ground floor was reopened and I could take my first bath in three weeks — except for the *bidet*), to arrange with the police about the fate of the Balinese midgets who robbed the house with much publicity a week ago and who, she thinks, live in the putrid belly of the whale now on exhibition *aux Invalides.* Marie Laure is first of all a child, second an artist, third a *vicomtesse.* (Isn't every artist a cross between a child and a *vicomtesse?*) Fourth she is a saint, fifth a masochist (because of Oscar), and sixth a bitch. (Isn't every child an artist? and every child a mixture of saint and bitch? and all *vicomtesses* bitches? and all artists saints?) In short she has all it takes to make blood flow fast and far from boredom. What I most hate is the nonimmortal quality of boredom. What I most like is intuition. . . . She, like Cocteau, knows about the beauty of beginnings and dangers of inertia; that art today approaches science (not really, but really). Above all she is generous, not to mention crazy. Aren't all artists and *vicomtesses* crazy? Though neither artists or children (and rarely *vicomtesses*) are generous. In the three lunches

I've had with Cocteau (at Charles de Noailles's, Julien Green's, Marie
Laure's) I have learned little, but am educated rather by his books.
And this is true again of Marie Laure.

Man Ray has finished my three portraits. At his suggestion I passed
by his studio in St. Sulpice Saturday afternoon to personally scratch
on the negative and add the inevitable soul's calculation (a music
staff, of course). I am unsmiling in the dirty white raincoat and red
scarf of Jerry Robbins. I like this better than those of Georgette
Chadourne, or Cartier-Bresson, who made me look like an oriental
orphan. . . . Friday I'll be thirty but the picture stays twenty-nine.

A moment ago midnight struck: it's the twenty-third of October and
at 2 A.M. I will be thirty. Just as a snake every fourth season sheds his
skin, so I learned when a child that man, bit by unnoticeable bit,
totally renews this largest of organs each seven years. In those young
days I longed for my fourteenth (twice seventh) birthday, feeling that
I then would walk about, clean as on my first earth-day.

Then on the evening of the 23rd I of course got drunk: dining with
Henri *chez* Francis, Place de l'Alma, we begin with two martinis each
(the *apéritif*), a bottle of champagne with the meal, two or three
Cointreaux in the Bar des Théâtres; then both on Henri's bike we
roll to the Flore; two more Cointreaux at the Flore, two *aux Deux
Maggots*, three or four beers with Terry McEwen on the rue Jacob;
then Terry and I take a cab to the *Boeuf sur le Toit* to drink there
God knows how much brandy and champagne, then the Club de
Paris, then back to the dangerous Pergola till dawn and twenty beers
and unremembered company and words. I wake next day feeling
very much thirty with all my money spend and everyone else's. I take
a ten-mile walk to collect my thoughts; toward midnight on the avenue Friedland a strong-faced sergeant says, *"Vous ne pouvez guère
avoir bien plus que dix-neuf ans. Je n'aime, moi, que des mineurs!"*
All this is a weekly occurrence, a weak and regular excuse for my

cast-iron innards to distract me from my music, my correspondence. Yet is it not an improvement from the American and early French days when I'd begin at noon and keep on for four days?

Are there today no Americans in Paris getting famous as in the twenties? In residence are only Tom and Theodora Keogh, Jimmy Baldwin, Julius Katchen. Maybe me and Noël Lee. All the others were "known" before they got here.

Spent a recent Sunday at the *Moulin* of Hervé and Claude Alphand. The "country weekend" is foreign to me, and here was the atmosphere of the relaxed high French bourgeois telling long jokes of infidelity after lunch. Am I saved when Claude picks up her guitar and sings to us before the open fire? Claude, the wan, her pale hair; Claude made of expensive wax, all elegant in her lavender skirt, her purple knickers, her violet *espadrilles*, flat on her back again before the huge fireplace munching rosy bonbons from a box of gray crystal, her olive hair almost burning. Her intelligent voice moves us, but one can't sing all afternoon. And as nobody pays attention to me I'm bored, but can't leave, being far from home.
     When will it snow?

André Dubois tells us that Poulenc has no awareness of the meaning of poetry (or literature) as an art. This is no doubt why he (Poulenc) writes such marvelous songs: he is concerned with words *only* inasmuch as they are connected with music. Auric, a real intellectual on the other hand, does not write successful songs.

Now I must go down to lunch. . . . Who are the other guests? Marie Laure's husband Charles (a story in itself!), Pierre Barillet, Van Moppes, Francis Poulenc, Hélène de Wendel (*pour faire gai!*), Jacques Bourgeois. . . . That will do. . . . (Two hours later.) Lunch is over and I am no smarter.

Saw *La Corde* last night with Marie Laure dressed all in fancy black with her little black basket, like a shepherdess in mourning. . . . We decided that though H. H. is physically dirty he is not mentally so; just disordered, as if instead of blowing his nose he swept his snot into a forgotten corner.

Who was next? Willy Kappell, and it was awfullest of all. Every American pianist in Paris was heavy with depression and I think none was relieved (relieved of his jealousy). Mother wrote me: "Nowadays when I hear of someone leaving this earth, it comes more as a surprise than a shock." But a plane accident: is it *leaving* the earth? or, rather, returning with a crash? Perhaps the soul rises as the body descends, even while we live.

Some people experience their strongest joy in physical contact at the moment they have become jealous of their lover. Jealousy, I suppose, is what accounts for the excitement in a *partouze*. And the *voyeur* is jealous but overcomes it. In Sartre's *Baudelaire* there are countless examples for those of us who rationalize:

> *Of the intellectuals of his persuasion, he recognizes that "the more they cultivate the arts, the less they can get it up" which could pass for a confession. . . .* [And:] *The voyeur does not expose himself; an obscene and discreet shiver runs over him, while, dressed to the gills, he contemplates nudity without touching it. He does wrong, and he knows it; he possesses the other from a distance, and he abstains.*

At lunch yesterday we talked about flying saucers (or at least *they* did — I never speak much) and science and robots that write poems and make love and calculate infinitely and are indestructable. And Thirion proved that the world (being an incomplete circle) will inevitably end in so many billions of years, etc., but hopefully by that time we'll have escaped to another planet. . . . All this depressed me yesterday, but now I'm out of the mood.

At 3:30 Hugues Cuenod came to rehearse my *Poèmes pour la Paix* for the Swiss radio. He brought two pianists and a creole baritone named Salvador Thomas whom I clearly remembered as the narrator in Juilliard's production of Stravinsky's *Oedipus* in 1948, since it was on that very night that I broke out in chicken pox.

Spent the late afternoon going through my scrapbooks at Philippe Erlanger's hotel on the Quai d'Orsay. He says I'm a hundred years out of my epoch, my style being like Musset's *La nuit de Décembre*.

Then I went to pass a torturous half-hour at the wine party of a Korean poet in a miniscule hotel room, rue Jacob, where long-haired dirty American girls sat on the floor (though there were plenty of chairs), and Daniel Mauroc declaimed like a monotonous genius, and the invitation had been typed without capital letters. This *naïf* bohemianism took me back fifteen years to Chicago's 57th Street and Gertrude Abercrombie (dear to us all) and made me feel old.

Quiet supper with Henri who gave me a little radio to keep me company when I'm home alone nights orchestrating.

An awful cold. Slept badly.

Friday the thirteenth, and like yesterday the sky is purple, clear, cold, sunny. After lunch with Oscar my flu was at its worse, so I took a *corydrane* which made me float as I rehearsed my astounding "Jack l'éventreur" (poem of Marie Laure) with the lush Lescot for the party next month. A little American Negro mezzo (pupil of Bernac: they're *all* pupils of Bernac) came to hear us: she'd known me "by reputation" in N.Y. where she'd studied with old friend Mina Hager, but had imagined I was fifty. Everyone thinks composers are either bearded or dead.

Marie Laure has some marvelous new hose: transparent red, transparent blue. The red ones show legs that walked through a slaughterhouse, the blue show legs which have passed through clouds.

One of the stringy-haired girls that I mentioned above at the Korean's party, had said, "One's public is one's friends." This is certainly not true. Joan of Arc, burning at the stake, had plenty of public who were not her friends.

The ASCAP journal is sent to me every once in a while—this time with an obituary column full of old pals: Albert Spalding, Berezowsky, Frank LaForge (a sugary quack doctor for whom I feel no remorse), and Eric Delamarter, the gentle Chicagoan who had good words for me when I was an enthusiastic composer of fifteen. Now that I'm twice that age I've only banal ideas: it all comes out sounding like Tailleferre. I'm too young to go dry, except alcoholically speaking. The genius of Mozart eludes me, and he was more than a man. No matter how much instruction we receive, we will never comprehend more than what is already in us. When I am given praise for my work I feel I don't deserve it; I know too well my dishonesties, though what I've made that stays beautiful seems only natural. When I do not receive praise I feel the world is made of imbeciles. I require the sensations of Saint Anthony.

No one—whatever his wish—can see himself growing older.

The only poems I've ever really understood are those I've set to music.

WHEN I WAS YOUNG SOMEONE SAID TO ME: YOU WILL UNDERSTAND WHEN YOU ARE 50. I AM 50; I DO NOT.

Quand j'étais jeune, on me disait: Vous verrez quand vous aurez cinquante ans. J'ai cinquante ans; je n'ai rien vu.

ERIK SATIE

L'artiste contient l'intéllectual. La réciproque est rarement vraie.

LEON-PAUL FARGUE

Coming back to my music after the usual dissipation is like returning to a starving dog—to a forgotten child for whom I'm responsible but haven't fed. It sulks and won't speak. And when we finally come to an agreement, it is with meaningless whines.

In New York where I used to drink for days on end, I would sometimes come home to find the child prostrate as a dead canary at the bottom of its cage without grain.

Then there are moments when this very remorse sets off a flood of inspiration, rich and thick as a hothouse tangerine, while periods of sobriety can be as dry as Ezekiel's territory, plangent with fake force and constipation.

Wish I could really learn to believe that the most expedient remedy for hangovers is abstinence.

My music *must* be instantly attractive; though I orchestrate skillfully, it is without chance or invention.

Finally saw Genet's movie. It was so much like everyone says that there's little surprise. (Jacob Wasserman's prison chapters were more remarkable but less pederast.) Creation is not based on experiences we've had, but on things we've imagined, woven, and finished: experiences we have not had. A great writer has not the time to live himself. . . . Of course the best scenes (which F. Reichenback projected on his wall, wrongly using Bartók for background) were not the out-and-out masturbation-without-climax "shots," but the smoke puffed into a straw, breathed and reabsorbed through the hole in a prison wall, from mouth to mouth by lovers who cannot, haven't, and will never see each other.

I CAN SEE MYSELF QUITE DRUNK IN THAT DRESS.

While watching the collection *chez* Balenciaga (whose mannequins are notoriously ugly), Marie Laure, at the appearance of one particularly frail gown, observes: "*Je peux bien me voir soûle dans cette robe-là!*" That also is my provision towards all attitudes I must assume.

And as for Virgil Thomson, who has known me since eighteen, I can't forgive his two remarks made on the lack of immortality now starting to shine in my arteries:

1. Having encouraged me to invite Boulez out for a night of brandy so as to "find out" more about him (which I did), he later reports by telephone: "Do you know what Boulez says of you? He says only, '*Quel sinistre individu!*'"

2. Having spotted me last fall at a New Friends' intermission of the Stravinsky cantata with J. Le Sueur, he later phones to say: "I notice you're finally going out with *younger* people!"

Virgil, who used to remark (when I was shocked by what I thought was Lucius Beebe's anti-Semitism), "Sincerity is your big number, baby!"

The phone: "But how will I recognize you?" "I'm beautiful."

Why not: the composer as disappointed critic.

Our fan for years, sweet Robin Joachim, name-dropper and lunatic, asks if he can dine with me. "Yes, but I won't be with a celebrity, just with a working-acquaintance." "Oh, that's all right," he answers, "some of my best friends aren't famous."

I'll make this a *diary*, a daily report for awhile (a discipline, since in any case I'm writing no music these days).

Philippe Erlanger says that superficially I strike him as everything a good mother would *not* want her son to grow up to be!

Dined quietly last night at home with Marie Laure, and afterwards we went to Gaveau to hear Cuenod and De Menasce. Later (Marie Laure having returned alone to meet Oscar) I went to discuss the concert with Poulenc, Sauguet, Jacques du Pont and Henri Hell at the Critérion near the Gare St. Lazare, where Huysman's characters used to evoke London. I had a bad cold and Sauguet said I looked thin and hollow. My voice doesn't go with my face, the former being deep, the latter being fine. . . . Wandered around St. Germain des Près talking long with fifty friends. Came home sober at 3:30 A.M.

Today slept till noon. Finished *The Duchess of Malfy*. Lunch with Cuénod (and his pleasant Swiss accompanist) to discuss his broadcast in Lausanne of my *Poèmes pour la Paix*. I'd already rehearsed them well last week with Perry O'Neil and Bernard Lefort; the latter will do them on tour with Germaine Tailleferre. . . . After lunch went to *Thérèse Raquin* (Carné film starring Signoret looking weird) with Henri, and we were depressed by the heavy Lyonnaise atmosphere of bourgeois murder. We were supposed to be, too. . . . Dined at the house with Marie Laure and Oscar. At nine had a date with an

Arab near Cluny and made love three times in a filthy hotel room: not very sentimental, but it sweated away my cold.

On second thought maybe I won't make a daily report.

Marie Laure says moodily at least once a day: "Youth is what will still be here when we have died."

A nice autumn. Even prettier as seen from Poulenc's apartment overlooking the Luxembourg at the fall of a clear day. I spent the late afternoon there yesterday with Henri Hell in order to hear the *maître* sing us the first three and a half tableaux of his opera. Beforehand we had hot lemonade and homemade ginger cookies, and talked of the recent arrests in England of Lord Montagu and John Gielgud. Then Francis played us what's written of the *Carmélites* and I was disappointed. Usually I love his music and feel he's the only one here who has not tumbled into that touchy masterpiece-complex trap. Yet this whole Carmelite idea seems so Catholic and wearisome that I just can't be moved. I didn't know what to say. . . .

Yesterday I didn't do anything sociable or journalistic; that is to say, I did everything: I worked. Began a cycle of coloratura songs with orchestra on Dryden poems for Miss Fleming. Today I continued. . . . At lunch there was Victor Grandpierre and a beautiful Spanish painter named Ortiz. Went to the theater this evening with Erlanger: Sartre's adaptation of Dumas' *Kean*—a confused virtuoso solo for the miraculous Pierre Brasseur. Opening night and hoarse voices.

Now tomorrow once again I won't have time for any creative work (but still we can't retire into the country and live among the bees and beasts as though they were like us). Because lush Lise Deharme is coming to lunch. Afterwards I must get the invitations printed for our music party here next month; then I must buy gloves and socks, and go to Galliani's for the complete Dryden; then American Express for overdue packages, and Durand's for manuscript paper; then visit Pierre Noël and bawl him out for not giving my sonata more publicity; then kill an hour *en ville* before going to the Quai Voltaire to pick up Gold and Fizdale, who phoned me this morning to say they're in town and with whom I have a date to dine; then meet Henri *aux Deux Maggots* at ten; then return to take a bath (I average three baths every two weeks, and the same number of letters home in the same amount of time). So the day is shot. And having written it all down beforehand, I dread the repetition in reality tomorrow. . . .

Who, nervous and unaccompanied at a cocktail party, does not think of *Four Saints in Three Acts*: "Saint Teresa seated and not surrounded."?

Vertès came to lunch, and afterwards I went to his exhibit avenue Kléber, but was too shy to enter, seeing so many people inside. His *vernissage* was the same day as Braque's and Nora Auric's: nobody was at Braque's but five hundred Very Important People were at Nora's. The celebrity of the Auric couple has overstepped their *valeur*, but they attend to their publicity with tireless persistence. At least this is the opinion of Marie Laure who quotes Cocteau: *"Ils ont l'âme chaussée par Raöul."*

And I shall always worship Eva Gauthier, if only because she once said (typical of her misinformation) to a pupil who was about to study Fauré's *La Prison*: "Now this song is on a poem of Verlaine which he wrote in jail where he had been put for cutting off van Gogh's ear."

Poulenc's music is adroit, clean and powdered, *dépouillée* yet expressive, economic and religious, careful, witty, uninhibited and schmaltzy. Yet he bites his fingernails dirtily and to the bone.

There is a story from Trieste of a drunk who mistook his wife's canary for a lemon and put it in the squeezer.

Now what do you think of that! In this morning's mail Mother forwards me the clipping of Paul Hume's column in the *Washington Post* entirely devoted to me and my *Corinthians*, which it seems Paul Callaway performed two weeks ago in the Cathedral with a choir of men and boys. (I never dreamed I'd have both those men and boys written about on the boat a few weeks ago!) Where did my oldest friend Paul Callaway get copies of this recently completed, unperformed, and already forgotten piece of mine? *N'importe!* Hume is in agreement with me when he says that though my anthem is perfect he doesn't know whether he likes it. With Margaret Truman he was more definite.

Reviews of my music have never taught me a thing. They are basically useless, and form opinions (*after* the fact) for those who have none. Therefore I like to receive only good reviews.

When the curtain goes up on a Balanchine ballet, it is as though the eyelid of an entire public finally opened to the truth. There is no *need* here to "understand."

Could this be a love story if a Peeping Tom follows a loving couple into a fairground and onto the Ferris Wheel? The Peeping Tom takes the seat behind the loving couple, the wheel begins to turn. Reaching the top he begins to descend, the couple already lower before him. He stands, extends his arms, falls, smashing his chin against the back of the couple's suspended seat, drops to the ground, dies. Can this be a love story?

Julien has an unpublished tale about a man who is killed crossing the street, while preoccupied with watching a beautiful boy pass by on the sidewalk.

For John Latouche's marriage Virgil wrote a prelude and postlude for organ called *"In"* and *"Out."* When asked, he answered: "What's a wedding!"

In reconsidering Poulenc's *Carmélites* I hear it as a *chef-d'oeuvre manqué*. For, moving though the music is, the scenario itself concerns fear, which the opera does not.

Art, sorrow, and beauty are perhaps useless, but no more so than earth itself. What is useful? Useful for what?

Rørhjem was our original name. In Norwegian it means "mixed home," but was shortened, as they all were, by immigration authorities—oh, a hundred years ago. Rorem in Latin means "dew." *Et rorem misericordiae tuae perennem infundas* (and shed upon them the dew of your mercy).

The prehistoric Henri Bernstein vanished here all normally, but Reeves McCullers committed suicide last week. . . . Truman Capote is in Paris for a month now, going to funerals and aged since I saw him last, four years ago: smaller than ever yet smart, sterile, and scary. I like him. His books bring me more comfort than his presence though. He should learn not to monopolize in the parlor with his special whimsy, for he's no philosopher but a poet; no Cocteau but a court jester. He lives fancilly in fear on the rue St. Honoré, and says unpleasant things about people which others laugh at without wanting to. . . .

　　　Old Satie to a friend: *"Cest sans doute parce que vous êtes encore jeune que votre musique est un peu triste."*

I spent the evening, rue Christine, with Alice Toklas (whom I'd never known, except for two seconds, years ago, at Nathalie Barney's) because I needed information about Stein's copyright, etc. And she is small and old as a unicorn flying through the sad old-fashioned smoke of other autumns; deaf, with Virgil's style and accent, quick as a whip. She seemed lonely in the endless suite of rooms filled with unframed masterpieces and electric heaters; and I had the impression she didn't want me to go. As I was leaving I noticed for the first time by the door three small and marvelous Picassos. Miss Toklas: "Gertrude always used to say that if the house were burning down and she could only take one picture, it would be those three."

For a month the weather has been all balmy and soaked in sunlight, certainly rare for a Paris autumn, especially when night falls at four. The French reaction to this good weather is of course suspicious: as soon as something doesn't go according to tradition the French suspect the worst — in this case it's radio-activity. And at the florist's window, rue du Boccador, there are orange roses on display, real *orange* roses.

Tomorrow is the luxurious evening that Marie Laure is sweetly giving for my songs with la Lescot for three hundred unmusical people. A house is not a hall and I am nervous in candlelight. Day after tomorrow it will be over. I'll get drunk with Heddy then, it's already planned. Monday I could logically be in dead crumbs from a fray like Poe.

Meanwhile I work: the coloratura tunes — and a love story for two pianos and two voices.

For an hour I've sat contemplating how the ball-point has formed the "*d*" in this sentence's final word.

Others die. But Lucian Freud has just married and we are glad for him.

Sometimes I've been able to consider excess as purification: to vomit is to cleanse. I've spent a third of my life in sleep, a third in drink, a third vomiting. After the music on Saturday I became drunk before three hundred people who had come to hear me play, and later went to the Pergola and Les Halles with Jean Stein in her Dior dress, getting our fortune told by a young man in lipstick. Awoke next afternoon at five, sticky from head to toe in the dried river of regurgitation which had smeared onto every object in the room with Protestant remorse. Then I began all over again, this time with Heddy, smoking hashish, swallowing *orthédrine* tablets, drinking beer into a state of numb stupidity. . . . This is the first time in a year that I've drunk for days in a row, and I'm thirty now (I never used to be); it takes a week to recover from the pained muscles, dried organs, depression and hate. The ensuing sleep is difficult and spattered with dreams of insane-asylums, slaughterhouses, and statues fully clothed and fornicating all twisted. Today I have a certain dignity to preserve as a composer I suppose: if I died, five hundred more people than ten years ago would recognize my name in the paper; that's all.

England, Germany, and Italy

Yes, I've been in London now for two days, asleep mostly, in its foreign mists, and staying at Terry McEwen's near Regents Park. The city is filled with Christmas trees, green and red store-lights, pink and white cupcakes, honest (I hate the word sincere) politeness, pigeons, and dears like Terry or Cecil Beaton or Jack Henderson, and bowler hats and hairdos with wavy shapelessness, and early dusk, and no night living. . . .

Nightfall's at 4 P.M. and I've been in London for a week and a day. Henri went back to Paris yesterday from Victoria Station all huge and hidden like an elephant cemetery. . . . During this time I've certainly done nothing yet worth changing continents for.

Wednesday: Lunch with Sonia Orwell, my favorite person in England, and perhaps my favorite *girl* in Europe. I tell her I've spent the afternoon at Buckingham Palace. She asks: "How were they?" (which could mean either the guardsmen or the royal family). Our entire conversation was of movie stars, the one subject that really interests me. The tragedy that television and easy voyages have made the flesh of the films a now-tangible thing, when in olden times our goddesses lived in the protective Valhalla of Hollywood. We hate the probability of Ava Gardner really going into the Flore like anyone else. . . . Sonia tells me Cyril Connolly's latest *bon mot*: "I'm looking for a publisher who's more interested in literature than money, and who realizes I'm more interested in money than literature." . . . In the black of six o'clock I took a cab to Cecil Beaton's crimson interior at 8 Pelham Place. We spoke only of sex. He always seems sad, though I don't think he is, and makes me feel vulgarly American. He has a marvelous portrait by Bérard, and several small Francis Roses which are the first I've seen and better than I'd expected. At seven Ruth Gordon arrived with Garson Kanin, and as I didn't know them I left, feeling depressed and envious before the camaraderie of theater folk who don't exist except in playful bitchy formal rapport with others, while a composer is necessarily alone (I'm shyer as I'm older, with a nuttier and more positive front, so that many people loathe me). . . . Returning home to generous Terry's, I find two young authors: Mortecai Richler (with mistress) and Negro George Lamming (with wife); I could suspect that neither has far to go. Writers' mistresses are jollier with laymen than painters' mistresses: the latter (I've known them in hundreds from infancy) are all stringy-haired, testy, full of culture (which painters are not), unmusical but love folk songs, and eat out of cans. They generally paint a little themselves, yet hate all but their lovers' work.

Wednesday: Matinée of *Hansel and Gretel* at the Sadlers Wells with Andrew Porter. No work. Evening: went to see Muriel Smith at Drury Lane in *The King and I* and afterward brought her back to Terry's to eat and talk till 5 A.M. Muriel Smith, the first ever to sing my songs, *Doll's Boy*. Is it already ten years ago that I wandered with her on Sunday mornings in lower Manhattan?

Thursday: Lunch at Andrew Porter's. Weather shimmering and clear and un-British. Nervous and bored, as I always am with people who know more than I do about opera when it means less. To a creator, knowledge is unnecessary, sometimes even harmful. Funny how little I think about sex lately. Maybe it's just the English. However, they are immeasurably more gracious than the French; too bad they're less attractive. . . . Christmas Eve and, bars in England closing at eleven, we went to an old Marx Brothers movie, and at midnight Piccadilly Circus was an inferno; even in New York I've never seen such puking everywhere: screaming young gents in rouge and feathers beneath the closed eyes of the cops, despite Montagu; cold whores in bare feet; unexciting sailors (*"la solitude est leur royaume"*); a crowd around the taxi of bleeding cockney rape; all retching, snarling, laughing, all tight, all with English accents on this English night of Christ's birth.

Thursday: New Year's Eve. Saw *Madame Butterfly* for the first time
since grammar school. Afterwards, gin-and-tonics until nine in the
morning at the madhouse of Piccadilly and later at the weird party
of a *couturier* named Bunny Rogers in a white lamé leotard and white
flamingo plumes, who received two hundred glorious guests painted
from eyelid to toenail in frog-green and hopping web-foot from room
to room speaking liquory Latin, or gowned in red bishops' robes
revealing the testicles, or in baby-bunting pajamas with a dagger
plunged in the spine and smoking quietly.

    Friday: Hangover. . . . A calm French supper with James Pope-
Hennessey who is nicer than anyone and who took me to the Fitzroy
bar where we saw an ugly man: asking for beer and not alms was a
Mongolian-idiot-type monster next to whom Boris Karloff resembled
Lana Turner; his right eye was where his ear should be, the left cheek
extended like a hump, on the tip of which was the other eye (closed),
a full seven inches from his noseless face. In my hangover this Bosch-
like creature made me faint, so that James and I had to walk to the
Circus struck silent in the iced wind to buy toilet articles as gifts for
Marie Laure.

    Saturday morning: Markevitch rehearsal of *Coq d'or* at Covent
Garden. . . . Dead tired. . . . Lunch tête-à-tête with John Lehmann
chez lui. Talked of sex and the new "little mags": his own, *The London
Magazine*; and Spender's *Encounter*. He thinks Eugene Walter is
the only young American in Paris worth worrying about.

Paris. Early morning: Awfully ill, iller than ever these two weeks
surrounded by my friends *les docteurs*. The hemorrhoids have been
succeeded by *la grippe* and my breast is a tight lyre of snot — snot in
tight wires. Nevertheless I must tonight take the sleeper to Munich;
for partner I'll doubtless have *un viellard qui pète* and may die. Those
who speak of their *aventures en chemin de fer* are liars.

Nuremberg: Still the silence of Germany which grows more penetrating after now two weeks, silence that gets louder. All I notice is
their difference from the French, who seem superficial by contrast.
If I'm lonely in this country it's because I see around me my own

introverted Scandinavian-ness put to practice, not my attractive counterpart; the Germans behave as I feel, walking glumly with the gentile footsteps of my mentality. Perhaps I've never before seen myself, yet I'm not at home. Of course I know only Bavaria: how they love blackamoors, hunchbacks, dragons and clowns, but not (like the French) *le crime passionnel*. They're scrupulously clean—more than the French—and their cooking's as good as it's bad in England. Slow. Like Americans, they wear glasses. The women are colorless though the men are "not bad." Outrageous aesthetic sense: store windows contain a hodgepodge of the owner's entire property, a mass of multi-colored sausages and lizard-skin radios sorted by a cyclone. At our concerts the audiences of even the smallest towns sit without a cough or paper-rattle, presumably loving music in general (with a thirst only for Lieder) yet hating themselves for hating our "modern" program. They applaud desultorily, without enthusiasm, that's how they are. Yet, if, as they think, they have a fine aural sense (unlike the French), they have no visual sense (which the French *do*). So Latins are visual, glib and dirty; Teutons aural, unsophisticated and clean.

The weather has been lovely and Heidelberg a cold dream, but what's all that without carnal delights (which, when we don't have them, we think all-important—though when we leave our dentist with one wisdom tooth less, we look about Union Square at the tramps and say silently and Germanicly: "You haven't been through what *I* just have") and when I haven't been in good health for a month . . . Here is the West's most sentimental people who weep at concerts and who die of broken hearts; these same who invented concentration camps. Their contradictions tantalize but irritate their American keepers who feel (with what appears a minimal penetration) that if they *are* rather sorry about Hitler, they regret much more having lost the war. Five minutes after meeting Herbert List he told me with intimate pathos that he must leave for Hamburg soon to bid adieu to a dying mother. What could I reply? Then he showed me his collection of photographs. *Très troublantes.*

It's the epoch of what Bavarians call *Fasching* when these sober sunken-eyed sullen industrious beautiful bees let down their Catholic hair. I, too, went to celebrate, but what happens? I get drunk, am

robbed without reward, and next night am questioned by a plain-
clothes man at the station where I've gone to wander from sheer
loneliness. Is *this* sentimental?

Later, long after midnight. Now I have seen Nuremberg and it
is attractive, at least after winter-dark beyond the parapets which in
warm times must flower with fruit. A kind of ironclad Florence. Roditi
undoubtably knew the manners here more than I who, at the sight
of what Henry James calls "the real thing," hide my head in a book.
The bright, jolly Saturday streets this evening (brighter and jollier
than Munich) brim with high Americans, quaint corners, moats,
portcullises and such antiquities; the men all wear hats, gay sweaters
and socks, Tyrolean feathers (and in summer, so I'm told, leather
shorts to enhance the male muscles of their bicycle limbs), though
the interiors are grim, and the ladies of the race are drab as ladybirds.
Dammit, those night alleys are agile with beautiful waiters, and the
beautiful waited while I, a fool, stay home writing a diary for fear of
what they'd think (not knowing they don't think). . . . The Pension
Charlotte at 18 Klaragasse.

Still I've begun to *feel* this country, the side of it that converts
called *gemütlich*. (In France I've never heard *savoir faire*, or *faux
pas*, or *pièce de résistance* except by Americans; the French say
présence, gaffe, tour de force or *plat de résistance*. Also their *music
hall* is what we call *vaudeville*.) But I've had no true contact with
any German. Last night we played at the Amerika Haus in Hof, but
after each concert (before we can mingle with the audience and drink
in the compliments any artist needs) we are whisked out of sight like
foreign untouchables by the authorities.

Paris, I miss you like a Frenchman during the war, and at the
same time how could you help but be changing for me?

Egk's music is a hash of reaction, yet during the war, and still,
he's the toast of this land. When he says he likes my music how can I
answer? Because he's in that school of *married* composers that bear
only tedious children. He has quite fallen for my Chloë Owen, the
constant presence of my provisional life, though as she is not *in* my
life I can say little more except that she's a superior soprano. How
many people really *in* my life do I ever speak of?

Germans. Their weak coffee. Their crucifixions show what I've never seen: the feet of Jesus quite puffed from the nails — which is what must have been the case.

Their lack of glamor. Yet they produced Dietrich, Hitler, Hildegarde Neff. Their lack of mirrors.

Their snowflakes the size of band-aids. Nuremberg: a décor on purpose, but the devastation is more than subduing. We Americans perceive a surrealist charm in balconies on wires attached to nothing, moats, church-shells and bomb echoes after ten years. But for the good Germans these landscapes are the artery of life, and the heart contains nothing but blood.

The audience is not permitted backstage afterwards; it waits outside to see us walk into the cold. But who are we? Nothing, compared to Neff or Hitler or Dietrich. They've never heard of us, but do want to say how they love music. We are touched more than they.

Freiburg: From my hotel window I look out (up) onto the Cathedral and down into the square which this morning is a market of improvised shops similar to those of Marrakech (and all German merchandising is deliciously snuggled into the flanks of the church since middle-aged times), with this Teuton sun of early spring that's been here since I came, beaming onto all, making happiness though I am a failure. Weather dictates my humor more than love or work and in this country of Johannes Brahms (to whom Alvin Ross used to refer as "Yo Highness Browns") the welcome has by the gods been tender despite myself so that "I'm beginning to kind of like it," as Garbo said in *Anna Christie*. That day of snowflakes in Père Lachaise seems now as distant as the moon, as Paris actually is. Is not my golden trail through this country already spattered with the red of broken hearts although I'm about in middle-aged times? Although I see just other Ned Rorems in the street liking Latins more? For now we're willing to travel halfway around the world for a good lay, but then we saw through a glass darkly and having all took nothing, not knowing what we liked. Oh well, it requires a lot of time, and time out from music, and anonymity occurs only to the anonymous.

The German reaction to my music is impassive, but with the question: have you—do you sometimes—or will you ever write in the twelve-tone system? If not, why? At Darmstadt they say: "Which of the works on your program was twelve-tone?" I passed Wednesday morning with Hartmann (Wolfgang Amadeus) who was prepared to dislike my music in the event that it was not *sérielle*—plus the fact that he hates Americans. (I found him charming, fat, vivid, and quite receptive to my suggestion that he employ such "unknown" Americans as John Cage, Fizdale and Gold, Nell Tangeman.) . . . When Stückenschmidt writes in the July '52 *Musical Quarterly* that "it is precisely the syntheses attained in recent German composition that show that every stylistic freedom is possible within the twelve-tone technique," how then account for Hartmann's statement that this technique is the *only* one that eradicates nationality and makes music universal —to contradict my remark that Nono's music is *malgré tout* quite Italian, and Stockhausen's quite German? So I amend my remark: if it's true this music is what he says, no matter from which country, that's because it all sounds essentially German. He laughs. Music is not a science of precision, but food for the soul (pardon the expression); not invention of sounds (which is only orchestration after all) but unalterable arrangements of tones made by a great man, relations of notes. Boulez has hypnotized Europe *à la* Hitler: even those who've never met him fear his charm. The force of a dictator (as of a saint) lies in the absence of personal libido; not *caring*, he can focus equally on everyone. Such a one in power is rare. So if Boulez (like McCarthy) were assassinated, a vanishing chaos would result, fertilizing the road of a genius whose ideas might be in absolute reverse. I can only say what I know, compose what I feel. Like everyone born in the twenties I have just discovered that today is yesterday's tomorrow and the velocity of living has quadrupled, hurling us—as invisible as cold cream—toward a death we thought would never come. Why keep a journal? It never records anything more stimulating than that in Venice one says: "Oh, but you should see the *pissotières* of Toulon," and once in Toulon you wish you were back in Venice to die like Wagner and Diaghilev and George Sand and Thomas Mann and the wings of the dove.

Later. The recital is over, Chloë in crimson and me in tails. No audience reaction: might as well play for the dying. Some nuns, and trains . . . trains . . . tomorrow we leave for Baden-Baden.

The disagreeable thing is to have been a child prodigy and then not to be one anymore. I have seen the rise and fall of Hitler, of Shirley Temple; I heard the last concerts of Rachmaninoff and Paderewski. People are for the Young (and they are right) and I think of myself as young, but no longer receive prizes or adulation.

As long as six years ago Bill Bergsma said (at one of those Columbia get-togethers): "You and I, we're no longer the 'young composers'; there's a whole new generation that's succeeded us!" The only thing more somber than the feeling-sorry-for-oneself caused by a hangover is the one that comes in a perfectly clear head. I recall the Hauptmann-Lindbergh kidnapping as well as this morning, yet Jean Stein was *born* that year. I'm no longer youngest, am often oldest. I read of a songstress being groomed as "a *younger* Judy Garland"; but Judy was a child star of my generation. What do they say of the music behind my back? Frailties, *démodé*, nothing at all (worse). For whom do grownups exist? Oh, I hate children and shall end up on the Funny Farm. Supposing I received tomorrow a five-thousand-dollar commission? I'm too lazy. Not too lazy to work twenty-four hours a day, but too lazy to make it *good*; I dread the admiration I so desire because I don't deserve it, and do. Mostly I fear the growth into being an established lesser composer. Yes I was spoiled by people I've now forgotten, who perhaps still exist, perhaps are still spoiling others younger, not envious that newborns breathe their air, and there's air for only so many. Already in 1945 Janet Fairbank wrote that I had a reputation as the most undependable lush in the music world — not winsome or glamorous as I'd imagined, just obnoxious. In Fez I showed the brothels to my dear Yvonne Loriod (who happens, at the moment, to be the toast of Germany — probably because she's strongly faithful to what she believes, which I'm not sure I am). There's a girl: but she was never young, so it's easy. Neither was Dietrich, and the two are indeed different. The chief of Amerika Haus tonight (dull and thirty-five) referred to "folks of *our* generation." His head is entirely gray.

I have crabs again! How do you say "Larkspur Lotion" in German?

During one of our long long train dialogues Chloë explained that although she liked to sing my songs better than anyone's, etc., they lacked "the virility of necessity," and I couldn't spend my life as the spoiled child. At this moment a waiter of the Speisewagen dropped a clashing platter, and though it was symbolic of nothing, I mention it for what it's worth. At fifteen I'd already written a novel. Virile. I've never been weak, have always known what I want. Do I today? I will not be dominated, but oh, I *will* be possessed. A two-piano team has not these worries: it's locked like Siamese twins who never go crazy. Now my head has fallen to my navel, limp as the Burmese lady's when the rings are removed from her neck. . . . Grammar-school days when Jean Edwards and I sprinkled pepper from the balcony upon an audience in paroxysms below, or spit in the fudge we sold, or swung high on the rings in the silent gymnasium while excreting onto the floor. When I'm drunk and meet a child-time goddess (as I did Greta Keller last Saturday here in Munich) I can only blubber so that she wonders what I am. When sober I am caustic and say to pregnant suburban ladies who already have a child, "Ah, one and a half, I see!" though they don't think this funny. Andor Foldes comes to stand with us as we have our picture taken. . . . Well, we'll do our last concert Friday with pomp and parties and then I guess I'll go to Rome — less for the beauty and music there than so as not to be forgotten as even Garbo cannot be when we see her glide nervous as a moth in that divine revival of *Grand Hotel* now circulating in Germany.

Pensione Rubens. Well, I've been in Rome nine days now. . . . Mostly I came to see my beloved Maggy and for Nabokov's Contemporary Music Congress; now Maggy too has left (this time for Genoa and Spain) and the music will soon be ending, so Friday my plane flies to quiet Paris from where I've been absent as long as when in America a year and a half ago. What can be said but banalities of this city where it is a tragedy not to be in love?

Leontyne Price, beautiful in a gown of blue sequins, sopranoing by heart and tonally (after hours of villainous bearded dodecaphonists), sang Sam Barber's *Hermit Songs* perfectly but with a trace of Southern accent, Lou Harrison's Rapunzel aria gorgeously but with a suggestion of Southern drawl, Sauguet's *La Voyante* in elegant French but with a shadow of Southern croon. Her success was so great that she was permitted an encore, and performed an unaccompanied spiritual *with no accent at all!*

It's the *talking* about music I hate; the redundant café intelligence makes me sigh. Who wants to be smart in Rome? This maze of concerts we've been attending has proved how little competition there is for beauty. It's shown too that old acquaintances after the years have simply grayer hair. But what can we say for Rome? The brightest love letter is banal. The whole thing's been equalified (thanks to Chuck Turner, who arranged it) by my meeting with the two French sadists who left me deliciously crippled in the apartment overlooking the Forum, and went off into the night on their motorcycle.

Charles Henri Ford, now a photographer, takes my picture. I tell him I want two kinds: some very *sincere*, some very *chichi*. "But sweetie," he says with a blue-eyed Southern lisp, "I don't know the difference!"

Broken German hearts. Letters from Germany tell what I've always been told no matter how I change (since even the brightest love letters are banal, etc.): that I play with hearts, but a day will come, etc. when I'll have no more friends, etc. If I could write a quartet as good as Elliott Carter's, I wouldn't care. Meanwhile I'm really in love (and it's sad) with those I sleep with, though ten minutes after I want to say, "Get out! I've things to do," as the Roman summer comes through the window. . . . The writer Miserocchi told me too that when we met at Bestigui's in Venice '51 he'd left a note at the Danieli saying that since his young friend's suicide I was the only one who could give him the *goût de vivre*. I never answered and had forgotten. If we are good to all who love us, what is there left for ourselves? Rome, Rome. Each one says selfishly: "No one has loved you as I do." . . . Mostly I've liked the many meals with Peter Watson, the lots of lunches with Ben Weber.

The only diary history of any import is of tedious incidents which publicity weaves into scandal: Stravinsky was refused entrance to the opera (Henze's *Boulevard Solitude*) for not being in formal dress. A real fight ensued. As Bob Craft was with him and Ned Rorem standing by, they both got in the papers all over the world. That's all. But I *do* love to see my name in print, even in the phone book.

Chez Jacques de Préssac: Palazzo Massimo. My final Italian afternoon and I am alone. It is raining so hard and long that it looks as though the plane may not leave and there'll be another interminable anticlimactic wait, which is bad, for in myself I've already quit Rome. My books are packed so there's nothing to do but sit, and the rain goes on. The toilet drips nervously, I'm bored and sad; crowds in the wet streets; across the way is Tosca's church, and the rain, and the rain.

The author at five years.

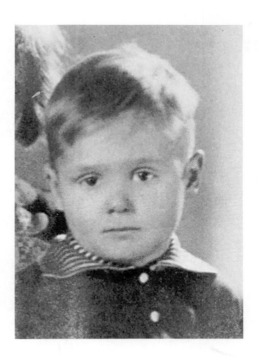

The author's parents, C. Rufus and
Gladys Rorem, Chicago, 1945.

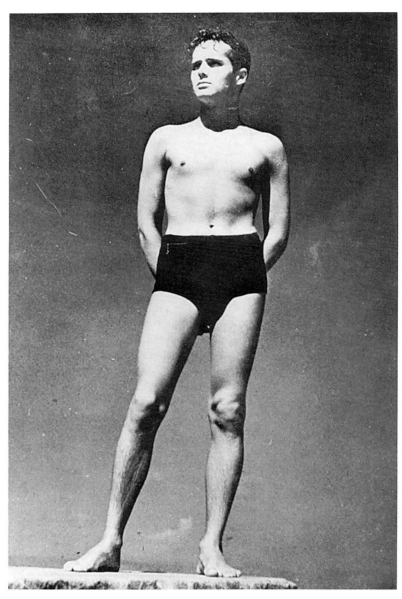

As an eighteen-year-old.

With Aaron Copland, Tanglewood, 1946 (© *Herbert Kubly*).

Morocco, 1949.

August, 1949.

With Robert de St. Jean (left) and Julien Green at the first performance of the author's *Second Piano Sonata*, Théâtre des Champs Elysées, 1951 (*from Paris-Match*).

Portrait of the author by Jean Cocteau, Paris, 1951.

With Jennie Tourel,
Venice, 1951.

With Shirley Rhoads,
Paris, 1951.

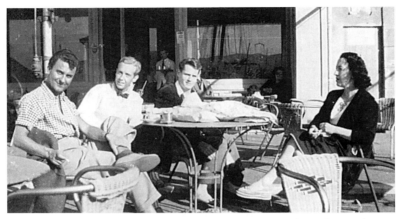

Left to right: Robert Veyron-Lacroix, Wilder Luke Burnap, the author, and Marie Laure de Noailles, Saint Tropez, 1951.

Marie Laure, Vicomtesse de Noailles, Paris, 1949 (© *Carl Van Vechten*).

Marie Laure pendant la guerre by Picasso.

With Julius Katchen,
discussing the author's
Second Piano Concerto,
Paris, 1952
(© *François Jeze*).

With Jean Marais, Paris,
1952.

Pencil draft of "I Am Rose".

Fair copy in india ink.

for Marya Freund on her 80th birthday

I AM ROSE

Gertrude Stein

NED ROREM

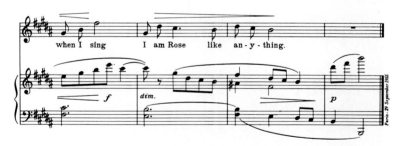

Edition Peters 6625

As published by Edition Peters.

Paris, 1953 (© *Guy Bourdin*).

In his room at Marie Laure's, Paris, 1950s (© *Robin Joachim*).

With Georges Auric, Hyères, 1953.

Paris, 1953.

This page and next: photographs by Man Ray,
Paris, 1953 (*above:* with music from "Tout beau mon
coeur," dedicated to Man Ray).

Hyères, 1957 (© *Ninette Lyon*).

Rome, 1954 (© *Charles Henri Ford*).

Dimitri Mitropoulos, 1956.

With William Flanagan, New York, 1959 (© *Gianni Bates*).

Paris

Marie Laure's in the Midi, so I'm alone and frightened. So much work to do, at a loss as to where to begin; so much music to write, books to read, so much love; if I could just be like the Catholic and ambitionless Romans who have only to walk into the street to be convinced it's no longer worth the trouble to aspire towards greater greatness: the greatest beauty has been there about them for centuries; and they live as was meant: by love, not work.

Two years ago Jean Marais visited me in my high sunny back room at Hôtel des Saints-Pères. (The desk clerk below, agog, had announced by phone: *"Le Marais monte!"*) He peered at my personal patterns, appeared tearful and confused, and finally said, *"Mais vous n'avez pas l'air d'un compositeur."* Indeed most people—musicians even— *do* think composers are bearded or dead, and I came across so many throughout Germany who'd been singing my songs for years that I felt both dead and bearded, abstract. I myself never existed for them. Just my notes.

Learned at the Roman Festival that I have minimal competition, and have never been afraid to say what's on my musical mind: I don't avoid the question the way Ben Weber does when he obliges his ninth-chords into an atonal scheme.

When I have a hangover I go down to Marie Laure's yellow and green ceramic bathroom and fill the tub with emerald bubble-foam and two kinds of bath salts (pink and blue gifts from Patrick O'Higgins). Then I get in and when it's over I'm sprayed and smeared with *Rose* from Rochas, and come back upstairs for Lanolin and Russian Leather and carnation talcum powder, not to mention D.D.T. for crabs and a suppository for piles. And so to bed: smelling like heaven and looking like hell, awakening again with a clear-fuzzy head and a broken back.

Last winter, just before leaving London, on a rainy day without much time, I said to Andrew Porter: "What kind of sight-seeing can we do for the next hour and a half?" "Well," he replied, "we could visit the tomb of Radcliffe Hall." And we did.

More than a month since I have written in this journal, and I don't remember a thing of these forty days back from foreign lands except having drunk and drunk and drunk. Yes, the concerto was played gorgeously by Julius last Sunday on the Radiodiffusion, and Villa Lobos conducted the other half of the program. He says I'm the only young American he considers, etc. I am drunk again with flattery all about. But these awful moments when liquor assumes a proportion far greater than music, *oh là*, I get scared. It *is* hard to write music — and when it's written it runs so far away. Editors are mongers, all or most — and years ago (dying to see my work in print at any price) I signed away my most beautiful things to cheats, to criminals. . . .

Anecdote: A large crown on one of my back teeth feels unstable, but I forget about it. After a private concert *chez* Mme. Verniaud last month I take my plate from the *buffet* and sit with Marya Freund (we all wrote songs last fall for her eightieth birthday). I bite into a sandwich and feel what I take to be a snail shell screech between my teeth. Unconsciously I remove the object which I place on the plate of Mme. Freund when her eyes are turned. Three minutes later, my tongue having found a huge hole, I yell, *"Mon Dieu, j'ai avalé ma couronne!"* and everyone comes running with advice: Eat this, drink that, so that it can go down and come out without injury to the intestines! I sit back, livid, resigned. Five minutes later Mme. Freund screams, *"Mais qu'ai-je donc là entre les dents?"* and they all come running back as she removes from her mouth my crown covered with spit and crab meat. Again I sit back, pale with humiliation and relief.

The artist himself is ignorant of the divinity working in him, he makes the music by inspiration and lives his life a pathetic blunderer; you

take in the music greedily and turn on him in fury. You are disgusting;
I bother to say it because I need your love and aid, you are the only
society that there is.

PAUL GOODMAN, The Dead of Spring.

I have dreamed of Boulez' approval as though I'd done something
wrong to sing my songs as I do. Paris is stupidly aclamor about this
"new" sonorous art, just as though I hadn't heard the same and better concerts fifteen years ago in the Middle West. Cocteau is also at
the Marigny (having heard the word *Boulez* only that afternoon, and
afraid of being left behind) shouting after the music is over, *"Mais le*
public, pourquoi il ne réâgit pas?"

A day like today all gorgeously sweaty in a summer sapphire sky makes
me too exhilarated for work. I need to gain weight, though nothing
is more gently sad than supping alone in a foreign city. Eugene Istomin
is in Paris again and he on the contrary needs to stop eating. (Why
are *all* pianists so obsessed with food? Singers need to use their mouths
in all the ways — but why pianists?) He tells me that our Xénia whom
I miss is staying with Anna Lou Kappell. Early last month in Rome,
on seeing Aaron Copland again for the first time in years, we decided to go sup (gently sad in a foreign city) tête-à-tête on the tiny
Piazza Mattei, and there he said that during the months after Willy's
death he sensed a *relief* in Anna Lou; that Willy, being her greatest
experience, was also her greatest strain; and now, even though crazy
with grief and emptiness, she need never again make an effort. All
death is relief, though it all makes us feel wrongly responsible; any
end is sad. Back in '46 when I first met her in Tanglewood, Grace
Cohen said I'd always have someone to look after me. And what's
old-fashioned one place is brand new next door: Cocteau is considered hot stuff throughout Germany. Generations touch me! and I'm
getting so old that I can see rises, falls. My own life and epoch of
Blitzstein or Latouche; influence of Falla on Paul Bowles; the "thirties"
which didn't exist in the forties (it was the "twenties"), but do now, etc.

While my fever was on and I lay in bed the friends came visiting. Patrick Burkhardt nicely brought a basket of too-red strawberries, and as I ate them (sitting in my bathrobe of strawberry-colored terry cloth and looking pretty because of the flush temperatures give to the very ill) he said they should be offered by cupids flying about my face. Out of the chestnut foam of my scalp, I quite agree, and the sensation of nails in my ex-tonsils. I did not know what Americans were before I came to Europe. The beauty of fever. In America I never knew the appeal of Americans, being one there myself.

Garland Wilson, the Negro pianist at the *Boeuf sur le Toit*, expired down in the rest-rooms there this week after vomiting four quarts of blood. It's said his liver burst from overdrinking. . . . And Roditi told me that my old puppeteer Frank Urbansky died of liquor two months ago (good Frank, who once related how, at an Alcoholics Anonymous meeting when all the members were grimly discussing the insurmountable difficulties of small problems like getting laundry done when one is tight, he simply said, "Don't worry, it'll all come out in the wash!" — which the A.A.'s didn't think funny). I can't help finding these deaths ominous, though doubtless I'm still not feeling so well. I get more frightened, more ashamed; ashamed of nudity. But isn't drunkness archnudity? The will power of a fern.

Old people, like babies, all look alike; time and art are fevers of the young.

But I'm not winning any thinking contests (no "heavy thinker," as Eudora Welty says) so I'd better go to bed as anyway it's late and I'm trailing ill. Tomorrow I'll have happier thoughts.

Rain, without cease, rain. For weeks it's been cold as November. Cocteau seems really dying this time (he's installed just across the square *chez* Mme. Weissweiller). Spent my last money on new clothes Thursday; Friday I immediately had the jacket stolen by an Arab in Les Halles. All day long I play and replay Kurt Weill's masterpiece *Der Jasager* on the piano, without understanding a word of the German about the child-student who kills himself. With my hangover Saturday talked long of this to Sauguet dining at St. Germain with Guy (who was in town for exams), and also Jean Bertrand and Jacques Dupont. Jacques has exhibited my rainy-pink-and-lavenders-ly portrait of three years ago in his show, and it's already bought by Marie Blanche.

In the cold of last evening I went to see dear Jean Leuvrais' outdoor production of *Bérénice* in the Cour de Rohan, with François Valéry who had phoned because I owed him money. Now for five years I have never particularly "dug" François, basing my opinion less on our "hello" acquaintance than on his rather cowering manner. But as is sometimes the case he turned out to be *sympathique* after hours alone during which we returned on foot through this mysterious summer-cold from those marvels of the *troisième arrondissement* along the Seine to the rue de Renne where we had supper and talked of all things until three in the morning. Of course his main interest for us is personal news of his dead father with whose works he nevertheless seems to be less familiar than other cultivated Frenchmen, which is not surprising in that most sons of the famous recoil from their parents' output in an effort to become individuals on their own. All the same I was distressed when he couldn't identify a quotation whose source I questioned. (Paul Bowles uses it in *The Sheltering Sky:* "The dying man looks at himself in the mirror and says, 'We won't be seeing each other any more.' ")

Hell gave me my semi-talents. Heaven gives man a whole talent or none at all.

HEINRICH VON KLEIST

The most discouraging thing I can conceive is that people should say, on hearing of my death: "It's too bad he didn't leave a masterpiece, to make his disappearance a tragedy instead of a farce."

No matter who you are you can't know Death's significance before thirty because it's a cumulative experience. I went to see Julien Green and we sat once more face to face in his "Vermont room," and had nothing to say to each other. That's being thirty and knowing change and death.

The twelve-toners behave as if music should be seen and not heard.

If you wish to raise your children well, treat them as though they were drunk.

If I — when we — remain jealously home at night, our loved ones out fornicating, how much more aching is the dying man's gaze from the hospital window to one walking by and vanishing into a vital tomorrow!

More and more, passionlessly, I don't, in the large sense, *care*. Yet doesn't this diary, paradoxically by its very being, show that I *do*? . . . And every day I am aware of growing older, not only in years and attitude, but in relation to the young who, with their inherent assurance and voracious inhaling, push me from the scene as a mother pig crushes a runt.

What can be said at all, can be clearly said; of that which eludes utterance, best say nothing.

WITTGENSTEIN

Reworded, the above makes music's definition. Because the astutest utterances *about* music (from Sappho to Suzanne Langer) are meaningless to someone who's never heard any. Music defines itself.

Last week Poulenc invited me for our bimonthly *tête-à-tête chez lui* so that we could play what we've each been writing, and drink some dubious-tasting lemon tea which the middle-aged French take for their *crises de foie*. Francis (*qui me tutoie* and who calls me *mon enfant*) never fails to amaze me when he speaks of how magnificent his own music is. It wouldn't occur to *me* to speak of my particular musical tricks or miracles for fear of boring people, yet I readily talk of how luscious my *skin* is. . . . He was in a typical swoon over my choral songs *From an Unknown Past* and, preferring it to my piano concerto, thinks *le choeur* is my principal talent. I of course return

the compliment — particularly as regards his heavenly *Stabat Mater* —
loving to enchant the man who has all the enchantment and instinct
of his country and who needs none of the intellect of his colleagues
to protect his talent.

I have committed only one pointless crime (Gide's *acte gratuit*). When
I was seven my old ill grandmother — full of love for me — was naked
in her bath as we laughed and talked together. Suddenly, when she
wasn't looking, I threw a glass of ice water on her. In her terror her
false teeth fell out, and she began to weep without defense. I fled.

Why have I only a lovely souvenir of Morocco? Because in spite of its
certain ugliness I have never been drunk there.

Since tomorrow I must leave Paris for a summer of work in the Midi,
this whole evening was spent alone, covering the city on foot looking
for love which (perhaps because of nearsightedness) I did not see, or
at least did not recognize, or did not admit that I recognized. But it's
the best way of becoming intimately acquainted with a town, and
special maps should be made of lovers' lanes the world over for the
tourist in a hurry.

Returned to see the Tchelitchew exhibit. Pavlik (who knew me
when I was what he calls a little boy) gave me a nervous lecture on
the evils of drink: the creator spirit is too beautiful and rare for voluntary ill health and the artificial stupefaction of drugs which have
never aided artists, but only (he quotes Tolstoy) "smothered the
requirements of their consciousness." . . . Of course I've heard this
argument inside-out a thousand times, but it gives me a start to be
scolded by the artist in front of whose "Leopard Boy" I used to stand
transfixed in the newness of New York and First Times.

PART 10
1954 and 1955

Hyères and Italy

Il se pourrait que la vérité fût triste.

RENAN

J'ai le coeur et l'imagination tout remplis de vous; je
n'y puis penser sans pleurer, et j'y pense toujours. . . .

MADAME DE SÉVIGNÉ
(in a letter to her daughter, October 5, 1673)

Because now, after five years of European living, I know less than ever what an American is. When *there*, being one, it never occurred to me to question. Now I see them: understanding less than anybody, am charmed.

It was while in Cannes for a few days last week with James Lord and Jean Lagrolet that I met Bill Miller and realized more than ever that I realized less than ever what Americans are, especially those cultivated ones without occupation, winsomely cruising the Continent more lost than the Jews. The secret of translation is not in the aptitude for foreign tongues, but in knowing your own language.

Summer loves. Ach! the wistfulness. How can wars teach us anything since each child must make the same mistakes, birth being always new, and no one's born wise?

A European can't know what a "camp" is.

All the French words, slang and medical, for the male members are feminine, and are masculine for the female.

Here, for my old age, is a chronological digest of the past six weeks or seven:

Before leaving Paris, Germaine Lubin spoke to me of her "friend Hitler," leaving me nothing to say. . . . Gérard Souzay sang Golaud beautifully, and during the intermission Leda Fournier announced she'd had a *rêve équivoque* about me. So did André Dubois, and now he's become *préfet de police*. . . . Cocteau nearly died of a rent heart after forty years of reflection on this organ. Poulenc too, so melancholy, feels death nearer, but it's imaginary. . . . Agnès Capri dyed her hair red, and Florent Schmitt is more tediously reactionary than ever. Alexis de Rédé gave a party and I went. I like George Chavchavadze and he's a friend. Little Jean Stein loves me. From a taxi I saw, on the corner of the rue St. Dominique, a fruit-seller who had no face, bombed—and lunched with Florence Kimball who seems to like *la foire*. That's all. In Paris. Silly to have noted it.

Since I've been in Hyères there's a steady flow of passers, with the regulars (particularly Oscar) behaving as dubiously as ever while a year older, and it's my fourth summer in this south.

I've been reading quite a bit: Petronius, Isherwood, Mauriac, Musset (in preparation for the Sauguet opera in Aix which turned out to be lukewarm), Maupassant, Balzac, Ray Bradbury, Christopher Fry (whom I never like), James (as usual), Apollinaire's biography, B. Constant (Adolphe), the proofs of James Lord's novel—and am studying Italian alone just because I guess I am in love with someone in Pavia.

The "semiregulars" *à demeure* (other than Oscar) have been to date: Robert Veyron-Lacroix (more sympathetic than ever, with whom I play four-hand Bizet at nightfall); the Aurics and *entourage* next door (Georges before supper intoxicates us daily, and then the supper with cider is divine); Dora Maar; Arturo Lopez and his followers (*pour moi une bande inconvenante*); Louis Decreux and Michel de Ré; a party for the gang who came to play Gide's *Saül* on the church steps; Denise Bourdet (we're buddies now) and Jacques Février (it's incredible how badly the French play their own music); Lily Pastré with *her* infant Boris Kochno; Milorad Miskovitch pretty as can be; Tony Gondarillas (old in his hill); the Godebski clan; and Diana C. disguised as a scarecrow. Also Claus Bulow.

Am beginning a requiem on modern poets (compiled by Paul in *The Dead of Spring*), and maybe an opera on James Lord's *The Boy Who Wrote No*. Receiving suicidal letters from Jerry Ackermann, and looking with wonder at photos of the Hamburg suicide of an adolescent torn to shreds in the lions' cage. Spent a night in Toulon with an Armenian met in Aix, the hotel surrounded by yelling whores, from whom (the Armenian) I've been receiving packages of oriental pastry ever since. Citizens of small countries are more consciously proud of what they are than big-country citizens. . . . In Aix, Marcel Schneider finally made me a translation of Weill's school-opera *Der Jasager* which for two months was the only music I liked. . . . Seeing movies, endless talking, manufacturing logic, reading Jünger, writing letters, worrying about money, eating well, seeing a lot of Philippe Erlanger, fiery or dull evenings in St. Tropez, long talks with Denise not only on death and the present sense of miracles, but about women who copulate with dogs and get stuck and are humiliatingly obliged to call the doctor, etc.

All of which stupidly brings me past a circle of seniors whom I perhaps wrongly overfrequent back to the trials of this minute which now seems empty since nothing exists in the present except an orgasm or a broken heart, neither of which I have. (The writing of music is not of the present, it is of a domain that has nothing to do with time.)

Yet with my elders in this my sixth foreign summer I've still had seasonal idylls. In Europe I've been twice in love, three or four times almost in love, five or six additional times (additional people that is) not quite almost in love; one or two (or three) hundred one-night stands (does one count such things anymore? if we were accurate we'd find ourselves far shy of the mark) which is inferior to the American score, if it matters; one or two hundred people in love with me, and this is the most important: it is greater to be loved than to love, it implies far more. . . .

Well, the reason I'm learning Italian since three days ago is because last week in Cannes I met someone who works in a *magazzino d'alimentazione* in the outskirts of Pavia (the Armenian works in a *magasin d'alimentation* in the outskirts of Marseilles), about whom I brood incessantly with that pleasant nausea that comes at the beginnings of love; and though it is a sheer invention that may never be of use, for the instant it's as precious as a beating blue heart in a crystal box. A feeling that makes us wish to say: I love you, so leave the room that I may suffer your absence agreeably, knowing you'll be back before the evening meal still with sea-salt to be licked from you; so leave now, I'm impatient for you to leave (though I only met you yesterday) that I may tell friends how happy I am; leave, so that expectancy for your return may be stronger than your return; or leave forever so that I may write you and suffer the only pleasant pangs that have any meaning, that make a difference; so that I may learn Italian and come maybe next month with joy to visit you and be disappointed because love was not designed for nourishment by the unfocusing imagination of absence, but meant for immediate consumption, and now it's too late; because, even though you might be better, you're not the same as I remembered. . . . None of which keeps me now from hours of practice at learning to say in Italian such useful things as: "Where are the monks? Are they in the refectory?" I'm glad to know that nothing, nothing will ever ever kill the capacity for wanting to fall in love, even when the object seems ridiculous or impractical, or when work grows hollow during such meditations.

In Cannes again. It's six-thirty in the afternoon. I'm feeling low. This is a town invented for pleasure, where one has no right to depression, where one must bed with as many as possible in the shortest space, where I'm useless and forgotten, thinking on Pavia (I've had no letter) with that stifling empty choked screaming desperate ill sleepless sensation that comes to persons in love, no matter who. No matter who you are, a sick heart is a sick heart. The choice of lover is one's own business, but if you're Beethoven in love with a hat-check girl, or a hat-check girl in love with Beethoven, or Tristan, or Juliet, or Aschenbach, or the soldier on furlough, the suffering is equally intense and its expression just as banal. Helpful friends saying "It's not worth it!" are of no help; logic does not enter this domain of helplessness. So here I am dumbly in Cannes again where the remembered cobblestones of any alley appear yelling for help — all this for someone in Pavia who "isn't worth it." . . . These words are as commonplace as all others in love, but maybe they aid me a little. Each morning when I wake up I say today I'll think a little bit less about it, and if I eke out a bit of not-so-good work all goes well for awhile, *mais vient cet horrible cafard d'entre-chien-et-loup* and I'm reduced to the state of wasteful reflection that makes fools of greater than I.

Then what have I done *pour soulâger* my long hangover (because I got falling-down drunk here Saturday with Robert Veyron-Lacroix)? Only the sordid encounters: it can't be believed, I want to cry. There's a club called the Casanova where a kind of man dressed as a kind of woman looking like a giant squid in drag, sings Auric's famous waltz; today I had lunch with George Bemberg after all these years and we spoke of the music we've always loved in common (Debussy's *Dieu qui l'a fait bon regarder*, etc.); afterwards in the afternoon I went for a rocky wet ride in the motorboat of P. le B., a lawyer vaguely Communist I guess and so forth. But none of these is *the* person, no words help, and all the brains and blood of the solar system don't mend the unmendable. So I dragged myself back alone along the *croisette* to the hotel, and here I am now.

In Cannes' harbor two second-rate yachts owned by Yankee gents bang together. Nine-tenths of what we speak think and write isn't worth the trouble — including this sentence. The other tenth? Not worth the trouble either.

The kind of remorse I feel after drinking or after lovemaking (though the first is a filthifier, the second a purifier) is of course strictly Quaker. For instance, I'm ripped with shame at returning the next night, the next year, to a place where I may have disgraced myself in a *déchaîne-ment* of stupor; whereas our painter Jacques Dupont, a Catholic in a Catholic country, declares that nothing *we* can do is "wrong," and he suffers even physically less than I the next day since it doesn't occur to him to have a conscience. Oh, Protestants sure made me real passive.

One must be really brave to choose love or writing as one's guides, because they may lead one to the space in which the meaning of our life is hidden — and who can say that this space may not be the land of death?

DEMETRIOS CAPETANAKIS

And Colette too has died these days.

James in such stories as "The Great Good Place" or "The Jolly Corner" has taken us into realms that are not concerned with death and life, yet he died all the same. These authors, those routes in time, with what we call the future which is just a series of static landmarks we approach and pass (since tomorrow already exists, why can't we sometimes reach it quicker?). Still they die anyway; our deaths are there waiting. . . . I have always kept a yearbook of appointments. I need only to refer to a given date in, say, 1947, to see what I was doing that day. Now, if it were possible to buy the engagement pads to be used from today until the end, the pile wouldn't be so high. Generously I'd need forty-six books between now and the year 2000, and I've already passed the lunch-period of my life.

Pavia (Albergo Moderno): A hangover can be transported from Marseille to Stockholm! You have only to get drunk and next day board a plane, getting off six hours later in a new country: a different language, but the same hangover. Loving hearts too can be carried about without harm, and, as Maggy used to say: "A good lay is worth going halfway around the world for" (to which Norris Embry used to add: "But I've *been* halfway around the world!"), which is exactly why I am in Pavia today and don't regret it. The tourist is truant here, and as I seem to be the only one I peer among the buzz of honest work feeling much as I did years ago when I'd ditched school, and having then nothing to do felt guilty at the sight of a bricklayer.

During the past three weeks in Hyères I spent two hours a day learning Italian alone in preparation for the magic Saturday when not three minutes after we'd met in the Milanese airport P. had slipped the gift of a gold medallion around my Quaker neck. Oh, the grown-up French and Swedes and Germans and English never were children, but Americans and Italians always stay so, and thank God I learned this language a little, for in Italy they go right to the point.

Today I will leave Pavia, go by motorcycle to Voghera which is cheaper, and nearer P.'s home-town of Dorno. Each tiny city in North Italy is sadder than the next, but this people has a different level of perception than the American and the poorest shepherd sports an enthusiastic heart. I've lost all sense of place, and being addressless, no "outside tie" could contact me. Am dominated by this impossible situation of love and no longer think of music. P., eyes all naïve, is excited by an article on me in the Milanese *Derby* which appeared coincidentally with my arrival in Italy Saturday. P. was born a twin and will live and die in poverty in that gloomy unheard-of village with a great heart, dear arms, animated ways, and preoccupation with what we ambitious ones name the "simple pleasures." Why are these worlds such oceans apart? Yet it is just the primary distances that make our chests bloom impossibly. I cannot live here forever as though I were like them, without those facilities which are myself. But then where *can* I live?

Voghera: Shorter days, a small town, a season is ending. After only twenty-four hours everybody knows me already as the stranger, and looks askance at my sloppy dress, the bleached streaks of my hair. The humblest Italian has more *chic* than the richest German.

It is six o'clock in the afternoon and hot. What a troubled summer it's been, the season speeding past like the wind of foul televi-

sion seen here from my hotel window smothering the modern streets
of this distant town. It is Thursday. Tomorrow P. will not come over
from Dorno to see me because the day must be spent killing pigs.
Maybe half my life is over. Saturday I leave alone for Venice, the city
of death. I could kill myself from the tenderness that chokes even
my impotence.

Yesterday we passed in the Chartreuse of Pavia, the land's most
luxuriant sepulcher with its hot gardens. But would I have found it
beautiful had I been alone? Afterwards we went to the church of
San Michele where once more I was ready to die.

Garbo in this language means grace (*con garbo — avec grâce*).

When I am a hundred P. will be ninety-nine. Our centuries will
always be different. Americans, Italians. . . . I was not ready to die.

The whole night long I cried, and again this morning. The strength
of an Italian peasant family which I, as a rich creator, cannot combat.
Even now that I have made this incredible *déplacement dans le bled*
we're still able to meet for only two to three hours in the evening
when P. should be sleeping, for the daily chores are far from here
and P. gets up at 4 A.M. under the continual supervising eye of the
ferocious *madre latina*, and the families of southern Europe are
indissoluble or they would simply perish. These two or three hours
then are pain to me and the other twenty-two or twenty-one I use up
in crying. There is no piano here (I wouldn't play one if there were)
and the city's without interest, dreary as any small town on earth
(not unlike my childhood's South Dakota), where the foreigner can
be only the intruder. This afternoon, with Gianni, P.'s sidekick who
runs a haberdashery next to my hotel, to kill time (before my projected
excursion into the wee weird town of Dorno tonight "to meet the
family") I went swimming at the new glossy pool of which Voghera
is proud. As I was moping at the water's edge reflecting in terms of
tears and considering this scarily banal vicinity and how love can
awe the vocal cords and cause a desire to die, as I moped, suddenly a
loudspeaker, silent until now, beaming on our drops, without pre-
liminary introduction began to emit the quieter piano music of Satie.
Of all things! all times! places! All the music of my babyhood and I

was overcome. What's more, the pianist turned out to be Poulenc, Poulenc's recorded fingers trickling out onto the ugly *piscina* of a town he's never heard of, while he himself lies delirious in Lausanne. Oh don't die friends, friends don't die. I want you always near, am in love, and miserable. We, we are in love. Don't, friends, die. . . . Perhaps I will never come back here again . . . it is easy to say. Now that my French is as good as English I don't want it anymore. I don't want music, I don't want the poems of Capetanakis (at moments like this the Bible, the solutions of poets don't hold up), don't care if Gold and Fizdale never play my pleasant piece with the voices they've not acknowledged, don't want good weather. I want you.

After a strenuous week in Venice where curiously the first people I saw (the sustenance of my stay) were Fizdale and Gold (with Jimmy Schuyler), I am now again, by contrast, in Pavia with much the same frame of mind as before except that meantime Derain has died, and I have not had a real bath since leaving Hyères eighteen days ago. This time my hotel, l'Albergo Corso, is across from the Monarchist headquarters, though the Communist headquarters are in a classier neighborhood. I arrived here Saturday night.

Next day (the second of autumn). I'm writing this because I have nothing else to do. It's grown cold and tomorrow I go back into France, back to Hyères first and the comforting of Marie Laure and strange contrasts. Then up to Paris for three months of work (finish the Third Piano Sonata, orchestrate the Christmas Choruses and coloratura songs; write a piece for flute, and a Pindarian Hymn for Nadia's contest). I'll be having another birthday too, oddly enough, and at the beginning of the year I'll *not* go to America but to Rome instead forever if I can find P. a job there and a way of living for myself, no matter how humble.

Of course all this is merely words and words, when really my one wish is to say I love you I love you and it wouldn't be the first diary filled with useless information, though really, like the changing weather the changes of the heart make about the sole subject worth discussing. It could never occur to me here now that a war or shift of fortune might arrive to disturb all this. I am in love and possessed and shorn of personality. Every time's the first time — thank

God for that! and that I have no pride in such affairs. And every time I say where was I and how have I lived till now though when it's over nothing can be more over and the possibility of resumption is less adequate than rape after orgasm. Meanwhile I spend my afternoons watching Pavia's cinemascope where during the intermissions even here we can listen to Johnny Ray exercise his contagious neuroses at throat-ripping velocity. Then after *How to Marry a Millionaire* I come out again into the reality of Pavian light (which to me is not so real) and wait, and wait.

Just now in Venice my first boss Virgil Thomson said in his dry Gertrudian style of this-is-how-it-is-and-there's-nothing-more-to-add: "Journals must be kept for their gossip value, since in any case the editor will cut all the sentimental parts." Also: "Come home now and start your career!" But I can't any longer base my living on other peoples'. If I choose to go to Rome and starve with someone poor from Dorno, while in New York without me swirls the sauce of people "getting ahead," it will be my choice, since this is the only life I know I have, and anyway I'll always write music. God told me to love. In Venice I saw David Diamond again too, about to have his fortieth birthday (I remember the screams on his thirtieth); he also has his life, nothing to do with mine; we have little to say. Why do I write all these excuses? Oh, I suppose it's just a Venetian report so that Virgil's "editors" won't cut.

On the evening of the ninth live pheasants pecked on the floor of the Fasani family's parlor in Dorno, the ugly town's dirt squares and limited life. The next day I stood in sweat on the train all the way to Venice where I arrived with a cold, sick and sad with love, left my stuff in the Albergo Paganelli and went onto the piazza to look for consolation and immediately bumped into Bobby and Arthur (whom I'd believed in U.S.) with whom I dined and had the first coherent conversation in a week because till then I'd been only blubbering in baby Italian. I spoke only of love. Next day came three magic letters from P. Spent the afternoon with Harold Norse who aggravates me; saw the new Chirico exhibit which is bad, and a thousand close friends in San Marco. In the evening Lenny Bernstein gave a concert with his new fiddle Serenade (built from Plato's *Dialogues*) played by Isaac Stern. Supped afterwards at the Taverna with Virgil and Mimi Pecci-Blunt, later Fulco. Everyone was the same only older, so I went home early to think about love and nurse my flu and be forlorn. . . . Next day, Monday, saw Christina Thoresby who's helpful but boring because of her psychoanalysis and because she wants to be *dans le grand monde* but isn't the type, and who's a dear friend of Roditi, of all people! Spoke only of love. Then had lunch with Raffaello, lovable as ever with a new double chin, successfully *mondain* but only pretends to be helpful. I spoke only of my love affair, though he flattered me on my work and on everything else, and said that geographical tribulations help hearts, etc. Studied Italian some more. At four saw Miserocchi who's a pretentious bore and still an opportunist at sixty. At six-thirty had a lugubrious drink at the Bauer with D. again and we spoke mostly of my love. In the evening a dress rehearsal of Britten's new opera on *The Turn of the Screw* which I liked immensely, and even if it's not a masterpiece it's the piece of a master which Sauguet's opera in July was not. And there I met Bill Weaver, my pleasantest encounter. With him next day, Tuesday the 14th, I sight-saw: the Dali exhibit which disgusted me, particularly since afterwards we saw again that Carpaccio had done the same more rightly in the little church of San Giorgio degli Schiavoni which is maybe my favorite place in Venice.

Virgil made me get up at dawn Wednesday to go (with Efrem Kurtz) to a rehearsal of his flute concerto, a misty formless piece, elegantly played by Elaine Shaffer. The work is apparently a portrait of Roger Baker with whom we then lunched as Virgil pursued his sardonic advice. I am too thin. Haven't had a drop of alcohol in thirty-four days. Thursday, lunch at the Chavchavadze's (where it seems one *has lunch* in Venice) both of whom I like. Played the record of my piano concerto for young Philippe Entremont, George's protégé. At six Christina took Petrassi and me to Peggy Guggenheim's whose collection is the same as Marie Laure's only one-tenth as good. The Twentieth-Century Music Festival continues. In the evening attended the second performance of the Britten opera (which Virgil calls "The Screw of the Century") with Denise Bourdet and "drove" her home in a gondola to the Bestigui Palace. In Munich last winter Peter Pears had already warned me that the little girl's role would be taken by a lady-midget of forty. Of course it was a flop. Why not a boy dressed up as a girl? At those ages there is little difference!

The last two days of Venice were a composite of the other six: same heat and water, same people and wistfulness, same realization that I have nothing in common with those with whom I have everything in common: those agreeable Americans in Europe I can talk to on the same level of understanding, but understanding isn't *being* and so I came back here to Pavia by way of contrast as I said, and am sad and must leave tomorrow.

Here I don't know a soul; here is where I collect my thoughts and that is the bitter truth; here is where I wait.

Gropello is the gloomiest town! Father used to quote: "God made the country, Man made the city, and the Devil made the little town!" Gropello is formed of dirt, saliva, bare feet, and bathos. That is where P.'s brother works in a ceramic-factory all day long, where I was given three *échantillons* (not too pretty) to take to *La Viscomtessa* — as Marie Laure is called here. I was horribly touched; the monotony and resignation of poverty is so foreign to me; I am at a loss.

Our flaw is to reject what *is* precisely because it *is*. We *are*, we met, took root, so gently, but inconvenience obliges uprooting. New frail conveniences will waft or fling us to where we'll *be* again, replant seeds, leave them too to dry, to *un-be*, to fear, from fear. Life is inconvenient. It's not ego or evil but sheer mediocrity that's killing the planet.

Hyères: There is nothing I need write to help recall the drama of parting yesterday at the Milan airport. The first thing to greet me when I arrived back tired and ill in France was a message (in what seemed to me perfectly literate Italian) from P.'s mother saying she'd discovered and read all my letters and that if I wrote once more she would notify the police. Her note was dated the nineteenth. I can't believe that her police could be interested in a correspondence between two adults, though those letters reveal sensual penchants more frankly than this diary. In any case, were I in Italy, this *virago* could probably be embarrassing, and meanwhile she's demoralized me to a point where I neither eat nor breathe nor sleep nor work. Oscar

and Marie Laure are as comforting as is possible, but these useless
ironies in a short life are impediments. Consolation is that God has
presented a trial of love, so I shall cope with it, dangerous patience,
though I don't know where the sickening business will end. Here,
. too, is where I wait. I think I see the first wrinkles about the eyes,
and my flesh responds like ginger ale at the thought of those hands I
love. I too have a mother and love her still and left her long ago in a
country of the present. We are all so different. And I am so tired.

Under my plate this evening James Lord compassionately slipped
this verse: " . . . and human nature is not conceived to conform to
human needs."

*On dit que j'ai trente ans; mais si j'ai vécu trois minutes en une . . .
n'ai-je pas quatre-vingt-dix ans?*

BAUDELAIRE

Obstacles. They are, in a sense, the chief impulse (inspiration) for
my every act and thought. And the long days fly past.

Some of me is gone and dead. Though I know these words don't have
meaning, make any difference, when I read them later. It's a dreary
September with the waiting days that drag by at a snail's pace. I've
lost ten pounds, worry and smother, life's lowest month (which is
saying plenty inasmuch as it's not yet accompanied by wine). I am in
love and wonder at the reason of absence in this too-quick life-span.
Nothing consoles, no book or speech or success. I'll be glad to return
to Paris Friday after three months.

Rome, via Angelo Masina, 5B. Haven't written this diary in over three
months: 104 days, to be exact. Not because I've been particularly
happy (and diaries are for the schmaltzy moments) or even occupied with music, but simply because I haven't had time, with P.
abandoning family, at my encouragement, to look for a job in Paris,
then leaving Paris to settle here a month ago, coping with the unrest

and scandal all this gave rise to. For if I live three lives I mix them together (wrongly perhaps) and don't keep problems to myself. Similar to Cuenod who, when I once observed, "But you pass with no transition from the subject of rough trade to Monteverdi as though they were the same thing," answered, "To me they *are* the same thing."

In the interim old Max Wald has died, my first composition teacher, Chicago. Also Matisse, and our Jacques Fath. . . . 1955, and is it already fifteen years (half of my life) ago that I was preparing to graduate from high school and had difficulty finding acceptance at a university because my grades were low? In the interim I received a commission from Louisville for whom I began *The Poets' Requiem*, and gave three concerts in Paris with my song in the mouths of Irma Kolassi and Miss F., the first a white jewel, the second a flop, though the orchestration of my coloratura tunes had the fragile sumptuousness of rope in ruby silk. I've hardly drunk; not that I've accomplished any the more for it (drinking was part of my rhythm), though I have more stamina to scratch in the knotty nest where I've voluntarily thrown myself. I've turned thirty-one. My craziest occasions were before twenty, but am I more balanced now that I recognize lack-of-balance?

Roses and zinnias: these are my favorite flowers. I am jealous even of your shoes, your sleep.

Hairdressers, harpists, cooks: most are women, but the best are men.

I have forgotten the hell-fire, the maniac, and dreams, my burnt letters. Alas, we can only be in love with those of our century. We should recall all: I can't wish even the most painful instants to have been wasteful.

Those are illusive (allusive?) words, I'm afraid. I grow lazy with the thirties. At least I have learned Italian.

What goes through the heads of parents reading their famous children's dirty books? Oh, the parents will do alright as long as the children are really famous and the books stay in print. But what goes through the heads of *friends* of parents when reading these Americans who so criticize their grownups? Just words (illusive), the fools! Don't they know a symphony can be twice as dirty? only nobody listens. . . . I for one love both Father and Mother tenderly and always have, though I realize the exception.

Let's get back to reality (the only thing which, by nature, we should seek to avoid; its definition is different to each of us although we must announce it as that which is *ugly* and should be escaped from — artists sometimes succeed): there's been so much of it these last three months! When I left Pavia to take my plane back to Nice (September 23rd), from my taxi window I spotted Peter Watson walking the dawn streets of Milan. So I shouted, and we had breakfast. Now it's never strange to see Peter in any city you accidentally happen to be in because he travels (despite his money complaints) into places where intelligent natures would expect consolation, and does it alone, hating train company and suspicious of love. I must not forget that the evening of the morning I shouted my joy to Peter Watson in Milan I was to receive the first of those letters (back in Hyères) from P.'s mother. Others. Oh Mothers! Really this now all seems so long ago it's a bore going through it again, and, as I say, in my thirties I grow lazy. At least I know more today than yesterday what an Italian is; if this people has no sense of humor as we know it (and as the French in a drier, bitchier fashion), it's because they *are* a camp, it's a national characteristic, and you can't be a camp within a camp.

Returned to Paris. How could my life *not* have seemed empty (though Larry Adler asked me to write him a piece without offering to pay) when only the uninitiated can believe that an artist goes on being an artist when he doesn't have what he desires? So that when P. arrived in France on my birthday I had what I wanted (though the "friends" were against it), but suddenly found myself for the first time being *responsible* for someone, which I still am today in Rome where jobs don't grow on trees.

I am now in the future. The present was love-time. Minutes have assembled and built towards this moment. Wind seen from above. Our smallness, our bigness on earth. *The Poets' Requiem* opens with a quote from Kafka: "You can hold back from the suffering of this world. It is allowed. It is your disposition. But it may be that this very holding-back is the one evil you could have avoided."

I am intolerant of those my age who retain faults I once had, and vanquished — particularly the fault of timidity. Yet, as I advance, the

more I grow afraid, really afraid, of everyone. Their indifference: a
cruelty I've not understood, being myself inquisitive.

P.'s gone now. An hour ago, for a long time to the North and a dying
father. Another day of tears and tension unrelieved since August 8th.
Back to that Pavian North for a death rattle in an *ambiance* of Catholic
solidarity so foreign to me. (Are these the same Italians who astonish
my tourist's eyes with their web of grafitti on holiest monuments? the
same who produced the assassin Cannarozza—famous this week—
who decapitated two ladies with a bomb in an Ancona cinema?) Yes,
I am loved and in love and have never been so unhappy, with answer-
less questions, from a situation without solution. Is it worth it then
to remain a month or four longer alone in Rome just to arrange a
little concert at Mimi Pecci's or with Michel Chauveton to play my
not-very-good fiddle sonata and not get paid, meanwhile not working and waiting and waiting for P.'s father to die, and then return to
Rome where neither in spring will jobs be found, and always the
money dwindles in spite of the three hundred dollars Miss Fleming
mailed from New York? I'm getting to hate Rome, archeology where
everywhere beauty smiles and smells of the dead, to hate Rome for
all its warmth where even January roses vomit out among broken
pillars in the Palatine, hate Rome (now all alone) in this good apartment at 35,000 lire with an out-of-tune piano on via Masina in the
shadow of that institute of mediocrity, the American Academy—
Rome, though in Paris with the animation there'd be the ice, and
also Howard Swanson sitting dark on a *tabouret* in the Reine Blanche
feeling sorry for himself. (Didn't I also look at Gina Lollobrigida two
weeks ago sipping a soda at Greco's?) Though I do not drink I have
bad dreams which I try to forget though they wish to be remembered.
    But am I Job with this decision between love and ambition?
Looking about, I perceive not only that indifference ubiquitous in
each land, but personal plights as powerful and pathetic, and the
sculpture of Mme. Ibert representing a mother who cannot help her
child (we know her shock when her daughter lay dead for days in an
elevator shaft); or the joyful Poulenc now with nerves and liver
paralyzed, self-torturing in a Swiss hospital where he writes saying
(because his circulation is bad and stigmata appear on his skin): "*Au
moyen-âge on vous brûlait pour moins que ça!*" All this! Are we put

on earth for such reactions? such wars? our miraculous brothers who slumber in the muddiest inertia too lazy to open their eyes? I've no more ideas, nor any desire to save our world. . . . On the walls in the crypt of the Convento dei Capucini, decorated like a wedding cake in human bones, are signs announcing that everything is vain save the humiliation of worship. I am more sympathetic to Rome's poet Penna who has given up versifying in favor of searching love in Trastevere's regions. But he is born of the Catholics. While I must continue writing music and remain alone.

By myself now in Rome and all by myself. Who'll do the laundry and bring breakfast in bed? I have never really been self-supporting nor do I feel this is necessarily a virtue. Today I'm exiled, wading from room to room in tears up to my knees, having the solace of a few American friends: Kubly, who after all these years, lives again next door; and Bill Weaver with whom I go to the movies, and who's writing me a libretto. Afternoons I play my old songs to myself (like the heroine of a silent movie munching bonbons between sobs) and wonder how I could have written any of them previous to this affection's puzzle. "Slow, slow, fresh fount; keep time with my salt tears." Proving once more that creation, coming from within, is extraneous to outer lights, though this one of my nine lives began in August. I have always hated cats. I write songs on the eves of great meetings rather than later celebrating romance with music, just as my dreams anticipate actions instead of recounting them. At bedtime I try reading Italian: Pavese, Malaparte, Moravia (the pride of their country) — or the weekly film magazines, which I prefer. As Virgil says: "Rome is the European center of the Catholic Church, the Communist Party, and the cinema industry." Movies are mine. Roman society is humorless and narcissistic; at best they imitate Parisians. I feel lonelier than Debussy at the Villa Medici sixty years ago. Those right and reasonable days of discovery when, at ten, I first heard his *L'ile Joyeuse* where a new existence was revealed. Today all fails at my fingertips. The Hersent's visit brought me together with Vera Korène who projected a great sound of mine (as we dined at Passetto's) for *Les Mouches* of Sartre. Now this too is canceled as I'm not a French citizen. As for the Romans, not *one* of the elegant names it was suggested I contact (Barromeo, Caitani, Volpi, etc.) has seen fit to receive me; in their boredom it is only their loss. . . . Would I feel better off in the mechanical rat-race of New York? or in Paris where H. L. De la Grange used to give parties so that I could play my tunes to Menotti? or once more in Germany where the people are too sentimental without the spontaneity of imagination, leading them far from individual decision? I am stupid about my medium, and especially Italian opera which doesn't interest me. Lenny Bernstein has become the rage of La Scala. No, I feel no wish to compose; am sterile, jealous, aging, cowed. I want only to love, and today this privilege is denied, I might even say by God. There is no place left where I am not a foreigner.

Hate again Rome and its imitation bright boys as at good Weaver's party all surrounding Visconti like Casals and Bayreuth or that God might even say by God—and I grew drunk and so dull, damaging those only possibilities. The almost-genius of Maria Callas was there too in a mink-gold dress. My work has long since ceased to interest me, nor do I any longer bother to bother; and once done it interests no one else nor even Maschia Predit with whom rehearsals are as difficult as teeth-pulling or borrowing money from the rich. Chester Kallman calls Auden "Miss Master." Miracles don't happen to me now. I wait, but they don't.

The hair of Iris Tree is still trimmed yellow in a china-poodle style. I never knew her in the February days of '49 when I did music to her play. Now she has here a teensy penthouse right on the Spanish Staircase and we're to write pop songs together for money-making. She lives with a pair of cageless doves, is completely daft. It was her birthday.

You are my leather and my honey, my yellow roses (like those in the Spanish Place), my electric chair, my drum, drill, sweat, and my thistle. I love you. Floods in Paris, and weeks of twenty-below-zero in Chicago. Now a new war in Formosa. Is it really five years back that Korea made me mute, that I wrote another string quartet? I cannot read.

My other starvation for books has all evaporated and I do not want to look again to see said better what it is all about. I prefer unable to sleep in the love rain and dying to ask what is it and receive my own less complicated more complex retort. How long could it all go on? Could we feel otherwise than that this time you are leading me smack to destruction in involition and whimpering? If I should die now here (I cry as I write it and it must be known), all that I have, money and music and trinkets and hair, is left for: P. F., via M———— 13, Dorno (Pavia), Italy.

Empty and depressed, depressed and empty, over and over again, that's all, for the same reasons general and private, waiting for a footstep, sterile disinterest in work, lonesome for Paris whose any ash-can is to me beautiful; lonesome most for you (for all words starting with "P") whose any geography I'd disappear to always. Families, money, distances, these make me empty, depressed. Maschia Predit didn't work out; empty things to do. This afternoon I'm off to see Petrassi again with a musical briefcase under my arm; unless he's very encouraging I'll return to Paris in two weeks, stopping in Milan to see *La Sonnambula* and try to put coherence into my love and my enemy Pavia. Tonight I am to dine at Mimi Pecci's once more with Rieti (who tires me) and Marcelle Meyer (about whom, like Germaine Lubin, they tell atrocities from the Nazi period. But who am I to enter in? I was not here then). . . . Iris Tree didn't say so, but she was disappointed by the songs to her verse, yet I ask nothing better than to abandon subtlety and make a fortune. Meanwhile she is off to Marrakech with the affected and drunken Diana C. who is Beauty become a urine-hued scarecrow. Well, let them leave and leave me to my empty problem. This war will hang and settle us all.

Tomorrow, as Ned Rorem, with Kubly and Bill Weaver I'll see Naples for the first time, and die perhaps (getting *that* out of the way), and this will pass time. Can I live only hopeless to cry sloppily again in the smell of those caramel triceps. This page, that tree, and love, will soon be long ago.

And I did die too perhaps. I'm back from the hot of the South of Naples which I hated and its beautiful house of opera. There your

chain and gold medallion representing *La Madonna del Dito* with
the engraved date of our meeting 9-8-54 were stolen by a trapezist
(though in my letter I didn't tell you it was a trapezist) and I am maybe
punished—though as Bill Weaver said, the chain may one day catch
in the trapeze and slit the thief's neck. Punished, I've said, for now
returned, Naples, my hemorrhoids have recommenced so viciously
that tomorrow I must enter the hospital. Thank you for your letters:
how I love you; you are my glass and my key. I long for the fragrance
of your arms far off which I see outstretched as we are crucified face
to face watching each other die.

No relief. Love means being together; as I am, I grow daily weaker
with my Naples illness rejoicing higher always so that I ache and
cannot eat nor think of working, going to the dentist. This weekend
I will come up to Milano to kiss your feet and beg you to leave and
humiliate myself by classic banalities, and you too will turn humble
and full of love, and we'll end at the beginning with the insoluble
dilemmas. Far from you there's not one friend who doesn't bore me.
As I perfect my Italian it becomes the language of my misery. Am
sterile and bewitched. The dearest, tedious: Leo Coleman smiles in
his Portuguese discs and Petrassi has lent me some rare Gabrieli,
but I'm now deaf and blind, and scribbling here has no relief.

Yes, P. came and went and maybe now will come again, and I am
going in a week. Back to Paris. After four months in Rome (during
which I still haven't finished my *Poets' Requiem* but am covered with
new acquaintances, also new wrinkles, paler and older, thinner and
smarter, more streaks of peroxide making me red-haired: not really
red of course: red hair actually is that usual baby orange of carrots or
flame) Mimi Pecci will finally give me a concert next Wednesday in
her castle where we'll try out (among other things) Frank O'Hara's
Four Dialogues for Two Voices and Two Pianos which we'll record
next day for the R.A.I. Then I am leaving (all of my new friends and
those who've passed by). Back to Paris. By way of Florence and Milan,
revisiting old friends and collecting souvenirs. They too'll've grown.
Collect too many souvenirs and the basket breaks: that's death. But
our baskets are stronger than we think! It's life. . . . I'm still in love

with you and it will remain so; you, so far from me in every way, loving me, back in Dorno killing a hog each Friday. It won't be long again now. Charley Ford says love means wanting *to live with*, and applies not only to persons but pets and works of art. Back to Paris whose every ash-can is to me a diamond chalice. Our friend Rochas has died in these days, leaving a beautiful wife.

Petrassi thinks that my music — irreproachable though it may be in its traditional frame — lacks the health of adventure.

Before the Evening Meal: I've always liked to do it best before the evening meal. Because thus with a new friend (or old one) we can go out afterwards into the early night's illumination of a strange city (or a familiar one, feeling in love, or out of it) and discuss it all while dining. And drinking; that's making friendships. It used to be that I would drink in order to go to bed; now it's going to bed to be able to drink after and discuss. *Ceci dit* I've slipped only three times since I've come to Rome: once a month is some improvement over once a day. If my hair is sunset-colored . . . if art comes of suffering as they say, perfume too is a monster's infection and sunsets are agitated dirt. Are whales, so good, monsters? Nantucket. Let's go to the islands, any from Nantucket to Lesbos. Real drunks can't sleep. Though I loathe crowds, I love light low closed hotel rooms alone in a huge bed, that magnificent apparatus.

Love before the evening meal in summer (though it could as well be spring when, with the newborn buds, we are moved to wish to utter those same old banalities of love, but to new ears). The first warm days and tinkling carts selling Good Humors in cool suburbs. I find myself whistling the song I made to Edwin Denby's sonnet. Yes, I can whistle and am also somewhat left-handed, can ride a bike "no hansies." (Ride a bike: but in my fantasies of love it is the opposite.)

In America ninety-eight per cent of us are from the "middle class." When Piaf opens her mouth the bourgeois man of France will swoon; she also makes Americans desire a Paris return. *Moi aussi, j'en fais parti.* People wonder: do I love myself or my music more. Is there a difference? I *do* protect myself and with iron ramparts. It's a great love affair! (and before the evening meal).

Florence (the Berchielli): Each cranny and odor I'd forgotten I remember now again in Florence after five years and not a barman's
face or restaurant's clientele has changed as though some charm had
stopped time with always summer weather here. Left Rome this
morning: all was completed there (all except my work in progress),
and I am tired, tired. Tomorrow evening P. joins me; then there'll be
Newell Jenkins' concert and tea with David Diamond; the same sight-
seeing (that is, the same sights seen with older eyes — but nothing's
changed, as though some charm, etc.). Everyone and everything I've
seen before I saw once more in Rome which means Judy Garland in
her new cinemascope vehicle *A Star is Born* (as long as it is wide)
which I admit I saw in Yankton with Janet Gaynor way back when.
Today the world's most beautiful woman is surely Elizabeth Taylor.
. . . Doctor Kinsey still sends his yearly letter to say he's following
my career (noted by way of keeping with the times). Rome did nothing much for my vanity (the flesh does grow weary, but alas the most
crumpled will still desire: that's the irony). It's no place for drinking:
the word *hangover* and its treatment do not exist in Italian: if you
have one it's unsafe to venture into the streets: there you risk seeing
a decapitated head, a stone dismembered foot, under other circumstances beautiful. Tullio Carminati (who, my age, cannot recall Grace
Moore?) flattered me, but what of the old? (when alas the most
crumpled, etc.). . . . Also I met Lord Montagu in flesh and blood.

Rome: its mediocrity: Favaretto (Italy's Irene Aïtoff). The scandal at the Villa Medici of Jean-Michel Damase (the only talent there)
suffering what Edward the Second suffered from the jealous hazing
of his fellows, and Ibert shaking his head as though this had not
happened. Doda Conrad quotes Nadia Boulanger who says, after a
conversation about today's young composers: "Well, after all is said
and done, there's really only Ned Rorem! . . .

PART 11
1955

France Again

Easter's gone.

Sick in bed, throat on fire, a French fever of 38.5. Every year I sink like this because I am a sinner and time grows shorter.

I don't like Paris anymore after these twelve days. I miss whom I love and that's all that counts. It has been months since I have had any impulse to compose and the word *music* causes a pang. I'm awaiting the doctor which is why I write all this. The *poubelles* don't look like grails anymore.

Sick from starting to drink, from thinking I'm the same person in the same place, from a cold and jealousy and boredom and laziness, sick from missing P. who bewitches me ever more tightly after nine months. Probably I'll move completely to Milan.

The doctor came with penicillin, and I'm weary still with throat aflame. Friends too have come and gone, bringing fruit and sandwiches. It's ten in the evening inside, and outside warm spring. I must stay abed and sweat. Friday if I'm well enough I'll go to Hyères two weeks.

Hyères: Einstein died today.

It *is* as always a paradise here. Oscar's a good boy. The Vicomte passed through again (he's a good boy too). The rest of us are correcting proofs: I with the luxury of adding new dedications onto my *Cycle of Holy Songs;* Marie Laure highly nervous about the forthcoming publication of her *Chambre des Écureuils* which seems to be a long-ago dream all the details of which are real but the *whole* becoming a newness from imagination (as in painting, says Nora, where each stroke is trivial while the ensemble is strange).

Poverty's fine at twenty. At thirty, it's unbecoming, being a necessity only to the very young. Today the *avant-garde* is *démodé.* We have other realms to bother us and true adventure no longer glows in the field of arts. I recall first introducing myself to Christopher Lazare by emptying a shaker of martinis over his head at a G.-Village party (he was enchanted). This was a good ten years ago and is the type of gesture I could not repeat today in even my maddest moods. Now we are not concerned with arts, but with jet pilots and atoms. As I grow older the desire for learning, need to read, health of curiosity, leave me increasingly. All answers have been explained and I've understood. But perhaps none of that is true. Why, having learned what there is to know from others, need I now believe in anything but the development of my dreams? I think more of sex than of music. (Should I say: I think more *about* sex than about music?)

In a way I'm still sick from my Paris flu and the everlasting hemorrhoids. But I've begun to soak in sun, and mornings when I pick my ears the wax seems a glittering orange on the nails of my tan hands. I no longer bite my fingernails, by the way — or at least quite seldom.

Couldn't sleep all night because of the strident giggles of Marie Laure and Oscar gamboling on the lawn, drunk, plump, middle-aged, and stark naked. At 4 A.M. Robert Veyron-Lacroix — distressed and bleary-eyed — came to my room for a consultation, and to eavesdrop on this amazing phrase from behind a cypress tree: *"On est vraiment des beaux gosses, n'est-ce pas?"* We decided that if in fifteen minutes they hadn't shut up, we'd douse them from the balcony with a bucket of ice water. Precisely at 4:15 we let the shower descend onto their unsuspecting heads. Then, of course, wide awake, we all laughed together till dawn.

In answer to "Why must painters distort?", ask "What does music mean to you?" People question their eyes, seldom their ears. Is it that since the ear as organ is so much more complex it sifts and chooses on less literal levels? An artist, says Picasso, paints not what he sees but what he thinks about what he sees. Can the same be said of a composer? of a *littérateur*? No. A musician writes what he hears, but *only* what he hears. As for authors, do they notate what they think, or what they think about what they think? No. They write down what they *see*; this holds for both Rimbaud and Daisy Ashford. All creators just see (the composer sees with his ear; mescaline so clearly demonstrates how senses overlap: we witness sounds, hear color, touch tones, taste blues), but since painters see with their eyes they are the most primitive. Gide constructed musically, or so he thought (*Les Faux-Monnayeurs*, if anything, is fugal, and a fugue is formal — rather than rhetorical — only inasmuch as its trademark is contrast of tonalities); in any case he practiced more than, say, Roger Martin du Gard, Aristotle's concept about tragical verisimilitude: "What is plausible and impossible is preferable to what is implausible and possible."

The beautiful are shyer than the ugly, for they move in a world that does not ask for beauty.

Some artists feel superior to this world they live in. But it's *their* world too. Perhaps they depict it better than others, but that very depiction is part of the world.

Eugene List and Carol Glenn are full of good peaches and cereal. They will never go mad.

Why not perfumes with fragrance of fruit as well as flowers? Apple cologne. Pear body-cream. And of course the immortal raspberry. To die in a raspberry. *La mort à la framboise.*

Cannes: It all began wrong. Despite the written invitation from Erlanger I was kicked out of the film festival première because I wasn't in a tux. But I saw the stars' entrances, their congealed smiles, the perfume and flash bulbs and furs, and I swooned a thousand jealousies, and dined alone and did a little walking in the semicold. I want to be a star too like them and have peasants agape at my falseness. Alone in this sexiest of towns I'm a slave to temptations which should never be resisted (our worst memories in old age will be of rejected opportunities), though I nevertheless returned wisely to the hotel (it's only ten-thirty — the Westminster where first I was with Guy six years ago)

and will spend the rest of this ruined evening reading the fatuous
new Montherlant play, because tomorrow I must rise early to meet
P. at the Nice airport. And tomorrow life will take a meaning here
where it began. Meanwhile outdoors the back streets are peopled
with easy love and I feel voluntarily cheated as in Nuremberg a year
ago. Poulenc is here also, and movie folk sufficient to enrapture my
wildest associations as in true American inheritance. But it's gratui-
tously lost for me tonight without a tux. Oh well! I've the memory of
last evening in the hills of Hyères between the arms of one "whose
business has to do with fish" (as Eliot explained in my sung prayer
from "The Dry Salvages" in '46). Fortunately P. doesn't read English,
for the above is a curious admission from a person to whom fidelity
is all. Really I am *putain*, not in its understanding as *whore*, but in its
French adjectival sense as, say, a dog who, with soulful eyes, knows
how to solicit a lump of sugar, or roll over to get his stomach rubbed.
. . . Cannes, darn it! this is a little girl's entry! My timidity soars as
did my snobbery in those poems I used to write. Heavens, what haven't
I done! Piles oppress me. When I'm thrown out I just leave obediently,
tail between legs. To think that for this I had lugubriously allowed
the sun to scorch me into a raspberry!

Our world's imminent end? Maybe that end came long ago; maybe
we're a race of zombies, the vermin that for millenniums has clus-
tered with increasing thickness over the earth's corpse.

Stage fright of a martyr: the simple Christian fears the lions less than
his first public appearance.

Plants do not wish to rule the world like us: they have higher concerns.

Paris: Finished today orchestration of my *Poets' Requiem*. Fiercely
cold, rainy.

Aaron Copland came to lunch today, having read the fifth volume of my journal and we spent the afternoon listening to records of my music. He says the journal expresses the unexpected violent side of my nature, while the music is the less inventive serene side. The music doesn't seem as *necessary* and varied (particularly rhythmically) as with a composer who has *only* this means of speech, especially considering I grew up (I too) in the jazz era. Does my exquisitely laborious manuscript in India ink on transparent onion skin (a *métier* in itself) represent the most perfect side of my music? Aaron I suppose is the "nice man" *par excellence*, yet my main interest in him is his in me, and if he still intimidates me it's because we first met when I was a child. His worry is that I seem as reconciled to my weaknesses as to my strengths, which indicates I will not change. And growth is change. But he too is a sum of his parts and who's to say where differences and relationships begin in others, let alone ourselves?

Winter's turned to summer in one feathery-yellow day; Paris roads are squeaky-stuffed with baby-buggies. But my nerves feel sawn and knotted: drinking again. Six times since returning on April 13th, six too many, and haven't once made love. Next Saturday I'll take the plane for a few days in Milan, as I can no more stand it alone. Why? when my "career" is abloom in America with fine reviews last week of the opera and symphony, and in a few days the première of *Design* in Louisville, and three concerts in Paris next month? Because I'm bored, weak, shy, lazy, and even the threat of those *lundis cafardeux* does not keep me from wine, with health thinning and fear of work, and the awful post-tender hang-over shaking. . . .

   Our writers today have lost a sense of words. Could we too say our musicians have lost the sense of notes? We can't now see Rome as an alive place, see a column and say Nero also breathed on this. Too far ago. Whereas the cave men are just far enough (like the angel Michael). Sleep after drink is a passion and for three days it's hard to have enough: we grow like the luxuriant ruler who enjoyed being awakened for the pleasure of falling back to sleep. Though *désoeuvré* and guilty-conscienced I'm glad to be going to Milan, to know that, if the plane doesn't crash, in five days I'll be in the grip of love without which it is wrong to live and with which it is also wrong.

Evening with Nöel Lee (who is thoroughly good without being wishy-washy) and played him *The Poets' Requiem*. He in turn played me his big cantata on Valéry's words which impressed more than any American piece in a long time. Afterwards, having dined rue Mermoz, on his motorcycle we investigated *à deux* the warm Paris roads for three hours, a thing that should be done alone, and I returned home unelated. The same happened last night in other quarters with Roditi. If love smiles bright in the street I'm too coy to capitulate and despise myself for it.

A month ago with P. at the Cannes Casino I gambled for the first (probably last) time. The thousand francs we won was spent on tea and two dishes of raspberry ice cream.

Poulenc was in Cannes, quite recovered from his long illness, but looking old and smothered in pimples. As he's always been rather *le cher maître* in my eyes, I was chilled by his talk of sexual success.

The movie stars in Cannes outraged my life-long veneration, for they behave like their own caricatures, not as legends. And they're so old! Movies nevertheless remain my preferred subject of conversation.

As Philippe Erlanger points out: *les vraies grandes cocottes ne couchent pas;* they are for show.

Italians: How many of them have said to me, knowing me to be Protestant: *"Ah! ma tu non potresti capire, siccome non sei cristiano!"* ... Their marvelous sense of luxury in disdain of the necessary: the poorest will go without a meal to buy a tie. Luxury (in the sense of a *need* for beauty) is a dying art; it has nothing to do with being rich.

Philippe Erlanger quotes P. in Rome: "Italian duchesses are better than French duchesses because they don't invite me."

Conversation between Mr. G. S. and Mrs. J. B. overheard years ago:

G.: "Everything's against me: I'm a Jew, a poet, a Communist, a homosexual, an alcoholic; everything's against me." J.: "That's nothing!
I'm Jewish, a poet, a Communist, a homosexual, an alcoholic, and *I'm
a cripple!*"

Which recalls Djuna's doctor saying: "A broken heart have you! I
have fallen arches, flying dandruff, a floating kidney, shattered nerves
and a broken heart!" . . .

What is bad cannot endure: it must grow worse.

Before leaving tomorrow again for Milan I'll write a little here to kill
time, for I have no more ideas in work, have orgied too much now to
orgy more, read all I can, and seen as many movies and friends as
are necessary to stay a bit the threat of obliteration.

Ida Rubinstein, who, for years lived next door to Marie Laure
here in the Place des Etats-Unis, has (they say) at her ripe age gone
as a nurse to a leper colony (just as it's reported that Garbo is to join
a nunnery). The Rubinstein house was sold and (to make way for a
French six-story *gratte-ciel*) has been reduced to rubble with nothing now left but Diaghilev's dusty recall. We've sniffed about in the
ruins of Bakst's blue mosaic garden where Nijinsky died at parties,
and Marie Laure, free of charge with her flair for finding the valuable where unexpected, dug from the crumblings twenty superb re-
productions of Sebastian (my least-favorite saint: I dislike and am
jealous of those who permit themselves to be riddled by soldiers)
which were used (caressed) by d'Annunzio and Debussy. It's all gone
away now; history is never fabulous as it's being made.

In the *Hommage de la France à Thomas Mann* which came out today
(ed. Flinker), I am humble at seeing my name as the only American
and one of four composers (with Auric, Milhaud, Honegger) among
the seventy-five or so French admirers. Because Mann began my
years of "good" reading, until twenty-five when my curiosity ceased.

As Quakers we never used to stand for *The Star-Spangled Banner* (to stand *up* for). Today I realized that this proved little.

An opera libretto cannot be multileveled psychiatry. It must be blood and picnics, hate and drinking-songs, love, ghosts, potions and posies. The music will give it subtlety.

Because I couldn't stand it any longer I went to Milan at the end of last month to see P. whom I adore after ten months of impossibility. We spent a day of heat in Como where one can no longer sip a pear-juice or nibble a pineapple-sherbet while moodily thumbing a guide-book *à la* Henry James on a solitary terrace across from the Duomo. Everywhere today friends must be met in that only place they come: *la tasse*. But we had love and cannot consider such things. Anything thrills me in P's presence so the cathedral was a marvel: more appre-ciable than, say, the Sistine Chapel which I'd prefer to admire by reproduction than by craning my neck in the Vatican confines sur-rounded by flocks of sweating Swedish female students who've come on foot from the home country. Claustrophobia's my fever and liquor my reward.

I went to Milan also because my body wanted love and I don't know how to look for this in any other way. I have not written a note in months and feel *désoeuvré*, idealess, filling myself with aches and gloominess, ridding myself of that by extended going-out to return with the extenuation of sociability, fall on the bed and cry, saying: What am I doing here? as, indeed, one could ask anywhere. Those dreamlike hours which accompany a hangover when carnal obses-sion attains a peak of daring *et le corps ne pense qu'à lui-même*. Certain others know this.

Lenny Bernstein has been once more to talk to me of me, and, though I know no one more astute, I cannot feel close to him because he *plays* at being close to one, *plays* at being "the real thing"; his reality's unreal; I like true unreality (hate reality); Venice is truth. There is no real difference between the *texture* of Scriabine and Berg.

Drink, and recover in order to drink (and recover, in order . . .). That's
how it's been during ever-awful June, and forever it'll go on, I know.
The tension with which I imbibe can be matched by the delicate
care I take to eat liver next day (to recover — and drink). Meanwhile
I don't work, squabble with laziness, postpone, let time pass.

> . . . *le bonheur d'avoir été malheureux.* [Gaillard on Francis I]
> *But the memory of past sorrow — is it not present joy?*
>   POE, "The Colloquy of Monos and Una"

During intermission last week at Ballet Theater I saw Zsa Zsa Gabor
en chair et en os (I had met her once with George Sanders at a party
years ago, the first evening of my psychoanalysis). She is the kind of
woman I love (all in yellow, blond, silver, false, beautiful, shining,
affected: the very definition of the Hollywood Hallucination, the
STAR). Well, if I could choose between remaining a friend of, say,
Paul Goodman or becoming one of Zsa Zsa Gabor's, I'd forsake the
former. For Gabor will not last, and was created to be encountered,
smelled, admired. But a great man is known by his work and is without interest in his private life. I am a child before the movies.

Aix-en-Provence: Heat.
I despair at twelve-toners: they have lost the need for pleasure.
Music's not written to be understood, but to be *felt* — and grown-up
imaginations cannot perceive it. (Not meant to be understood: yet I
am happiest when composing to a vocal text. Is vocal music an im-
pure form of this most abstract of arts?)
At six we are going to the Casino for the new Boulez work *Le
Marteau sans maître*. Boulez has won through intelligence and personal charm (he looks like Gene Kelly), not because his music heats
hearts. The critics and musicologists, those sterile ones, are agog before him since finally they can "understand" an emotion explained
by words. But where is that necessary union of beauty with the all-
important *form* of Nerval, or Piero della Francesca, or Haydn, each

filled with the health of inspired bees working toward their hazel-perfect honey?

Hyères: Jean-Louis Barrault and Madeleine Renaud stopped by yesterday on their way back to Paris. They've been preparing their forthcoming production of *L'Orestie* at the nearby nudist colony of l'Ile du Levant. "Communal nakedness, after the first embarrassed hour, is quite antisensual," maintains Barrault. "For stimulation you find yourself saying: 'Get dressed *chérie*, and let's make love!' "

My philosophy was entirely based on the Quaker Church and American cinema.

Drifting back: to earliest high-school summers, midnight swimming, Tom Collins, slow dancing and car radios, learning about sex (which I still haven't learned about), etc. Of course no parent wishes the child to grow up, nor does a child wish his parents to know he has grown up—if he knows it himself, usually too late. My father, in his sixties, tells me he still tells himself: "Tomorrow, when I've grown up. . . . " Children just assume their elders know more; what a disappointment to grow up. Because standards stay stationary: I recall my shocked child's tears at old ladies seeking nourishment in ashcans, but it is no stronger than my grown-up amazement at fellow mediocrity and the laziness of human scavengers. Not that the old ladies were "mediocre"—I had just thought they were like *me*. Poetically speaking, growing up *is* mediocrity.

When I go somewhere today with Marie Laure and Oscar I think people no longer turn to say: "*Voilà la Vicomtesse accompagnée de la Belle et la Bête.*" We went to lunch *chez* Christian Dior near Grasse, and he ate hand-in-hand with his Arab acquaintance who's been *rapellé* by the Army. The world's going badly.

Here is the beginning of the end of a season which I seem to have passed without at all writing in this diary; now it's not easy to begin again in a new book, all the more so that I have other problems in progress. But a congenital air for order as well as a fear of chronological loss (like the tourist-monsters incapable of seeing a masterpiece without taking a snapshot of it) make me start here once more. And what have I done in this summer? Contradictions:

Venice. A city where birds live on the ground and lions in the air. . . . Venice is a *chef-d'oeuvre* out of context, an isolated masterpiece having nothing to do with Italy, just as *Bolero* can't be included in Ravel's "normal" list of works. Venice is where we quarrel and then make-up, eating grape ice cream on Florian's terrace and watch Chirico stroll by in a yellow sweater as natural as the sunlight. Contradictions of the mid-twentieth century: In Tiziano's portrait Sacred Love is naked and Profane begowned. The *C*'s of Correggio, Carpaccio, Caravaggio once confounded me as did the *M*'s of Maurois and Malraux and Mauriac. Contradictions: Last week was my eighth voyage into Italy where everyone's either rich or poor. In America everybody is *bourgeois*, the poor as well as rich because they live in a place of *bourgeois* habits (just as American Catholics have Protestant natures *because* they inhabit a Protestant country. In France the contrary is true.) In France the friends of Julien Green believe him to be a French citizen; he is not: he's a Catholic convert (to the French it's the same thing).

The worst surprise was discovering grownups had all the weaknesses of children, and none of the strengths.

Marie Laure having gone to meet her mother at a *fête en Arles*, we dined last night in Toulon—Nora, Jacques Février, and Guy de Lesseps whose ancestor, in digging out the Suez which so worries us today, left to his progeny a wit equivalent to the Canal St. Martin. After getting laid (*mon "tapin" quotidien*) in a sordid Toulon room, I joined the others for a good sea-food meal at the Calanque. There is nothing American in this city which entrances me with little lanes, ten thousand sailors, women dining or ironing behind the summery windows at street level. Le Papillon at eleven was jammed with military dancers and intense whores, and a cruel accordionist yelling into a microphone: "Don't forget, *messieurs*, today's Friday, and these ladies have just had their medical; so you won't risk catching clap. Go to it, *les gars*, grab tighter!" My hair stood on end mournfully at these unsmiling faces on the eve of their departure for Egypt.

When I arrive back soon in America (and particularly Chicago: there have been nine years; and I knew each alley, every taste) it will be bizarre as a doll's town frequented by a giant seeking with thick lenses or newborn retinas the old familiar patterns. Less poignant than not recognizing the known, but more alarming, is the reverse phenomenon: recognition of the unknown. Though this occurs for me rarely, it happened again just recently. While in Parma fourteen evenings ago, with P. and Anterro Piletti, we decided to dine in nearby Salsomaggiore. Now I had certainly never seen nor even heard of this bathing village, but the moment I got off the train I knew it all: any signpost, every store-light, each alley or mixture of tastes was familiar, and especially a soaring park seemed more intimate than my pocket. I have known this town only by evening (daylight changes everything); how have I already been here before? in a dream last night? last month? This dismay is familiar to many, intangible and disagreeable.

Later. It has been raining hard for hours; the air and countryside are heavy brown and drenched with ozone, a relief after the continual honey-glitter of the azure coast.

I am exceedingly discouraged about my work. For months my only ideas have been a pallid unspontaneous musical mass of treacle.

Rain, and the room where I write is agrool with a buzz of mating flies who get caught even in my hair and make me shriek. If only this rain could also purify my music, for I don't know into what generation I've been placed. I employ twelve notes designed after a pattern that my own ear craves (all honest composers must do this *d'ailleurs*). But am I too young to add new ideas to my elders who are my influence (and who say, "If it were twenty years ago I should follow these children")? Or too old to amuse myself playing with the experimenters who are not precocious but grim? The worst of it is that I just don't care. Meanwhile I read and read, not as an intellectual (I don't seek to instruct myself) but for my realest joy. And meanwhile I play the

piano some: the Chopin *Ballades* of my childhood, or old songs of
my own making. And meanwhile, it goes on raining.

I have just counted in my Agenda the number of times I have been
drunk since the beginning of the year: eighteen! Eighteen times in
about thirty-four weeks, or an average of once every twelve days
(though in the summer-country I drink once every five weeks, and
in winter-Paris twice a week). This is more than I suspected, yet a
certain improvement over the years between 1944 and 1952. I haven't
drunk two days in a row for over three years; and between drunks
when I don't drink, *I don't drink.* Not even wine.

These days, I am no longer interested in filling my address book with
grand names, but am turning back instead toward those who've always been solid: relatives, first friends (as for the ego, I would rather,
in any case, have the parasites chatter in my small shadow, than to
chatter myself in other shadows). Yesterday, despite my continuing
difficulty in remaining seated (because, I guess, of a troubled prostate),
we drove, Marie Laure and I, to nearby Collobrières to visit the chestnut forest and take tea with *marrons glacés.* As a child, I once screamed
to mother, "Look!" as I swung daringly in a tree; but it was not so
much the skill of my swing, as the narrowness of the twig I wished
her to see. . . . P. told me that recently with companions in Dorno he
burned a snake alive: at the moment of agony it thrust forth four
tiny legs. I was shocked. It was not at the unlikelihood of a serpent's
latent extremities (a serpent already *is* an extremity moving: hence
our fear and fascination) as at P.'s childly cruelty.

Maybe I'm too literary for music. When at work on a sizable piece
I'm bored before it's a third done: being able to see the bridge's other
end eliminates the need for arriving there. I'm too logical. Yet I *réussis*
short songs best (they being composed *en un souffle,* in one intake
of breath, one "inspiration") which is doubly illogical, song specialists (dealers by definition in poetry) being the least intellectual of
musicians.

I am not an intellectual, because I read and reread not to instruct myself but for enjoyment and from curiosity (there! I *am* curious). I adore discovering origins, seeking comparisons. For instance: Is not *Dorian Gray* a combination of *Roderick Hudson* and *La Peau de Chagrin?* (It's certain Wilde knew Balzac, but could he have read James' book that came many years before his own? James, the only author of quality to straddle the century-point. And who — as Mauriac recently pointed out — troubles us more by what he didn't say than those since Freud who say what *is*, and talk of love in terms of love.) Yes I read and I read and there is never a time when I haven't two or three books under way. But I read junk too. I read more than I compose. I never read what bores me, and cannot read to learn. For we find in books we like only a rewording of what we already knew. Everyone sees the same thing so differently: look in my *Poets' Requiem* at how Gide and Rilke spoke almost simultaneously of animals' liberty; and then I wrote here last May 25th of Nöel Lee's *Cantata* in which Valéry says differently the same words about beasts. It's in the air. But Nöel's notes and mine, as interpretations, have no resemblance (or rather, they *do*, but it's the same difference for the point I'm making). The creatures of Colette, of Butler, are the same, but all sets of eyes converge upon them with separate sympathies. In beauty we discover only what we can understand. The author's name beneath a masterful or mediocre portrait can, alas, adjust our appreciation (Koestler talks of this in his nice but limited essay on snobbery in *Encounter*. Limited, because there's no mention of snobbery's aid to, say, Haydn or Leonardo).

Mother has just sent a copy of *The Friends' Journal* (a Quaker monthly) in which there's a quotation from *Time* about my opera, saying that Rorem "is, at 32, a master writer for the human voice." First of all I am 31. Second, this opera was composed when I was 26. The public assumes that the date of first performance is the date of creation (not *création*, of course, in the French sense, which means "world première"). Hence, I was a "master writer for the human voice" already at 26 (and, I believe, long before), but this opera is now far behind me and today at 31 (not 32) I'm busy with other interests; it's even possible that when I'm 32 I'll no longer be a master of the human voice. Naturally what I compose today — though perhaps different (if no better) — could not have been done without my experiments (successful or not) of yesterday. Each new work is a result of the preceding one; there is no such thing as a first effort, not even birth. As Gertrude Stein says in a letter to Fitzgerald: "One does not get better but different and older and that is always a pleasure." . . . To return to Wilde by way of parentheses: he (of all people) is represented on the cover of the Quaker journal by the following quotation (undoubtedly intended for future twelve-toners): "He who is in a state of rebellion cannot receive grace, to use the phrase of which the Church is so fond—so rightly fond, I dare say—for in life as in art the mood of rebellion closes up the channels of the soul, and shuts out the airs of heaven."

Are geniuses ever unsure? Because, my God, *I* am!

Julien Green once said that anyone seen with me—man, woman, or child—would automatically be compromised.

Auric, who is doing the music for Clouzot's film on Picasso, brings back this troubling story from Nice. The Master speaks: "The tragic deaths in war are not those of children, but those of the old. A child is quickly replaced (anyone can make one in two minutes) whereas it takes years to make an old man . . . " This is a *bon mot* which, as a pacifist, I don't find amusing.

. . . of all natural forces, vitality is the incommunicable one.
                                          —FITZGERALD, The Crack-Up

Because of my health I haven't been able to work for a week; and while everybody plies me with amiable advice I can just smile and remain in pain. Nora has given me the name of a specialist in Paris where I'm going tomorrow, ruddy as an almond and blond as a peach. Probably I'll get drunk when I arrive and that will settle everything. A summer of witnessing the boozey downfall of others has been

instructive, but foreign fire is not our own. I'll learn my lesson when
the time comes (as if I hadn't already learned it a thousand times).

What a good little boy I am, back in Paris now and working (songs,
and a libretto from Petronius) and seeing all these nice people before whom I lower my eyes, shocked, when Boris Kochno's habits (or
somebody else's) are mentioned; but if they knew of the sweat in
pure gin that smears my corpse, or my libidinous promenades, their
hair would stand on end. Or would it? The truth is I have never really
known how to be *bad*. Sometimes I'm compelled to flee attempts
and go south to produce in a disturbed fructuous chastity. For this I
can say that, since I've lived in Europe, Marie Laure and Guy Ferrand,
in harboring me, have been my closest acquaintances, both in connection with liquor and musical puzzles.

Bright blue smoky clean brisk autumn temperature which every
year has that fragrance of trouble and delight that means "back to
school" in a bonfire, and I see that shy boy, as through the wrong end
of a telescope, growing smaller and smaller in whirling leaves — but
for once it's rather pleasant: in less than two weeks I'll be thirty-two.

Marie Laure is still in Hyères (having rightly decided that *Paris
sait attendre*) so I'm alone in the great house having breakfast on a
platinum tray and sometimes a gold lunch as though I too were rich
and noble, and my life is one of movies and American friends, and I
take bouquets of yellow roses to lady friends I haven't seen since
spring: Lise, Rina, and Denise *chez qui* yesterday I lunched and had
a picture taken by Cecil Beaton. *Voilà.*

Yes, I love to gossip, and I'll narrate the most intimate details of my
libido, of a libidinous encounter, to almost any companion (men, not
women). But I am discreet, even here in this journal, about what
really preoccupies, about concrete problems.

The older we grow the more our first experiences turn sharply
etched. The first time I smelled the liquor of a red rose or the honey
of a yellow one is clearer today in memory than the seventh time.
Problems or joys or terrors or discoveries or hates from ten to twenty
now seem in less confusion than from twenty to thirty; and at seven

we have so few years upon which to look back that the smallest thrill is all-important, being always the first. But even if I still feel seven, nothing more seems new (though I sometimes *think* so when I'm drunk, while it's only an age-old situation in a reversed scenery at a slightly older — should I say newer? — age), though I suppose *blasé* is life's most insidious adjective. My thoughts feel tarnished; as I said, I'm ill; and, as it's late, I'll go up now to bed.

May I quote myself? "We are only jealous of the young, and we avenge ourselves by falling in love with them. The odor of youth can never be disagreeable."

Poulenc has grown a mustache: his pimples disappear.

The Spanish are dancers; Italians are singers. The Italians have no ear; they *see* their music by substituting themselves for the *prima donna*. Nor can a Spaniard be a spectator; and if he's obliged to sing, feet come clacking out of his throat in a strained *flamenco*. Just as when an Italian dances his feet turn into vocal cords.

It was understood beforehand that during the three-minute wait in Valence I would get off the train a moment to say hello to my friend Jean-Paul Gaël who lives there and was expecting me on the *quai*. Which I did. And before he could open his mouth I began with that timid hilarity which the restraint of time requires me to spout: *"Oh, te voilà! tu es donc venu! Embrasse-moi vite que je te tâte, car les trépidations du wagon ne m'ont fait songer qu'a ça! Et comme je suis nerveux, nerveux! Je sais qu'en te quittant tout à l'heure je me trouverai subitement envahi d'une bizarre tristesse due sans doute à moitié au paysage crépusculaire des environs de Valence* (it was five-thirty in the afternoon), *et à moitié aux cinq minutes impuissantes et fugitives passées ici ensembles sur le quai. Parce que je suis non pas seulement entre deux trains mais également entre deux pays après ces plus de six années françaises. Tu sais que je m'apprête à partir aux Amériques* (I always say it in plural). *Six ans ou cinq minutes, c'est bien une chose fragile que celle des rapports humains vis-à-vis des soi-disantes éternités que l'on passe renfermé en soi-même. Et je me sens ridicule devant ton ami. Ne m'y attendant pas, je n'avais guère préparé mon 'effet' lequel m'est toujours si important.* (He had brought a friend with him *pour éviter la mélancolie,* he later explained in a letter.) *Au revoir."* And so saying I went back into my compartment leaving him stupefied and mute to watch the train pull out a little while after.

Paris. It appears to blossom at the moment of my going, blossom in fall. *Oh bien sûr, tous les emmerdements habituels:* I have to renew my *carte d'identité*, passport, pack my trunk, see individually six hundred musicians, the numerous details which give me goose flesh. (Jean Rivier, he's the poor man's Florent Schmitt, and that's very poor.) But I'm scared to go, everything stands still, eyes governed by heart see what they're told, and I adore Paris, am scared to go.

The past. New York. Twelve years ago I came wide-eyed into the sin and chic of the Empire City, fresh from Curtis where Menotti was my professor — and professors are above suspicion. Now in those days the specially chic audiences of a particular brand went only to concerts of Povla Frisjh (or Landowska, or later Tourel, or Fizdale and Gold). What was my surprise at seeing Menotti at a Frisjh intermission! These are the contradictions of growing-up. Today Guy Ferrand comes up from the Moroccan nightmare with tales of terrors he was obliged to witness: pregnant women, disemboweled, with small dogs put in the place of embryos; or old women whose vaginas are stuffed with flaming straw. Oh where are we? Oh what I *could* have done. Moravia just wrote about it all in the magazine *Confluence.* I'm so nervous, nervous, nervous, and the tragic liquor of departure. It's Sunday. The nowadays' *entr'actes* will say farewell to me next Wednesday when the Barraults with Marie Bell give their *L'Orestie (musique de Boulez)* which everyone says will be *très long et très beau,* but nobody says *très beau et très long.*

Our sensitive André Dubois is marrying hard-boiled Carmen Tessier.

For years he was a promoter of the "underprivileged," both generally and specifically: he negotiated the Jewish exodus from Germany, and championed Boulez before anyone else did. For years *she's* been Europe's answer to Louella Parsons with a daily column in *France-Soir*. Though *he's* now Chief of Police and known as the "Prefect of Silence" (having forbidden honking), *she* continues professionally to be called *La Commère*, or The Gossip. *He*, for years a Gidean admirer of tasteful youth, now says to *her* at parties, "Raise your skirts, *chérie*, and show us the bruises we made last night!" Well, we all evolve; and opposites attract, as Cocteau couldn't help pointing out: *"Le Préfet du Silence épouse la Commère."*

Well, in what country *am* I? Finally I heard the tape of the Louisville Orchestra playing my *Design*. The mechanic of the studio said to me afterwards: "But you aren't of your time." But of course, I am of my time, only it is not of me.

La pire chose, c'est de vouloir être à la mode si cette mode ne vous va pas.

— FRANCIS POULENC

Rain, drizzle. Rather soft autumn weather. These are my final Paris days (Auric thinks they're the final days *of* Paris) because in two weeks I'll be on a boat going home. So everything—friends, lawns, neighborhoods, the sky—takes on a deeper, more immediate meaning.

Rubinstein gave a *souper chez lui* last night after his great Chopin concert at the Chaillot and there I found a gorgeous series of former lady-friends who didn't recognize me because now my hair's its normal color. Before them I asked François Valéry (whose dream it is to die in the lion's cage): "A male or female lion?" I guess it's an indiscreet question.

Bernard Gavoty, a sad Monday, tells that Honegger spoke of me on his death bed in these words: *"Ned Rorem, lui est vraiment doué avec son goût de la féerie triste. Ce beau nordique, ayant tout, devrait sauter de joie."*

Barring death, there's no old lost forgotten friend we'll never come across again some day. It's a matter of living long enough to learn the size of cycles. But sometimes it would seem better to keep far-agos buried instead of always wishing to find them again, and seeing only wrinkled lovers without conversations. I cannot help the overwhelming memory of snow and poetry in Chicago, at Northwestern, those days, during the learning cycle; the smartest thing I can now do for that lovely sadness, is to keep a thought a thought and not try to remake it squalid-real by stamping back after ten years to find all diminished nut-sized. I knew Roditi when I was a child there; years and years have gone by and now today here we are in Paris which too will be recalled. Roditi who recently used these astounding words: "Well, the suffering is over now"; whose little poem of jealousy I've just made into a song, my only valid gesture since returning to Paris twelve days ago, twelve days of tension, all the hysterical nerves of my departure for America without a cent and full of debts: all these big, these little problems cease the day we die. This hovering around the past: I remember in 1936 when as a family we visited Europe; at the American soldiers' cemetery of Belleau Wood I saw mother cry upon the tomb of her young brother buried there long before my birth; I wondered at her tears for something so remote to me; today there is less distance between the first war's end and her tears, than between her tears and the present moment—yet our summer in 1936 is clear as crystal to me. All these are landmarks static in static time; we move from one to another down the road until we reach the one melodramatically signaled with our own end. Then, for all we know, it starts or stops again.

Aboard the S.S. *United States*

Saw Julien again before leaving and we walked ecstatically through the Palais Royal (where we had been in other weather) into the rue Vivienne (and Julien showed me a house "where wicked things take place — very wicked!" though he wasn't sure on which floor), and on to the little store of the Bibliothèque Nationale to buy a pair of earrings designed as Merovingian owls for his sister Anne, whom he has never allowed me to see.

But none of us is really interesting in what he *does* (even Don Juan, even the headsman) and so an artist invents a marvelous world to which everyone runs with tongue hanging out. I have seen real live princesses; but how old they are, all snobbish and battered. Nobody warned me of this as I read my fairy tales. My tonsils, my hemorrhoids, were torn from my adult body and aged me a decade. Why write of this? I'd rather tell lies.

How many thousands have I spent on perfume and alcohol, cigarettes and Turkish baths, disappointing trips and third-class movies; how many months in silent bars or parks, expecting, in a chair with a book not reading, or waiting in line, waiting in line? Who will tell me it's a loss when I know life must be for pleasure? The parks were balanced by museums, the baths by oceans, bars by composition, and the dreaming chair by books finished. Nothing is waste that makes a memory. Only an American bothers to consider such "justification," turning out souvenirs on the assembly line.

All last night a storm: the boat rolled, stretched, sagged with such energy that I was frightened and envisioned myself on a raft eating my fellows. Today the sun, and we search for whales. I also saw a small blue bird, but none of us knows from where he comes. Toward

two this morning I opened the watch Henri gave me before I left,
and read again what he had scratched on the metal while a prisoner
in Germany: "2 7-5-40 (and other dates until '42) Maman, cafard,
faim"; also a flower engraved with infinite patience which, in a prison,
would be called boredom (though Maurice Sachs maintained that
there one would make love with the whole universe — and, like so
many others, he only found real peace in jail). How could I not be
moved by these scratched words, I, who was in no direct intercourse
with the war and therefore am free to create the wildest inventions,
sufficient to flatten out and mute me for life? Yet all around is talk of
new conflict as though each rising generation would feel cheated if
terror should happen to forget it. Nobody learns, and it is hard to
take advice despite five thousand years of fatigue. Must I too die and
be replaced?

Is art odd- or even-numbered? The Rockettes are even-numbered
(6 × 6 = 36) but the best *corps de ballet* seems odd-numbered —
or even-numbered oddly distributed, whereas how can you distribute
odd numbers evenly (i.e. in pairs)? Yet iambic pentameter, which
would appear the ultimate in odd-numberedness, ends up being in
six, since there's an instinctive pause at each line's end. Look at
Stravinsky's early odd balance, or Bach's even unbalance. The unexpected (which is art) is always odd, but (as art must) it always evens
out. It's as clear in space as in time. One square is a bore (hence the
slang; square) while circles are forever magic.

To sleep with a person and be stimulated by images of another. Then
to sleep with that other and "succeed" only by images of the first!

In three days we will land in America. I fear a new young electricity
after my lazy years. I fear that the streets will be broader or narrower,
the days longer or shorter, human smells brighter or duller than I
recall. Tricks of memory. Just as our music sounds either better or
worse, but never identical to what we heard as we wrote.

On a postcard from Elliott Stein in Yugoslavia: SEE DUBROVNIK AND SPLIT!

Sober, the business of *daring:* daring to react, be alive; drunk, the avoidance of living, i.e. boredom or breathing. The *courage* for writing music, the obscenity of it! Art means: to dare — and have been right.

Morris Golde tells of the explorer who, age twenty, vanished in Siberia. The widow and young son mourn him long and obsessively. Finally the child, now thirty-five, vows to retrieve his father whom he will recognize by descriptions of clothing last worn. Indeed, after perils and adventures, the corpse is found in ice, a perfectly preserved twenty-year-old with red lips and black hair. The son examines his father now fifteen years younger than himself.

They say women outlive men. They say also that seventy-five per cent of crimes remain unsolved. Now, of these crimes, most are rural poisonings. Is it that wives do not naturally outlive their husbands, but simply kill them off?

Theme for a tragedy. They meet in the morning. By afternoon they are in love. That evening one of them dies.

At the rate of one pack a day for twenty years I've smoked one-fifth of a million cigarettes. And I've passed more time on movies and movie gossip than on music and music copy; my hours of research on Marilyn Monroe alone go beyond those on, say, our lady-authors (I've read them all), not to mention the complete history of music. So life is spent, with crossroads and choices.

Suppose that from the safety of a subway platform you throw a kiss to an unknown paragon in the slowly departing train. But the train *stops*! Its doors reopen, the paragon emerges and approaches you! How much will the knees shake? How will the paragon express unprecedented derision? How will you explain yourself?

Is death an end of illusions? or the ultimate rewarding illusion when we'd thought there'd never be another?

All men are forced into one of two categories: those with eleven fingers and those without.

> *Oeufs à l'aurore*
> *Gigot de Chevreuil*
> > *Sauce groseille*
> > *Sauce venaison*
> *Purée de marrons*
> *Salade*
> *Endives braisées*
> *Charlotte hongroise*
> > *Sauce chocolat*

This was our last lunch at noon, typical of the menu twice a day for four years. Back in 1951 my obstreperousness in the company of Marie Laure was both feigned and short-lived: an expression of dazzlement at so easily meeting half of legendary Europe at her table. Once the novelty wore off, my Quaker sense informed me that, above all she's offered *the leisure to work*. She has not only provided three pianos, sponsored concerts, clothed and fed and housed me, but has been the main cause of my staying on to compose in France for so long. The glamor of daily life in her mansions of Hyères and Paris — among the richest and yet most "livable" on the Continent — has been balanced by emulating the discipline of her working habits, and by finding the talented child within the spoiled viscountess. (Her unchanneled glee at receiving my gifts of American toilet paper! her French refusal to stop a conversation even while on the *bidet*! her suave ignorance of my midnight strangers in her purple sheets! her tolerance of cripples!) She has been my chief *confidante* and adviser; as sheer instruction goes, she corresponds in the French fifties to what Virgil Thomson was for my American forties. My parents excepted, there is no doubt that she and Virgil are the two "older" people who've most influenced my thinking and my style.

If I could live hidden as a hermit I should be utterly happy, but having been born for notoriety my nature will remain obstinately sad. Nevertheless the moment of making is at once the loneliest and happiest one can have. It is the time between these timeless outbursts which excruciates, as it's then we're lost. What difference if our art has been spoken before: every new generation demands in living words the same morals, horrors, same ecstasies, which have already been as frequently reproduced as the number of seasonal rebirths since earth began. There is no evolution, we never learn; we merely change language and styles every decade or so. The marvelous clamor of science has aided in little things, lengthened our life, but has never made us good. Is it any wonder my father has signed up to go to Mars?

When idiots on boats say, "Where do your ideas *come* from?" I answer that it can't be explained. When clever laymen ask, I discuss the process at length. But when other artists talk of this, I say, "Ideas? I *steal* them." And they understand. Sometimes I rob myself.

The entire ship's been interlaced with a series of temporary ropes, as complex as the thongs in a spider's web, which we must clutch, as more bad weather's expected.

A diary has impact only through the accumulation of unlimited observations (of which many are obsessive and recurring), never through the development of themes (for then it would no longer be a diary). Works of art must have a plan; beginnings and ends. A diary necessarily has no form beyond the accidental one of improvisation; hence, though it cannot be a work of art (improvisation precludes this), perhaps it *can* be a masterpiece.

The fact of writing here turns an experience into an idea. If I were to keep a diary instead of a journal, I would ultimately forget having lived, would remember only what I'd written about having lived. Man's horror is language: Chaos and Order are mere inventions. If, ten billion years back, one cell had slipped a fraction, how different today would be our concept of things.

John Ashbery says: "Once you've been happy in Paris you can never be happy anywhere else — not even in Paris."

Alas, I am happy! Despite complaints or broken hearts (my several hearts); despite this sometimes mournful book that demonstrates less the need to explain than to document myself; despite the hangovers which, like mescaline, make me a vegetarian; or that hardly a day begins without my wondering if I'll die before dusk; despite the schmaltz of eternal youth — I eat with good appetite, sleep and screw well when not working well, and am, as they say, *appreciated*. And so, though the style was always tragic, larger than life, today I'm happy, alas! (happiness, for me, being contained almost exclusively in routine and good weather).

The day after humanity dies there will still be huge atmospheric storms in midocean as there were ten thousand years ago, but nobody left to imagine them.

Yesterday was my birthday. Tomorrow we arrive in New York. Already it appears to have happened to another child. Who knows if America might not after all be the country where my *realest* problems, for better or worse, will eventually be solved?

I asked her if I would find love again back home.

    But Marie Laure replied: *Quant à moi, je n'ai plus envie de faire l'amour, je veux faire l'amitié.*

The New York Diary

PART 1
October 1955

Aboard the S.S. *United States*

If you look back, you risk turning into a statue of
salt — that is, a statue of tears. . . .

COCTEAU

It's not that I'm more self-involved than other people, I'm just more free about showing it. Exhibitionist: that has the ring of a dirty word. Yet an artist is an exhibitionist by definition, and an artist cannot be dirty.

Now shyness forces me, all seasick, back to this journal. Hopefully it will be at once less frivolous and more outspoken than those Paris diaries. One grows increasingly unconcerned about others' eccentricities if they begin to displace one's own.

Where am I? The man-as-artist can begin again only in midstream, that place where there's time for time, where the future can't loom, the past sheds its skin, and where we finally find ourselves *in the fact.*

Yesterday was my birthday. Tomorrow we arrive in New York. Neither event particularly thrills me this time although both involve years and years. All appears already to have happened to another little boy though I can still clearly see him running about. Will taxis *never* learn where we live? Must we tell them every time?

My Paris weathers have grown into a tremendous conglomeration so it's somewhat of a blur; later we are more clearly nostalgic about places least frequented since we have only *one* memory of them. It is no accident: a new explosion of events on the eves of leaving. I've too many recollections of the Gare d'Orsay for a general sentiment to remain hovering, but to these was added a particular tussle at the *commissariat* on the eve of my going — and Paris was quit with a bad taste. Not to mention an array of old photographs Denise Bourdet showed me of today's dead and dying in their beautiful time. Well really I can't tell what's waiting for me "back home" (as travelers say) when the psychoanalytic examples (now, to me, long forgotten) come flying through town more messy than ever in monster egoism.

Come snow, clean us off a little! The mediocrity of this ship's passengers is beyond belief. But the mediocrity of this ship's pen impedes me from developing more *là-dessus*. How could any psychoanalysis help but be lugubrious now? Life's too long and there seems nothing I cannot understand. Though sometimes I pretend ignorance just to make time go by.

The French speak for exercise, Americans for self-expression. Paradoxically the French speak on many levels but Americans on only one. Americans say what they think, the French think what they say. As for me, I take everything I hear literally, and mean literally nothing I say. And still hide all knives before going out, not knowing whom I might bring home who'd stab me.

America is not a place one speaks about except in retrospect, so the next months may be silent — that is, too noisy to think.

Yet to think — even to talk — about your life is, in a way, to stop living, so a diary becomes a breathing corpse which eats into the present. Possibly writing music is also a kind of self-denial (as well as self-indulgence), but no one can assert that it's autobiographical. Music and prose satisfy two distinct drives in me, though each involves anesthetizing life temporarily to bring order from chaos. But the music is sacred chaos while the prose is ordered profanity. Being today involved in the latter (and time stops in midocean) I halt to pluck green memories and mount them in this scrapbook like drying fall leaves, leaves whose veins still flow with an inextricable poison that pervades and blurs the very system that formed them. . . . But I *do* have to live, don't I? No, I'll leave that to others. I just have to get my work done.

Et pourtant. . . . Recurring obsessions. The anguish of alcohol's danger, however imaginary or exaggerated, pains me still, and will doubtless continue until death, as will legends of Eros and fright of people and boredom and guilt about work. Still, we continue to live in order to be loved and maybe to love. There's little else.

Adolescence is the only period when being-in-love is a potent force, for that's when the heart first breaks, breaks out of the placenta into our poignant confusion and reaches a quick peak. The average mind is adolescent. Therefore the run-of-the-mill have a truer capacity for love than intellectuals, who should know better.

The hoped-for never materializes. Still, one cannot be positive of exactly knowing when the End's around — and who can say whether doubt might not be the ultimate joy?

In art spontaneity must always be calculated. Simplicity is complex, to be easy is hard. Why do I compose? It keeps me off the streets. (At this moment I could say: keeps me out of the waves.)

We live mostly in the past or future. Music and meals and sometimes mating are all that exist in the present.

There goes the dinner gong. Despite seasickness I shall reel down and eat. Because I've paid for it.

Then, to make time go by until we land (pretending ignorance), and because America is not a diary country (its inhabitants preferring to make others live their thoughts) let me look back to reactions of those three months three years ago when I first returned there. At the Chelsea Hotel, autumn of 1952.

New Yorkers, the New Yorkers who were my friends, had made a shroud for the city during that period of the Eisenhower election. I saw this both half and twice as well because I had never thought about it and still was a stranger come home. The delirium of old acquaintance past, and I nearly saw New York as a new Frenchman, had forgotten its former power over me as amply as that of an old love affair. And what if this were to happen as I went back into France? When and for how long would I be able to stay there once more before the arrival of death, which I now believed and feared and knew the secrets of? If I am special, then I can love only a daily person, but for this, or even for its memory, I would move to China. Should it be the opposite? No, as then there would no longer be love for me: the man not born a genius may know family joys but not those of travel; he must wait. The famous will displace themselves for the unknown. Or so I felt in '52.

It had been about four years. I read death on old friends' faces suddenly as an overnight change. Home in Philadelphia I thumbed through forgotten scores, heard old records, spent hours with baby pictures and high school annuals; nothing that was real had dimmed, rather had become surrealistically clear. I recalled each scratch on the family furniture, every piece of silverware, all curtains and smells and bedspreads, the same, the same only smaller, like photographs in dreams, or like being on a train taking my youth farther away. It was more than I could stand, even when I turned to look the other way. And oh, the anxiety of parents when they know together how far off this all has grown since they saw the first nasty glimmers of love and talent that kidnapped their child. . . .

Although I drank, I did not make love in New York. (Do I write this in hope that love may arrive tonight, even as I write of atomic fright feeling that written words prevent the reality?) Although I had again fallen down there and seen a thousand former friends, not making love made me miss insanely my Paris. The streets were full of the globe's cleanest sunshine, but Americans seemed afraid of love, still talked psychotherapy as though I'd never gone away. All about me on Park Avenue in the bright of noon I saw people, young people, vomiting, bleeding, lying on their backs with vacant stares, begging, limping, having epileptic fits; old friends were dead, disappeared, in asylums, or forgotten in medical wards; these street-sleepers were invisible to my friends who live there, but I saw panic at any corner turned and not a trace of the marvelous indifference that the Latin church affords. Even their music had hysteria, and what didn't exist in France existed too much at home.

There was no place I had not been, nothing I had not done or seen, nobody not known and loved; yet all of it wrong. For I had not been able to observe the cinema of myself. Why do I keep on, making every gesture in the fear and hope that it will be seen, remembered? Or for what reason can I say that this or that of me I have made indelible, when with a final gulp I, too, have admitted death? And when I die people may talk a little while, ten, fifteen years, saying, "Remember when he did such and such a thing," or, "It's tragic that with such a talent and etc. . . . " Then those who've said it will also die, and fifty years after, it will be as if none of us had ever . . . etc.

A printed song is no longer *me*. I hold out my arms for a bit, but it gets away, and I must start again. When it is sung in concerts I cringe that a half-recollected infant of mine may disgrace himself. If ever I am spoken of in whatever generations may have the funny miracle of being born, it will not be Ned Rorem *himself* who is remembered. I loathe this thought.

I went alone one evening to the Chaplin movie *Limelight*. (Like all great comics, Chaplin lacks a sense of humor.) Afterwards dined alone in the 23rd Street automat (an old beef pie, spastics, ladies with runny noses, people who don't say "Excuse me!"). Then returned to the hotel room alone feeling like Tobias Mindernicle. Nothing to do but finish the book I was reading, take one of my rare baths, go to bed: terrible remedies for a big city. France had saved my life four years before and would do so again. But the weather had been heavenly since my return and I felt neither sad nor happy. I'd seen so many people good and bad in so short a time that I had no moment for ideas.

Alma Morgenthau asked me that autumn if being good-looking had caused difficulties professionally. Others had wondered this, and what is the answer? I began writing music at birth, before knowing what composers were supposed to look like. The surnormality of "creation" hit me before I was aware that problems divorced from art show up for any adolescent. Nobody knows where talent comes from, whether it's cause or effect, but it seems clearly not inherited since it grows so rarely and in such diversified climates, and usually becomes apparent before worldly stimulants could direct it for better or for worse. I would have been a composer no matter how I looked; had I been born deformed I simply would have made another kind of music.

Appearance has never fundamentally helped me. Those who have been most useful are people I've never met. Artists are artists because of, and despite, their environment. If his father is great, no son will equal him, so that son must choose either another profession or suicide.

Intelligent beauty (a contradiction in terms) moves over an earth that never asked for beauty. Therefore beauty is shy. Not to have the problem of an awful face is to create different problems, different faces. We know what's great mostly by hearsay, by what surrounds us in the streets. I'm not sure that the first reading of an unknown Shakespeare would suddenly call forth his famous power. Beauty's not instantaneous (necessarily). Once the thing is done, dragged up by pain from nowhere, it seems simple. "I could have done it," they say. Yes, but did they? "My child, my cat, could have made that line, this noise." But they didn't.

Staring into the Chelsea bathroom mirror, I placed those scissors in my nose, a prong in each nostril, then opened them quickly — and zlish! blood everywhere! The pain dissolved into ice as I observed a diffuse orange glow like a halo around my skull. . . . Then I fainted. I was going back to France.

"I'll love you forever" may be said by one person to many others with equal honesty. Time in love and time in life are unrelated: forever exists more than once. Where is P.? Alive. But no longer in the time of forever. Expose yourself to hurt, to love, or why live? Do we then have to live? Is working living? No.

Of course the America of 1955 will be different. No, nothing again will ever be new, though every return necessarily indicates a change. At least I felt this on arriving, and said, "Here is the last marvelous displacement I will ever know: the bitter sweetness of a first homecoming." It's not true. The same voyage will always be new, and we all have perhaps but a few moments more. People, that's not memory. Sentiment is a situation recollected, the fainting taste of skin-covered blood. Greenwich Village, they say, is revitalized, though upper Broadway has always represented a land of the dead. But do we ever change? No.

Yes. Life doesn't stop. I feel myself involuntarily flung forward into 1955, even as I wish in this book to rush back toward unforgotten formations as though they made a difference. How I wish that Ned the grown-up could stand back aloof and cast a jaundiced eye at Ned the growing brat, conceited and insecure, could watch him misbehave and suffer while knowing full well that when he becomes the Ned of today he'll still suffer and misbehave as before.

If there *is* always tomorrow, the tentative appeal or hope-giving element lies in the utterly unknown. The past, any past or present may
form in a palm's lines, but never the future. That future, said to be
divined by the extrasensorily perceptive (a mother's warning of her
son's death overseas), is only an intensification of the present stated
in terms of the past. Nobody knows the future. Cassandra saw only
the illogical logic of human nature.

Three weeks ago in London I bought a giant tube of K–Y. It is still
unopened.

Who knows what New York may bring? Nell Tangeman will
sublet her far-west 23rd Street apartment to me during the winter.
But first I'll visit the family for a week in Philadelphia. Neither place
can I yet perceive tonight because there's snow all over the ocean.

PART 2
Spring, 1956

New York

One lives by memory . . . and not by truth.

STRAVINSKY

Ages since I've written here because, as prophesied, New York with its noisy pollution is where, unlike Paris, we look at our feet instead of the sky. No "inner repose" needed for journal writing. I'm not sure this is true. *Is* it repose French diarists possess?

In any case, Americans are not especially concerned about whether they're going to hell when they die, and that's the theme of a French diary. I'm not at all interested in what I now write here after such long months, and cannot imagine adding anything not already said at more urgent minutes. It's not simple to summon sufficient interest for starting again. We all lie anyway at the really fascinating time that makes a difference. When a person has gone to pieces — really to pieces — he is no longer capable of maintaining a document about himself although this is the crucially interesting moment toward which he has been directed, because he's no longer in a position of caring. Not that I've gone interestingly to pieces, *au contraire. La preuve*, I'm writing a diary once more.

America, the new slang: goof — to miss, make a mistake. Flip — to swoon with enthusiasm. America, the new compulsion: male impersonation. In his *mépris* of women a young man refuses to caricature them; he becomes instead a male impersonator by affecting leather and dungarees (male symbols, it seems). He attends S & M meetings (i.e., sado-masochist or slave-master) where truly gory doings are rumored. Yet, when I question Bill Flanagan about the details, the Third Avenue bartender, overhearing, intrudes: "Don't kid yourself — they just hit each other with a lot of wet Kleenex!" Perhaps it's in mimicry of divine James Dean (already immortalized by our Frank O'Hara); still, it's a cause and not an effect: James Dean would not have existed without them.

America, my "success" — otherwise I'd have been a failure. I learned that a composer, whatever his reputation, must be (as opposed to a poet) on the spot. I also touched Talullah Bankhead (thanks to Bobby Lewis) and dined with Dietrich (thanks to Truman Capote).

Neither of these ladies knows I exist. *Et puis après.* Talullah rose
from her couch and exclaimed: "I'm not so old yet that I can't stand
up for a young man who wants to meet me." As I was speechless,
even *her* conversation lagged, and that was that.

As for Marlene, there we sat in El Morocco at midnight, she all
in black, with Harold Arlen, downing a four-course meal including
an oozing *baba au rhum*, and Truman's three other guests pretending
she was just someone else, and she so bored, while I longed to lean
over and whisper, "Oh, Miss Dietrich, I loved you in this, and even
more in that, and especially in *Song of Songs,* which nobody knows,"
but lost my nerve and stayed mute, and she never looked my way,
but remained thin despite the *baba*, hummed along with the solici-
tous pianist playing "Lili Marlene," called over the *chasseur* ("How
do you say *chasseur* in English?"), to whom she gave a phone number and said, "Tell them I can't come," without explaining who she
was. Even grander was the leave-taking: when Arlen gave her a handful of change for the powder room she complained, "Oh no, darling,
I need a bill. After all, coming from me, *noblesse oblige!*"

I prefer to recall my enthusiasm of 1944 when, drunk at 5 A.M.,
I would phone from veneration to Povla Frijsh, then hang up when
she answered. Today, knowing her, I am disenchanted. Or knowing
George Copeland or other idols of my babyhood. More and more,
despite myself, I am impervious to those about me and wander through
daylight past all reactions like a somnambulist, aware only of me, or
vaguely of the family unit, which takes new meaning. Before the
age of thirty we can't know this, being charged with only accusation.
There's no longer the desire for gossip to interest others. What's a
diary? Write about the rain.

I made discoveries in New York and know it as one can only in
getting away. Write about drinking in America: *je m'y connais un
peu, quand même!* The best thing for a hangover (next to not drinking)
— and this I hadn't known before — is that Manhattan array of rhap-
sodic turkish baths which answer so well to your one-track carnal
awareness the afternoon after. Days, days can be spent there in the
sensual naked steam of anonymity disintoxicating the body (always
the body), while outside it ceaselessly rains, glumly rains to your total disinterest. It was my discovery of America and must be shown to
all Latin visitors as an Anglo-Saxon attitude.

Nothing exists unless it is notated, not even the smell of wind, much less the sound of pastorales. I remember sounds with the eye. Even love and lovemaking are unreal except through a recollection which grows faint and disappears unless I print it here. I can't "just live," but must be aware of being aware.

"Why do we live, since we must die?" everyone wonders, whereas the converse could as logically be asked. Maybe life is death and death life—like Pascal's sleep and waking. My sleep is so light, so light, just Miltown at night gets me through it. Quite simply, the purpose of life is to seek life's purpose; to find the right answer is not so important as the right question. Where we came from, where we'll go, and above all, why, we'll never never understand.

Can you polish a phrase about tears in your eyes with tears in your eyes? Yes.

Who am I to say that Delius stinks? Every nonmusical association from my sexy adolescence shrieks of him. Wagner too I love, if I don't have to listen to him. For nothing *works* today. Things must work: love, music. Or if they flop, they should flop tragically, not tackily.

Title: *The Rewards of Boredom,* i.e., of sobriety. No one believes it, but I'm much more timid than these journals indicate. Yet the fact of their existence proves it. If I utter brasheries when dead sober it's to prove I *can* dead sober. I'm no longer "mean" when drunk, just weepy and redundant. But my bite is louder than my bark.

Some of my best friends are 12-tone composers. David laughs for Absalom. Fugue is as suspect as its opposite, improvisation. (This applies to present decades.) Opera should be seen and not heard— needs letter scenes, toasts, instruments on stage, candles, dream sequences, and women dressed as men. (Men dressed as women, however, can never be taken "seriously," i.e., as people in love.) The bad old days. Two nuns take leave of each other saying: Be good! Stravinsky—Cocteau *Oedipus*: a telegram from Sophocles. I deserved the Gershwin Memorial Award (1949), but the piece I wrote did not.

Now I've known so many that'll die soon: Carl Van Vechten. Who? Peter Watson and Cecil Smith. Honegger's dead too, and now little

Bernard Charpentier — *de la drogue.* Myself from champagne, that easy way away from tension. Aphrodisiacs used to be put, for children, into candy which is dandy though liquor's quicker. . . . We do not need graphic sexuality in letters. Nineteenth-century restraint's more troubling than today's one-dimensional violence. . . . Taffy-colored taffeta drag: old-fashioned.

Seven years' absence. Old friends in America are now settled into their mold. I am left out. Conservatism comes with age.

The long lazy heat of childhood summers in the first heavy odor of zinnias, hollyhocks, bumblebees, summer with his hot yellow smile at the summer maid who sniffs the dirty laundry of the boy she loves.

All we need now is one genius, just one. There aren't any more. I'm not as glamorous as my friends think. But more than they think, blind to the rich man who, in his huge and unrequited love, finances the lover of his sweetheart. The French have no word for vicarious.

Embarrassment composing at the piano when Messaoüd was in the house. Messaoüd, our Moroccan servant in Fez, 1949, in every sense a Moslem and centuries away. Embarrassment that he might find the sounds I struck too corny.

Embarrassment as a child at the semi-annual arrival of the decorators who pulled away the bed to expose the lower wall onto which for six months I had smeared deposits of mucus after picking my nose in the morning.

Sober: the awe of death is — is *sharper.* But sorrow is useless.

Drinking, like anti-Semitism, is unintelligent. But must we always be intelligent? Probably.

If through skill in false premises I annihilate a less logical yet more honest adversary, I later cringe with wonder at the pleasure in my wrongness. To be confusedly right (though ephemeral and smug) should be higher satisfaction, should it not? Does my conscience tell me *not* to kill because my wish tells me to kill?

If I've learned one thing in my travels it's that Europeans, Arabs, Negroes are not "just like everyone else" but quite different. That difference should be coveted, not thwarted, for it provides an attraction which could prevent rather than cause wars.

In war the first thing to go is the truth.

People are mostly alike; one hopes for a difference. When a crippled girl entered the restaurant tonight I mused that there at least, by definition, was a difference. But then she brought forth *The Readers' Digest.*

Discontent with work, vaguely but regularly saddened by the gorgeous weather — sentiments not wholly lacking in charm. Meanwhile the weeks slide by like a funeral procession.

Another day. . . .

The superfluous is all that counts — art, screwing, ice cream. As for sleep or taxes, they don't *count*, do they?

Painter friends accuse me of blindness. It is because I'm internally visual. Even my musical memory is visual, not auditory. For instance, if I'm on a subway or somewhere and think of a tune, I inscribe that tune on a mental staff, photograph it, store the negative elsewhere in my brain for development later.

Nor can I "just listen" anymore: whatever enters my mind must be inscribed on psychic paper. Do I *know* music too well now to enjoy it? In any event the layman's hearing is inconceivable to me; my nature always asks what makes beauty beautiful.

And silence? Becomes the sound of our world whirling through space.

A poet may look like a janitor, a janitor like a poet. Art is the only domain that resists generalities.

Why not a popular song extolling New York as the French, with accordions, have so often extolled Paris? Because one can only extol in three-four meter and Americans are too hurried for that. Why *be* in New York? Because it's where you *have* to be: for better or worse it's the center of the universe. Which is why I'll leave soon: I can only feel adjusted off-center.

If I retire forever to write, does not the very act of writing contradict retirement? How can I wish to chastise Man in words or notes unless *au fond* I want his love? Yet the most agreeable sorrow (the pleasures of pain, the pain of pleasure) is in contemplating the Jersey flats on the train to Philly and wondering where that one reed (that one in billions) will be in a year, in a minute, when the train's gone by.

Finally heard Liberace. Extraordinary, his fingerwork! He plays all the right notes wrong.

At loose ends on a Thursday evening, I phone Paul Goodman and invite myself to his group-therapy session. In preparation I wash my hair and don the famous black turtleneck jersey.
        Of those eight or ten present, I know only Paul and Sally. . . . Long, very long Quakerlike silence which I finally invade by exclaiming, "Well, since I'm the new one, maybe we could break the ice with someone telling me about the procedure." Silence again, pregnant and sinister. Then Paul speaks. "Ned, the artifice of your social style, your charm, will be your downfall." This drop of blood set the group on me like sharks. At a total loss, I exposed myself to their teeth; mute myself, I was tossed from one stranger's mouth to another; following the leader, they ripped me to ribbons. At which point the session was over. (Charm or not, I *had* been the center of attention!) Then we all had tea and cookies and were filled with

fraternal love. No question of a postmortem; only Paul's complaining of always being Father. But he can't have it both ways. As for me, I felt like another Faust: he sells his soul to the devil, then shows his pretty body to Marguerite, who declares, "Oh, I'm sorry, sir, but I prefer older types."

We can sing it and say so, but how can we be truly glad for what we have or are, since we cannot know until we have not or are not anymore, and then we are no longer glad? Glad for what we've gained? But at this moment we have forgotten yesterday: five minutes after weeping, our tears seem silly. Should a cruel king fall to low place, repent and do good deeds and cry loud and love God, once reascended he will again be cruel. I have never been shown that there is a connection or growth from day to day: it is as easy to forget as remember, as logical to be happy as sad. People say, "I would give my kingdom, my riches, my fame, my soul, for youth and beauty." I have beauty and youth, though how can I know their value? I want a soul, fame, riches, a kingdom.

A priceless bird hides hardly fluttering in the cage of all our chests, a bird we are not allowed to see until the moment it decides to leave us and fly away forever. How could we have known it was starving inasmuch as we ignored its existence? So as not to become tiresome to others, I oblige them to fall in love with me.

As I grow I become more and more curious about things, but about people less and less. It's rare that I am not bored by the average person within two minutes and by an intelligent one within two hours (excluding, of course, the physically attractive, who cannot be boring). My only curiosity about fellow humans concerns the waste they make of themselves. Why, I wonder, have even the ugliest been so magnificently constructed: that labyrinth of artery and nerve, more exquisite, fragile, and complex than a beehive's gentle machinery? With what is this mechanism occupied? With sleeping, eating, fornicating, nothing more. Its reason serves solely destruction. Still, it takes nine months of building, more magic and intense than for skyscrapers or ant hills, more patient than for blueprints of pyramids or atom bombs, a muscular waxing, the infinite house of the brain which finally uses about 3 percent of itself. All this emerges, works for years in spite of itself toward a total perfection which will live in the charmed construction incrusting the earth like a transparent jewel. But why, seeing that all this is good for absolutely nothing?

Unimportant that people exhaust their hearts and die at the end of a given time, if only they would ask a question one day in their lives. Yesterday evening I was exposed for hours to the laughter of five ridiculous girls. Never have I been so bored. One can say, let them giggle, it's a stage they're going through. But *I* never went through it; I read and asked questions, not of others but of myself; the others bored and frightened me. One says too: they are only girls and require gentlemen, though gentlemen serve the purpose of their mechanism to even less effect than animals or vegetation.

If in half an hour I can make an indelible impression why, when I go away, must I want to rush back for fear of being forgotten? Three seconds can inspire a lifetime of loathing. . . . If a person dies later than he thinks, only a handful more people will recall him, and already with less mystery. We are immeasurably more curious about Mozart, Lautréamont, Maurice Sachs, than about Richard Strauss, Voltaire, Gide.

How, sometimes, could I not compare myself to some god come down to earth when I look at those about me? Suppose it were true but that the knowledge for some reason were denied me: would this keep me from suffering any the less in a contest for my life? Is the trial of a god like any other when the judges are blind?

Donald Gramm and Mattiwilda Dobbs, each in Town Hall the same week, sang premières and beautifully for me. Also my little opera *A Childhood Miracle* received its television debut in Philadelphia, thanks to Plato Karyanis, Wayne Conner, Dorothy Krebill, Benita Valenti, and a bunch of instrumentalists from Curtis conducted by Donald Johanos, all of whom donated their services. But what else did I get or give in America? Since not a day passes without history, there are those who say it should be recorded or lost. But such is a chronicle, not a diary. And history recorded tonight would not be the same if recorded tomorrow. It is not what you say but what I say you say.

I drank a lot, was sober a lot, saw a thousand intimate friends, made some new ones, lost old ones, parties, parties, accumulated fans and clarified my situation with the music publishing world, was hated and well received, grew up and got younger, refound my marvelous mother and father, had a Thanksgiving, a Christmas, and Easter, and no longer believe in my own immortality.

It is the rainy month of May and next week, after six months, I'm going via London to Marie Laure's in the south of France. I'll be back in the Europe I've missed. If it please God, I'll also be able to miss home.

Is it the memory of New York friends that might make the heart ache? Or will it be rather more difficult to shake the souvenir of sitting in my late-night, early-spring apartment on 23rd, and the window-street sounds of tires on warm-winter New York rain ten stories below?

Around the Mediterranean

The very act of writing stops thought by making it
dependent on words for its expression.
We never think that what we think conceals us from
what we are.

VALÉRY, *Monsieur Teste*

Hotel Majestic
Beer bullets. I'm in Cannes, again with an awful hangover. Jacques
[Février] drove me here yesterday and we dined in Antibes *chez* Marie
Blanche de Polignac, after which I got very drunk and was brought
back to the hotel at 5 this morning by Tony Pawson's blond friend,
who proceeded to beat me up. Now I'm black and blue, alone with a
headache, rather gloomy, my hand shakes, throat feels trodden by a
Simenon *personnage* wearing spiked shoes on a murderous night *aux*
Buttes Chaumont. Am I rewarded by the staggering sumptuousness
of these wild scorching September sunsets hurled here by the mistral?
It borders on nature's bad taste. A low whistle! I'm in a state of sexual tension which evokes certain memories of the future. It's just
seven in the darkening evening and I can't write here any more but
must go out into the old quarters and search for odors to excite me. I
like to imagine myself admiring the fountain of Toulon's Place Puget
and the sudden sweated matty voice of love over a shoulder. But no,
I must seek, then avoid it, myself.

A purge. Not the city, it's *myself* I hate in Cannes: sneaking
around black corners, shaking and scared (shaking from yesterday's
beverage, scared for tomorrow's war), inebriation on the eve of perhaps a new war (I never learn anything either), as if I couldn't remember like yesterday the wars of sixteen and six years ago in the
world and in Korea.

Our new religions have an interplanetary inspiration. Mars: the
new romance. God of war, this star this month is next door to Earth.
The old say the young have no poetry. Heaven, once a reward, is
now a probability. But we are not all so *désabusés* as Françoise Sagan.

The boredom of completion. When I see the end of a work in progress,
when I feel a piano piece under control, I'm no longer interested.
This can be dangerous, but I stifle with polishing. My little opera
The Robbers is two-thirds composed, the remaining third must
be the difficult padding of coordination and that is what disturbs

my laziness: because it's no longer a question of *souffle*, of inspiration, of pulling the strings all together so that the well-trained marionette can dance his tango without tripping. But when we finally see our destination at the far end of a long bridge, we still have to take the last steps necessary to get there. And these steps are the most fragile: anyone can have ideas, though only *we* can spin them into solid shape.

Who has a *face* nowadays? My mother, *she* has a face.

Cannes has always formed the portrait of my dilemma by putting into flesh what I fear. What am I doing in France? Can't I say that for the rest of my life wherever I am?

Write an opera on Buzatti's *Siete Piani*, or on the suicide pact of *Hôtel du Nord*. Operas should have a nightwatchman (*Meistersinger*) at end and beginning as binding factor. And begin right out (and end) with the *big* aria. Opera for *one* person (on my own imagination).

Write a book (I've begun!). Reverse insanity. For instance, the ending of Paul Gadenne's *Invitation chez les Stirl* might be interpreted by showing that the hero was insane in thinking the others were, and the letter he receives was his own automatic writing composed while asleep. Like *Le Voyageur sur la terre*.

Perhaps I could put this in my book, my opera.

All this, however, is what the French call *bloc notes*, without development. I wish I could keep a more gossipy journal.

Bad cold, aching back, general fatigue. Wild dream of a razor slicing off the knees of children.

Poulenc's maid speaks of R. the chauffeur: *Vous savez que Monsieur trompe Monsieur.* He's a cross between trumpet and weasel and signs his letters Biquette.

Le morse, la fouine et la trompette
Se réunissent en une biquette.

Pisse-en-lit, pet-de-nonne,
Je suis terriblement putain
With a green heart *en etain*
Which will not know what it has done.

What am I choosing!
On this same road where hand
in hand I fell in love,
today I'm cruising.

Because it's Cannes' bullets of gin that riddle me whenever I hit here. Probably I've spent a total of three months in fifteen visits, arriving for a sensual purpose that's usually deflected by my own Venus Fly Trap oozing with booze (what a sentence!), and the trap made of a flesh that I'm told is as far from me as Jekyll from Hyde. And frequently I wonder — on awakening in strange rooms with my mouth like the bottom of a monkey cage — who pulled off those half-remembered crimes last night.

It's 6:30 of a hot Sunday evening. Spent the afternoon at the Plage Sportive with Jean Marais (must he always stay beautiful?), Claude Bénédick, and Philippe Erlanger. Philippe, who neither smokes nor drinks and retires early to work on his Diane de Poitiers, tells me (though I can't remember) that last night I persuaded him to make the rounds by the following logic: *Pourquoi passer la soirée avec une femme morte quand tu peux la passer avec un garçon vivant?*

Now I'm alone writing this on my tan naked lap. Soon I'll go out again. Then tomorrow, passing by Grasse, I'll motor back to the seriousness of Hyères with Marie Laure.

Again it's late afternoon and I'm preparing to leave Cannes where nothing much has happened (except those long pointless misunderstandings with sick Virginia F.) because it's no longer a town of lovers but of whores (mostly Algerians passing themselves off as Spanish), or else I'm just older and beyond the spontaneous honeymoon stage.

The sunlight's been massive with spasms of blue. This year the azure coast bores me and I want to work. Excuse me.

Hyères
For how many years (when practicing the piano) have I thought of
myself as subject to this possible torture: obligatory sight-reading
when the first false note means death! But who are the judges? Freud
was born a hundred years ago today.

Reading Zweig's weird life of Mary Baker Eddy reminds me of Father's
joke of the rabbi explaining about certain of his disciples turned
Quaker: "Some of my best Jews are Friends." Zweig says the man
with an *idée fixe* is always the strongest. Now it seems years since
I've been consciously passionate enough about *one* thing (except
myself, in general) to wish to move worlds through persuasion or acts
of conviction. I just don't care, and am amazed by those who do. This
is untrue. But why did Mark Twain get so excited about Mrs. Eddy
making all that money? Couldn't he foresee Hitler's remarks on the
Lie in *Mein Kampf?* or the fortune our analysts receive from listening?
(They too wish patients to *earn* the money they pay with.) As for
Zweig, he doesn't once mention Lourdes, or the Congo tribes who
dance impuniously on live coals.

Suddenly I can stop dead in my tracks alone (so seldom) on a summer country road at the odor of day's end recognized in a vanishing
flash as the same I knew at sixteen, sixteen years ago, at Northwestern or with my father in Taxco, where barking and fountains grew
more agitated than bats at sunset. Then I ask myself why, when I
first breathed autumn's new cold or looked for love in Chicago's
parks, couldn't I have savored the firstness of this love, that cold? It's
smells and streets and situations of the past one misses more than
people. Now at thirty-two I know what I could have done bodily,
but I've restrained myself (often in drink) as an artist more than
most, content to know I could have, or could still. Age is the begin-

ning of the memory of survived anguish. It is also the awareness of being young.

Responsibility of death. The personal guilt we feel at the dying of a loved one. Now the boy who knew summer fragrances was myself, but he's dead (though I didn't kill him). Youth's departure is a certain dying. We only say "if only" when we knew the person well. That boy who had all the opportunities he didn't take: I wonder what I've missed! I can still smell the clove, carnation, cinnamon, but through a new nose (could it be then a new smell? after all it's not the same clove, etc.). . . . A pungent past has nevertheless not kept me from almost finishing the first draft (libretto and music) of my opera *The Robbers*.

Last night's dream: Oscar Dominguez takes me for a ride in his new flying saucer. We glide low and slowly between tall city buildings whose windows show lamplit scenes of little girls in the white gowns of their first communion. The tail of the vehicle begins to sag and I am frightened. We land on a steep cliff in the forest. Marie Laure is there and takes the hand of Oscar (he's now my father) and they walk off, but I cannot follow because the rocks of the hill give way and I slide back (ugly Oscar was also the violist of the L. Quartet — they once played a work of mine — whose name I've forgotten but whom I thought beautiful in 1947).

In the water of our morning swim we can already smell the trouble across this small sea, of war in Algeria and Nasser in Egypt.

When I have written that I've never understood a person's "*caring* enough," I realize now it's because I've never *had* to.

Miracles happen only in novels. But for long years my life was like a book: I took the fabulous for granted and wishes were realities. Today is today, yet a moment five minutes ago is already memory mingling

with fifteen minutes, or weeks, years past, more and more confused.
What is present? Or which accomplishment can we enjoy in this
second, since it is immediately the past? Death is the straw that broke
the camel's back.

Happiness is a mediocre desire which, if granted, would result in
stupor. I don't want happiness, I want the life of curiosity which,
mostly, excludes joy.

The past is more important than the future — I know them both so I
can say. It is patience; the future is impulse. The past is also longer —
from where we stand today. I live there. Probably I write these words
because tomorrow scares me, but anyone can make a future without
even waiting, whereas the past (as we see it here) becomes a slow
and grand accumulation of uncountable millenniums.

Am I alive in what I do? Or standing on the outside looking in? (As
though what's inside made any difference.) Sleepwalking again. My
not caring as to the import of great or small events occurring before
or to me (including the happy hypnosis during creative or loving acts)
makes me more and more into a sleepwalker. Though I notice that
my not caring doesn't prevent me from writing here that I don't care.
        I said my life was like miracles in books — taken for granted. Can
I have already reached a time when I'm open-mouthed at the memory
of afternoons (not so long ago: and past is more than future) when my
beauty, conscience and constitution allowed me to drink, in Greenwich
Village or St. Germain des Prés, and pick up strangers, so as to have
that out of the way before evening when I could drink again with real
seriousness — and then write symphonies next morning? That's Auric's
first recollection of me: in 1949 perched on a midnight stool surrounded by the aged and eager, bright hair askew and wild eyes and
beer and cognac flowing fast. And that is how Auric must open his
biography of me.

The bright realization that *must* come just before death will be worth all the boredom of living.

Was it Landowska or Genet who, when someone murmured *"Un ange passe,"* added: *"Qu'on l'encule!"*? Such libidinousness I long to retrieve in a few days going back for a little tour of North Italy, if it still exists. Sadder than *Death in Venice* would be the death *of* Venice and let's try to visit there at least once more before we die. Unless we're already the vermin that for thousands of decades has been clustering with increasing thickness over an expired Earth. If last night I dreamed of being dead, how can I know that in "reality" the reverse is not true: that this morning my awakening is a dead man dreaming he is alive? Have I explained it in music with *Another Sleep?*

Inconsistency is the diarist's privilege. In three pages I may contradict what I feel in knowing too well my love affairs and prefer the harsh suffering of a scene through the keyhole. I keep making lists of what I must do when I get "there," but once I get there I forget, the lists being of past desires or acts accomplished. For instance, I tell myself that when I finally get back to Chicago (it's been ten years) I'll have to take a look in Tin Pan Alley on Wabash Avenue, hoping the siege of marihuana and admiration, benzedrine and beer that carried me through my seventeenth year will bless me again. Now I'm not even sure Tin Pan Alley still exists. How well I comprehend sketches of winged genitals on prison walls! All my daydreams are of former dissipation.

Rapallo, August 15 (Assumption of the Virgin)
We sit at the port cafés and watch faces and faces go by, many unchanged since Giotto. But this is essentially a vulgar town, and also noisy (noise of loud Lambrettas, klaxons, strident voices all night): Italy is the noisiest country in the world, and noise for its own sake is my worst torture, probably because I'm a musician and my ears . . . etc. . . . . Now, Bergamo with its quiet mountain square two days ago (today ago I ache from no sleep) was called by d'Annunzio the city of

silence; it's half true: Donizetti died there. I let myself be carried into convulsions by noise. Probably I reason too much to be happy. But physical delights are my shame and ordeal, and even sexuality seems a burden. Maybe these are just Rapallo thoughts because Mary assumes too much today.

Later. We've just been moved to another room on the floor below, having complained about the noise. Darkness into darkness, and I feel quite ill. P.'s at the beach while I lie down in an expensive chamber. We sit on the port watching faces and eat *fragole con panna*. Is it why we're born: to ask no questions? I'm a little disappointed. We're given only so many thrills to a lifetime and (though I try to disguise the fact even to myself) I feel that most of mine are used up. Music interests me less and less (though when I say it I don't wish to be misunderstood; I can still melt, still think that this new room on a quiet court is trembling with Italian guitars) and literature more and more.

My latest affectation is to leave my hair its natural color. It hasn't had a drop of bleach in ten months. Nora Auric (between throws in a game of *pétanque*) says it's the color of better Swiss chocolate with golden highlights. Delights of the pretentious natural: I feel "haloed." I am less sure of myself than most, but I admit what others hide. It is stronger to be loved than to love: it implies *having something*. To love is passive blackmail.

My first regular drinking was in Duluth, Minn., summer 1939, when Mother and I would have two bottles each of beer at the end of every afternoon. That was sixty-eight seasons ago and the summers float by our stationary bodies (ever more eroded) with the blandest unconcern. A week ago, I heard Denise Bourdet say to Jean Godebski (both ending their fifties): "*On dit que la vie est courte. Ne trouves-tu pas — nous qui avons le même age et approchons le crépuscule — qu'elle est plutôt longue? Pas trop longue, mais quand même très longue.*" . . . I don't ever want to say this! In spite of any blasé bitterness I might show today I want always to think life's great surprise is just around the corner. After all, I'm a good composer and many know it and this is a satisfaction which 99 percent of the people don't have. I take all I see and make it my own.

NEW YORK DIARY

We went to a revival of *Scarface* and, God, how *démodé* it was. But Paul Muni is heaven. Look at me in the darling little sailor hat we stole from Simone Berriau: I'm as cute and *démodé* as one of those frightful Oranese postcards of lipsticky boys offering candy roses to insipid damsels. But I liked me that way, so did Denise (as for hours we went screaming through opera scores while Simone and sixteen others played poker loudly in the same room).

This paragraph is a "delight of the pretentious natural." I have beat André Masson at a game of *boules* (he too knows what drinking is; his wife is troubled for my future, but he, dear man, is worried at the small dent he's made. *Ce n'est pas la peine* he says each day — then paints a picture).

But I'm back in Rapallo (I've never been here before). Now I'll leave this journal and, during this small vacation away from a piano, will write some storylets in the beautiful album engraved with four golden moles (the animal) which Nancy Mitford gave me.

Florence

We thought of staying in Viareggio because P. needs seawater and animation after a year of routine in Dorno, but not only couldn't we find rooms, the town turned out to be a vulgar steaming wound like a Texas outpost overrun with tourists. So we continued on to Florence last night and here we are in the Pensione Aprile. Far from the sea, even this paradise swarms like the tower of Babel and we've just bumped into Alvin Ross, who's coming here to dine with us. He tells sadly of the death last month of Alan Ross MacDougall; the swirl of those Drossie Restaurant days revives to overflowing here in the Piazza della Signoria as Harold Norse and others from then come by, all older, to interrupt the meditations in our peach ice cream. And floods of August visitors who cannot look at a great work except years later in their own snapshots (when a masterpiece rises up their eyes go down on the camera). Dougy is dead and nothing's static. When people ask me if my year of psychoanalysis did me "any good," I say: "How can I know really? Since I was a year older at the end." Was it analysis or the passing weeks that changed me (if I changed)? I'm a new person with different problems every day; analysis tries to remold the same old lump of clay as though time were static. Of course maybe time *is* (depending from where you look) but not on a level which concerns these doctors.

Any cloister anywhere with weeds, abandoned, makes a vision of peace. . . . My health feels *scabreuse* again. The usual hemorrhoid condition. I am never comfortable. . . . Deceits of meaning, tricks on the ear: as a kid in French class I used to hear in "Frère Jacques," the line *sonnez les matines* as: "Sonny laid Matina! . . . Does *dégoût = d'égout?* . . . This afternoon we're going for tea at Harold Acton's La Pietra.

Tea turned out to be cocktails (I had lemonade), H. Acton's Jamesian mother, and the most beautiful gardens in the world (with a gardener still more beautiful than his roses). The roses were haunted. The old mother said: "All *my* friends are dead!"; and Acton looks like Henry Cowell. When I asked him (just to be pleasant) if he knew my friend Douglas C., he answered: "In my house don't mention the name of that loathsome hypocritical snake" etc. . . . The same thing happened a few hours later as we were dining (in Harry's Bar) with John Pope Hennessey, of whom I asked Violet T.'s phone number: "Why do you want to call *that* stupid pretentious lady?!" Really, rich English art historians put one in a *situation fausse*. It's so hot you can't breathe. This afternoon we leave for Venice.

Venice — Pensione Paganelli
Why does Venice seem always to mean the death of someone? Why don't maniacs more frequently put rocks on tracks to cause train disasters (it's so easy) like the Hungarian lunatic who used to stand off in the woods to applaud the mass of twisted steel and broken bodies he'd just caused? The endless tunnels Italian railroads go through, as aggravating as a woman's purse! So I bought *Time* and read it from cover to cover as is my habit once a year (never oftener) and was struck in the eyes by the "Milestone" column announcing the end of John Latouche at thirty-eight. As one does in such cases, I let the train clatter on and closed my eyes to review a relation with Touche from the time we first met one dawn of 1944 at Valeska

Gert's on Bleecker Street, till our last meeting two or three months ago when he talked (in the French style) to me and Larry Josephs late into the night. During these twelve years he was the symbol of immoderate freshness in a country where assembly-line resemblance seems the rule. The attack on his heart was only appropriate (I hate moderation in any form), but the attack on our own provides a sad and damaging shock. *Où sont les nègres downtown?* . . . Poetically speaking, growing up is mediocrity. And this week more artist friends have died never having had time to realize they'd grown up: Professor Kinsey, Brecht, Jackson Pollock, Papini. Now Oscar tells us that Dominguin has returned to the bullring. How admirable. Becoming adult is acceptance of going no farther. Where is the use of saying I have all, money, love, fame, etc.? Rip it down and start over like a spider aiming higher.

Rushing with Jean Stein from the Piazza toward the Accademia bridge, we came to Mary McCarthy, whom I do not know. The thrill at witnessing the famous hairdo is that she's good and I'd dream of librettos from her if I weren't now making my own.

A month ago I'd written in the new notebook: " 'The Fall days known as *glorious* were over.' McCarthy's chapter-start could only be by a woman (such an attitude from, say, Thoreau, is unimaginable; even James would not have conceived it just this way), but a very special woman, for Millay might have banally declared: 'The glorious Fall days were over.' It's the word *known* that indicates the cold avoidance of romanticism, i.e. the Fall days are glorious to others but the reaction's only known (not felt) by us intellectuals who find beauty in rarer style rather than in Nature's dubious daily taste. No male writer, however effeminate, need prove his maleness, so may be as perfumed as you please. But women just can't win: their style's either so feminine only they could have made it, or so masculine only they could have made it. ('No one's going to call *me* a "woman author"!') Does McCarthy realize that her sentence, nevertheless, could be the opening of a sonnet?"

Dream. We were a slippery gang of boys, eleven, seven, naked as a sky slashing in a country lake. Our voices not yet changed squealed like girls' speeding down the slick tin toboggan flashing into water — the echo of our child-voice lashed the lake with a shudder of pleasure: we were clean American Protestant Youth. Now lying weary on the still naked bank we (being clean) began mutually to clean our ears. Those of us who didn't bite our nails could dig out with a little finger-tip nice globes of reddish wax; the others managed with toothpick and cotton. Picnic of hairless bodies glowing sleeker than pears on a hill. In cleaning one's own ear it is easy to gauge the recesses, the unbeat drum, the necessary depths. Somebody else's cave though makes as slippery a danger as our lake. Suddenly among us stood a sailor. No one had seen him appear, he was just there, a little sad and virile, soiled and unsmiling. How were we meant to act before the adult whose muscular neck burst tired from a cloth? It was known in a look that I must clean his ears and, standing on a stool beside him, I began. Here I am faint at the fragrance of a grown-up man whose violent biceps rich and thick could smash my veins. Odor of muscle. Sniffing the oil I can't comprehend I shove the cotton tooth-pick into a wax like cheese. I do not know how far to go, no one says Stop or even seems to see. With a thrust the drum is split and the sailor in slow motion falls like a jelly. The children all have disap-peared, and across the cadaver I perceive a dark tall woman who evidently is not disapproving though she doesn't smile.

I see myself as others see me, for I can quit my stationary body and walk around myself examining at ease this immobile boy sitting in the country church, and sitting on as others file out forever into the sun. But is it seeing myself: one part observing another? Any-way there's a child in black short pants there gritting his teeth or running his tongue about his lips craving, craving with twitched mouth but riveted to his seat. Three: like a double exposure I can see the same child rising from himself (leaving me the sitter nevertheless) and straining toward the open door through which he even cannot pass. Here it's white and clean; out on the church lawn is laughter. The boy sitting sees all, would like and would be welcome to partici-pate in the happy flashing through the door — a tongue sweating. Still, he remains.

Why does mediocrity have that nervous laugh? Those overheard beach conversations when someone says, "It's a hot day"—and then snickers. Or something equally banal which just isn't funny. Does this dumb unfelt giggle impose assurance onto insufficiency? Or is it a groping toward poetry (if you'll pardon both terms)? There should be a prison for the mediocre, for those who laugh too much, who overreact. But then of course there'd be so few people left.

A man who had tired of this same view of the rainbow longed for visions at a new angle. But when he gave his soul to the devil and stood looking from where we cannot see, he knew that on the rainbow's other side there was just more of the same color as though his mirrored self were observing a live body in reverse.

Kenneth Pitchford writes from Seattle that the *Black Mountain Review* considers me the worst American composer. Not just second-rate or bad, but the *worst*! Is being thus singled out as unique true glory?

An intelligent fool, I am also *une allumeuse* setting traps which catch only myself while other hunters vanish and leave me agape. "For once I'm telling the truth," he lied.

Hyères, September
And drums and beasts and fancy gowns. A week ago I got back from North Italy in a plane so small it was like riding a kettledrum into France. Returned to Hyères just as Denise and Jacques returned from Bayreuth full of *The Master Singers*. Jacques breaks the piano daily practicing Ravel's Concerto—the one for two hands I played at Northwestern in 1940.

Autumn seems now to have come with dark winds and cold incessant rain keeping us indoors in bare feet after a troubled summer of restraint. But maybe it is just this restraint I half-involuntarily self-impose which brings out the best in whatever work I may accomplish.

This of course is balanced by the artifice of my famous binges; I so seldom abandon myself to joy and fun (relaxed and natural) that I'm capable of realizing I've *forgotten* to get drunk, *forgotten* to make love with myself or go to the bathroom, as though it were forgetting to buy a loaf of raisin bread. But I prefer my intimacies by correspondence, am embarrassed (no: annoyed) by time-consuming actuality. One can be tongue-tied with exasperation at a thumb sliced by a rim of paper.

I am reading a history of Quakerism (Howard Brinton), though concentration is dubious when each morning the news of Nasser's Egypt appears even heavier. Actions seem arbitrary, pointless, and a coming war feels almost aimed against me personally. When I was a child I thought "growing up" would supply rational answers to the dangerous games of war which I could not yet understand. Now I am adult and the accepted contradictions of propaganda are just as baffling: overnight the Japanese (whom we were required to hate by caricature in the early '40s) became our brothers, the German changed from ghoul to angel, North Koreans were bad and South Koreans good (simple as the nursery rhyme), and Russians are dumb when they show themselves intelligent. I didn't, and do not, comprehend. "Thou shalt not kill," we were taught, so how, how do we reconcile that command with compulsory military training?

All this was complicated a few days ago by the sun producing an explosion stronger than a trillion atomic bombardments, giving that star this morning a silver instead of gold look. But of what consequence are children's questions?

Where today is that slip of paper mislaid for twenty years on which Jean Harlow wrote her autograph? Burned? Then are the ashes fertilizing graveyards? Jean's long dead and her celluloid's yellowing. My loves for music and movies were (still are) joined and confused as Siamese twins. Soon I wrote fan letters to John Alden Carpenter whose replies I treasured. Then suddenly (was it only yesterday?) Ravel died. Twelve years old! Twelve years are a great many when they're all you have. When I was twelve in 1936 that distance from

NEW YORK DIARY 247

my birthday seemed as far as it does from today because I had fewer comparisons. What the French called *le recul du temps* is only relative, because the stretch from my birth to my third birthday was so vast I couldn't even remember it. And night before last seems ages ago when you're only one day old. (Or one day dead.)

At fourteen I knew by heart the poems of Cummings. Could I arise today in Quaker meeting and discuss the pacifist use of his personal pronoun "i"? Or at least if we must capitalize it, let's do the same with You.

Tuesday I take the Mistral for Paris and a brand-new summer is gone gone gone. I've read fifty books, slightly traveled in strange towns, written stories and an opera (though not orchestrated), gleaned and forgot, feared a war, praised *Le Balcon*, learned Catalan and Provençal, and visited the ruins of Edith Wharton's nearby mansion barefoot with Nancy Mitford who doesn't like Americans. I awaken daily filled with morning sickness like a pregnant woman: it must be a holdover from Cannes, or the shock of Henri *le maître d'hôtel*'s statement on Charles de Noailles, or my heart touched by Dior's praises of Chicago, or embarrassment at the proud gardener's very crippled son who writes awful music and wants to join the Société des Auteurs. Now Yves Nat too has died. Maggy has finally renounced me and married Richard Fisher after sixteen years of whirlwind courtship. And Xenia (Shirley Gabis Rhoads) has a baby boy. But I go on forever. My Second Symphony, written last winter in New York, just had its premiere with sweet reviews in La Jolla. And the First Symphony (1949) will have its eighth performance this month in Oslo.

3:30 A.M. (*aux cabinets*). Went to bed sick and now am sicker with surprise. Sleep is a noisy ocean which I hope to cross from night to morning and arrive cured.

Next day: I must stay in bed, an olfactory kingdom. Lily and Marie Laure stuff me with laxatives, prunes, blue suppositories. Outside it's hot and bright. I'm feverish and forceless.

A journal gives a false perspective, for sometimes the entries grow congested as accordion pleats, while other times the spacing is wide enough for storms to enter and evaporate. For instance, the sixty or so pages of the present book cover more than a year while my first volumes were stuffed with weeks. But in flipping through the leaves we often disregard a date so that living seems a matter of daily crises.

Put down the book now, look up, imagine that what you've been reading has become real: that a burglar will crawl through the window, or that you will truly have to face a world battle unless you curl up into a shell of insanity which in any case means change.

PART 4

Autumn, 1956

Paris and New York

God knows it's little use;

God knows I have spent ages
peering like a stuffed owl
at these same blank pages
and, though I strained to listen,
the world lay wrapped with wool
far as the ends of distance.

And what do I hear today?
Little that sounds mine—

W. D. SNODGRASS

Returned to Paris night before last and immediately had my first *cuite* (with Elliott and Kenneth Anger, who met me at the train) getting *that* out of the way! Yesterday, the long sordid promenade of recuperation, and a movie (Renoir's *Eléna et les Hommes* — boring fun), great fatigue. Today routine begins. I'm writing naked in a sunny window. Now on the telephone I make a hundred dates (both G. B. Shaw and Freud are a hundred), particularly with Tom Keogh, whom Marie Laure's commissioning to do the sets and costumes for *The Robbers*, but also my dear Jean Leuvrais (he's in Julien Green's *l'Ombre* which I'll see Sunday), Gary Graffman, and Ninette of the Parc Montsouris.

A visit to Victor Hugo's house, now a museum in the Place des Vosges, where in the folly of his dotage he carved furniture — *with his teeth!*

Cocteau once said that Hugo was a madman who thought he was Hugo. Do I think I'm Ned Rorem? No longer.

Certain former winds passing with a cool touch of the almost old-fashioned can nevertheless intone in a manner unbearably sensual. For instance, Debussy's *Jeux*, or *Ces Plaisirs* of Colette, which I've just been reading. No word is out of place nor superfluous and the images spill overlapping and silver with her polished unrestraint.

She never drank, having that writers' curiosity for observation which only sobriety can provide. My drinking is an order perhaps, and part of a larger self-organized control; however, boredom (which only "intellectuals" can feel) and big cities and nervousness before others lead me daily, at cocktail hour from 6 to 8, through an anguished struggle to which I fall victim at least one time in seven (too often!) and awaken with the *bonne mine de la fièvre* that vanishes the second day and leaves me a ghost. That is when I walk the streets, too tired to consider anything but my body.

And that is when I learn the language of the spider nests (known also as confessionals and centipedes), so-called by myself because of the female thinker in the middle, legs apart, awaiting the gobble on which the whole organism is focused: *Occupe-toi de mon maximum,* or perhaps: *j'enfile mon fils,* followed by (in a different script): *tu n'en es pas le seul!* Let's place a silent camera well-aimed in these domains and leave it twenty-four hours; then (with adroit cutting, *bien sûr* — not just *anyone* appeals to us) show the results some Sunday at the Cineclub accompanied by Debussy's *Reflects dans l'eau.* And why, after all (with *Feuille de rose*), doesn't Dior use "blow" as a cologne title? *On ne rentre pas avec qui l'on sort* is a slogan of the upper classes who attend the theater with a white-minked lady and are sometimes written about in readable novels; but, to my conscious knowledge, it never happens to *me*, and this, *enfin*, is what my journal concerns.

Bright blue smoky clean brisk autumn temperature which every year has that fragrance of troubled delight, and means "going back to school" in a bonfire, while I see that little boy, as through the wrong end of a telescope, growing smaller and smaller in whirling leaves — but for once it's rather pleasant. In less than two weeks I'll be thirty-three — and next February 23, 1957, I'll be a third of a century old!

The remorse I still (it's physical rather than moral, I suppose) feel from my *cuite* of Thursday shows always that *au fond* I am really a middle-class American. The morose and agreeable vegetation from a hangover in the wombish bed a bit humid with the comforting smell of my own fingernails, perspiration and yesterday's breath — a false hunger from which I get up and go to the baths Rue Cambronne where I soothe a smashed knee. Only ivy-league babies make rubbing love.

Ernie is of a rare yet solid breed: the annoyingly delightful not-too-young expatriate sensitive lush living off an untalented intellect and a small but regular allowance from somewhere in Vermont. He is ubiquitous: you leave him dead drunk at the Flore, take a plane to Venice, rush to Harry's Bar, and somehow he's already there, dead drunk — and has seen all the movies. So you ask him how they are — there being a local rush on old Dietrich — Garbo — Davis films. "Why, they're having a George *Brent* festival!" . . . I mention all this as introduction to his disappearance. Because his passive ingratiating presence hasn't been about lately, and when you're not trying to work his bitchery is always welcome.

Well, this afternoon at the Montana, wretchedly hungover, I was sitting alone having a pick-me-up, dizzily dried-out and susceptible: even the ashtray looked menacing. In walks Heddy de Ré, plump in her jeans and still fresh after last night (How does she *do* it! By putting Privine in her eyes.) "Have you heard about Ernie?" she asks eagerly. "You know where he's been these last months? Killed!" And she has the nerve to tell me, in my condition, of his murder in San Francisco: two drunk sailors tied him face down on the bed, thrust his curling iron into the rectum, attached the electricity, and vanished into the night singing sea chanties. Next day he was found in black powder.

Women as fish on fire. Sapphire sharks. Flaming water. Ocean of glaciers, a shifting of blood on the globe, black bleeding glaciers, so nothing stays static.

For *The Robbers* I want an opening curtain (as beautiful as Picasso's for *Parade*), a scrim through which, after the shriek, the three men will be perceived half-holding-up the corpse which they let fall gradually as this inner curtain is slowly raised and the light grows for the first words. And at the end I thought that after the leader says "help!" and during the final bars, the door might open slowly, but the curtain drops before we can see who is about to enter.

The delicious simple one speaks: "I don't believe you really had that dream. You must have made it up." What is the difference?

Midnight, in bed with a cold. I'm daily more and more obsessed with sex. My fancies fly to any doorknob, drop of water, loaf of bread. Yet public baths and casual contacts (so very casual!) leave me toughened and unsatisfied, wanting the personal smash of lips and arms. But found, why do I let them go? Why do I stand them up? There in a line, swarthy, loving me, they were everything I pretended to desire. Why then did I ever let them all get away?

I have a conscious dread of my own intoxicated spells whose approach I feel as a kind of awful duty required, like epilepsy, by my demon half.

I wish my work weren't more important than my play.

These three paragraphs seem like uncontrolled conflicts. But if I'm as advanced as the baby who throws his all-day sucker out of his crib and then cries for it back, is it balanced by the restraint in my drinking knowledge? And I *do* wish I knew how to play really well, and not just how to work *fairly* well. These tedious eternal Journal Queries.

Last week at Jean-Pierre Marty's: birthday gift in the form of a thunderbolt. I am in love again for the first time! Exuberant need to giggle and screech. The bloated earth already seems too small for the sky which stabs drab Avenue Marceau with yellow rubies although for weeks the fall sun's been typically tight over Paris. Yet my childish heart claps as though spring had come bringing the urge to utter those same old corny lines—but to new ears. *Oh Claude, Claude, Claude, Claude, Claude, je t'aime encore plus que tu ne m'aimes!*

—*N'ébourriffez pas mes cheveux.*
—*Pourquoi pas? Tu as toute la vie pour te les repeigner.*

Time Out for the Dying, Pleasures for the Dying. Because for a person in any way condemned, living takes sharper meanings. His letter might read: "I cannot say I take 'time out' to write you; the very writing is a pleasure in this time-limit of which each second I protract into an immediate memory. For the remainder of my stay is so short that I allow no waste and am *aware*, joyously, of every hour. No sound or color, nothing of taste or touch goes by unnoticed. What a luxury!"

Claude woke me up to say Hungary's been invaded by Russia, they're massacring people right and left, all Europe's threatened.

This afternoon Maurice Gendron, just returned from Vienna, tells of that city filled with bulldozers arriving from Budapest covered with blood. I don't understand.

Halloween
Winter's awfully here with another war seeming well on its way like a searchlight wail of mammoths straining the sky. All around in Africa and Hungary is such positive and bleeding unrest. I'm scared. Is it any wonder I always say: sleep is no waste? More than ever in this week that I've been thirty-three I need nine dream hours from which to wake and learn again secrets from a spidery world (language of the spider nests). Everyone's glued to his radio, newspapers, words heard on a bus through chilling fog that now covers Paris.

Gieseking has died. The last issue of *Folder* printed three songs: one by John Latouche, one by Ben Weber, one of mine. Now Touche is dead. Which one will be the next? Who will come third? and how? When I was your age I understood everything, got the point, had all the answers; today at my age I understand nothing, don't get the point, have no answers.

Lightning changes, politics switch overnight, revolutions all about, and discontent, tension, fright, depression, sorrow, nerves, war scare. Yet out of my window the streets look just the same: leaves fall, the sun sets, children laugh as though nothing were up. Last night, dining uncomfortably, Rue Mazarine, with Elliott Stein, Henri, and Kenneth Anger, the strain of conversation terminated thus:
Henri: *Enfin, on verra bien.*
Me: *On verra mal.*
Elliott: *On verra pas!*

Nobody talks but of the stupid crumble, and my only hope, notes, this little book, so perishable. Of all nervous diseases, hysteria (as in Ionesco's theater) bores me the most.

Another afternoon with Alice Toklas. This woman still in the company of *that* woman whose power was such she even influenced her predecessors (as I'm influenced by the future). So many of us, and even dogs, have survived the rise and fall of Hitler. She loves politics but I hate them. Again the near-dying. Her explanation (not mine) of the American male's eternal youth is that, wanting to be like his neighbor, he's unable to change (whereas the Frenchman, for conversational exercise, on purpose takes a contrary viewpoint). As for American women she says merely: "Yes, *aren't* they though!" And also, "Quaker? it's the only thing to be!" How much farther does she have to go, and will we meet again? Correspondence is a pleasure of the deaf. Is it why, as a musician, I write so many letters?

Played my opera for Poulenc today and he says to call it *The Novice.* I will. Sauguet, *lui*, tells me my ideal opera subject now should be an American comedy based on the Marx Brothers' *A Night at the Opera.*

André Fraigneau and Sherban Sidéry, bored by my singing of *The Robbers*, swoon at Mattiwilda Dobbs' record of *Pippa's Song.* But the opera, I tell them, has just as gorgeous a vocal line. God, but I'm credulous, and never cease to be astonished at how everyone's out for himself: Marie Powers, Françoise Sagan, Ella Fitzgerald, these ladies (and each, except Marie, with a special poignant surprise of her own) have no time for the works of others. The tedium of arrival. I lose ambition. I drink as a robot wound up whose springs go wild from tension. It's regular. I'm *pince-sans-rire* (they tell me), passing spare moments these perilous days in making narcissistic collages which I mail unsolicited to certain friends and friends of friends.

In a week Claude and I go to the Netherlands. I've never been there for tulip time, but in November it's ideal honeymooning because of an unchallenging blandness, a sort of Germany *manqué*. The men all look like theological students and the women like gym teachers. Six years ago with Julius Katchen I remember those vast long surrealist snowy beaches covered not with winter swimmers but with ladies in muffs drinking foamy chocolate, and Russian wolfhounds in sleighs.

Amsterdam, Hotel Victoria
Hardly the moment to write in diaries: time's suspended. But last night in The Hague we went to hear Monteux conduct Irma Kolassi's *Schéhérazade*. Claude was moody throughout: time's too precious for us to spend concertizing. Afterward I went alone backstage, telling Claude to wait at the bridge. I returned to find him vomiting copiously into the canal. Why, why? Because in the morning, after a big Dutch cheesy breakfast, as he sat on the great Dutch toilet thumbing through this diary, he came across the cruel couplet of a few weeks ago (—*N'ébourriffez-pas mes cheveux . . .*) and felt it applied to him. Tomorrow France and reality again.

Who walks into the Montana last night but Ernie! I'm stupefied, and somehow embarrassed. "I thought you were — " He comes to my aid: "Dead? Yes, gossip *is* unclear at times, isn't it?"

Since birth I don't recall a month the world could enjoy the ease of peace. It's a generation enveloped by dangerous dispute. But with what necessary quickness we grow used to calamity! For instance, now we take in our toughened stride Hungarian news, and African, the worst is at our door, *tant pis,* when only twenty days ago we shook. But I work, go on. If I don't live on today's earth, when, on which one, *will* I?
    It is snow time without snow: a rather blurred desire for flakes through which gray sun rays come lying onto this page. It is also Monday. We were in Holland, Claude and I, a week ago four nights and days. Must happiness be paid for? The radio is spouting horrors about new concentration camps in Egypt, the kidnapping of Nagy, the shock of hate all over, the exodus into Austria, and crimes, while I dream on of the movies in Amsterdam and scarves and pastries, of the *zeebad* honeymoon in the Kurhaus Hotel at Scheveningen near The Hague, a wintry actionless dream of Dutch beaches, that coun-

try scraped clean of character offering the ideal anonymous décor for new lovers passing tens of hours in bed. Nail me to this wave. Must this fragile book too vanish? Can the dead fall in love with the yet-unborn? Let us be thankful we're of the same generation. Or look at poor old Joan Crawford in *Autumn Leaves*, the poor young murderess of *The Bad Seed:* these American age phenomena are passing simultaneously now on Champs-Élysées screens. Cinema in general pleases me so much more than theater. Like panic, it is the art of my time.

Last week when Dora Maar finished her final and best in a series of charcoal drawings for which I was the model, I gave the beautiful result to Claude to have photographed and framed. He forgot it in a taxicab! No frantic searching of the Bureau des Objets Trouvés has availed and I'm as sick from this loss as Gide from his burnt letters. Yet I'd rather have Claude than Dora's picture, and wonder how in five days I can leave a *garçon* who strongly looks after my weary gums in his midnight dental office *à la* Villette. But I will leave, and his drawer stuffed with my daily *pneumatiques* speaking of a good love time. Nothing is harder with these sentiments than to write convincingly what one does not feel: the disorder and lonely panic of a shopgirl's love letter is more moving than the greatest sonnet using the same words in different order. In speech anyone can lie well with a manner of eyes or tears. Writing has no sound (we only imagine it has the sound we imagine it has). My letters have no lies; it can be seen; he will know it. Nevertheless I will leave.

Speaking of eyes, a ragged lady accordionist yesterday in the Place de la République had a pair of false ones in dolly-staring glass all immobile in a scorched face. Why? Because this shock inspires no pity, and the blind have other means.

December 9, on board the Queen Mary
A week on water is about as far as you can go in boredom. Great creative plans projected for just these days of irresponsible bliss all fall to monotonous pieces which regroup themselves into a portrait of waiting, waiting for the meal gong or the next movie. At least this time I have a cabin alone and not with my usual four octogenarians

who fart and snore and leave the light on all night and crowd ill-tempered around the morning mirror in their dirty socks. So my cabin has grown into a world apart where I keep myself from the sunny Atlantic and write to Claude for hours on end, playing "the mysterious passenger" who talks to no one and refuses the intrigue of the evening Bingo game.

Always more, how I shun the ordinary. I want to be the luxury of lives, and have a lover be my long dessert. Is it why I've so often been divorced? I won't now believe that Claude's familiarity too will tarnish.

If you take the No. 75 bus to the end of the line you will go up a street in the 10th Arrondissement called *La rue de la grange aux Belles.* Here is where I choose to live with all it implies of love and slaughter. Oh, I am devoured by the greediest masochism and want it, want it four hours *à bouche pleine* before you pin to his dying the glad shaky moth. *N'est pas aimé qui veut.* Is a man who "possesses" another, twice a man? Or the contrary? It depends from where you look. If you're on the bottom, crushed, back toward the bed, don't forget your gaze is skyward, that the bottom is the bass, the very foundation on which a male's melody role is constructed.

From 1925 to 1950 American women have been Mae West and Martha Graham, Billie Holiday and Marilyn Monroe, Djuna Barnes and Maria Callas (who just makes the time limit). The first two are conquerors, the next are victims, the last seem troubadours for the others, and all grow immediately legendary.

Since tomorrow, Friday, at dawn, we are — twenty-four hours late — to arrive in New York (where Jean Stein has found me an apartment in the East 60's, of all places), I may as well put a few words here this evening since I probably won't be writing again for months.

The whole trip's been a bore: a sort of *huis clos* on the waves transporting; but a calm preparation to the ambitious frenzy waiting.

All the time's passed in moping for C. When in love I oblige everyone else to love my lover too, and hate them for it. People don't turn to look at me as much as they used to. Nothing is aliver than falling in love, but, when over, limper than a dead fish. The contrast is more than black to white. Is sleep a waste? Never.

Who has the right to camp? It's a matter of *seeing* yourself doing what you *know* you're doing—like having the right to say "Moonlight Sonata" . . . (the third convolution, etc.). Also Rae Robertson just died. I got in at the end. Because, with his wife Ethel Bartlett, he recorded my old Siennese *Sicilienne* about seven months ago.

Adieu little friends: Vera Korène, with your husky sapphic contralto and your guitar on a couch; good Heddy *de mon époque Heddy* never to be refound; Harold Acton, Roger Peyrefitte. Hello again: Greta Keller and Carlo Van Vechten. Some, but not all, of you are part of me. John Lehmann sent my stories back saying "they just aren't very good." I want newer smells and wider flowers, a life in the country with fresh eggs and work near to Claude, for whom I compose letters I'd hesitate to reproduce in a diary because they are too right and true and dirty and loving and unstyled and selfless and mean. I am a musician after all.

New York City, January, 1957

Why? I have everything, I have you. Why then? Yet hardly a day goes by when at bedtime—for reasons unknown to myself—I don't contemplate suicide. It's the kind of extravagant romanticism I should have shed ten years ago before my excess forces could tire of unnecessary thoughts. Now today is again in a worldly state of useless chaos surrounded by expensive mistakes, and tomorrow so quickly grows into yesterday that I feel a prisoner between two seasons: no place.

I've been back in New York a month and there's bright electric snow with a thousand friends. Where could I rather be without love? Americans penetrate the heavens but not the earth; they don't know how to copulate, but build skyscrapers. The rich here, as everywhere, seem to have that "misery priority" which makes them ignore a poet as though everyone didn't really love everybody for at least one ulterior motive. I am *mondain* but not very sociable (there *is* a difference).

Having crossed an ocean again, now, at thirty-three, I begin to situate myself. At that age, by standards here, one ought to have "arrived," and of course I have come where I've come, not yearning for the old times of discovery (Carl Ruggles' *Sun Treader*), but still not caring much. The concrete 12-toners think they are recovering primary sound, but they are only uncovering surface noise. Ansermet said the other day that music isn't concerned with *sound*, but with *notes*. Etcetera. Still I'm not interested. Oh, I phone and orchestrate, write letters and go out scrounging, don't drink much and lament over money, don't feel like composing but don't talk about it. Actually the miracle moment I'm waiting for (thank God we must always have this) is Claude's arrival in seventeen days. And now I already feel better.

When I am in love I must gobble and rip, demoralize and entangle, ensnare and devour, desecrate and be enveloped, snip and run off, suck and weave webs, be stroked and be penetrated, become idiotic, shrieking, followed, coy and mean, scared but destructive and ferociously passive. These are needs, with traps that help work. The moment has almost come. Let us orchestrate.

  Taking it out of your *braquette*, and feeling as the crazed lioness in the arena who, with a brief flashing claw, rips open a martyr's chest and sweeps forth a bleeding lung, a heart, steaming guts, and devours them. You've spoken of the ecstasy of torture which I fear so. Being in love and mutually, I place it above all art and reason, blush that you understand and condone my needs, and even offer to aid, excited. Adults keep children's sillinesses but not their wisdom. I'll make your triangle tingle, or see that noisy sleep which sings into the kingdom of a bed.

Could Rebecca West's *The Return of the Soldier* make an opera? Is there a letter scene? or colored streamers? or people in disguise?

  Mexico's poverty is Catholic dirt, and that is why it depresses us more than Morocco. There's nothing in the Bible when you really need it. Elliott Stein to the Mona Lisa: "Wipe that smile off your face."

American Negroes since the Puerto Rican emigrations have lifted themselves up a rung. A taxi driver, black as coal, will now say: "You can't move a foot without bumping into some Spic!"

Tomorrow Claude comes. Anemones fill the room.

   The French preoccupation with God and the devil now seems both farcical and humorless. If the devil exists, if he's as powerfully sly as Catholics believe, isn't it possible that their image of God is Satan in disguise? After all, the Church's history was more diabolically bloody than any other.

   Situation: the Protestant in a confessional.

Weak men are so often portrayed by strong women: Sebastian, Octavian, l'Aiglon. Why not Joan of Arc played by a man? And I like Félix Labisse's notion of Hamlet acted by the dwarf Piéral. Who decides? Couldn't Cleopatra be done convincingly by Tony Perkins, Blanche du Bois by Edwige Feuillère, or Macbeth by Marilyn?

Just as the emphases of musical generations alternate forever between contrapuntal and harmonic (meaning sacred and profane, and these in turn alternate between church and street, and sometimes it's street songs which are canonic while the mass grows lumpy), so society's sexuality is covert or overt, Victorian or Bacchanalian. Today music is contradictorily contrapuntal (holy) in contradistinction to our uninhibited sex. Though really there's no difference, really both are eternally equally present.

He came and stayed three weeks and left. *Quel gâchis!* The bottom has fallen out of my life.

Letter to Claude:
New York and Paris

Ce n'est pas dans Montaigne, mais dans moi, que je
trouve tout ce que j'y vois.

PASCAL

Cher Claude,
       You've come and gone.
       I write to you now in my journal because I no longer dare speak. You've imposed a straitjacket, though if I could get out I'd be more useless than before: suffering only seems unreasonable to those who cause it. Yet haven't I in these very pages exclaimed that hysteria (as in Ionesco's theater) is the nervous disease that most galls me?
       And I'm writing in French, because when I think of you it's in that language, and I think of you always. To hear it now hurts the heart. I've tried to rid my room of your traces, but go into the city only to find you there again in fifty souvenirs. I can't stop shaking. Every morning at the mailbox, knowing there'll be no letter, fearing what you might or might not write. All composers, like dentists, become, through the years and unbeknownst to themselves, sadistic, by dint of doing a job that obliges people to shy away. I reread new meanings into everything, from your first impotence of last October to your indifference of last month. Was it that in having, you no longer wanted? You said you'd loved me in secret four years before we met, for *my* indifference, but wasn't the result more conquest than affection? It's harder to investigate the shadows of one's own soul than of someone else's, but we've got to try, or we'll never know each other (though must people know each other?). You criticized me too much for me not to suspect a lack also *chez toi.* How many times a day you'd ask: "What are you thinking about?" You must contribute too a bit toward something you've half-invented. A touch of tenderness doesn't necessarily imply *ménage.* This apparent lack in you is what gives rise to a hazy suspicion about your very nature.
       Once you wrote that I belonged to you. That meant ownership, not affection. To be jilted unexpectedly is rough. It's crazy what two people will do bad to each other, as though the world weren't going to anyway. Flay each other without anesthetic. I've never been left before. Yes, my vanity's touched: why not? Happiness is made mostly of pride. But I'm sad by what will have been errors in judgment, in having selected someone unable to get over the shock of clay feet,

the vague conception of what virility is supposed to be in anyone. Thank God I'll have learned it soon enough to be able to find a taste for life again—though not soon enough to have had heart bruised or ideas altered about what used to be called human relations. Now you lower your eyes before the deluge you've provoked.

I tell you all that, but do I believe it? Inscribing mad solutions to enigmas too close to be seen. What's clear is that I love you and could die of it—maybe all the stronger in that I'm no longer anything to you. *Tu m'obsèdes.* The mind reels. Let me see you again once, twice, or seven, or twelve times, no more, please, normally, if only to be rid of your phantom. We were both too terribly impatient. My mistake's always been in committing suicide on the eve of a revelation. Certainly there's an antidote against the poison you write of; could it be friendship? Could it? Could I learn to loathe you?

You used to miss me when I went to the bathroom. I'd based my life on such myths of charm. Now it's sickening to watch weeks go by without the relief of change. A month ago I stopped living. One word from you (which will never come) and I'd start all over. It's not your fault if you no longer love: it's the one thing we don't regulate. Yes, yes, from the beginning you glimpsed unnatural lights, why did you lead me on, slaughtering? Why did you lose faith? Oh, such holding back when I make these reproaches: you too must have unanswered questions. The irony is that so recently I was saying: "Finally, happiness, I've got it!" No sooner said than gone.

After strong pain could one end up loving again the person who caused it? *Réchauffer la soupe?* Before seeing that person one plays the martyr through inventions of memory. Suffering of which we ourselves are the cause is harder to conceive; conversely, inflicted on us, it becomes all we know. What's pathetic is that the end of unbalanced love (what love's balanced?) is the sole situation we can't control. Less than war. When I think of all the hearts I've hurt! Yet now have nothing more to look forward to—anticipation being the very nourishment of life. Oh God Claude, Oh God Claude, *je m'étouffe!*

This journal's always reflected reactions without giving reasons for them. My bed, only, has become a white wound licking me into itself. Art, the genius of choice, obliges selfishness. Joy, the art of resignation, pale, unselfish. You never indulged my "faults" (though I promised to repair them) and falsely accused me of atrocious motives.

Thanks to David Diamond, who had introduced us a week ago at the Scala restaurant, last night I visited Mitropoulos. Arriving at his bachelor quarters in the Great Northern at nine, a bundle of scores humbly under my arm, instantly I sensed his goodness, his open warmth, his resignation. We sat down to tea and honey. Ten minutes later I could no longer control the formalities and broke into tears. Mitropoulos closed the music he was examining, and asked me (why?) if I were being blackmailed. I began the story which flowed out like time and the river. He said look, let's forget the music for tonight and I'll take you to supper at the Blue Ribbon. Two hours later he said, as we sat over our empty cups of kirsch, looking straight at me, at the state I was in: "How I envy you! How I'd love to crawl, on the floor, in the mud, at the feet of one I loved. If you're strong you can rise from it all reborn, a new man with solider values. But I'm too old now!" And we walked back to his hotel through the warm March wind as he told me stories of his youth. Those words, his more than gentle force and beauty, were like an icy balm for the moment at midnight. But all melted again this morning.

On the phone across the ocean you advised patience. Patience, my God! Obviously there's a difference between a little patience and the paranoid hell of waiting, waiting. I swear, that phone call will be my last abject action. No, it's dumb to swear such things. But I'll make a monstrous daily effort because I want your esteem as much as your love. As proof of goodwill, I've already stopped drinking. Almost. I'd say even it's . . . well . . . licked, and I'm a little scared, because not drinking is like not masturbating: explosion lurks. (Can explosions lurk?)

It's the first morning of spring and I wish I were dead. Got up at noon to see a sticky sky and one season leaking into the next as though the earth had stopped in its tracks, as though the hate and venera- tion which ooze into love were an eternal repetition of those tears which won't stop flowing, not to purify, but to insult the mud. Oh, I'll get over it! Meanwhile nights are sleepless or if I drop off it's to a recurrent dream in which you take me back, and I'm filled with joy, and wake up to the hard truth that everything's over and done, done, done, and the day's started hopelessly like yesterday, like last week and the week before. Sexual tension's been horrible: there may be pleasure with others, but they don't exist when I think of what I liked from you, and you in me, and I catch fire and can't put it out. Are any two people alike? Your New York humiliation was beyond control: far from your milieu you functioned only as my friend. In Holland we were in the same anonymous boat away from daily responsibility, but we'll never be again because we like our work. Don't we? When one person's on vacation and the other not, sparks fly unless there's a compromise. You were by definition in a *situation fausse*, and what could I do? Discretion now seems everything, now that it's too late. I'd even prefer that no one ever see us, that we meet in secret. I don't know what I'd prefer, I'm thinking out loud, where, where did I go wrong? To need you so much sometimes I could die, and dead could wait!

One afternoon you offered as sedative to poor B. (who still bemoans his unrequited loves) the idea that a thing desired, once had, loses its interest. That concept's more typical of Americans than of French: the latter are less quick on the trigger of novelty, stick closer to one circle of friends, dig deeper rather than adding layers. The spineless man (I say it rationally) is one who refuses the responsibility of a relationship, who accepts the dessert without the spinach (to coin a phrase); the most deranged drag-queen is more valid because more honest. Your attitude of "I don't want to help you nor you to help me" is nonetheless more French than American: during a century France has known how to accept defeat, eyes closed to her wounded pride. You'll say I'm far from the truth, that all these arguments have nothing to do with you, that you're quite simply sick of the whole bloody business. Jesus! Me too. Sick of self-pity, but I'm talking from limbo solely with the hope of deliverance. And so. I mean you meant to conquer first, love later. No, Claude, I don't mean that, forgive me. You've got to have strength to construct a working liaison without getting confined to middle-classness which tempts you, I think, as much as me—which frightens us. (That awful word "us.") You have preconceived ideas (who doesn't?) and loved (idealized) me before knowing me. My ideas are postconceived, I loved you for yourself. An *ideal* should not apply to an idea which changes constantly.

Yes, in New York I knew everyone, you knew only me and the need to get used to dozens of new circumstances in so short a time. I mustn't defend myself too much or we'll never be on equal terms. To be able to say: music must always come first! But I read and reread your letters, between the lines, a thousand new meanings. To have been so blind! and today clearly see those many moments you tried to escape at intermissions. How I understand your impatience to quit the bad dream of New York where you smothered like a kitten beneath a sow. Now it's I smothering, but don't need to kill myself. You've done it.

The lover renounced becomes a bore because he no longer functions as human. With the death rattle of any affair, they say, there's always one hurt more than the other. I love you, joylessly. Oh, still to write you dreams of vacations, tell you what I'm doing, ask the same of you, sexy letters! But this shock made life mechanical. I'd so love to have the word which would inspire me to go buy a ticket for Paris, a word saying: let's at least try to mend this mess enough for the remembrance to be nostalgic and not sordid, enough for us to see each other as friends and not monsters.

Should I admit what I did? Two years ago I met a baker named Marcel on the Avenue Friedland. He specialized in pastries to my delight, then to my disgust explained how filthy his work was: peach pies covered by smoke and saliva. Anyway, we got better acquainted in a hallway, and saw each other maybe twice later, and then I stood him up, and that was that. Well, two weeks ago in fierce loneliness I sent a letter, a love letter, to *Marcel le pâtissier* with no last name on the street without numbers where he once lived. The letter was returned: Address Unknown. . . . In *Other Voices, Other Rooms* there's a character in love who no longer knows where his lover is. He writes the world over, care of General Delivery — to Oran, Frisco, Shanghai, Frankfurt, in vain. He hadn't got it through his head that the incident was one-sided, that it was finished, that his friend no longer cared. Today I'm that character, nor do I know where you are, nor have I got it through my head that you don't care, but continue to hope against hope and pray on my knees for all soon to be better between us. The worst moment of a life is when you look in the mirror and say (knowing it to be true): "No one wants you anymore."

I think more about you in not having you than when I did, my cloud, my steed, javelin, sapphire. I've never loved anyone but you — the others were. . . . And I'll love you always. . . . We endow our poor lovers with godly traits, then destroy them for being mortal. Make

one repugnant gesture that would permit me to despise you, a release from this tender anguish which I stalk, stroking the brief past
with its thorns and afternoons at the Pont Mirabeau or the Buttes
Rouges, and the first evening when I sang you my songs, which you
pretended to like. Love with its soggy crust and petulance must come
before the music it's now hard to hear because I ruminate too much,
too much on you until there's melting in tears six times a day. Yet
what can save me, bring me through the universal intestines — music
staves which resemble bars — if not the sounds I'm supposed by God
to write?

How far France seems! Her smells and rivers and nights and
streets. To return for a long stay! It's not a question of money or desire,
but I won't go back until I can honestly admit it's not an attempt to
reactivate a union (dead on one side) whose recall will always be the
most precious of my life. Half of that life's already lived and I can
count on the fingers of one hand the number of months I've known
peace. Is it worth the trouble to languish over someone five thousand kilometers away who doesn't give a damn? Am I not another
person than the one who wrote that giant letter from the boat in
December a century ago? A century ago, when a green world seemed
to open where tonight there is only a void. You dropped a bomb without turning to see the explosion, leaving me to limp through the ruins.
But maybe he who's left is the more powerful — he held on. But the
cause, the causes! You tell me that the mass of contradictions are
contradictions only to me. Well, sure! And so?

I won't rest until they're swept up. Was it conflict of careers or a
jealous disdain of my hamminess that got on your nerves? But I don't
want your slavery — except to my body from time to time.

Why on earth write all this? Nothing but an insignificant wind,
a sentimental breath which sounded feebly in an immense Sahara,
heard by no one, by nothing except a heart that drips, loves, bleeds,
snaps, wants still to give itself away. You sought yourself in me but
found nothing.

Today's your birthday. Is it possible to dwell on you more intensely than I've done for the third of a year? Not a minute goes without wondering where you are and who you're seeing. It's classic — the
banal fixations of leftover people. But one mustn't, at such moments,

expect consideration from anywhere. Nor is there consolation in thinking back to our frequent conversations which remain my most valuable possessions. Your image persists like my love, my love and dreams
vomit up a thousand pardons from which I awake each day with a
face drenched in tears.

   You left America a month ago, and since then there's been not
one gentle word from you. If you could have foreseen the aftermath,
would you have tempered your revenge? No. By accusing me of irony
do you clear a bad conscience? But letting myself destroy myself is a
sin. Was I too weak or too strong for you? Could you tolerate such
fishwifely questions? You make me dance to a whip of icicles yet
won't listen to the musical shrieks I can no longer notate, notation
which no longer makes a difference, the difference in your future
loves will be lukewarm, but at least you'll never be the same again.

   The weather's still marvelous this morning, sweet and silvery,
bringing a terrific urge to make love, not done (or hardly, or badly)
since you went away. With whom? The bizarre mixture of my talent
and physique loathed or envied has never brought much more than
sadness. Everyone thinks my narcissism is unequaled. *C'est faux.*
I'm less sure than most, but openly admit what others hide like
gangrene, and it's a fact I've been more loved than I've loved. To love
is to put on the spot, whereas I take what I see and make it mine.

   Love, which fascinates a lover, is tedium to nonparticipants. In
the act of love I see myself . . . *comment dirai-je?* . . . like a child
simultaneously tortured and protected. It's not perilous. Nothing's
more perilous than reproaches: the act reproached is, five minutes
later, far in the past, and people alter. I'm capable of visible motions
of the heart; yours are invisible, therefore stronger. A blindman knows
how to garnish his dream. I've gone too far to pull out now. I never
forget a thing.

   Do you know what it's like to wait? Are you able to be unhappy?
(Love's just a habit, only a habit.) Does loneliness never seem sad to
you? (They tell me I was an eleven-month baby.) Can you ever be
jealous? (I've asked you seven and a half times.) You're in my life but
I am not in yours.

   I love you. Because you don't see as I see, you miss everything.
But if you saw as I saw I wouldn't love you, for I need only mysteries.

Music is a mystery. To *understand* music is to love it less. (I love it less and less.) Nor do you know much about me. It's better that way. I want to be *the* person for you, meaning the one thing beyond your work you need. Thus I could spend years away from you. Yet alone my successes would be empty: they need to be shared.

You simulate all emotions—which gives your face a stingy beauty. If my principal quality (quality, not virtue) is frankness, yours is concentration; you never lose a minute. Thus all your minutes are lost. Though maybe nothing's lost. Or gained. No love is happy. Art is happy, though life is drab. An only son is a child in a tower who, when he becomes a man, holds onto his independence as to his mother, that is, to something inexistent. . . . A free man? Free of what? For solitude does not exist either.

I show my foliage too much, heart, ruses, I shouldn't: I'm the mountain who goes to Mohammed. But no one changes anyone. Since no one has anyone, how do other people pass the time? Love is impossible. But when it becomes possible it's no longer love.

Thinking incessantly on you, you infiltrate yourself like a jiggly flame between myself and the music staves. At heart I'm a good person; one's never credulous enough—not the French. My passivity is active.

To a point of sickness you're obsessed with freedom. But, I repeat, freedom from what? Liberty's just an easier path, and you'll find out one day too late. Love's a specific renunciation you ignore—a race in a labyrinth, and only young love lasts. One must descend, descend to the chest's roots, a hard trip for two. You travel the world without really leaving home, without investigating foreign manners, elbowing true feelings which make you shiver though you cross an ocean to see the one you maintain you admire. But you remain a tourist too in love. You made me crawl, the easier to despise me, and despised me, the easier to rid yourself. So doing, you've grown to a giant, are all I cherish, block the way to new experiences, to work, and won't disappear. *Claude? Claude? Tu m'écoutes?* Our recent *rapports* now seem as strange as a detective novel made by an illogical poet, so I contradict myself (a privilege of fluid souls), though not in the essential of what was named Charity that day we rode over Washington bridge in Morris' car. If I praise myself it's self-defense. Because you've cut off my feet, then laugh when I limp—buried me deep and ask why I stifle.

All this is no more than the blurred angle of a dull story you'd prefer flinging to silence. Such arguments could no more interest you than your ability to see through my eyes as I see you—like divinity and ghoul. I observe my errors. Don't you prefer someone soft whom you can, without complication, dominate. Are you "my type"? What's a type? Did you take for vanity what was enthusiasm? Do you have my number? Speak my language? Dig my camp? No. You don't realize that, like you, I'm French, and though the French might wittily be true to speech, they never, like Americans, boringly speak the truth. To speak the truth is to speak one-dimensionally.

I'll keep these sinister gifts in my red red heart until they mix with my blood through the dissolution of sweet events in a future as uncertain as your feelings for me, but no, no, what's the use, I give up, give in, surrender. Thrown to the ground I'd paw it, but no longer have the strength to say *au revoir* or *adieu*, because I can't stand anything anymore. A venture on which two beings mutually embark—if it must end, must end mutually. But that's easier said than done. Let me now take my will in two hands and rebecome myself without you.

We see among the perfume bottles, plants, and bedclothes a murdered woman's head; but where now is the decapitator roaming, what thinking? Or we see sparrows lying in the snow, fallen from their sleepy perch when the young adventurer with a thoughtful sword slashed off their legs; but does he linger to observe the agony? Or through a keyhole we watch the doctor gaze into a twitching orifice recently disturbed by some rugged phallus whose carrier is today far off (while the victim stays in the office). Victim? . . . The tree was grounded by the hunter come and gone. The girl's heart's broken by the now-invisible lover because present is immediately past. Who, what, where are *these* hours, those all-powerful ones, walking, who couldn't remain to consider the sexy suffering? We see the kisser and kissed and though the kiss can't be undone the kisser will run off not knowing because not caring the same way. We see those tenacious kissed ones lament the ever-changing replacements, wishing like mad the present were fixed and that they in their turn could have ripped off the live bludgeons of their thoughtless divine assassins and kept them to own always in an attic of mementos. . . . You long to be free. And everything living wants to live (does an orchid try suicide?). Yet the new convict can't wait to see his future home. Yes, all long for freedom; necks of shepherds and sailors strain against T-shirts and wind.

You're indefatigable because you economize the efforts of your heart. You will say: "What a beautiful picture," but not that Mary Magdalene was *amoureuse*. You appreciate a *chef-d'oeuvre* more than the heart that made it. That strength is in lack of reaction; those who don't react are dead. People passionate about the arts are heartless: green oils and high strings come before "real life." Yes, you do react, but it's so rare that the glow in your eyes is that of an unknown planet which I catch and freeze and hide away in a private treasure chest. Perhaps only artists (so-called) can afford the luxury of love or madness which empties and fills them, a lonely luxury by definition. I only like what I can't understand. But all masterpieces are a bit boring; it's hard to catch on quickly to new rhythms. You are a bit boring.

I have been too much loved, which has led me too much to drink. Truth to tell I'm shy with people. And animals. I drink only for the hangover from which emerges the moment of truth, the *coup de grâce*, the involuntary detail, the All of engrossment underlining laughter of human hyena females on a subway. Trees, porpoises, don't bother to laugh — or are they always? It's not that they don't give a damn: they don't *not* give a damn. There's a demon in sobriety causing wars that could be avoided if the sober realized they're really lushes who don't know it. Unfortunately most people aren't drunk most of the time. It helps in meeting people, a hangover, by its power for concentration: concentration toward a spot on the ceiling which eventually moves (it always *did*, but we never waited long enough in bed). When our ears ring do we listen? When the larks flap before our very eyes who sees them? . . . Hangovers make you receptive, hot and hungry. A stupor of illness permits focus on a thumbtack generating light of its own, a luminous jewel and our sole gift to the unknown. There's a fourth dimension to the hungover world through which we perceive the fifth-dimensional one of sobriety. Another is sobriety's prisoner with only three auras.

How *do* people meet? There is a look of possible love exchanged by strangers (at a party, on a bus) who, through shyness or duty, never speak—and spend their remaining lives regretting the fact. Sometimes I feel the most faithful union is that sealed by a glance from a passing train to a boy in a pear tree.

Your systematic and somewhat inhuman way of seeing everything could end up exasperating me, making me so ill with jealousy I'd roll in your old sheets, bury my head in that drawer of soiled clothes like a bee in gray roses eager to retrieve your crotch and underarms, needing to possess your yesterday's sweat. An envy of shoes for being closer than I to you. An itch to crawl under the sleeping eyelids so that no dream could waft you where I was uninvited. Now I cannot think of any of those others without crying, and I think of them always. But this time I'm not going to cry, not this time, oh no!

You compartmentalize emotions as you do teeth. You are not made to comprehend artists whose "curious" lives have always been my daily bread. But you comprehend other things which will reunite us.

Today an envelope from Pavia encloses the despair of P. Which leaves me indifferent. See how the years pass? How now I am groaning for you who seem to need nothing? Or do you? Don't tell me. Insistence leads to lies. Don't judge America through me. Drinking again helps remembrance of things past, though will permit scant recall of what's now occurring.

Always injure the perfect in a flash, then choke on your own sweet time, the virtues of idleness. (Play hard to get in haste, repent in leisure.)

What on earth can you this afternoon be thinking there in France? A glance would show you my change of heart if you'd look here just once more. No, having failed to demolish you some of me died instead, the part that alone you could retain: your notion of me. Can we hurry to make new friends and be reborn in their ideas? But what of those I've never known who, from a distance have seen and loved me—and who have died? Did I feel, far off, that piece of myself which they possessed, also disappear?

What an ugly sunset!

Yes, we act according to our dreams. Let's act according to our real needs and not have wars. Dreamer, I built from something real (our meeting) something unreal (your devotion), but since public opinion sways you, you strangle me at the very moment I cry out: *je t'aime!* Happiness is the perfect balance between work and love. But balance is stupid, and happiness should be aimed at only secondarily. Can you dream, you? Have you recognized yourself in any of these words? You bastard?

This is a love letter — the last of so many. Never sent. After such vows, with a desire to rediscover myself and be alive again, I look continually over my shoulder nevertheless and understand nothing. So, seeking librettos, I read *Camino Real* and immediately see:
"The little comfort of love?"
"Is that comfort so little?"
"Caged birds accept each other but flight is what they long for."
For myself I dream of being tied down. But can any self-made oath truly help us change? How can we keep from being invaded by a sort of hazy sorrow at the futility of any try at loving? Finally love becomes only a frail scabrous game; and if, proudly, you show your tactics too much, you've lost before you've started. I don't know why you suggest that out of bed I may show no real interest in you, but you're not the first to say this. That bed, that wound, and I recall my long years of lying there inert and alive with a hangover late into the warm wet spring afternoons of darkness with curtains slightly blowing, and from the outside world came the far sound of separated children laughing or hammering, or the ting-a-ling of a Good Humor cart. You were then not yet in my life, and today I am no longer in yours though not two months ago you came over a toy sky to find me. And I'd even thought of suicide to clear up the mess. But one can see. Suicides which work, fail: having your cake and not eating, or something. So I try to be persuaded that music must always come first (will always be the one faithful love), and that creation is the genius of inevitable choice and elimination and seeing things as they are not. Thus seen, they become, since all exists. Literally I'm dressed in the skins of former love. And a lover is the worst rival since there is another ego to feed.

Nobody, even if he's fed up, has the right to do to another what you've done, in changing without warning, condemning without trial. Yet haven't I done it myself so many times? You claim you're the least complex of beings, and it's true for you who've never tried to know yourself as I have tried to know you. At such moments we find reproval or seek consolation in any breeze, and I came across a Whitman verse of unrequited love and set it last night to notes. . . . The headsman locks the dungeon and goes off forever calmly. Put an ocean between you and the prisoner and you've no more worries. Unless the prisoner escapes.

Love is mutual respect; I'd forgotten that you existed too. And love is always a game. And an invention. And what we learned in the last affair trains us what to unlearn in the next; yet when the next's over we realize that what we now refrained from was just what should have been done.

You helped me look into myself, so I love you, to know how to live this little life, and also, curiously because you didn't encourage me to love you. I love you for what you are not, with a constructive ego, the best way: one can't healthily love without faith in oneself; and though I haven't it anymore, it will come back.

April 1st. *Poisson d'avril!* Have lost nearly all the false narcissism which was nevertheless a refuge for one who lacked a base of self-assurance in spite of appearances. If I could replace it with faith! Only we know such good resolutions aren't easily realized. These kind warm days of early spring I perceive through a fog seeping down my throat that makes me cough up dumb old things to be thrown at new ears.

Today if by chance you were to come across these pages you'd hate me in not finding yourself because you don't see yourself as I do yet you think you see yourself entirely. Never again will I believe what were nevertheless the dearest words I've ever heard—those murmured by you in discovering yourself *grâce à moi*. Pray God that if ever I'm granted another love it'll be on another plan or plane, because one can't ripen by always following (as one evening we longly followed your Canal Saint Martin) experience after experience in exactly the same fashion, unassured and possessive epoch after epoch. But this future love: could it be again with you? Even though you've withdrawn and taken back all you gave? Even though you've cultivated my soul while deriding my family? Even though we're new children about to inscribe on the erased blackboard? Even if I've started again to drink like a fish in former routines? Even when you deny old desires while the whole autumn through you struggled with me against an innate laziness (even to the point of wanting to do a libretto), and regretted only that you weren't the first of my loves (although you *were* — and I can't stop harboring that)? Even if you knew that now I stuff myself with sleeping pills (which used to appall me) in order to forget you a few hours a day? And even if you knew that I roam around each night looking for just anyone to fill the wounded bed which seems all the same to stay empty, empty, empty, empty? As long as you're sure of me this will be impossible. But the neurotic me (*le moi nevrosé*) of whom you once were sure, he exists no more. How I loathe you.

How I love you. Face growing gaunt and lips tight. Handsome does as handsome is. This is brought home so strongly now when entering a bar, and no head turns. Does a tiger consider the antelope's pain? or an Iroquois administer anesthetic before scalping? Suddenly today I am standing apart to see the young among themselves, their arms frailer than spider strands and voices like spider breath failing. But what unrehearsed voices! what strong, strong arms! Old songs, their skin, the tears, the expressionless, the isolating, the young among themselves. I used to think that being conscious of your own youth was a first sign of age. Nevertheless, the young, with all their teasy ways, *do* have smoother skin and see their whole lives before them. Or minutes. But minutes are life, and what can I look forward to but years?

Yes, now I can see the years and how the past drags like a peacock's tail ever longer which yet erects a luminous fan blowing and hiding and sweeping the traces and helping what might come. How exclusive they get! — or rather, they've no need of exclusion. (Where now are all those who once said they loved me?) I can stand off to see — how clearly? For to children together age grows invisible, no outside exists. Through mists the world interprets, forcing wars upon them with bad senility ruling. Yet to whom the fault? Age, or rather decrepitude, is boredom of body; it's not that we're no longer able, just that we're sick and tired of putting the same old carcass to the same old uses. But while the seasons unquestionably repeat themselves we go to pot. . . . Enough is too much. Still, a little too much is just enough for me. I yen for you whose musk inebriates across the ocean. Who can add more than bromides to the universal plot? Children enamored are self-sufficient, blind to repetition of fault after fault. Age, the world, plots (having no more to do); and what can it comprehend—except through remembrance—of young love occurring far from time? Far from space, love young, love young, for whom even force of wind or smell of sweat is new, all new, learning what I've forgotten, remaining alive when I'm dead, who (being born each minute) breathe more and more the oxygen I've less and less of.

For me there are no more first times. But at least the Lovelies of our cinema have more in common with me than with Poppea—or even Lillian Russell—for the simple reason that we're all living now. And whether or not the Lovelies like it, they and I will forever breathe parallel lives. That's one consolation. Except for me, can the naughty old world pretend to give a damn (since it does give terrible damns), spinning, trapping, recoiling, conspiring, leading them to misfire? How *not* be consoled in knowing they'll finally die! Dear one, everything dies, even our children, even the sun.

Today I received this letter:

Dear Mr. Rorem,
    Your frankness, and urge for outburst and exhibit of your distress is exactly the most important element a creator, a composer must have besides his knowledge. That is why your music spoke to my feelings and that is why I programmed it for the evening of 12 October 57. That is for your information, and as a kind of antidote against your actual poisoned condition. May thus, the power of a spiritual sperma annihilate the power of another wasted one!!
    With many friendly feelings,
                                                    Dimitri Mitropoulos

Do you recall, in that Amsterdam hotel, the plump Negro girl whose window gave onto our courtyard, and on whom we spied at midnight as she, naked, fingered a silent keyboard with two dictionaries on her head? . . . But where is a homeland when you've stayed

away as long as I? America always seems home while away and a
return is as inviting as the renewal of an old love affair. But being
here, I haven't yet really *seen* New York, not knowing where I am
now, nor how to take hold, nor the way to truly love myself, which
would help me learn to love you. These many French pages indicate
this, for I criticize you at being incapable of an "errand into the maze"
and speak of the wounded bed as though it were a title. But have we
a right to accuse others of failing at things we ourselves don't dare?
Today is gray and hot with a lacy rain, and we're well into April.

How little nations understand each other, or try. That's said from
the impotent placement of a poet who's spent a good part of his life
liking an earth he's not understood. In Paris, an uprooted American,
he was held secure by the balance imposed on a false shelter by two
powers like winds battling. And learned never to expect anything
from anyone except himself. Now he feels the start of a wavering.
Which way? When, if ever, we see each other again, we'll be the same
actors but in a new play.

After midnight. Weather's turned cold. Back from the movies,
the movies where you always liked most to look at me — in profile with
glasses. How I adored being alone with you! Never take a Frenchman
literally: promises are no more than exercises in style. It's not for
you I say it: you with a chest frozen before the prospects of a marriage
which would have comprised so many readjustments. So you returned
to a rich solitude. Where now are you going? who frequenting? what
indeed was your former way? . . . Was I perhaps less capable than
you of holding the reins of that heart-shaped horse, but don't realize
it since you in detesting me make me want you all the more? From
the start we'd both based the whole thing wrong: you on vanquished
fantasy, me on unmysterious possession, whereupon I lowered myself into a disguise as an owl showing shallowest sides (saving the
good ones for work). Rejection without advice.

To live is to make souvenirs, both in romance-memories and those
left through solitary production. To love is to desire to live *with*, and
is more than only life. Without it there is no reason, though reasons
for it have no definition. Sterile today and tomorrow I'm making no
memories. Have I an unrequited love for myself? "You're beautiful."

"So are you." "Well shall we come together and make something ugly? Thereby producing from two negatives a positive."

There can be he who kills himself at the death of a loved one *not* so as to retrieve the lover in heaven, but so the two can be in the same position in relation to the world.

Later is too late.

To say: I love you. Look. A perfectly lovely sentiment. Those words speak louder than actions though I don't know it yet, for knowing would mean I'm no longer young. Of course thoughts sound louder than words even if, alas, we only grow old above the waist. To think: just two days ago I was always the youngest at parties.

Well, that's how love is—don't we agree? Clenched heart, a parade of good-byes, then the long good-bye, a long postscript, an expedition of waiting. I remember the muse of love growing larger as she walked away with no cure for our sentiment trailing like a sick rat on a leash. But the impossibility makes love love, whose only clinching vow (we all agree) is dying. The desire fulfilled to be indispensable turns out duller than the disciplines of art. Oh, that dumb need to share. . . . Here lie I, caressing my thigh, and calmly file and clip and trim and smooth the ends of my chewed hands, lying demurely with lowered eyes in the midst of our vertiginous galaxy, for comfort offering order to the sky that doesn't know that it doesn't know. What goes wrong with chaos that we must classify? Must invent also a trap for the heart (I, for one, always fall in), hoping permanence squashes solitude. *Such* a habit! Yet try to retrieve it and find that now old lovers have new lives too (or has anyone anyone but himself?): that mysterious surprise makes us love them all the more. Absence, it's agreed, stimulates fancy. Wait, wait, and wait—kill, kill, and kill. Oh, I love you. . . . But when the door's finally knocked, *how* to react! Open-armed?

Depuis que vous avez quitté New York . . . since you left New York you've not unhappily left me but settled like lead even when I come home late on purpose from hollow exploits, torso gnarled as a cauliflower and nape bruised by strangers' teeth. You, though, smashed the heart into gelatin unable to harden toward new adventures as I stagger blinded among grimaces. The *cafard* is insistent,

ever present, like a sentimental poison numbing. I feel I've no longer
any power over anyone. Your letters which envied the joy I may have
known previous to knowing you, which promised relief, now burn
these fingers which begin to find a joy owed to nothing but self-
inquest. I'm destined to live with myself so must get used to it. Later's
too late, and you were too strong. Happiness may exist only in sharing
and lovers have a marvelous solitude à deux. But it's also a selfishness
à deux. How boring are loving couples to their friends! bereft of
elegance or dignity! Whenever a friend gets married we lose him.
How stupid the happy lover! and how stupid the rejected one! Fickle
as fairies who break each other's hearts more easily than peasants
twist geese necks. . . . You must never learn how indispensable,
irreplaceable you've become, how I seek you in nightmares, and by
day pitifully in the features of others, in wet places, bars somber and
stuffed, or rainy streets or public baths, bottles of gin, or slimy mouths
offered risibly. You resent what I've been able to keep of you in me,
the you of yesterday who is no more and whom you've forgotten.

The sad thing is that we were both so weak, so dumbly weak
after such wasted investments. Anyone's capable of 90 percent more
than he does, but only inertia keeps us going. This evening I'm so
depressed in remembering all the failures of my demi-life, in knowing suicide solves nothing since we won't hear the aftermaths. With
all my heart I wanted this to work. It's the disappointment of a life.

Oh those I've loved and never seen who've inhabited my body,
shouted through my lips, or sometimes cried, all those. And our styl-
ish books on love as a sharing bit: they presuppose mutuality so never
propose solutions to the unrequited. If I wrote songs the choicest verses
would be those weeping down from latrine walls.

For days you don't leave my mind. That smile hurts, the smile
pains for weeks, a star pressed on the brains. I carry it everywhere
like a briefcase from city to city. You can board a plane, you know, in
Stockholm with a hangover, and land a few hours later in Casablanca
—with the same hangover. Or the same banged-up heart or slap-
happy smile—what's the difference! I've done it. But hurt does die.
Things do, you know. Or do you? A force of love builds prisons: in
memory of a nightmare. Or maybe the nightmare is just its being
over.

Love is a fantasy and no one's fantastic anymore. Shall I invent a fantasy for you? Listen. Since Youth is Body, that's what initially attracts. One step beyond creates a really physical romance. If the outside delights us, how much more gorgeous is the interior's clockwork of artery and purple nerves, its maze of muscle and yellow organs! Let's take a doctor as hero, since he (not a dentist or Jack the Ripper) normally explores the corridors around our bones; he, and only he, sees past the silly beauty of a face, can slash open his mistress' belly confronting all color, construction, and patient evolutionary threads. When alone he longs for the sight of his lady's lungs, the touch of her real heart, her cold odor of blood through a honeycomb-skeleton. He hears her veins and would lick her spine. . . . It began when an unprepossessing woman entered the office of my surgeon, who ignored her face and chest and tiresome complaints, but the instant of incision smashed heaven's doors: never has he known such a velvet liver whose cancer flows golden. With unbounded affection he weeps into her wound. . . . But she heals and goes off. He grows lonely, sentimental for that distant orderly inner room. Can his nostalgia prepare a trap into which she'll tumble and break her stitches, bringing her back exposed to his arms which will caress again the long pink warmth of her intestines?

Mitropoulos is right: remarkable health can result from abject dejection, and from rejection wherein one is nothing, nothing. Yet what's the use of being healthy in a sick society? I miss you as one of my own members which however I myself tore off in trying to understand, like children rip open their dolls. To penetrate and receive in giving and taking through these two acts (which are really one) is to love. Each note of music is written for you, whether you will or no, so strong is the need to give, to give; and I need you because I love you, though I don't love you because I need you. I hope. Why not marry? You can't live amongst the willows and wasps as though they were your neighbors: man, dreadful as he is, is all we've got. Don't keep yourself from it.

I really liked being in your company. With P. in the old days I always felt: "Go away, so that I can see us in relief." With you it's: "Come back, because I can no longer stand to think." But you're far off, and will stay far off. That first evening, you said: "The sad thing is that Americans must eventually go away." Later we concocted a love without identity.

During the past two months and for perhaps two months more I'll have gone from shock to paralysis to astonishment to rage to despair to *l'anéantissement* to uncertainty to resignation to selfishness to indifference to remembrance to forgetfulness. I don't wish you to be my life, but to be part of it, to help me again to hear the sounds of nature. These ears have grown numb in trying to become your equal. When we first met the days were growing shorter, colder. Now they're lengthening into springtime and it's possible that soon I'll return to Paris. To be acquainted with all the seasons in you so as to better analyze the source of this failure, to better feel Ives' music named "The Unanswered Question!"

For weeks in the middle of the night I've burdened the saintly Morris Golde, wept and pleaded for advice as for a drug. With endless patience he calms, suggests, tolerates, comprehends, lends his time as I crumble, and aids genuinely. Next day another shot is required. But I'll be forever grateful.

We failed thanks to the twentieth century. Because one flies over seas. Because one's in a hurry. Because so many of us see love as being loved (and we're right) that few are left over. Because of the difference between falling and staying in love, because we confuse relief-from-loneliness with infatuation. Loneliness is hard work, infatuation is laziness. Not just anyone can be unhappy — *n'est pas solitaire qui veut.* Laziness takes us away from the *practice* of love, like practice of music or dentistry. We're certain of only the past and death. *Et encore!* We're ashamed of love though it's the cheapest remedy for solitude. Or is love evil because it destroys the necessity of aloneness? Art's a substitute for love, but paradoxically on a higher plane.

Having read and drunk everything, what's left but you? Still, we threw ourselves into a disintegrated fusion where, once bars were down, we were quickly without the miracle of astonishment at those discoveries which must constantly renew themselves, that two become one yet stay two. Is love the act of giving without sacrificing? Even in receiving one gives in sex they say. Bromides of responsibility, respect, love is the offspring of liberty, the do-it-yourself banalities of Erich Fromm, who has recipes for every kind of love except the unrequited. (My self-love is unrequited!) But respect is hard without knowledge, and we're unknowable even to ourselves. I had desired, Claude, that you relinquish your secret in making you suffer rather than in liking you.

It's very late at night and I'm back from the Tourel recital with Jean Stein. Over the weekend I was drunk to obliteration, which somehow cleansed me nevertheless, awakening early in the head-ache haze to look closely and in a single dimension at my blanket of red and orange which became *childhood colors seen again for the first time.* Only a hangover can reproduce such a focus.

Have always felt a little guilty at liking what pleases me. From that comes excitation for music, pastries, and for certain acts of love. And from that comes the sadistic fear, alcoholic.

The courage of upset starts to evaporate thank God and I don't much want happiness but vital activity. A dentist plays God by fabricating a true part of a human body which his customers will carry around until death and long after. A composer can't say as much. Not to be able to love doesn't necessarily imply not to be able to love Ned Rorem—though you'd never believe it after all this. Nevertheless, disenchanted, you couldn't prepare me for the downfall. In *The Robbers* I have the Novice say: "There is a difference between the planning and the act." Can false love (oh my) be so fast substituted for true, as you maintain, without infection having germinated from the start? We never calmly asked where are we going? have we tried to keep first impressions which are finally all that count?

Failed thanks to the century. . . . The French fright of being caught by feelings. Everything's now more hurried than basics, we've no longer time for anything. Americans are cured through excess, the French through ridicule. Modern life, alas, is no longer adapted to the Tragic. To perfumed wounds. Ridicule? An American's ridicule would be to go back to Paris and find you once again involved with a phantom. *Mais il faut être capable de tout.*

Am I going mad? Unfortunately not. Insanity means being unaware of insanity.

Drinking too much again without question. Between two binges, float foggily to the surface and learn that finally I've been granted a Guggenheim. I'm gladder for my family than for me. But it will be a living for another year or two, and that, plus the inclusion of my works on programs of both Ormandy and Mitropoulos for next season, stabilizes somewhat these shuddering months. Now what do, where go this summer? Stay in America? That would surely be wisest. Until you've ripened and met yourself I cannot meet you. Or is it my business to love — the leisure to love — yours, to fix teeth? Maybe you're too young for me. But to deny me tenderness just because I request it seems perverse. . . . So much indecision these last two months! So many new loves signifying less than cricket tunes in other summers! So much clairvoyance when I thumb through this very diary of ten years ago!

Patience is a virtue of petty souls. Credulous as a child, I maintain trust despite contrary proofs of this fickle menacing world. The trust is painful and silly and valuable, I wish not to be cured. *Par cette foi je veux vivre et mourir* — sang Villon. And without it, how write music which no one will hear as I heard it?

Well, now I'll retire with a kiss on your forehead. (Don't recoil like that! Stop fearing what isn't!) *Ciào!*

It's not the unapproachable noncaring you that I like but the other so kind from yesterday gnawing my souvenirs like a fragrant cancer. If I could only retrieve that yesterday through you of tomorrow — for meanwhile my soul lacks entrances for creeping beauties, strangers all. Naturally it's stupid to go to America and expect the Netherlands. What you French call liberty is really a type of discretion, which doesn't keep you from making mincemeat of foreigners' frankness. Our affair (problem) was never resolved (ended) in a fair (intelligent) fashion, which is why I so want to see (disdain) you again, and may buy a ticket to France (the past). Being unsure of yourself you broke off unfinished business. And yes, happiness is paid for. You knew it, paid. While I've been accusing myself too much, to your advantage, am now but a rag with eyes watching the gas stove. No longer accuse anyone. Your cowardice gives me force.

Happiness paid for? Yes, if you've not the nerve to sustain it free; if you can't resist rendering ugly the most touching notions; if

you search for it instead of a rebirth through it. Happiness in itself is
ineffectual, a fragment unaware of its cocoon. Though of course there's
the passivity of reflection that we of the west ignore.

You'll never be at ease in love for the simple reason that you
seek an ideal. Now your ideal, being unique, by definition can't be
found in another. All dies and passes: plans, youth, genius, love, com-
bats, worries, works, and simple hearts. All passes and dies: young
people with gorgeous genitals in decay, day and night and life and
death die. A ship can sink at daybreak. What we've waited for all
our life can come and go away without our recognition. Deceptions,
disappointments disappear and die as well. . . . And my ultimate reaction is of great disappointment. Then, too, I'm a little scared of
you. You, you, you! *Oh, toi!!* Otototototototototoi!!!

Easter Sunday. Awful hangover. Awful cold. Awful aches and
pains from yesterday's excesses on 28th Street, awful heat. Finally
will be the approach of an end to something when you no longer
need worry about where your next screw is coming from. "And why?
Have I been too much loved," I wrote in June of '52. "I think I have
been too much loved, and a little success is the same as a lot."

One reason the collapse of a romance is boring to outsiders (not
to mention participants) is that it contradicts both natural structure
and the structure of art, a postcoital paralysis that disintegrates rather
than builds, and goes on too long. The end of love is like the *Boléro*
played backward.

He's too "sure" of himself to progress, ego too solid for ameliora-
tion. But egotism's fine and positive when it doesn't harm others —
sometimes even when it does. Now however he tells himself: "I no
longer love. I'll write a letter, and that will fix everything." Fix everything! Obsessed with detail, he sees nothing whole. What made him
think out of bed no one took him seriously? Fix everything! The letter's sewn total disorder. We can only see things as we see them.
Your red is my green. The redder it seems for you the redder it stays,
a red decided since your first infant red (or in any case the red you
think you see), and one can't change reds in midstream. My green
stays, alas, my green! Certain puzzles nevertheless suddenly solve
themselves: the answer smacked us so hard we couldn't feel it.
They showed me a million other greens I'd never suspected, and

several were even stained with red. And you—do you see them?

Rejected—*plaqué*—atrocious word. Admittedly of course I rationalize, ball you out, sing your praises while looking, looking for an urgent alley of explication, while the plain truth is that I miss you insanely. Tomorrow therefore, and wrongly, I'll buy a ticket to Paris, where I'll pretend to be indifferent. You see? . . . I'm less deceived by your attitudes about love than by your ignorance of friendship, your blind good conscience, by the risks you run without running risks. For instance, our last morning in Holland you said: "Well, tonight we go back. The pain if you said what a nice outing, and now *adieu!*" Tables turn. You speak in formulas as you act. I'd not understood, that night in Pigalle, when you said a *voyage à deux* would be determining, for usually others tired of you in a fortnight; I'd not understood that "others" meant yourself. Not understood that, like 90 percent, you existed through habit by surrounding with halos all passing excitements. But to have humiliated me! I've thought too much about you lately to have anything left to say when next we're face to face.

Why did you come to America if you knew from the start you hated me? A demolishing Columbus needs funds. It's curious, even amusing, how two beings tonight are intimate as twin embryos and tomorrow as distant icebergs. You were the first to say *je t'aime* and the first *à rompre*. Show your photo to another person and risk losing a bit of yourself; show a whole scrapbook and you'll lose the other person as well. Happily life starts (or starts up again) when love starts up again (or starts), and it's unimportant (*et tant mieux*) that these actions reflect themselves infinitely. I've said I love you to I don't know how many, each time was the first, and each sincere. For the "always" of lovers is a Time set apart and out of daily usage. One has time for everything if one wants: being busy's a pallid excuse. You'll see when you grow up. When I grow up I'll have lost curiosity. Anger begins to replace languor, it's health, are you glad or not? There remains simply the question of faith.

In a dream last night an infant, dark and adorable, has his tongue ripped out without warning by bandits. I care for him, curing, cajoling, and his trust returns. Now Gilles de Rays fondled them *before* the torture, so if one succeeded in surviving, his faith wouldn't necessarily return at the same time. It's up to you to see the relationship. . . . If you knew how I still vainly wait for your impossible note, indirect news, even a phone call. For two months and twelve days you've been gone, not even disliking me, and you're still here squelching each minute. *Je t'aime.*

In Bernard Rogers' opera, Delilah blinds Sampson with white-hot pokers, then asks: And how do things look now? In *The Big Sleep* Humphrey Bogart says: They knock your teeth out, then accuse you of stammering! How's your quiet conscience? All around I see the same drastic mistakes re-procreating themselves as if adults never had time to learn from their children. In just two weeks I take a plane for Orly despite awaiting perils. I'm afraid of nothing. But rumors of war thrill me less than the thought of seeing you. (We'll know the answer in three minutes.) You dissimulate your game so well! Not a game? Yes it is: silence is already a game. I lied from the start. The result sickened and cured me. We've never been friends. Just lovers a little, never friends.

Quite sick and full of codeine. The smell of your sleep awakened me. Hysteria's turned to disgust. Kissing is a waste of time. My strength is stronger than myself. I've a terror of being forgotten, from which comes the strength, stronger than me, preventing fear of being forgotten, etc. The Nordic says love me or I'll kill myself. The Latin says love me or I'll kill you. . . . It was not the palpable You I loved but a shadow's shadow I walked beside as with a cadaver on those *boulevards de l'extérieur.* Sweet memories will always be soiled by your action. Loving afternoons on the banks of the Marne before we met are preferable now. And you name me cloying because I'd rather be called angel than bitch. My life did not start and stop with you; it did, however, stop and start with you. I know of torments better than movies to distract you. End what you begin. Faithful to a type. You were intimidating because we never laughed. Love commences with shock and continues through habit. Six years ago I wrote: I'm the image of love, not the thing itself, and can't be slept with more than statues, though one takes statues to bed with faces impassive and shoulders stony. Which is why I weep, stones weep, because I was granted all, not part, and all can't be shared. Only the incomplete can enjoy love.

It's you who were mistaken, I remain consistent in still adoring you. It's up to you — the reparation gesture. . . . He said: "I love you, I love you, I love you, excuse me, I have a date, and anyway I've changed my mind." Watch out! Before you jump from high stone wings aim straight or your fickle blood will infect the pool of neighboring swimmers and you too. . . . You were the flop of my life, meaning: my own flop — as though you said: I was the flop in Ned's life. Ironically I no longer remember the names or faces of so many whose hearts withered through me. There's our justice!

Still ill as a dog, sinus infection, high fever, wandering about watching the quick flame of spring fertilize Manhattan, which bursts each moment into hot emeralds, all suddenly more close and precious, as always, now that I'm so soon leaving. The great heats, jonquil orgies on Park Avenue, and Central Park's again a cathedral of green lace over croaking kids and whining frogs in crocuses which strike at the heart like rattlesnakes, and the sky has a cloudless yellow smile as I've grown fond of someone who aches at my leaving and will maybe be glad when I return next fall.

Instantly there I am fortuitously precipitated into a monster gulf, a void, scabs ripped from the wound. Gradually the gulf fills up, with our own blood, blood of dizzy forgetfulness, a bit melancholy. Such are the ways of nature. A public cherub. With that face of yours *on te donnerait le bon Dieu sans confession.* But let's recall Marie Laure's first word at your photo. *Sadique!* . . . I remark, seeing someone in the street, *je serais bien dans ses bras.* You remark, *ça serait bien dans mes bras.* So who's a mirror? And you're quickly discouraged. I've never been in so many beds as during these last ten weeks. You never especially pleased me physically, love seldom can. I'm quite another person from the one you last saw. A week from this afternoon the plane leaves for France. Lou Harrison has always seemed to me America's most *inspired* composer. Paris will disintoxicate these blue thoughts. We're all just customers to you.

Tomorrow I go to Paris. With a camera's accuracy I recall mirthlessly every minute we spent together. Am feeling little friendship for you now, letting myself be so guided by the heart, but was it really to the detriment of work?

Paris, chez Marie Laure
Well!! We've met again. Last evening. *Nous avons même fait l'amour.*
And though it didn't work too brilliantly (as you say) it was not so
much from my shyness as your casualness. Yet I think we both were
moved, that you were even lonely and would start up again (on quite
another foot, of course — we're no longer the same people, etc.). Maybe
I'm wrong. You know, I rather despised you later? All the same, in
the taxi home there was sorrow caused by the strange-familiar streets
of your far part of town, your slaughterhouses of La Villette, the heavenly prison of blue Paris again. I'd sworn never to confront you with
injustices, nor will I (*d'ailleurs* you'd shield yourself French-style)
since vengeance is not a strong point. But neither will I ever tell you
my true feelings. But will tell you this because you want to know:
yes, I still love you (what a dull word now) but with a love denuded
of gentleness, one doesn't feel gentle toward the heel of a shoe. So
much was, and will remain, unsaid. No doubt best. I only ask to see
you amicably, painlessly from time to time. But yes, I detest you
somewhat. So take it easy for God's sake, you are a careful surgeon
after all, and your hand's too magic on the flesh — don't step in those
screwy corners of my lungs.

I'm not sorry you didn't suffer, Claude; I'm only surprised you
think you're incapable of suffering. But you don't give yourself time.
Try. Less masochist than a sleepwalker. (Though I've seen you suffer.)
Anyway *I* have, and can't begin again as though nothing had happened. Do my ears deceive me! You speak of trips to Rome, joint
excursions to the *fête à la* Place de la Nation or the Château de
Vincennes! Remember my memory and wait a while. . . . Yes, I was
tempted to write you. But you never answered my last (the one that
began with the passion of Hungary), and besides, what's the use?
On the other hand I wrote all these slobbery pages with the half-
veiled notion that one day you'd look. And you will, maybe not right
away, maybe with a little embarrassment and a lot of boredom because
you won't find yourself but you'll find me and understand the privilege of contradictions uttered in self-defense to keep me breathing.
. . . Do you know what touched me most last night? When you said:
"No one phones unless they've got a toothache." Know that I'm here,
like you, am glad to see you, have some things that belong to you.

I've no more time to lose with those who don't pay me court. It was myself who made me suffer, not you; myself who was able to endure the purge, not yu. Anyone else could have been an indirect cause. Not you.

June 1st. Eight years ago today I first came to France. I miss your conversation and your arms. Close up the worst and give of yourself, everyone. It's only innocent people who feel the need to justify themselves.

Oh, this wonderful hot weather! Beauties come out now on the streets, *débraillées*, and Paris light stays until nearly ten in the evening (and dawn is at three) with a lemonade glow, and the streets seething with the nervous and happy. The season changes, bringing the past like a flashlight into the Chicago parks where, as an adolescent, I lay (ignorant of danger: hence safe) in the arms of adults smelling of sun and gasoline and strength, the spring human smell of the *débraillé*. . . . When was it? Where have they gone? Today we have lunch in the garden. I go to the movies, one cannot be an amateur of both theater and cinema: I choose the movies.

For nineteen years I have been making love. Eva Gauthier used to tell her male singing students: "Just be glad you're not a soprano obliged to give a recital in spite of her 'period' when with every high note she feels blood rushing downward and prays that the audience be unaware of the red puddle forming on the floor." . . . These steaming spring evenings what else can we think of? love and sex along the river bridges. I'm different in summer than in winter, different in Paris than New York. And I see the arms around that little boy grow tighter, smaller, more distant, and somehow I'm no longer jealous of my childhood.

The heart—his heart—will shrink in its safety vault; I can't begrudge that unconsciousness, any more than the little bitch of *The Bad Seed*, the final revenge for my indifferent innocence. The *petit bourgeois* of the 19th Arrondissement, hobnobbing with artists and playing Don Juan, can now go stew in his own juice. Because we see each other as monsters, each unfair to the other. Kick me in the mouth like Bogart. I've too much heart, and you: none. (But am your equal in bad manners.) One doesn't torture another almost to death only to be later merely vexed that the "victim" misunderstood. You pushed to the utmost limits, cat and mouse, exasperated. From self-protection here's the definitive break. I've had you again and am not interested. Therefore I dump you — *je te plaque*. As conquest I cost you plenty. It's always a mistake to show one's love too much. You bastard.

These are the calmest, the least mean words with which to end this letter addressed to a misunderstanding. How changed a person I've become only someone else will tell. But I would rather have as remembrance the smell of those arms in a Chicago park tighten sharp around me nineteen years ago again tonight in the heat of France. *Salaud! Espèce de maquereau!* you pig, you real pig! you bad damn son-of-a-bitch, you prick. You shit!

PART 6
Summer–Autumn, 1957

Paris, Italy, Hyères, Paris, New York

La maladie de l'Europe est de ne croire à rien et de prétendre tout savoir.

CAMUS, *Réflexions sur la Guillotine*

Paris, July
Again tonight in the heat of France. Intelligent waste. Some wise
mistakes:
    When I reread this it will be cold somewhere, months, years,
from here. But this evening I seem alive by myself and can't believe
the risks I've run. More like a nun alone at sundown through the
cloister garden for the ten-thousandth time thinking on her first arrival:
same trees, same grass, same sun, new nun (old nun). That's how it
goes, as we grow on, not learning much, stopping dead in our tracks:
the honest man this morning may murder tonight, just as now the
lush on self-patrol may yet be drunk again so soon; the atrocious ex-
ample of others is useless, *on se fait des raisons.* I carefully build my
health up to a weekly breakdown. Year in and out this pattern's gone
on too long, and what once had elements of fun is now sterile humiliation, demolishing, *ennui* (but drinking too starts from nervous habit
of boredom). It's as though I self-imposed an impediment to hamper
work, slow down life. And the reconstructive week of movie-going
(oh! nothing with *shooting*! think of our headache!), I've said it all
before, still start and start again. Kell Kweet! If I am an alcoholic I
still hate to drink. Even more, I hate myself when I drink.
    Again tonight in the heat of Paris, hot Tuileries fountains sur-
rounded by wire chairs upside-down in lights from the ice-cream
shacks, heated flowers in darkness, and wandering couples, the mad
long streak of summer lanterns all the way up to l'Etoile. I spoke
with a stranger there, but it led to nothing.

Concert of my music at the American Embassy. Because soprano
Ethel Semser's nice leg was in a plaster cast she could not walk. We
therefore kept the curtain down, posed Ethel beside the piano like a
statue in an evening gown, and were both on stage when the curtain
rose. Then, my God, it wasn't us but the audience which seemed on
display as we gazed out over that Proustian assemblage of heads.

Composing, since I have become a "professional," has long since ceased to be a spontaneous gesture, but a laborious responsibility needing more reflection than the youthful inspiration we take for granted.

I like the image of Saturday night in a packed city bar outside of which there is only prairie for a thousand miles. And I like those who stay home rehearsing for days so that they may come and "sight-read" before respectful auditors of the intimate chamber music gathering. . . . All told, and in the long run, it's the old proved classics which move us the most when we still take time to listen instead of hearing with more careful ears the glitter of our own modern music almost snowed under by the sciences. But, too, the classics are what truly bore us the most.

I rather detest with good reason (the stronger that they are beloved) these seven: Hemingway, Eartha Kitt, Schweitzer, Samuel Beckett, Joan of Arc, Casals, and June Allyson.

Just had the first polio shot because if I hadn't and got infantile paralysis I'd kick myself. Or as Joe LeSueur pointed out: "If you *could* kick yourself!" Joe, who has written a book called *Answering a Question in the Mountains.*

For three weeks I've been back, though not back. Yet no longer either in America, but at some midpoint without a particular happiness or sadness, a little bored, no strong *goût de vivre* nor anything settled to look sentimentally forward to. Still Paris is flaming with those wild spring storms that smell of summer while I take long unfocused walks alone to dispel the fourth hangover. At least now I've resolved as well as it can be done the problem for which I've arrived — that louse — and would be ready tomorrow to go back to New York, if it wasn't a waste of money, toward a grass no greener on the other side of the ocean. I'd also be ready to fall blindfolded into a brand-new affair, credulous, passive, jealous and demanding; *l'amour, quoi!* Meanwhile I write song after song on poems of Elizabeth Bishop, and see that although France has somehow gone on without me, it's also reawakening like the sleeping princess at my return. France doesn't know she gives no more escapes to someone, older, for whom pedestrians no longer turn around much. That's why we write diaries: to scold a public which doesn't react.

Feeling lonely. No one writes, nor telephones. It's dark and raining, depressed without tension, a need for anticipation. Few ideas, a little reading (Bernard Minoret, E. M. Forster). A head full of tuneless songs. The truth is I haven't yet come back to life. *Nullement sauvage, j'ai horreur d'être seul. Je me sens malade.*

Write a poem on the ruses of cruising, fears in the street, long strolls seeking those who run away, "looking for love where it can't be found and waiting for love where it will not come," how to evade with the happy foreknowledge of being caught, how to reject gracefully and ungraciously, etc. And call it: The Art of the Fugue.

Americans build toward the sky, the French make love toward the earth. The French (visual but unmusical) create a snobbism about the harpsichord, which is dry and precise, but around the harp (blurred and luscious) no snobbism can be built, for sensuality— though we fear it today—is popular. There is a repellent female approach saying: "Music is a privilege, a relaxation." It is not a privilege but on anyone's doorstep; not a relaxation but a positive ear-opener for the auditor willing to work at letting go and forgetting the less complex structure of mouth and eye. This I have explained in Philadelphia to Edna Phillips. To my father, weary of the rivalry and altercations of communal work and desirous of joining an "outfit" that knows its own mind and functions as one, I explain: "How can an *outfit* know what it wants? By definition it is made of mind-groups no two of which can ever truly agree." Our earth is the same, but I believe it's the only one we've got.

I am still convalescing. That is why this pale enthusiasm is just nourished by watery broth and no spermy ink. Art (that!) is simply a series of inevitably correct but accidental choices. [Explain why *He has come over a toy sky to find me* is a distortion from myopia that formed grace.]

Marc Blitzstein in New York took the time to help me translate my libretto to *The Robbers* from (as he said) English into English. Since then I like the work less but Marc more. Menotti has let me see that one of my songs is worth the whole opera.

Let's translate *l'amour est terrible* by Love is Terrible. The distortion is amusing, and thus two nationalities are angrily fused.

Le Partage de midi is a combination of *Camino Real* and Rita Hayworth's old movie *Gilda*. Its greatness keeps it from cheapness, it's sensuality from tedium. And of course *la Feuillère* is today's best actress as actresses (*les belles fausse*) go. Who wants real life? Good theater in its form and concentration improves on God. If you know a lot of people it's easier to replace them.

I've been back in France four weeks. Still not back, etc. But *l'épisode Claude* is over and closed with the ugliest finish imaginable. I have no more force to note the details (though when I spit in his face a molar fell out!), nor does it make any difference. Yet I think often of it with a heavy heart, and still feel lonely. I'm lonely because I know too many people, and pacify myself by writing letters, it's my habit: the literature of separation. Drinking too much. No sex (nor feel the need, though feel I should feel it). I grow confounded by the intimacy of such acts where two bodies strive so tragically to be one, and the empty-stranger post-orgasm abyss. It happened last night: the frenzied pathetic joy of a child before his birthday cake, followed by the tears of abandonment when the last guest is gone. I'm ready for the calm assurance of a single person, the thatched hut, a cabbage patch.

It's chilly for June and river lights have no heat in the wind. We can only see ourselves when away from home. Gide's funeral was nearly

seven years ago and all Paris seemed in mourning. Could it happen
that way in America for *any* man of letters (even Hemingway)?
Prokosch told me yesterday he needs to live far from America's
"vulgarity." Now I no longer (nor did I ever) see it this way, and want
more and more to leave the France I know as well as my pocket through
which I've suffered. And I'm bored, and bored, bored.
> *J'ai le cafard.*
> *J'ai le cafard* (another day).
> *J'ai un peu moins le cafard.*
> *J'ai le cafard.*
At least our friends console us by growing simultaneously older
and recalling like yesterday those popular songs of the thirties.

It's early in the morning. *J'ai découché.* It's my Robert Hillyer song.
It's hot, *et je ne le fais jamais.* I relive my songs, though I'm not always sure of the poem's meaning as I write the music. I compose not
through past experience but what *will* happen to me. Today I create
(not *the*, but) my future—and, years after, I whistle my own tunes
while practicing what they preach.

Some people recover, improve, and advance: Nell Tangeman, after
a session in Saint Vincent's, is now a new and glowing person. Some
people relapse, disintegrate, and sink: Boris, after dubious years of
secret Russian charm and a *litre* of pernod per day, is now a bloated
mass of scabs in his tuxedo mumbling like a forgotten moron. Some
people seem to stay the same through the years, and they are frequent,
frequent. Those who advance, learn and work with flying saucers.
Boris lives on the Rue Bleue, between the Rue de Paradis and the
Rue Papillon; lovely names, but the *arrondissement* is overrun with
Arab assassins. It is very hot and rainy, a late Sunday afternoon. My
eyes look out on a level with the treetops and my head and heart
swim with an overuse of alcohol these last fainting days. Overpre-
occupation with detail, trimming to perfection, is only laziness. But
the performance of a Schubert trio must be a *ménage à trois sans
bagarre* which, in real life, just doesn't exist. My breakfast is of red

foods: apples and peppers, cherries and tomatoes, strawberries and rare meat. In which category do I fall?

Since leaving school nearly ten years ago I have lived more or less exactly as I pleased (have I been pleased?): going to bed and getting up when I feel like it; answering to no higher boss (similar to my friends in art — though not to those in romance who've been obliged to keep my schedule, thereby falling ill); living where I wish, seeing and eating who and what I want; writing the music I hear; desiring to have what I desire when I desire (from the very start I was a spoiled child); enough money, no real material fears; overdrinking, but with the time always to sleep it off. Now, with this mass of leisure I have, through the years with a Protestant order, accomplished more in sheer mileage (if not in quality) than any other leisured innocent I know — living immoderately on both sides of the scale, but with an almost desperate sentimental restraint. And I have been reasonably happy. And I have been reasonably successful (by American standards). The beautiful have a more drastic challenge than the ugly in aging, for only they must habituate to a change.

Day after tomorrow, the Mistral for Toulon, leaving thus the anonymous peace of a big city for my routine summer industry. The heat wave of this past week has been the strongest in France for eighty years: all one can do is lie around, reading a great deal in a suffocated semisleep which is rather pleasant. Nobody and nothing interests me, though at least in my present state of convalescence I can again concentrate on a page or an air-cooled movie screen. The heat. Already six, seven, eight years back I was lunching with Caïds in the Moroccan desert, blond as the sun, while the weeks slipped by invisibly. Am I only capable of a passion in lost causes?

What comfort is there in pederasty to one who's not a creator? In love, something more than just itself must be an issue. Since the war we've come away from three thousand years of art into an age of science where flying saucers as easily nourish intelligent souls. Young American composers today are early-married professors with steady incomes and no further need of competition, writing square works for their babies. Only I (ten years older than they), poor, but living in a French house of luxury, seem out of joint suddenly in what I sing.

But if I am "not of this time," couldn't it be *au contraire* that I feel
this Today so well and much I've got to leave?

My last largest works I've escaped and never heard: the Second
Symphony, the Woodwind Sinfonia, *The Robbers* will sing first without me in September California. Does my logical intelligence eliminate a sense of taste? "Good taste" has never (like courage and
sincerity) been of my concerns. Taste, like intelligence, can lessen
the necessary abandon of creation, though intelligence and taste
have nothing to do with each other. I've no taste. But intelligence
wants me to keep this diary when I should be musicalizing. And I
read too much. Ought to fornicate more (now while it's still available
to my age)—I feel the need—instead of talking about it, walking the
streets and combing my hair for it, left unsatisfied like a strangled
belch.

Hyères
What a reassuring pleasure it is, summer after summer while the
world goes to pot and sizzles there in precipitous change, to hear in
the marketplace and alleys the Provençal language still being spoken
and even by seven-year-olds who weren't born when I first saw this
town.

Faisons le bilan. During just three weeks in Hyères I have completed two symphonic movements and God knows how many songs,
including a short cycle on Whitman poems for Wilder Burnap and
his virginals! "I pour the stuff to start sons . . ." wrote Walt; and now,
with a brand-new friend (PQ. medical botanist and physical *mélange*
of Jean Lagrolet, Dane Clark, and Noel Lee, with a *visage crépusculaire* which climbs me like a tree but leaves me limp), I'm off on a
car trip to the isles of Naples.

We leave Saturday. . . . We are what we make of ourselves; artists are "makers of manners"; could I be that composer who remains,
for love, always in France? In any case today it's the only country of
conversations, and here in Hyères at Marie Laure's we are living
amongst the pleasantest company of our century.

French society consists of those who pronounce (Lord and
Minoret), those who are pronounced upon (*les dames du monde*),
and those who sum it up with *le don de la réplique* (Cocteau, Noailles,

or the middle-class talents: Mauriac, Bourdet, etc.). For years Marie Laure called me Miss Sly, the foreign absorber. To myself I seem the sole remaining Romantic, a languisher, moving through black mornings or anguished dusks with an ardent wish for awakening into another dimension. It's not a female impersonator's name—like Miss Citronella Snowdrift—but rather a title for one of Father Divine's humorless daughters.

The Italian trip will help to take up and sort souvenirs as a box of colored candy, as the sumptuous order which only lady authors—Colette and Woolf—feel. With a certain relief I see disappearing the *joli garçon* I used to be (I used to take my own breath away), while dipping (how gracefully!) into the thirties' duties. Beauties have two lives: the old, the young. Uglies stay always the same, no matter how smart, and will not hear that embarrassing knock on the door of orgasm—or just when you sit down with a book on the toilet the phone rings (it's never anyone nice either). I knew I was grown up before anybody suspected; I remain a child with no one knowing. I understood grown-ups as a child (I have nothing of my own Corinthians), and today can see a child as clearly as day before yesterday. How different these lives and aims, among all my lovers, a spider-web railroad leading and lost into the desert.

I am never idle. *Les vacances c'est là où on travaille ailleurs,* said Colette, and sunlight with sand for me must be accompanied by letters of order and hot thought.

Il faut cultiver sa légende.

Auric recounts the cremation of his Protestant colleague, my former master, Honegger, the first of *les Six* to die. A coffin, like any other, is lowered into an oven in full view of the collected mourners. The door is closed as upon a final act at the Folies Bergères full of flowers, and a dull burning machine sounds in the distance. Eulogies begin, speeches, epitaphs with tears. Twenty minutes. The minister motions to a choirboy who opens the door, looks down the shaft, shakes his head, withdraws. Not ready yet! Nervous silence. Another speech. . . . Finally the coffin, shrunk to the size of an urn, is given to Madame Honegger, who holds in this jewel box the body of her husband.

Telegram from Charles-Henri Ford. Tchelichew is dead. Gone in an Italian summer like Latouche a year ago, the end of one friendship as long and desultory as the other. What can we remark anymore about these recurrences which increasingly attack our own selves? A bit of me too is gone with Pavlik.

It was as long ago as 1945 that I implored Parker Tyler to introduce us. The fantasies at the Modern Museum were haunting me as was the painter's own head glimpsed across a room and mythological. Parker arranged a *dîner à trois* at the Russian Tea Room, but I was shy and Pavlik ailing (older than I'd expected); I recall nothing but his river of talk, the red ribbon on his wrist "to ward off evil spirits," and his surprise that Parker had brought him "a child." A year later I wrote music for a puppet show called "At Noon Upon Two" authored by Charles-Henri, designed by Kurt Seligmann, manipulated by John Myers, presented at the Old Knickerbocker on Second Avenue, and attended by everyone of those days including Pavlik, who said on seeing me, "My God, he's an old man now." I was twenty-one.

Our final meeting was last year in Frascati when P. and I went for lunch and saw nothing but Charles-Henri's pictures. And now what is there? I feel sick, for no special reason.

Hubert de Saint Senoch and Charles Hathaway come around occasionally. They own a pair of Rolls-Royces. The larger is for visiting duchesses. The smaller (to avoid ostentation) is for cruising the *bas fonds* of Toulon.

September. Who seeing Paestum for the first time would not wish to die there? It rips out the blood and the Greeks have peacefully won, they remain, while the Roman ruins aren't crumbled but melted like ice cream. . . . It's a month later (retrospective journals are less fun but easier) and, Yes, I spent August in Italy with PQ. If nothing else, it purged and scraped me clean of that gray anguish in the Spring of Claude.

The mountain comes to Mohammed.

This was my eleventh trip into Italy and in three weeks we did 4,000 kms. in PQ's Dauphine. Dark, a cloudy lover settles like a storm on top of me. Can I only only like *that*? (Yet certainly I'm growing no younger.) All my gorgeous honeymoons, and that regular magical hour of the meal with a lover. I am dying not to die. I repeat: what we learned from our last love affair teaches us what *not* to do in the next; yet when the next is over we realize that what we refrained from doing was, in this case, just the thing we *should* have done. Now can this help itself from being again the summer romance which fades like a suntan in the fall? A professor of botany has concrete duties and only artists can afford folly. But *justement* they are alone in their folly.

Amalfi
Silver stalactites. And all this world's history oozing from the old Mediterranean's importance; what was I, an Anglo-Saxon, doing there? Being in love? There's nothing to cure that. Near Genoa we look at the sunset as powdered rust sprinkled onto blue whip-cream. Rome: thick ivory sun on the orange city where the always unbelievable Italians wash their cars in the spray of Saint Peter's fountains. And PQ is shocked if, with a whore's address, I enter the treasury room at Saint Peter's and say: *Ciào tesoro!* But pays no true attention to me: we get along fine, but I could as well be anyone else and not Ned Rorem: I could even be the Miss Millay of my childhood saying (what was it?) "I am in love with him to whom the Hyacinth is dearer than I shall ever be dear." But it's my first botanist, for whom I'll one day be as dusty as Pompei. Gardens. Hans Werner Henze showing us the sights of Naples says in his special French: *"Et voilà le jardin méchant!"*—which of course has nothing to do with botany, but which can neither break our hearts like a sunset on the Appian Way (what poem as a child did I write of "Five O'Clock on a Roman Road"?) nor bleach the souvenir of my palm on the driver's thigh.

Capri's a work of the devil, Paestum and Ravello seem nearly things of God, but Rome shows that as usual the best work's done by man. Go into Florence's Accademia and know why Valéry was right to say "A work of art is never completed: it is abandoned." Not abandoned are the life-sized statues in Florence's cemetery: tasteful Carrara marble replicas of the deceased in Ginger-Rogers-type 1930's page-boy bobs. Where do I go from here? And in love? What love affair has ever not been impossible? The hills of Rome as breasts are brave little pears, but often Nature makes a mistake when she thought up love affairs. We are more forsaken than the ship *Mary Celeste* in 1872.

The actual truth is that, except for an occasional song, writing music rather bores me. It is a necessary chore, and the wisest are the laziest. Control of laziness is a secret to success, but composition of tears is given only to a few despite themselves. Knowing, then, that I must "make," what *is* it I seem to crave as well? A need to share? Nevertheless, the constant molding of attainment toward romance as I seem to want to keeps me in a state of tension preventing work. And still I work. That's how it is.

The Big Dipper couldn't care less. "Controlling" our nature, we do the same to music: do you suppose a phrase is happy knowing it falls into a 12-tone orbit? Or that a tone is less lonely to find that it has overtones? You can't go home again (but you can, I have). No traveler returns. And no one really has more than himself.

Monologue of a Fairly Young Composer. Gardens Without Pity (Nîmes). Deception deeper than heaven, and hellish as the Aven d'Orgnac. Why do I write all that? Because yesterday evening I returned again to Hyères from a five-day excursion, with PQ, of Provence and Languedoc. Where weren't we? The same almost as Henry James' little tour of France. In any case it's not possible to go farther from a skyscraper than to the *manade* of Jean Lafont. Imagine (*au Cailar* where his Toril and tiny half-finished house are) dining by lamplight in the dark chilly garden. Five yards off, the end of the universe. At midnight a full moon, and we go to watch the sleep of two hundred kneeling bulls in a fog thicker than butter and *Boris Godounov* sings from the radio. That's where Jean Lafont lives with an adopted adolescent. *Je n'invente rien.* And discretion's a quality more precious than the sugar of sincerity or noblesse; with it, any life can be led.

Masterpieces are all boring. It takes time to appreciate the syntax of new loves. But at least in Arles or Avignon or Aix I've made love. In *Mes Apprentissages* there's a letter from Jean Lorrain, who says, "*Oui, le hâle fait les yeux bleus plus bleus, mais l'amour en*

Provence les cerne comme nulle part ailleurs!" Leave Arles, leave
the cloisters of St. Trophime, les Alyscamps, the theater and dangerous arena, leave Arles for the remains of Mont Majour nearby, where
you'll smell honey so thick that the sound of bees, the sound of yellow,
is in the fragrance. Do it with a lover. Look at Daudet's windmill if
you wish (from a distance) and lunch at Saint Rémy after a visit to
the high mausoleum which the peasants of that region call *Les
Antiques*; this too is far from skyscrapers. Buy some candy at the
springs of Vaucluse, and as you chew try thinking of Laura and
Petrarch if you're not too nervous for your lover. Les Baux is worth
an afternoon, and the Val de l'Enfer. Then go to sleep in Avignon or
Villeneuve d'Avignon, but do it with a lover. The beds are good. Next
morning in Orange there's the orange Roman theater (and a trium-
phal arch), but later at Vallon is the incomparable nature's Pont d'Arc
(Utah has no equal) where you can take a river swim in the Ardéche
(naked), then the grottos of Orgnac, and along the roadside *les
Dolmens*, where the Gauls sacrificed their friends a thousand years
before Christ said not to. Uzès, where Racine lived a while. And oh,
the Pont du Gard. In the evening at the Nîmes arena watch a game
of Rugby with a live bull added for complication, laugh with a lover.
And go to bed and quarrel. Montpellier with the esplanade Peyrou,
and far out of town hidden near the wild beaches is the old church of
Maguélone. Have lunch in the ugly resort of Palavas on PQ's birthday (Sept. 9), then take a train back alone to Toulon with tears in
your eyes.

I cannot wait until tonight to say I love you.

Now Marie Laure has forbidden me to write letters. She's right.
Their wings catch fire and spray friends with ashes.

Yet I must, and will do it here. New friend, you'll admire my
silence when we meet again to say good-bye in Paris. *Donc:* [Here
follows, believe it or not, a forty-page treatise addressed to PQ
between the time of our Provençal excursion and our farewell season
in Paris a few weeks later. I have neither the patience nor the esthetic
to translate and reproduce it here. Suffice it to say that Marie Laure,
after reading both this and the letter to Claude, commented simply:

"I'd put both those people in a box, tie it with a ribbon, and throw it in the deep blue sea." N. R. 1967]

Knowing I go Thursday to Paris, and now is Monday, I've already left, yet still here time drags by at a snail's pace. More trying than an arrival too soon. Meanwhile I've not had a drink for two months and roast myself all naked daily in the last sun, for the Ile-de-France will be cold they say. I compose and onanize and read, liking my Third Symphony, the human body firm and fragile as a paperclip.

Boris Kochno mailed from Switzerland a letter in lovely script to Marie Laure in which he speaks of himself in the third person as someone met on a beach who asked after her — but he was unable to reply. My friend Jean Leuvrais solves such puzzles irrefutably: those he admires or loves he makes a part of his life whether they know it or him or not; he works the strings of people a hemisphere away — their least decision has his approval. He's not bothered with the flesh. News flash: Nature improves on art.

Paris, early autumn 1957
Yes, I've come back to Paris two nights ago and have already had my homecoming *cuite* of disgrace, face a bit hacked, which comes (as we know) from the jerky shaving with a hangover. Cities, cities, cities as doll-town mazes. My hand's still none too solid and the Paris air is heavy, cool, dark. I am blond, depressed, tan. If, like they say, I have no living "sense of theater" it shows more in the dying sense of compulsive occasional drinking. Everyone has his particular *sens du théâtre*, which is not necessarily the sense of *spectacle*. *Au fond* I'm really a very good person and too credulous. Sick of suffering: there's been too much; and I long for the opportunistic thrust which could help me select mates to help a career. Why not? Oh it's dark and I must go out. . . . PQ has arrived (must watch my P's and Q's!) and tonight, with J. P. Marty, we will dine. It's nervous-making. Raining hard. And Sibelius finally died today. Also the king of Norway.

Yes, I've had beautiful women also in love. Now the incomparable Madame T. Perhaps after all marriage is the happy solution.

Tu es orgueilleux, mais non pas vaniteux. Chez moi c'est l'inverse. Voici la différence.

Maybe: A Symphony of Poems
Orchestrate: *Visits to Saint Elizabeth's*
Title for a painting of Dominguez: *Cercueil de Vitesse.* Noisy Coffins.

In last month's *Poetry* David Posner has dedicated to me his "Poem for Music." But Paul Goodman quotes my style in last year's learned review *I.E.*

Looking back—now that three seasons have come and gone—at that endless letter to Claude (and it was only one of the many not sent), I feel both embarrassment and impatience. I now see myself as a self-indulgent nag, in view of what I've since learned (do we learn?). True, that suffering was close to unendurable, though in viewing it now (but one doesn't "view it now"—such things freeze) my anxiety was less from love or even privation than from insult, an insult spewing a blank year of recovering from two months of bliss. Still, is time lost in mourning time lost?

Today I marvel only at the energy of that sorrow. No mention, however, is made of my Third Symphony, begun and completed that summer. It's bemusing to consider the lacunae in musical subject matter here. In that whole winter's writing to Claude not only did I seldom allude to other persons, but in a hallucination of one-track-mindedness there was complete omission of the news that *The Poets' Requiem* (then my most extended work) had its world premiere.

Like God, made in our image, we endow those we love with imagined timeless qualities which they neither possess nor (usually) want us to think they possess. When, then, our disillusion of necessity arrives as we witness the collapse we've forced upon them (but for which we take no responsibility), we hate them; and, like God, they can only stare back with that blank surprised dismay of corpses.

While sipping anisette on the terrace of the Royal Saint Germain we see Jean Genet stroll by on the arm of DeNoël, to whom he is saying: *"Mon Dieu,* since that damn book came out [Sartre's *Saint Genet*] I can't even pick my nose in public without someone whispering 'Oh, that gesture refers to so and so and you can read about it on page such and such,' and so I . . . " and his voice trails off as they disappear into the crowd, for he never sits down. But we sip more anisette, and observe the next passersby.

In thirty-six hours I leave in a plane for America. Here it feels as though winter's come. The weather's made our Paris world like a cave. Will I come back with the buds? As all grows smaller we still spread out. PQ goes to Algiers. Now we pass our days doing Seine things: the old Venus de Milo and the Gioconda smile (ripe ladies when I was a child) appear adolescent today. Works of art do change; not because we become more intelligent but because we grow older. Writers have always influenced me more than musicians. And who's done more than I in music for American poetry? Why doesn't Carnet do a movie of me? and write a score for my own soliloquies, precise with contrasts and all bars down—like the Balinese.

   Yes, going away once more. Good-bye and good-bye, can it ever stop? Will I have another American cold season writing letters to North Africa? No: suffering *can* be controlled: when it starts, think of your toenails. Work's no real answer, but replacement or substitution are.

   I've written as much as I can.

New York
Thursday October the third the sun came up over Europe as usual, only I wasn't there any longer to see it. Being now in America with no New York lodgings, and the Philharmonic's opening concert can-

celed for the first time since Lincoln's assassination (*Design* will not be played), I wonder to what I've returned. Nevertheless, PQ, I'm glad we left Paris at the same time, each to a city the other ignores.

Day after tomorrow I'll be thirty-four. Since Christ died last Easter, and I didn't, perhaps, I have a long way to go. Going professionally (or "career-wise," as they say in America) things seem fairly smooth at the moment, particularly as I am to do the music for Tennessee Williams' new one-act "shocker" *Suddenly Last Summer*, and Mitropoulos has scheduled my Woodwind Sinfonia for November 10. Also I have a place to live: back again on Thirteenth Street after thirteen years. But the ways of the heart seem null and void in this country, and though drinking bores me I do it all the same. The tenacity here, and fear and money and ambition and blindness begin by fright and finish in contagion. When have I not wished to be the direct cause of every spasm, all orgasm in the world? But so do all others now. This competition troubles because work wants quiet.

I must buy a checkerboard. And a red vase for yellow roses, a yellow vase for red roses, a red and yellow vase for roses red and yellow (as well as red vase for red roses, yellow vase for yellow roses, etc.). Would it be a good idea if Marc Blitzstein wrote a libretto for me? Last week in Bloomingdale's basement I find Grace Cohen Jaffe, beautiful Grace from the happy summer of 1946 in Tanglewood, where she says I said: "Ah, Gertrude Stein is dead. What a pity she never knew me!" Did I? Yet today don't I reproach PQ for a similar reflection in Montpellier?

Dior died. I'm thirty-four.

America. I seem to be back. But how can the shock of it not shock me? Art here is more of a comedy than ever (I meant to write commodity), and anyway the twenty-year-olds — those who count — don't care, being more interested in science now; and science (except for love) has all and more than art had: mysticism and mystery and romance without sex. But I am from before and America's grown unreal. I am more and more afraid of people, and in this city of money, of comfort without luxury and violence without erection, I am lost and wondering, having never in any way prostituted myself nor dealt with people I didn't choose. How long will I last it? Until I too become hypnotized by The Big Money? But lazy habits and creative needs have now gone on too long, and we cannot even smile without paying cash for the halo-frame about the lips.

Tonight we are going (Morris and Marc Blitzstein) up to Juilliard to hear the new Copland piano piece. Why does he apologize? It's all we ever do. And the bars! Such frozenness! What couldn't I say?! At least I have . . . what was it?

John Latouche: "No, I'll meet you later — after your earlier appointment. Like that you can have your date and eat it!" He used to get drunk at his own parties.

Here in American hotels are no *bidets* nor room service for breakfast. Again the Protestant shock. Take a whole bath then, every day, so as to smell better standing frozen drunk in the frozen bar and saying fearfully: no, not *this* one yet, for the next may be better. (Americans of course take too many baths.)

New York

Whoredom and wine and new wine take away the heart.

HOSEA

Who hath woe? who hath sorrow? who hath contentions? who hath babbling? who hath wounds without cause? who hath redness of the eyes? They that tarry long at the wine.

PROVERBS

Theme without variations. Eight months ago on my return to America I stopped writing here. And now, with winter gone and heat slapping the sexy sidewalks, I start again having nothing else to do, having finished the Third Symphony and all the rest, having stopped and recommenced and stopped with love once more, and having no plans at all. I seemed to have reached a stalemate and necessary point of reflection in work (how can I rejuvenate it?) and living (I shall not return to Europe), neither happy nor sad; though some days just the sight of a lamp, a dog, a barrel is enough to start the tears. Since normally I'm in Paris during the spring weather-change I'm moved to think of May rains the year before, but now it's been ten years, or forty seasons, since I knew New York in this season, and I think back, always back, on nearly twenty years (eighty seasons) past when in Chicago I behaved pretty much as now.

Now I know how the past gets dragged like a leaden tail. It's all red like the rain or rubies and roses and cherries and blood, sunsets and wine-drops and raspberries and Scarlet Tanagers, Cardinals and stained glass and Jello and devils, flame and hell and crimson cushions and strawberries, anger, and red as a heart. The only one I miss in Europe is myself; now that self is irretrievable, so why go back? There is nobody I particularly look forward to seeing again. The church and heaven of adults are children's former fairyland where I cannot go without serious suspicion. It's been a good ten months since I've had "satisfactory" sexual relations! Can a fish on the hook enjoy it as much as I? (But only in love.)

Dream (on the Ides of March): burning lions and horses falling in sparks from a skyscraper as I, fixed in space, look down and watch in terror those animals which were pursuing me. (It occurs that the foregoing—written in March—has the "doublings" of orchestration: the winds of "burning" is doubled by the percussion of "sparks"; the strings of "lions" by the brass of "horses"; "look down" by "watch"; "falling" by "pursuing"; etc. Doubling is dangerous: for what thickens by simultaneousness in instrumentation only confuses by redundance in prose.)

Oscar Dominguez is dead. At the end of the year, to our sad astonishment, he finally fell into his own trap of threats and, across the ocean, severed wrists and ankles. The things which cannot, but *do*, happen will astound me until my own dying. Both Hart Crane and René Crevel wrote of their *type* of suicide before it happened. And so it was with our Oscar, whose souvenir I brood upon only through one tiny painting and a hundred soothing and cruel words. Why is what is prophesied never believed? Can I lump them all together like the current mode, "the sick joke," those darlings whom last winter stole while I wasn't writing in a diary? George Davis (leaving Lenya with a German husband buried in America, and an American buried in Germany); Robert Kurka (teaching a lesson to his colleagues); Mike Todd (as spectacularly as his life); W. C. Handy (the evening sun *went down*, if you'll pardon the expression); a Greek-tragedy murder in the family of Lana Turner (she was always a girl-of-the-heart with whom I closely identified). Finally our precious Marie Blanche de Polignac, yes finally (thus ending an *époque* which cannot be revived in this lifetime). Loneliest and nearest was Oscar, though too distant for me to write it now with feeling. In my own ever-increasing interspatial transports how often do I ask why we spend money to keep ourselves alive (buying teeth and doctor bills and cabbages) when it's easier to kill ourselves? The child's revenge of dying gave Oscar the courage of his convictions. And yet I loved him. When I can't sleep I think on movie stars. The presence of beloved parents prevents suicide. Yet some of me died with Oscar: the part he invented through need, and owned.

Elliott Stein writes from Paris of sailors with machine guns pointing from trucks, and war again, or still, seems whizzing around with wings so vast that even the sunniest of these first hot days which make the city streets steam with sex are clouded with the perpetual and necessary hangover, and I go "on the wagon" only to better prepare myself for the next drinking bout—the sooner the better. I miss France to a point of anguish, but through that American sense of *place* (not to mention lack of funds) I remain. The winter's accomplishments (and my sister Rosemary is pregnant for the *fifth* time: it will be born in July) have by-passed my own personality, making me, to an extent, a public figure remote from myself. We can make few generalities on how a composer should live. But don't I know how correct is Waugh, who says that Charm "spots and kills anything it touches. It kills love; it kills art. . . . "

Today I'm as sweet as a violet cream pie, and tonight with the bitchiness of liquor I can spout the aggressively self-assured nastiness which, like Mr. Hyde, good doers must possess. But I've aimed it badly, and seldom in my work. Often composers compose like what they think they are not. Look at the uncomplicatedly sensitive but basically joyous work of David Diamond during his flagrantly disordered war years, and now that he's stabilized in a Florentine villa his music's grown knotty, complex and sad. Observe Marc Blitzstein, whose private ways are circumspect, even to mystery, yet whose music's direct, earthy, of the body. Or myself, who say and show all anywhere while notating sounds repressed and puritan as hymns. Still I know my origins even if I may see influences less objectively than an outsider. *"Je méprise les fils qui rougissent de ressembler à leur père,"* says Poulenc. I always prefer the movies, and anything I do which is not "me," is still "me" since it's *I* doing it, and we know that consistency's the hobgoblin of etc. . . .

That question of *influence* is elusive. Composers are always being asked about it. Yet more interesting than their knowledge is their ignorance concerning those outer rays that blast them. When I first arrived in Paris, it was with embarrassment that I showed my little pieces to everyone, feeling those pieces to be too outrageously French, too lush, too self-indulgent. Yet Poulenc exclaimed (as did Sauguet, Boulanger, Milhaud), "Let yourself go! Why so careful, so Nordic, so Protestant, so unsensual?" Of course, what even the greatest artist expresses is nothing compared to what he represses. . . . The question of *style* is even more elusive. Sam Barber, for instance, has no truly identifiable musical syntax, yet he has nonetheless identifiably influenced our Charles Turner. Still, Charles' music (at its best) is his own—though nobody can tell you why.

Last winter's accomplishments: yes, Ormandy played my piece, and Mitropoulos, and I wrote music for Tennessee's play about a poet eaten alive last summer by children who cut him apart with tin cans. Success and establishment, like education, are cumulative, and for a composer it's never financial, while Tennessee with all his acclaim never sees a minute's rest and is given to public confession now. As for Mr. Inge, he's shown me a libretto about a sodomite undertaker who is required to embalm, on stage, the person dearest to his heart.

How could I not be discouraged about librettos, at least for a while, after last month's ignominious failure of *The Robbers*? The production was an outrage, with the three actors looking less Chaucerian than like Jesse James, Leslie Howard, and Harpo Marx. To add insult to injury, it was co-billed with Rieti's *The Pet Shop* (renamed "Amelia Goes to the Dogs" by Elliott Stein) which received all the praise from *les petits amis*. The damage of "charm" again, but for once I am not the sinner.

June

For weeks, for weeks now, in this heat, I have been just staring around this room or out the window which has grown so full of leaves I can't see up to the sky. Or drinking heavily three days out of seven, spending the intervening hours recuperating in nervous sleep. Or waiting for letters from Europe which don't come, or for the right person to make the phone ring (it doesn't). Steambaths are time-consuming and expensive, but I spend and consume. Certainly I do not work (except a few songs for *The Ticklish Acrobat*), just gaze at the window and cry and cherish my tears like a lady her diamonds. To sum it up: today it's June and I've no summer plans, no money, nothing to work on, no love; too much liquor and leisure, too much sleep, and too much worried humidity all over the whole world's sky. I'm thirty-four and waiting: it isn't easy.

The dark will always have it over the light. Around 4 A.M. The day is no longer long enough to drink in. The proof: I'm still able to write it.

Well, Nell Tangeman and I've been going to A.A. meetings now for three days, and will continue until I go home to Philadelphia for the 4th of July when Rosemary will have her fifth child. Certainly nothing can be said against their logic: I've thought the same for years and don't want to spend, without help, *all* the rest of my life in that shadow wet with unknown bleeding. But . . . I don't know. I'm not a "group type" (many say that) and do not wish to be *absorbed*. I'm used to being the *only one* at the party, and falling in with a commu-

nal plan is a worse change for shyness than going alone onto a long
wagon. I'm hell at a party, but heaven on stage. We'll see, I'll give it
some chance. Because God knows I'm bored with the boredom of
Monday's gin and I don't interest myself anymore. Liquor's black
magic, and I'm a mortal with no talent for combating sorcery. My
"fabulous life" which astounds so many is now a heap of tedium, and
the fatigued wrinkles of my forehead make a drunken demonstra-
tion even less dignified than in my earlier youth. And I *do* care, in
spite of all the "slips." I care more than all the beat and cool epochs.

Music is seen and not heard by them. Every time the curtain
goes up on *Suddenly Last Summer* Bobby Soule's set receives ap-
plause but no one ever knows there's music. The surrealists had no
ears and so banned music; the new generation uses its ear as a phallus,
and is violent only in its lack of violence. Had I been born just four
years later I might have fallen into this age which takes the atom
bomb for granted (I'm told that even the moon—that dreary suburb
—is being prospected only as a military base) and lacks all curiosity;
as it is, I remain romantic, liking excess, worrying still on waking up,
a broken boy.

Wilhelm Reich is dead also. The times advance with always more
embêtements sans poésie (as Philippe Erlanger says), and some grow
sterile before dying. Last night we saw *The Goddess*, for which Virgil's
music is a flaw. His defenses are more brilliant than what he defends.
Some people are easy, some hard, to talk to. Virgil talks at and of or
through, not to you. But monologuists are better than those who just
wait like lumps. A successful conversation is as importantly difficult
as a working love affair. Aaron attends, Marc shares, Morris ploughs
on, Tennessee stagnates, Marie Laure declaims, Virgil pontificates,
but Latouche knew the art more congenially than any. I want to be
enveloped (the better to blind by closeness and gobble up), and have
no need to envelope; am also a nomad—the faithful nomad—grinding
teeth and chewing nails, both of which are now impossible. Our
friends do reform. My favorite Heddy over in Paris, now all slim and
remarried, no longer tells of orgies and new bars but speaks instead
of the fluctuating price of cauliflower. *Oui, je te pardonne. Mais
seras-tu jamais réconcilié au fait qu'en essayant de m'aimer tu avais
découvert quelque chose en toi que tu aurais préféré ignorer?*

I could no more dare make an authentic list of loves than a total list of *cuites*. Europe is away from my life. And Maggy Teyte and Zorina are (or *were*, a few years back) the cultured American's idea of a Frenchwoman, unrealistic as Fifi d'Orsay, or as we think Beckett (whom I hate) or Ionesco are French. Small wonder that the moon is sought just by soldiers. We are unclear on our nationalities. Yes, conversations are a chore, and as we grow on the efforts of a diary are increasingly tedious.

> *... that doom of genius — the individual's powerlessness in the face of his own powers.*
>
> ISAK DINESEN

The compulsion to compose was with me, until the age of about twenty-eight, as intense as the compulsion to drink—and I was helpless before both: music flowed out of my body like a sweet but slightly sick liquid, and liquor flowed back into it during increasingly frequent periods of *violent relaxation*. This all began in earliest childhood, for both the alcoholic and the creator are latent in the personality long before the first drinks. But today I have much less a *need* to compose than to be appreciated through my composition. I know of what I'm capable, so the muse becomes less significant than the goal. Excessive drinking is a sign of "immaturity," yet the fairyland of youth is the one thing, if when lost, loses the artist. Drinking is childish, creative activity childlike. These two qualities are similar only as black to white and must never be confused.

Summer feels finally here; we've had no spring, just a long mild winter during which there were flashes of summer (not spring) showing the way Mrs. Depencier (our fifth grade teacher)'s silver blouse used to shine through her slashed sleeves twenty-four years ago when our minds were less on the blackboard than on the sound of a Good Humor wagon through the math class window coming with the first odors of forsythia and roses and the first fragrance of young boys and girls. This I mention because yesterday Bruce Phemister and Charles Mather came to dine with me on Thirteenth Street and we literally wallowed back with giggles to mutual recollection of our communal nursery school in Chicago. Then Bill Flanagan gave a debtor's party for a few composers and nobody got drunk (even Mark Bucci and Lockrem Johnson) because I've been in A.A. for five days (tonight I'll go to still another meeting with Bill I., who's been in for ten years).

Summer feels finally here but yes, those announcing flashes were showing as far back as March 1st when at Larry Rivers' I sat for the portrait which was ultimately rejected as a music cover because Mr. Hinrichsen thought the fingerprints looked grimy (which they did, but they were part of the picture). So the August winds of March floated through the rooms as I sat face to face with Larry whose large sketch pad was upon his knees spread wide apart and my eyes *had* to concentrate upon this zone while I wondered how can all those rumored drinks and pills allow him nevertheless to get up and paint compulsively through the day as I used to do but do no more!

With the wind of real Augusts I used to walk with thin Nancy Mitford in those endless mountains behind Hyères between goat bells and sundowns, while today I can't I can't I can't go back to France. The murderous vain dumbness of our strong new scary world makes an ever-huger moral distance between here and there in space and time; there are not poems, but science, and I'm four years out of my generation; what's the use now of recalling the snow dancing around the Paris gaslamps or the summer smell of boys far off? Even longer ago in Morocco with Guy we drove Yvonne Loriod over to Meknès where in an old schoolroom she played for us Albéniz. Today she and all the others, except me, follow their interests with focus (or do I just *think* so?); it's recent enough for me still to identify — and I've too much empty leisure. What lasts?

After nine years across the ocean in countries crammed with historic masterpieces, I've returned (for some reason) to where there are none: to mediocrity in high position, to no more true terror or art, just small *ennuis*, science and jealousy. New York streets, an avalanche of realities like rent and taxes and laundry and canned beans and earning a living and dying. At least it's definite now: Lenny Bernstein will do my new Symphony with the Philharmonic next April. How will I wait? and what shall I write and love between now and then? "In the Summer House"? There was a festival for San Antonio on Sullivan Street, a slum proudly ornamented with great electric clover leaves studded with ruby bulbs, and they sold pink-candy-cotton in the undrunken dancing and pinball machines. I liked that! It's summer all over.

Sauguet says, when I offer to pay the check after our first meal in a restaurant together circa 1949: *"Non! c'est vous qui payerez quand vous sortirez le compositeur de huit ans."*
　　When, for Ulysses Kay, I judged the B.M.I. competition, there were entries by infant composers whose *métier* was phenomenal. That's just the trouble!

Bill Connors, at a bleak midwestern roadhouse counter, asks for a hamburger. The waiter yells the order through the kitchen porthole, then goes immediately *himself* to prepare it. No one else is in sight.
　　In the New York autumn of 1946 I made these entries in this diary:

> No one is in sight. This three-day phase of willed waste was climaxed and can be temporarily dismissed. Rolled and beaten seven times this month, and room robbed twice. If only I could be generous of myself. But when my madness reaches a pitch the nastiness is highest and my shyness seems coldness; when I manage no responsibilities and don't write any music then the total stink of my character becomes insupportable to the nose of the whole city. Picking my nose this morning was like applying a small sharp shovel to a shredded velvet carpet. The visitor didn't mind—even gave *me* a dollar, longshoreman from Jersey. David says my tastes are masochistic—but even the cruelest need loving. I have a half a bottle of Calvert's left, but as usual I spent all my money again. I'll stop drinking now for a few days to finish my organ piece for Paul.
> 　　Yes yes, it's come to that. Nothing—sex, nothing is so important as alcohol. And yet returning here alone I sit inert. How I envy. How I envy. And overcome this hideous shyness drinking, drinking.
> 　　I confess that when I contemplate suicide as I do daily there's an element of sour grapes. I don't know why I want to. Don't know why. I've been drinking every night for a week. All I want is to cry. I'm jealous and dishonest. If I don't get laid soon I'll collapse. Yet I won't allow it. Don't like people, really. When I go out tonight I don't care if I come back dead.

Was interrupted (at 3 A.M.) because of Eddie's arrival directly after the soldier left. As for returning dead, of course I didn't, but with Alfonso Ossorio we all went to hear Billie Holiday who came to drink stingers at our table and I went down on her in front of everyone because of her extravagant beauty and because she smells like a Catholic church, not perfume but incense. But I only toyed with her legs, for in that shallow grandeur is an austere intimacy. I find Alfonso charming.

So of course I hinted all my troubles to M. and she is worried. Having been raging for over two-thirds of the past three weeks I've nearly lost my face. To reassure the family I say that I shall discipline myself without the aid of an analyst. God but we are truly of one blood. M. and I may be self-indulgent but that doesn't make a personal world seem less cruel. In phenomenal promiscuity (during which there's certainly never been realized "the function of the orgasm") which is sublimated to alcohol, am I retreating from love or doubts of talent?

This evening Janet Lauren did two of my songs on her program. I was moved. Paul Goodman was here and comforted me. Jim O'M. just went home, wouldn't come in. I can't formalize or write or write or write!!! Yesterday was lost.

Tomorrow Grace and I will go to the dance class. Tonight I must stay home, and alone. And read *Dead Souls*. How long, O Lord?

> *And in those days shall men seek death,*
> *and shall not find it; and shall desire to die,*
> *and death shall flee from them.*
> REVELATION 9:6

How long — was thirteen years.

At fourteen my first liquor was tasted with friends as an experimental joke, but doubtless I had the liquory temperament (or disposition) long before. Being a younger-brother who from the start was never discouraged in his talent, I dearly loved my entire family. Still do. We were Quakers of the intellectual rather than the puritanical variety. Nevertheless, the Friends Meeting (which in form and content is not dissimilar to A.A.) lacked an immediate poetry which I later sensed in the silver incense of a Catholic mass, eventually in musical composition, and finally in rye whisky. But Catholicism was forbidden: Quakers inspire restraint which, in my case, was manifested in shyness.

I loved those first drinks. And although the gaudily imaginative and experimental set in which I moved drank a good deal, I needed more. Of the "upper-middle-class" with few financial worries, by eighteen I was already a "problem drinker" without realizing it. Never a social drinker unless social can be called forcing friends to stay out all night. Never a morning drinker, unless morning drink can be called the one taken at noon just before going to bed. Never a lone drinker, unless alone can be called the last one in the bar. Sometimes I'd have a first drink alone (I've never taken only one), but its taste brought desire for company and I'd call friends, or go out to *find* friends, to have *fun*, the fun that was later to become frightened boredom, a soured magic. Any friend will do: an addict spends years of melancholy obliteration with people inferior to himself: an intellectual half-nourished on garbage which shames him the next day.

During college the drinking was periodic: exaggerated affectionate weekend binges. At the same time I was passionate about music, and like most young creators would forget myself in work for fourteen hours a day. Because I have never believed in (or at least been able to practice) moderation, today still, and probably always, I do all to excess, am hooked on work. On the wagon I feel *immoderately sober*, never wanting the poison of liquor to infect the now-purified system. . . . At sixteen, when still living at home, I used to have acquaintances phone my parents at 5 A.M. to say I wouldn't be back that night, and would end up in vague hotels. I drank to be grown-up—and the word *alcoholic* had a ring of glamour; I wanted any and all to know I drank: it was "interesting," romantic, to be a lush! Not for years did the lying begin, and I would invent a cold to avoid appointments, instead of admitting to the hangover of which I was formerly so proud.

I am thirty-four. Drinking has occupied two-thirds of my life, and already a combined total of several wet years, has, in a way, been effaced from memory. How did I ever get all that work done? Yet professional success began quite early; and the reputation, which is generally odious, of most drunks was, in my case, one of eccentricity, since artists are conceded to be unmanageable. And when tight I was able to overcome the heavy natural timidity and carnal inhibition which I still retain.

But in my early twenties inordinate rationalizations (which only other drinkers can fathom), procrastinations, undependability, irresponsible reputation, ever-increasing hangovers drenched in self-pity and remorse, all converged in a plot against me, and, to preserve sanity (and also due to an innate sense of order and well-developed ego) I began this diary devoted in part to musical notions, in part to alcoholic reporting on hallucinations and all they imply. Now the *word*, once written, is infallible to the gullible, and I felt, with depressed reasoning, that I could allow anything so long as it was in systematic narration. This started a period of self-indulgence maintained here ever since.

I was inclined usually to write mainly when sad, omitting expanses when reasonably happy or too busy to report my slips. Nevertheless in rereading I am touched by the weight of oppression through the years: how many hundred times did I move in an unremembered dream from party to bar, and room to room, falling, collecting unaccountable scars, playing the fool and confusing the days, wetting the bed and awakening on pillows caked with vomit, hand too shaky to work, tongue bitten like a sponge, character too humiliated (in moments of sobriety) to look anyone in the eye! Work and play became separate as Jekyll and Hyde, and I learned to divorce drink completely from music. Sometimes after a week's carelessness I returned home to find my talent stifled, like a canary lying in the cage dead of hunger. Blackouts so-called seemed less and less amusing, would awaken in beds of strangers, any age or creed or sex, monsters miles from home. The glamorous taste and miraculous effect of the first drinks taken in respectable company would lead deep into evenings of dubious encounter when I'd swallow anything, mix gin with rum, beer with wine, whiskies with each other, averaging twenty-five a night. But not all nights. I was never hospitalized, never had D.T.'s. Despite an enormous capacity I always *showed* my drinking, though far back in the brain perhaps there lurked a secret ordered lucity.

In 1947, at the suggestion of friends and in acceptance of the then-cultural vogue, I began psychoanalysis, heavy Freudian sessions thrice a week for a year. It's hard to know if this helped; I'd ostensibly gone to be rid of causes, and though I had occasion to speak of only myself and adventured deep into the ever-widening cave of the heart, I did not amend my pattern in practice. It was always easier to give "shocking details" to close friends than to the doctor. After a year I was wiser maybe, but can one know if the couch or just living was the means? At any rate I stopped analysis abruptly in 1948.

Because I won a cash prize (and instead of wishing to spend this on the analyst) I decided to go to France as a summer tourist — but didn't return here to live for eight years! The first of these years passed in a fairyland which only the "ex-patriot" who thinks he's shed his origins can understand. I had *not* left behind in America the infantile qualities of background which made alcohol appealing. Drinking is contagious and I will grow nervous at being near when I cannot participate. But I swallow differently, will not do it alone, therefore try to drag all others down too. The classical pattern: split personality; with the first sips I grow elated and "witty," then turn to nonphysical belligerence, twisting a knife in a companion's most vulnerable wounds, finally crumble in a babble of self-pity and obliteration of unhealthy sleep, awakening twelve hours later in aching remorse to find the typewriter stolen and blood on the bathroom floor.

I have two needs — to compose, and to drink. These comprise good and evil, white and black, high and low, agreeable responsibility and total perdition; they are intermingled and at swords' points; conceivably one could not exist without the other — but the conflict (and the possibility that it may always be present) saddens me.

In Morocco from 1949 to 1952 I abstained, partly for love and the routine of work, but also because geographically the country is not given to the bar life of Anglo-Saxons. Without, therefore, the possibility of drunken adventure with other drunken adventurers I remained under control and accomplished a great deal during this happiest period. On intermittent trips to Paris, however, I made up for lost time, and would then return to Fez with a sense of having again wasted myself in gratuitous binges. As though the ways of our world did not punish us sufficiently for us not to add a new self-punishment! "Is my flesh of brass?" said Job. Yet we continue. Yes, I am thirty-four, but still for nearly twenty years I have drunk to stop time, retarding myself to a simpler speed. One by one I nervously saw most drinking friends amend their adolescent habits, shape themselves into what's called the *normal* life; "nervously," I say, and vaguely surprised, for at the start, just as everyone on earth was a composer like myself, I also casually assumed that everyone had a liquor problem. Only in later years did I feel isolated or individual. It's not that I need to be understood, but I need *not* to be misunderstood. "What a pity," they said, "that nice talented boy willfully destroying all God gave him!"

Yes, certain geographies do not lend themselves to contagions of drink. I have been drunk in Italy, but only with Americans: that country's temperament is not alcoholized. Oh, to invent a land within, which could withstand the insane rationalizing of the alcoholic who feels his imminent fall! Oh, the desire for cleanliness that comes after drinking: you even wash the soap.

The joys of a clear morning head are preferable to weeks when knowingly I didn't bathe, masochistic netherland of sweat, anonymous hotel rooms, hotel rooms where heart and bed seemed bursting with urine, bleeding and blasting through my anvil head. Could I force myself to do sober what was avoided when drunk? I accept the sterile abyss behind, but the prospect of being unable to plan because of similar abysses stretching (half-voluntarily) until I die could cause a suicide today. No man's an island and half my life's been lived; liquory joys have long evaporated, yet I crazily persist, trying to *swallow myself into the past*. And hide it. And the mocker's mocked. And deathly sick of the make-believe hangover-sexuality when only the body is present. And having written this, and all this through the years, knowing, hating, I am still capable of going out now and getting blind drunk. One must have the conviction that alcohol is negative in order to give it up. I'm not convinced.

New York and New England

Rien que cette jeunesse qui fuit devant la vie.

ELUARD

At 1:30 A.M., back in the New York of May 29, 1947, my purple ideas on sound were as follows:

Music is the greatest art, the only one which removes us utterly from Earth. Other mediums do it partially but none so completely — that is, for a long enough period to instill at least a temporary change. Music puts us where daily things (living or inanimate) are not. Painting removes us only to another worldly place, another position from where we see objects or landscapes, not with new eyes (naturally) but from new angles. The validity of an art's strength is judged by its magnitude of transport (i.e., does it *send* us). Others try to incorporate into their expression the necessarily abstract impulses found solely in music, for it is toward music which they involuntarily aspire. Painting enlarges scope, literature renovates psychology, but both refer to the finite. They can be eternal, but music alone is infinite. Science excites romantic contemplation on other eternities, dance inspires our most antique catharsis; but definitely these are never all abstract, and total abstraction artificially produced is the nearest thing to sense-genius. The nearest thing to music is mathematics, they say, but also the farthest in that mathematicians are not concerned with exciting our emotions. (Musicians can add and subtract pretty well, and mathematicians like to play in string quartets. That's about as far as it goes.)

Enjoyment I cannot conclude from atonality in music or surrealism in letters. I like surrealist paintings and movies, and these mediums in employing expressionism I like (the latter would correspond to atonality). I think it is because dream, or nonconscious symbols (surrealism being psychoanalytic) are essentially visual, and hence more convincing in painting, which can separate comic or tragic variations in form and bright color, than in poems, which put into words that which in this case is not spoken. Expressionism is a detailed re-depiction of basic sensations (ordinary objects become emotional experiences), so music could of course never express this — not being concerned with objects — whereas in poem or piece of art such as *Caligari* it is successful. Atonality, then, by this definition, cannot work. But many atonal compositions (12-tone or otherwise) are certainly convincing and beautiful.

This is because their core is tonal, and they are expressionist only in that the whole is made of many segments.

Today I'm not clear what I was driving at. But I am clear about the only trouble with Milton Babbitt being that he still takes music seriously. As though it mattered! Still, if he's going to be serious at least he should be consistent. In his recent article he not surprisingly gives the impression that whoever doesn't think as he does doesn't exist. But quite surprisingly he illogically equates music with mathematics by suggesting that a concert audience should be as formally equipped as an audience at a lecture about advanced mathematics, as if science weren't a means to an end, and art an end in itself. They all speak of progress, of evolution, as though these terms were more inevitably applicable to a healthy musical growth than to a cancer.

Summertime in a great city and a damp musky summer *entrejambes* stimulating fragrance sets my expectant nerves on edge but I never give in. I could almost enjoy the relief of suffering again: it's been long and living's drab without it. One does, and doesn't, grow out of the habit. Looking gold as a peach and fragile as a fawn, without knowing how to *give*, though ripe for midsummer orgies with soldiers as in those first war years. If my enthusiasm for work has grown blasé, could a new intimate body in love still let me share Kepler's exhilaration when, after 6,000 years, he found the solar system's movement like a labyrinth of silvery veins and vessels and blood color of jet, platinum, and cobalt?

A composer isn't necessarily profounder than "real" people, but what profundity he does have he necessarily communicates.

Tomorrow I hope to clinch the rights for *Mamba's Daughters* with Audrey Wood and Dorothy Heyward. But if I *do*, then I'll have to write it, and (for the record) I've been drinking stupidly again and feel uninspired. Despite my complaints do I really want love? The fussy order of my habits keeps everything at arm's length. Day after day of heat and rain has brought insects to Manhattan, and I sleep badly. Because abstinence through A.A. has been an endurance contest and not a state of grace.

When he sees a beauty in the street, Norris Embry says (in parody of an A.A. slogan): "There with the grace of God go I."

If I abandon alcohol, what will become of that dear obstreperous kid I've been taking out on a leash for years? I've never made a clean break with another person, much less with myself.

Have been rereading my diaries: eleven, twelve, thirteen years ago was the same drunken slobber about the overwhelmingness of liquor as a beloved in this life. What does not happen to me is my own fault. Another love will be resignation, an event impossible to evade. But sentiment, like history, does not exist while it is being made.

Living by formula if not by order, yet suffering daily from someone new never seen. Those first diaries showed a world detachment much more *accusé* than today.

Like Roosevelt I will always have friends, though my life's seemed scandalous to some, and a total freedom for work which has never "paid."

Stockyards are concentration camps, butchers are undertakers. It's exciting. A funeral in the treetops.

Spray Beach. So here I am at a Jersey shore hotel with parents and two nephews for a few days of sunlight and a hair-raising glimpse of Atlantic City. A little bored, it's not unpleasant. I love hotel rooms anywhere in the world: Oran, Santa Marguerita (a year ago), or Germany. Concrete worries are only that the rent's too high, and how will I practically reconcile the joys of unemployment insurance to a month's absence in Peterborough during September?

Already at fourteen I was anxious about rum cake, or sherry in soup. (*When* will they pass a third round of drinks, O Lord?!) In the freedom of sobriety I grow nostalgic for my prison of the past. I, too, thought I was insane. Consummation can come to the hysterical approach.

Gertrude Stein writes a French English. Julien Green an English French. Hence the disturbing appeal of their styles. Because who before has ever used Gallic wit and compression successfully in an Anglo-Saxon tongue? or written of miserly Protestant small-town American old maids in the sensual Latin language?

A plague of children. NO LOITERING. The importance of odor. The ecstasy of the armpit, the right crotch, the loved human breath, fragrance of one's own knee in the sunlight (smell of the sun), or of your best friend's hair.

Still in the evening New Jersey lobby and about me radios, the *Saturday Evening Post*, Scrabble players, a defunct sunset, etc.

   Again A.A. I also cannot sleep and grow irritable at the time of the full moon. The star pupils of our meeting are Charlie Jackson and Bill I. (A month ago, on finding himself alone with me, he jumped into my lap like a Saint Bernard imagining himself a Pomeranian.) At the "closed group sessions" long hours can be spent on how to alleviate melancholia. But this ain't an "alcoholic question" (better stated: how do we avoid *drinking* when depressed or elated?). As Inge justly quotes: "To know life is to know conflict," and the soberest teetotalers can be suicides. At least after two new weeks of sobriety my fantasies are not of golden martinis floating through the sky, but of fudge sundaes or cherry-cheese pie. . . . After the meeting, cake, soft drinks and coffee are served, with a special late-late coffee hour at the nearest Schrafft's. Standard classic slogan: One drink is too many and forty aren't enough. Jay Harrison suggests that the meanest man of the year would be he who spikes the punch at an A.A. meeting! Meanwhile we all grow fat on milkshakes.

Plan a study on lawless misdemeanors in the Old Testament, and name it "Go Down Moses."

   I came to pray and remained to scoff. In spite of nineteen completely sober days, some mornings I still wake up thinking "hangover"; my relief's a clear wind. On correct calculation I have, between the first of the year and June 23rd, been drunk forty-six times (or an average of twice a week), and four times since my first A.A. meeting June 25th.

A nonalcoholic takes a drink or three or sometimes even gets drunk without worrying much about it. But I think and think and think and think. Normal responses which most *living people* take for granted have now for me a new unfearful significance and a sort of charmed open joy: mornings with a clean head, grass and water, a shopkeeper's smile, work without fright. Nor do I even consider its continuation.

I am wrong to say a drunkard's only a drunkard when he's drunk. Alcoholism is a state of mind which can continue even after years of sobriety. A thought of wine can be as sap to a rose or maple. Loud lamenting on sterility soon makes me potent, silent. Suddenly I'm writing four orchestral poems at once: *Eagles, Pilgrims,* a *Chaconne,* an Overture (which was to have been for *Mamba's Daughters*).

The end of a beginning. It is 2 A.M. Starting the 27th day of new sobriety.

For how long have I been thinking All's contained in me? It's the afternoon of my 35th year when I admit that, if I am of our world, so then are the subtle inventions of my dreaming from the flesh or dust or faint recall of it. If the molecules of my imagination are part of the solar system, did they exist before my birth awaiting my organization? or were they contained in order even then? I wrote that I "knew all about life except how to live it." It's difficult to believe that, although an alcoholic personality is formed quite early, a solution for its outlet can be discovered before puberty. (If Utrillo was hospitalized at ten it must have been for malnutrition and the wine that's in all French families.) The full moon prevents sleep. The saint in hell. "Old-fashioned" in music is self-imitation: the *new* is outmoded with Billie Holiday: her oldest records remain the truest. Black-male.

In December of 1952 while thinking and sitting alone in my ninth-floor room at the Chelsea Hotel in the rain around 2 A.M., I passed the most peculiar moment of my life without action or décor. What else can be said? Because a strange sensation may not be notated and still remain strange. But later, far down in the street I heard the automobiles driving by, driving by in the rain and one of them skidded, then drove on. Where, at this minute, is that car's driver? Where was I? Where will I be in ten minutes? Creation is the recall of something which never occurred.

      False pretenses? *True* pretenses!

Miss Marva Torture. The violent sea storms which have been raging around here are officially given girls' names: Hurricane Daisy, Hurricane Cleo, etc. At Schrafft's is a confection called Amber Mist. Like female impersonators others are: Heather Burns, Pleasant Change, Sylvia Sorrows, Sandra September, Sally You, Witch Craft, Hanna Henna, Miss April Friday. And a new perfume called Get Her. Miss January Summer, Miss Arabella Fantasy, and Miss Fern Sherbet. A massacre of mascara. His ideal dream— *To Be Fucked by the Unknown Soldier.*

Today I have been five weeks "dry." On Labor Day, I leave by plane for a whole September of work at the MacDowell Colony. I've sublet for $135 this apartment in the building where twelve years ago Kubly lived twice the size for half the price. Yes, our living is circular. Being obliged to forego the $45 weekly unemployment insurance, I hope to resume it in October.

Peterborough, N.H. September, 1958
The leaves, the cleanliness, the cool sun, the steeples. I can't believe it! Not since childhood have we been here. Our living *is* circular.

Begin article (or program notes, or something) with Yeats' quote: " . . . those dying generations at their song." *Making Pieces Today.* . . . Anyone goes nowhere. But a painter's blood drips precision and his weakest canvas glows a healthy red. Etc.

End: An artist should think he is able for all. Though nobody goes everywhere. I'm thirty-four. For twenty years I've had an "alcoholic problem." Today a group therapy helps battle compulsion. Has anything been lost or repaired, after or before? The artist's Bad is as good as his Good if not too many dishes are smashed in domestic quarrels.

Picasso: Every artist is half man and half woman, and the woman is usually insupportable.

Harp, Flute—Boys, boys
Flute, Cello—Boys, girls
Fruit Jello—Girls, boys
Cello, Harp—Girls, boys (for parties)
Harp, Flute, Cello—Boy!

The metronomic value of my normal heartbeat is 74½.

I love profoundly, and always have, both parents. And used to be shy. Logic helps to overcome it.

Question: Do you like Keats? Answer: I don't know what they are. (Brahms and Yeats may also be used.)

She combs her hair, not brushes it. Like painting a jewel, not polishing.

This morning Ralph Shapey came out with the old romantic banality that the basic instinct is fear, birth a traumatic shock. But *why*? What of the frisking newborn colt? Or the throbbing cocoon from which a near-finished butterfly strives to emerge, a tiny rainbow, and fly far off? Or the mass of eggs bursting together into the yellow contentment of perfect chicks? Maybe the infant makes a screech of joy from his successful effort to escape the black unfragrant womb. In all the universe natural life seeks light. The joys of being born. The joys of birth. The silence of real luxury. The virtues of idleness.

Blaze of change in the healthy green and ill red of fall each morning as I trot to my quiet studio for long hours' work, and the routine of each day is unchanged, offers no problems. A luxury prison. The necessary Prison of Creation. The MacDowell Colony. It will soon be a year since I last left Europe.

Here in New Hampshire I'm up every morning before eight — which is a good three and a half hours earlier than for years I've been rising in the city. When I return to New York in October I will have accomplished a great deal: in eleven days I've already finished *Pilgrims* (based on *Le Voyageur sur la Terre*, the most disturbing story I know) and am well into the orchestration of *Eagles*. There are few distractions — just a nonsexual routine. If there are no "possibilities," neither are there temptations, so one thinks of other things with evenings passed in the unstimulating though pleasant enough company of "average scholars," mostly playing Chinese checkers with Louise Talma. It is the abstinent productive countryfied solitary cooling time of year when one "takes stock." Suddenly, after a decade and a half of obsessed song writing I find the human voice hateful and opera silly: singing is bastard, pitched words superfluous, and I want to write just music with titles. This is what I feel while building the morning fire in my isolated studio and smelling clearer than yesterday those fires of olive wood on winter days in Fez as I orchestrated the First Symphony nine years ago. And I've never liked anything Spanish: zarzuelas, black enthusiasm, castanets, the corrida. Why? My nephew Paul, age five, asks: "Are you a grown-up?" How do I answer?

The surrealists were positively anti-music. In fact the only literary movement ever to take up music is our own America's "cool generation" and it's done it all lazily and wrong.

Woolcott Gibbs, Vaughan Williams, and Florent Schmitt have just died.

I know more people than anyone and, what's more, they believe what I say, which is always surprising since I never say what I mean and up here they don't dig my number, which is *pince-sans-rire* and "I love the movies more than anything" though I've overcome my timidity through years of persevering logic, and other people are dumb too.

The entire sun belongs to that lizard stretched naked beneath it there.

No longer the spoiled child of the Paris years, nor as young as I used to be. My work must now speak, if not *for*, at least *with* me. (I couldn't convince Audrey Wood through charm alone!) When Thomas Mann in 1940 came to lecture of war at Northwestern I disguised myself as Tadzio and sat in the front row of Scott Hall imagining to divert him — without avail. With Bruce Phemister in grammar school in our unchanged voices we phoned expensive restaurants commanding rare menus never to be paid for (that was when I learned of hollandaise sauce), or from the florist ordered gardenia ships sent C.O.D. to rich classmates. When Dietrich said "noblesse oblige" that night, my reaction was: Who does she think she is, Marlene Dietrich?

Working well: a long fructuous spasm. That's why the diary's dull. Rain, rain and a state of unrest here because of a strange series of thefts in the colony studios.

I recall an uneasy breakfast ten years back at five in the afternoon with poor Peter Marchant (dead now, leaving Van Vechten's biography unfinished) who said that constant carousing had come to make my cheeks look like lard and ashes. Always in music I overmix colors as I do perfume, flowers. Rain.

Music titles: The Jail of Rain, Invisible Cages, Chaconne on Drowning, A Quaker Prayer, Homage to Movies, *Le Pardon de la Mer* (a custom in Brittany).

The poet always knows where he's going, though he doesn't always know he knows. He works in showing what he didn't know he knew.

My romantic defeat is in desiring the role of Innocent Master. Love without love: the melancholy of masturbation: builds to nothing.

We think of Death as White Dressed in Black, but dying foliage takes the color of human health. Why in fall are red leaves red? Because that season wounds the forest. And I seem to pass my days in wounding orchestration paper with a razor blade. . . . My dreams are so real that the pain of daily awakening is like pulling a scab from the wound of day. The pain of missing Europe is sometimes unbearable. Yet I can get up with joy in the early country. My passivity has more power than your aggression; your action's weaker than my passion; my passivity thicker than your activity.

Moon. The crescent sets fire to platinum trees. The pain of burning logs which take so long to die. Not being a poet by trade I can afford the banalities of nostalgia while smelling back through the years those childhood apples of Oberlin or Yankton, and later of Fez. The nights are already very cold and the days rainy and isolated. New York will be shocking.

This afternoon during an hour at Esphir Slobodkina's cottage, I painted a picture which turned out to be a cat's face. Now I've always hated cats (being jealous I suppose, because I'm like them, and wise to their crafty ways). This cat is seen inside out, his purple flesh and chartreuse arteries lay bare to the surgeon's knife. But I didn't know what it was until Esphir told me.

We never really get accustomed to beauty, nor to eccentricity. I learn too quickly, I get the hang of games and trades, and so lose interest in the concentration of perfection (or at least of certain perfections). But we never forget our first step forward though it is followed by an infinite number of identical steps. I can recall the circumstances of each new French word learned, yet I have used them all ten thousand times since. And do not the reflexes of Jean Lafont oblige him, after years of feeding his bulls at night, to recoil before the fiercest, even as I, a novitiate, do? We are never reconciled to beauty, and I am glad to see Marie Laure still clap her hands at what I'd take for granted she takes for granted. What! does the artist pause before the empty canvas, the white page, the blank staff? The beginner doesn't know that this first pause of "where-am-I?" will be forever repeated.

After a dark New England week we are now released from our prison of raindrops. Half of the colonists have already left and I too will next week if Mother and Father come to drive me back. I am always austere.

The Young are always young, but the Old are young and old, and so the Young have the advantage.

Bees, hornets, wasps, spider webs, gnats, ants, daddy longlegs blur and imprison my reading in the sun. Apparently I once had appeal: I was led to believe and said it myself often enough. I am weathering well: not resignation (which I dreaded) but simply through involuntarily new interests. The pleasures of insanity.

Yes, the leaves by the billions have a stained glass pale orange and pink. And on the 30th (after a month of this sexless and profitable protected pastorale) I return to urban agitations via Boston, where I'll spend twenty-four hours just sight-seeing alone.

Since tomorrow I leave and time will start again, I'll write a page here while there is still no time. Intoxication. I used to drink because I thought I ought to, though an acceptance in politeness could start off days of oblivion. Yes, I am aware of all the true reasons *why* I drink (as well as the false ones *when* I drink) but knowing them is no prevention. I've been "dry" now for ten weeks, the longest in my life (longest *what*?), though Eleanor before I left New York had "gone" nine months, the length of a pregnancy, which makes her an honest woman. There is no thought of alcohol in the MacDowell Colony because there is no life of either past of future but only a storehouse release where the concentration is on forming memory from memories.

New York, Autumn 1958
Thoughts from Boston: All that can still inhibit me is the living proximity of a myth: the possible lover, the famous poet, the beautiful actress; that is, someone who can *do* something tangible (or changeable) to and for me. So I'm struck dumb.

The museums there showed John Singer Sargeant, the Henry James of pictures. The Harvard campus, alone, early evening and the dormitories begin lightening as the students (nervous from first late classes) return to jerk off. Those varied and vast minorities to which I belong.

Pain of good-bye. Yet I came back a week ago, afraid, inhibited, and broke ten weeks of abstinence built carefully as a web. *Back to unreality*, I like to call it; for when, in New York, are we willing to find five reflective minutes?

The hideous hours of early evening.

Yesterday night, after the A.A. meeting, Norris and I visited Eugene [Istomin] who is now *the* "successful pianist." (The pope died as we were talking.) Norris on the one hand, just home from Greece, is more shaken up than ever, needs a lawyer, has no focal point of American ambition. Eugene on the other hand is calm and established, professional and uncreative, rich in the way he wishes. There I lie in the middle: well-launched but without a performance, the envy of many but without a cent, and miracles no longer come (though we get out of only what we put into our miracles). Art, if you'll pardon the expression, is dying: its audience has grown huge while its makers have melted into such tiny specialists that there'll be no miracle here. Certainly our eyes admiring a masterpiece cannot see the same thing as those that looked one hundred or two years ago. As for A.A. its principles don't evade the agreement of my intellect, but it's no easy joke to relinquish live drinking, to become a dead drunk (meaning a *former* drunk). I am Saint Augustine still moaning. Lord, make me good—but not yet! A drunk in the back row complains that women on the wagon grow frigid, to which Ann G. retorts: not frigid, just fussy. There is nobody but people around. I am all reticence or dogma,

deaf also, and they don't listen anyway. I said: there is no more connection between a novelist and playwright than between a dancer
and an actor. Eleanor says: but didn't Ruby Keeler happily combine
the two?

An American composer must live here whether he likes it or
not. Whether he knows it or not it is here that his most interesting
problems will at least be presented if not solved. Norris (always in
trouble) says the Sartrian French agonize in the shadow—not the
substance—of the past. Who then are *we* while over there? Hermits
in a bird sanctuary? living in nature as though we were it? We aren't.

PART 9
Autumn, 1958

Pennsylvania and New York

In some strange way we devalue things as soon as we give utterance to them. We believe we have dived to the uttermost depths of the abyss, and yet when we return to the surface the drop of water on our pallid fingertips no longer resembles the sea from which it came. We think we have discovered a horde of wonderful treasure-trove, yet when we emerge again into the light of day we see that all we have brought back with us is false stones and chips of glass. But for all of this, the treasure goes on glimmering in the darkness unchanged.

MAETERLINCK

In madmen the fascination of the aberrant idea, the fascination of the thing that should not be done, operates by virtue of the same laws that govern expression and the works of art in general.

HENRI MICHAUX

The Mescaline House. Although tonight I'm exhausted from the weekend John G. arranged at his house in Crescoe, Pa., so that Paul Bowles and I (and he and a friend Anthony) could have an experiment in mescaline effects, I want nevertheless to note here the sequence of reactions while they're fresh.

Preliminarily let it be said that two exterior elements of preconditioning prejudiced — or at least tainted — my relish of the drug. First is a relation to Paul, who fascinated me from our first meeting in Taxco 1941 (I was sixteen) until our orgy of hashish on Rue de la Harpe in 1949 with Bill Flanagan and Shirley Gabis. I need him to know I exist, that I too am aware of evil (which however I am not in the sense he is). Second is the unheeded warning from Jane F., my A.A. sponsor, about whom I constantly thought.

As to a knowledge of mescaline itself, I'd read Huxley's first book, but felt already experienced in all that detail. But other fanatics, particularly Bill Miller, had so long sung its praises with such determined astonishment that I could no longer wait. They had explained mescaline as neither a soporific nor a stimulant, but a legal non-addictive device for showing how things are — not how they aren't (as do alcohol, heroin, or the self-imposed dullness of daily living). The pill is theoretically obtainable at any drugstore without prescription, but is now nearly obsolete, its medical function of inciting artificial schizophrenia never having been verified. By diverting us from the constant protective concerns of food and fear, by melting the censorial barriers of conditioning and removing us utterly from ourselves, by chemically lowering the armored instinct of self-preservation, mescaline heightens an awareness of what is about us always but to which we have blinded ourselves in order to live. It deflects from the business of our own death and permits full concentration on the slightest fact of surroundings. Under normal circumstances, perceiving the always present fact is no simple matter, even for the detailed maniac, or the genius who has occasional minutes of illumination which he strives to retain in memory and then preserve in marble. Today, on swallowing a tablet literally anyone can be ex-

posed for hours to a "miracle" which hitherto only an artist or saint
had known in scattered moments.

I had heard of this drug's ability to advance us a million years in
evolution (or does it, rather, advance us backward to how we reacted
in earlier states?), arousing an instant knowledge of true and false,
an intuition of the speech of bees and unspoken thoughts, a recognition of color too bright for casual vision, a sense of electrons revolving in steel one trillion times per second, a sound of the live earth
breathing into the feet—in short, a conscious observance of the never-
still skeleton of our universe: no longer to see "through a glass darkly"
but through the night rent by accurate lightning that continues its
glare making a plausible world of every raindrop. And I had heard
that all this was encountered without loss of control to body or mind,
and no hangover! Who would not be tempted?

So I took mescaline, quite unprepared for what was to be thirteen hours of horror.

John drove Paul and me to his country mansion four hours from
New York. (Anthony joined us later that night.) After some nourish-
ing meals and a wonderful night's sleep we awoke into the fairest
October Sunday one could hope for: acres of personal sky and miles
of forest with blue and magenta leaves in total quiet. Europe may
have the edge on us in many wonders, but nothing equals America's
autumn of which this day was an ideal sample. The house itself was
pleasant enough: Cape Cod cottage combined with heathen seraglio
heaped to bursting with incongruous objects: stones, pods, Audubon
prints, Persian editions, incense, velvet, chains, colors, stuffed animals,
and a live female mongrel named Erix. This décor must have been
established expressly for the use of mescaline novitiates.

We could have chewed John's dried peyote buttons, which are
what the Indian discoverers use and cost seven cents, but as these
cause nausea and hallucinations we swallowed instead, precisely at
2:15, the fifteen-dollar pills—although neither button nor pill was
advisable for the weak liver of Paul, who was submitting to the experience as to a necessary operation.

For an hour, no effect. Paul and I strolled through the forest to a
little river while the others weeded the garden. Then began an
agreeable withdrawal as with an overdose of codeine. Things seemed

the same (meaning beautiful as they should be right then) but lips
grew icy, and face, and finally whole body, and as Paul was shivering
we returned to the house. Neither of us had expected physical effects,
but they grew worse. Our host and his friend now reappeared with
prehistoric grins, and henceforth all came thick and fast.

We were invaded by violent lassitude in which the visual was
superclear. John took me to see a rose in the cool sun shuddering
with luminous crimson pleasure: a puff of cigarette smoke and the
flower recoiled. The cigarette was ludicrous, tasted false. We walked
through a wood where trees murmured with reason: each seemed
at once male and female embracing itself, arching toward the sky, to
live, with ten thousand leaves twittering correctly. All was Life: the
sky streaked with ivory veins, the hills breathing, nothing still, everything motion, inhaling, striving, fluttering, speaking delicate wounds.
Whole outdoors a labyrinth of hypersensitivity: the sound of sap in
the maple's arteries, the emerald chlorophyll throbbing through apples in the grass as I stepped compassionately among them. Nature
in her force cares nothing for us except as we unite with her like a
"thinking reed," more reed than thought. Mescaline banishes ambition along with vanity; cigarettes taste false because they have no
part of living. And while on the verge of knowing the animals' language we have no desire to "write all this down for later." We are
Now.

So the effects increased and were not all pleasant. Manmade
insertions into this scene were outrageous: a slash of paint on bark,
a bridge, strips of barbed wire seemed contradictory as death. Autos
on the landscape were ridiculous, even indecent; all human indication
was a blotch of blood. Blood everywhere: the wooden fence was a
tree skinned alive, and a poplar whose low branches had been hacked
off seemed really to gasp. Nature weeps, and though vegetation is
not human we experience the lacerations of fruit or leaf as though
they were ours. For all outdoors is flesh, even the wind.

My own physical state became at that point atrocious and I had
no sense of touch, my body was glass and fear, and both Paul and I
were taken with jitters, chills. Observing the faces of these friends, I
saw only varicosed monsters of arteries and teeth. Teeth (and the
marks of teeth in food) are the ugliest human possession and the real
from the false are instantly perceived. Like cannibals we bite into a

stalk of celery. Once back in the house ice became epileptic fire. The shocks continued.

Looking into a Goya reproduction the artist speaks out and you see through layers to canvas. The three-dimensional photos and advertisements in *Life* magazines scream with the mediocrity of all that's man, and men are vicious sheep, sad and scared. But my own hands were beautiful: a few days ago I had ripped open the cuticle of my thumb: now this small red hole was a great glowing pink marble entrance through which I could gaze into the mechanism of my inner body. I was afraid to turn around, felt menaced from all sides by my companions no longer human—or rather, more human than I, and so ugly. Knives. Everywhere knives and breathing veins. The presence of those kitchen choppers made me want to escape while too heavy on my feet to budge; not the familiar unsteadiness of alcohol for which I am prepared, but a new sluggish lucidity of dope from which there is no turning back. I felt out of control without knowing where to find the safety valve. No blur, it was freezingly clear, a total awareness of the state of unawareness, forced to examine, examine all in novel detail, like it or not, untrained, without order, not understanding pictures which spoke, moving objects, blood on the ceiling, knives, knives. I feared sharpness and being cut or cutting. Outdoors animals screeched, animal night noises all around, the dog looked at us and knew. (Or did she?) Matta's oils bled. My eyes bled. Paul, without feeling it, had a liver attack, his bony hands, luminous green and transparent, clutched at the organ and tore it out as he grinned, his face all molars. Each "normal" experience was now an involuntary experiment of perception. To satisfy this awful energy I drew twenty pictures in five minutes, all of them huge eyes. (John later declared them to be groins.)

Because of how the others looked, I was doubtful about seeing myself since I knew the reflection would be *a truth of flaws* to which I might even be indifferent; yet upstairs in the bathroom mirror I saw no change (except, of course, teeth, always yellow fangs, skeleton bursting out of our mouths, plus a few bemusing wrinkles I'd never admitted), and would have stayed riveted for hours if some flies with monstrous eyes buzzing about the bulb hadn't frightened me. I screamed for help and Paul came up and swatted them. (Poor precious dear sweet brother flies now stupidly dead there in the toilet bowl!)

They said my little speech defect had gone. Colors intensify greatly and take a new sense: synthetic dyes are immediately distinguishable from true vegetable tone. Blindfolded, one tells black from white by touch, and after the first frozen shakiness has worn off one finds a certain level of calm on which to examine. Authenticity can, to an extent, be distinguished from fakery, and the painting the artist made from his wife's menstrual blood looks just that. The stars, the whole mass of heaven, take on a bony form where the planets can be *seen* whirling through space at unthinkable speeds and all movement is related to all other movement. The very globe of our world heaves and perspires beneath the feet. My own face seemed unmarked by the eternal qualities of avarice and anguish, etc. John later said it was a *pure* face as opposed to those other filigrees of rings and shadow. Since I am not basically visual, everything I saw was a revelation, but my reaction to music and literature, which normally mean most, were without interest: it was difficult to concentrate on the printed word, and my discernment in music seemed unchanged although the quality of performance is more obvious. (I would like to have heard some of my own with the intention of finding where I may have "conceded," but I doubt I'd have learned much.) Appetite is decreased and meat—especially its odor—is out of the question. For instance, when the dog was given her supper, the smell infected the entire house like an *abattoir*. (Incidentally, I felt no empathy for the dog because, as Michaux points out, dogs haven't any.) If there is a craving it's for oranges, tomatoes, but it's cruel to eat even them, they shriek.

Loss of balance. Sexual impulse reduced to nothing, though certain affection came after fear of being attacked was overcome. I did not want to be left alone with my razor which gleamed on the table like a gypsy crystal—didn't wish to be left alone yet kept leaving the others to find my own boredom of discovery out in the night which also scared me.

For night had fallen now. It was a green doped nightmare in part quite vulgar. Ambition was plain silly. Paul sometimes reverted to babyhood and I grew protective: qualities opposed to our natures. Of the four, Paul appeared the validest human, especially after nightfall (because sin is for darkness). Then Anthony brought me a welcome cup of tea in what I think was the Holy Grail. Outside we examined the heavens, their careless logic, felt Earth's revolving purpose rightly placed and spinning about the neat framework. Then I peed for the first time since morning.

All had been foreseen in that cat's face painted last month at the Colony. There was nothing, nothing pleasant about it. Around nine the effects wore off, thank God, little by little like petals drooping back into place. During the long postmortem I was told my preadolescent erections were inspired uniquely by sado-masochist images. John said my whole nonpleasurable tantrum was because I just couldn't face the truth mescaline offers. Is it the truth? After twenty years of drinking I am less a prophet for alcohol than he for this. At 3 A.M. after thirteen hours of unbroken tension I retired to a battered insomnia relieved only by an unusual nosebleed. I really learned little, though John's pose of sophisticated despair and nineteenth-century refinement was quite dismaying. (He's always struck me, at least in his writing, as the poor man's Paul Bowles—though of course much richer.) I'm already a selfish poet and since childhood have found flaming cities in the porous furrows of a common brick. Any poet has seen this, though perhaps not with such relentlessness, seen the stars fly and grasped their relation, felt the earth revolving, himself carried along through the galaxy like a well-built boat in the sea. I prefer to learn, to hide, in my own Ned way and never to meet them again.

The truth of beauty was evident, certainly, but had to be counterbalanced by the truth of ugliness. There is no shortcut for paradise, to coin a phrase. Today my eyes ache from having seen too much. Otherwise there is no hangover, the incident is finished. This morning (Monday) before returning to New York we inspected everything again, the trees and skies, the dog, the velvet. Everything looked exactly the same as under mescaline but also exactly different, without the vibrant hideous charm: all was, thank God, now quite banal. I recall the episode as "Dead of Night," a filmed country orgy far off, disagreeably weird, a fourth-dimensional fever, not forgotten but over, unnecessary surgery, a gash in consciousness and conscience, a slash in a vacuum, an acrid perfume which had always been around unsmelled. But I am a nearsighted Norwegian nun who still knows that vision is important only to the blind.

Lions and the sun, two happy fixations. I could wish to be absorbed, gobbled up in the sunburst of a lion's mane. Drowned by the sun.

I've never conceded, nor can ever ever accept the world on its own terms. Because they invent their own rules they avoid the true challenge, and confound creation with color. I pretend to enjoy myself but haven't for years. Yet I fool even me.

Rain, dreary, hangover, weary, it continues. Tomorrow I am thirty-five.

Today I am thirty-five.

Fifteen years ago I had my first public performance of importance: a Psalm for male chorus with woodwinds, played by Bill Strickland with the Army Music School in Washington. I was nineteen. Since then I have written so much vocal music in so many different forms that suddenly the whole effort appears shredded by ridicule and now (for the moment at least) I loathe the human voice, opera's a mockery, songs a profanation. The end. A.A. gave me a birthday party last night at which I didn't show up. And Jean Stein (my "fiancée" who'll be married in a month) gave me pink pajamas from Bergdorf Goodman's. Uncle David died today, And the Harrisons' second daughter was born, named Troy Nedda in my honor.

"Is the bath water hot?" he inquired.

"In a way," she replied.

"And will you go out afterward?" he interrogated.

"There's no place to come back to but home," she retorted.

"Well, did you see Helen today?" he queried.

"Well, in a way," she noncommittalized.

"She *is* very lovely," he exclaimed.

"Vaguely," she proffered.

"Has she been divorced? and did you water the plants?" he desired to know.

"Sort of," retaliated she.

"Whatever became of Maxine Sullivan?" he mused.

"I wouldn't know," she avowed.

"Do you enjoy Michelangelo?" he suggested.

"Oh, somewhat!" she quipped.

"Well then things are back to normal," he ejaculated.

"Or almost," she alluded.

"Oh! la la! and whoops Bessie!" he sighed.

"Soft gentle pussywillows," shrieked she.

"Time is nearly up," he joked.

"Hardly," she agreed questioningly.

"Is the bath water cool?" he stated, amused but bored.

"Kind of," she asked.

And then he added: "The insanity of innocence is also the smile of danger."

The smile of danger. Mescaline. Extreme naïveté is certainly akin to the one-track mind of madness without the art or crime. Ignorant of danger I died of joy a thousand times in the Chicago park of my early teens.

Mescaline: the distortion of accuracy (or vice versa). I'll never be the same again. It functions like the apple of Eden. And I saw death at work in faces, molecules whirling in tables, heard the speech of flowers. There was no place to alight.

Peyote. Today calmly I ask: how does it benefit those plants (99 percent are born to blush untasted) to contain that which may enrich or demolish not only an animal body but a mind? Conversely, could certain flesh produce a corresponding hallucination in certain vegetables? Picture a dahlia raving mad!

It was the most significant single event of my life. By which I mean: self-contained experience within a specific breath of time. Love, for instance, is a continuum. Nor is a wedding an experience, but the preparation for experience. Other events may have been more "important," but less compact, less singular. Nevertheless it is wonderful only in retrospect. Now when passing a meat market with its pink cadavers hooked in the window, or rushing through Times Square in a swarm of apprehensive stares, I say: Thank God I'm not seeing this with mescaline. But on days of pure nature, as with an autumn rainstorm, I wonder nostalgically how those myriad crystals might look if observed through the telescope of our unveiled eye. Or a gigantic microscope. The sky was a naked bulb lighting a concentration camp, an eye that saw all and couldn't shut, the power of lightning that cannot be extinguished, the truth glimpsed by a dying man who cannot expire. Mescaline does for the eye what marihuana does for the nonmusician: helps to dissociate the solos of a jam session. What effect has it on the blind? On lovers? What does love *mean* under it? For it can make us critical but, alas, not creative (though on the surface it would have a specific allure for artists). And lovers are ambitious, whereas with mescaline ambition (i.e., gain) disintegrates.

Which is why the desire to smoke was eliminated as futile, human meanings grew pointless, nature (or an object) represented only itself, what happened was what happened. Eden's apple glowed a warning against exploring the independent inner mind. Nature, ignoring us, lives her own life. All moves. Nothing in the universe is calm. Perhaps an Angel is Stillness. The conscious, stripped of an instinct for self-defense, carries us to a luminous island of innocence.

Does a person carefully reared in Nature have any need of Art?

Since my mescaline excursion three weeks ago I've read the last chapter of the *récit* by Michaux, who after an overdose six times stronger than "normal" takes the reader into a new plane, and Huxley's second book *Heaven and Hell*. I don't know. As a family the four of us were accustomed to communal nudity. From birth to adolescence I saw my parents and sister naked without thinking twice, and I assumed other families followed similar comportment. Only I, at puberty (for other reasons), covered myself; but even today the rest are as they were. My behavior with persons remains as it was when I met them, i.e.; with Paul Bowles today I am again sixteen in Taxco. With someone met a week ago I act a week younger. I have separated personalities (none of which is *me*) for everyone, and with two or more persons I become what I become by rapport with the room's strongest character — or else I go "on stage" (and may be pushed off) — even when both Love and Seniority are present. Tonight, for instance, I have asked Morris, Marc Blitzstein, and Virgil T. to dine (we shall have a sirloin from Esposito's, baked potatoes with a half-pound of butter, salad with thyme, Mother's gorgeous homemade plum jam, ice cream with tangerine sauce, and my niece Mary's cookies). I shall be a child then, until the after-supper guests arrive— a host, nervous, *désintéressé*.

Joe LeSueur, as everyone knows, is Menotti's secretary now. All day long he hears the maestro composing a new opera in the next room. Gian Carlo emerges for a cup of tea and asks, "Well, Joe, how does it sound?" Joe, at a loss for words: "Well, mmm, it sounds as though something terrible is going to happen." Frank O'Hara later adds: "Something terrible *is* going to happen. He's going to finish it."

Music I hate: Flamenco, Berlioz, Viennese waltzes. Maggy, who knows I also can't stomach Schweitzer or the blind, proposes a hell wherein the good doctor conducts, throughout eternity, the music of Johann Strauss to which sightless couples dance with Spanish gusto as Hector applauds in my ear.

Last night Lee Hoiby played us his opera which only confirms my new convictions about the overall silliness of the genre. Why bother to sing such exposition as: the chamber pot has disappeared? Dwight Fisk fingered a continual elaborate improvisation as literal background to the text. His music wilted into descriptive padding but was funny because of it. Which is not to denigrate Lee, who's serious in spite of it, and whose talent is singular and necessary. Yet jealously I see these boys, all younger than I, pulling down plump commissions while I go on living with $45 a week— *too lazy to be untrue to myself*. But at least today (and tomorrow?) I am not drinking, am feeling well, not compulsive. Autumn with cold brown rain is here. Indoors it's warm and bright.

Indian Summer. How many bars have I been thrown out of or not served in? 11,509.

Mescaline. Recognition of the unrecognizable. Unfamiliarity of the familiar. The opposite of a dream. Horror of eternal repetition.

Last night again I gave a little dinner party with the same menu as Sunday but different guests: Bernie and Bob Holton with Marvin Levy, and as star Bill Inge. Later came Bill Flanagan with Edward Albee (whose new play about Bessie Smith is dedicated to me), and also Kenneth Pitchford with a poet friend. Such gatherings in my small room are expensive not only financially but in time and tension since I must not only cook but keep the conversation going without a drink myself. However today I've no hangover and there can be fire without smoke (and when some people die, they just die, and that's the end of that). Edward's cordial but pointed retort to my contention that there's been no literary theater for 150 years, is that I listen for meaning and not for sound. He feels he's been more influenced by his composer friends than by dramatists, that he will write a phrase like *"Help!"* or *"I want to go home"* less for intrinsic meaning than for its rhythm or echo of what comes before and after. As for Marvin (who one year ago devotedly helped me furnish this room from the Salvation Army, only to find the luxuriant bed a seething nest of bedbugs), he is as fond of opera as we are of the movies, and perhaps we'll find out that he (being Jewish) retains that grand tragic sense the rest of us lack. Meanwhile Kenneth's friend, who doesn't know Inge is Inge, says Inge satisfied needs of this decade (as America's foremost uncontroversial playwright) but will go out with the sixties.

This afternoon we're going to play *The Ticklish Acrobat* for Libby Holman, whom I love and when I grow up I'd like to marry, and this evening I dine at Jennie Tourel's: a day with the glamour girls. On seeing Montgomery Clift drunk as he was, how can I not recall what they all say of me: why? he's young, famous, talented, rich, handsome? why?—and there's no answer. To make a work of art does take a certain minimum of happy concentration. *Maria Golovin* herself is without interest. A month longer and she could have been.

Sobriety does not provide (for me, anyway, yet) climaxes, landmarks. A time span has usually been punctuated by a binge. Sobriety for the moment lacks contrast and life has stopped at a comma, a vast hesitation, a dull though not unpleasant disappearance of danger. My flesh is willing but the spirit is weak.

Most people aren't drunk most of the time. But: most people don't dream in color most of the time.

Had a very busy day today: very busy sleeping. The other ME is always on the verge of knocking to get in (or out), and he gets out (or in) with increasing frequency. Sunday after three dry weeks I got drunk and it took me four days to recover from the shock. It was from perversity of tension. Is it "right" to purposely sicken myself? Am I (inversely to what I've always thought) a composer to justify my alcoholism? I wish I could be nice like everyone else. Entire days pass when my only wish is to cry. I will try A.A. again.

Thanksgiving is gone.

Anything *nuancé* or delicious I might consider notating will be obliterated by a *cuite*: Sunday's was paralyzing. Beginning with a party of heavy martinis for Jean Stein at Ruth and Zachary Scott's (from whom I stole a Persian perfume bottle of apricot crystal) it finished in vomiting bile. Well. Newness is a constant change of mental decor. But Greenwich Village has lost its lights for me.

Sartori is the note G. Write a piece with the calm G (open string of second violins) sounding throughout but which we do not discover until the end. Bombard the G until it's hit. Mescaline again. My picture painted in New Hampshire was a prophecy, not a reflection of the experience. A piano is a tree flayed living with hanging brass veins. The wounds are coated with varnish.

Tyrone Power is dead.

More Titles:
    Malice in Wonderland
    Emergency Artist
    Gorgeous Numbers (essay on geometry)
    Indecent Proposals
    Certain People
    Sun
    Certain Parks

Someday the Rain
Water Music
Dignified Funerals
Many Many Movie Magazines
The Question Remains Unanswered But Is Resolved
The Answer's Always There But We Never Listen
Smoke Without Fire

The Ticklish Acrobat. To John Myers, exasperating though he is, most of us owe a lot. Publicly he remains in the background, but it's curious to realize that a decade ago he was New York's chief Renaissance-type promoter for its own sake of the then avant-garde — whatever it was. If George Sanders worked in the *commedia dell' arte* that would be John, glass in hand with swirling cubes, moving unshyly with shrill opinion among the great or the grand, making them (through convincing persuasion or plain annoyance) cough up. It's beside the point now to say that if he never existed we'd have to invent him, or if it weren't him it would have to be someone. It's time to give John Myers his dubious due. Although fidelity is a question of dates and I now feel hampered by John's endorsement (we can't remain eternally beholden for past favors), he was nevertheless directly responsible for my introduction into the *View* milieu; for all my early theater music from Kurt Seligmann's puppet shows of 1945 through Maria Piscator in 1949 to *Suddenly Last Summer* last winter; for Larry Rivers' portrait, and my collaborations with Herbert Machiz; and for being a friend of music which he really knows nothing about. (But who does?) At the moment he's flattered me and Kenward Elmslie into nearly completing a musical based on Hivnor's *Ticklish Acrobat.* ("Ned darling, you've got to make *money*! Put your fingers in *every* pie! Take Broadway by *storm*! You're more gifted than *anyone*! Herbert will make you *famous*!") However, I doubt if this collaboration will leave ground: it's difficult to be simple. Especially for me — accustomed to writing recital songs, straightforward but for skilled voices with wide ranges — it's harder to tailor the tune than for, say, Auric, whose "serious" music is so knotty that when he sits down to compose a hit he throws long-hair ideas out the window and comes up with a masterpiece like *Moulin Rouge.* Besides, it's not talent that gets you to Broadway, but patience and push and

kowtowing to those tacky vulgarians who pull the strings. Money's
not my goal, my ambitions lie elsewhere. And so do John's, really.

Mary's Bar on Eighth Street. It is already eleven summers ago that
John Myers and Frank Etherton worked there, whining the tunes
Paul Goodman and I composed for them: *Bawling Blues, Jail-Bait
Blues, Near Closing Time.* Occasionally, for comic relief, Eugene
Istomin would play *Ondine* on the tuneless piano and the drunks
would actually stop talking. Eighth Street's changed a lot but we have
not. We are all for sale. And let's be careful. Because we aren't much
maybe, but we're all we've got.

Like sieves we should retain only what is needed. A first impression
or sweet recollection can be wrecked by reworking. In before-&-after
ads, in Hollywood overhauling of starlets, it's always the first version
that's more authentic. A ballet rehearsed on an empty stage, an unfinished poem, seem often more expressive than a final product, for
in them we perceive the honest labor procedures which artists later
hide. As soon as the painter's given what he wanted, his job, for his
purpose, is over. Of course there's always the being nice to rich people,
though finishing schools (do they still exist?) don't make finer folks.
Do I mean all that?

Tomorrow I will make a record of five of my songs with Patricia Neway.
And after that I'll go to the ballet with Libby Holman, who's lately
been trying to convert me to Zen—except that I've always "had" it;
it's just that now it's been given a title. It is the poor man as creative
artist. There are thousands more saints than great composers.
        The demon of sobriety. Perhaps all sober people are really drunks
who don't know it. It's not fright. It is boredom.
        For the past year my sexuality has been shabby, to say the least,
through an increasing inability (or un-desire) to concede on American terms. Suddenly I'd rather live alone and hate it than *à deux* or
en masse and hate it, and France seems so far off. To think I used to

introduce myself by enclosing half-naked pictures in letters to people
I'd never seen! Christmas will soon be here.

Menotti concocted a truly eerie get-together at Chandler Cowles'.
"Everyone" was there, from Auden to Zadkine, but mostly younger
genii gleaned by Steven Vinaver. The purpose was for Great Minds
to commune and eventually collaborate, at the fee of one hundred
dollars per contribution, on what would become an evening of Album Leaves next summer at Spoleto. The eeriness came from the
silence, a silence not of communion but of embarrassment, since conversation between Great Minds is not easy and we know what its
dearth leads to. So at the liquor tray near which I'm standing demurely
in a pink bow tie given me by Bill Inge, Jack Kerouac approaches
and, with a twick, undoes the tie, saying, "You're a doll." "So are
you." "Yes, but I like girls." "Well, that's your problem." . . . Edward
has already finished his *Sandbox*, Lukas Foss his *Hellos and Good-
byes* and me with Jay Harrison *Last Day*. [Not one of which was
done at Spoleto. —N.R. 1967]

Diner en ville with Marc B. and Libby. Then the latter and I go to a
church lecture by Alan Watts. Libby Holman is not only the world's
one real female baritone capable of sustaining a consonant (and it cannot be done!), but the world's thinnest lady with a plump character:
joie de vivre of Sarah Bernhardt. I think I love her.

Last night late and glutted, stretching like a reptile and blasé as Nero,
I rolled over and said to the twenty-year-old: "Now I crave some-
thing new: nightingales' tongues or twelve red flowers to swallow."
This morning I received a dozen roses with an attached note to hope
I was still hungry. There are, then, pleasures from pain (or is it the
pain of pleasure?). The consolation is in knowing that half of New
York is as devastatedly dehydrated as I from the Christmas holidays.
But I have not written a note in three months—and that can leave
me even higher and dryer.

It's a nice day. I'm reading the Pasternak novel with passion. Dear
Eva Gauthier has died. Tomorrow is New Year's Eve. I could wish to
be elsewhere. Here I don't speak of the world's state, but I suppose
my own echoes it almost blow by blow. China like an enchanted princess comes out of a thousand years' sleep.

And why do I keep on writing this journal? Probably nobody else
will ever read it, and when *I* do there is no chronology to keep interest nor have ideas been helpfully clarified. Fear of anonymity can be
also a terrific time-waster; and finally, in the third convolution which
brings us back wiser to the starting place, all that really counts is
eating and sniffing and dreaming and hearing parrots scream and
seeing stars and faces and feeling speechless love—but *knowing* and
being *aware* of these things. *Not* diaries, for God's sake, and no
lamentations! All I've spoken so longly on what the artist is (he only
for whom there is no definition) has been merely a rational evasion
of my own lack of dedication through too much concern with personal physical effects: my living's too divided between sociability and
creation: hence alcohol as blinding joiner. Age, or rather, decrepitude,
is boredom of body. I wrote before that our flesh is willing but the
spirit grows weak, repeating ourselves nevertheless in spirit like the
seasons which rejuvenate each year as we crumble, crumble. What
we are, and what we think we need, can be mutually exclusive. Wanting love is not coping with love. I have nevertheless always had my
cake and eaten it. Tonight to end the year I'll get drunk at Norman
Singer's.

New York, Saratoga, Buffalo

As for me I would exhibit my qualities, but I am not
hypocrite enough to conceal my vices.

LAUTRÉAMONT

1959, New Year's Day
And I did. It's raining. Have an awful cold. Excess is my name. But maybe why I stay young is that I never *spend* any of myself. Does this mean I've never bought anything with myself? Beginning with the word "treble" I knew I was going to commit suicide, and was glad. As recently as six years ago I didn't know (or rather, consider) the difference between a soprano and a mezzo. Yet some of my best vocal works had already been composed. Suicide from boredom. Suicide of boredom. The suffering of boredom. Suffering of waiting. Of expectation. . . . *Male* is the principal character of this story. His younger brother John grew up nice and normal. (Remember to reread Kafka's *Metamorphosis*.)

In spite of it all (the conditioning) I am American and eat just in order to smoke, drink to screw (the next day). But the next day (hungover) I do not smoke (though I do eat). Oh, I do feel older and not "with all my life before me." The separation of the generations is so apparent, and here am I at the turning point, on a cliff. And still having the power to *will* love, yet without power to undo the suicide of waiting. American, without power not to feel guilty not to have created in months, but to have drunk, to have waited, to have squandered. The joys of glory are slim but doubtless tougher than the joys of failure. The real glory is *during* the work—when it doesn't count. (America, America.) Pasternak has certainly a different will from mine. Americans have never taken time for The Tragic. I said we wrote diaries to scold a public that doesn't react. Falling in love is always wonderful, and being in love always a bit boring.

It is very cold, very sunny. I am about to write a ballet with Valerie Bettis whose father just died.

What is waste? Where is it real, i.e., unhelpful? Is drinking, is masturbation, waste? Is death? When can we learn from it? More and more (in flashes, but increasingly frequent) I am concerned with dying. But don't let anyone stop me from crying: my routine cannot change.

What's the difference between angel and ape? There's nothing like the regrets of a hangover to keep you in love. Those self-imposed obstacles that make plants bloom.

At least the well-ordered man has time for everything. If he says he hasn't *time* to read it's just that he doesn't *like* to. He has time to love and read and work. He has time even to waste time. He's capable of all, and all these things run parallel but at different speeds, like our two lives. Time's one thing we can helpfully waste. It can be done, though not by Miss Average Man.

Beauty centers in the eyes. Narcissus is ugly since his eyes do not look out but in, projecting nothing.

There is no man who differs more from another than he does from himself at another time.

                                                            PASCAL

Saratoga Springs, June 1959
Here at Yaddo I am far from writing the nature of things I would have written if I'd written here these last five months of silence because I'm far from the things that obsessed me staying near them, namely too much of the city and its contents.

For the record it should be mentioned that last spring two of my symphonies were played in New York within a fortnight of each other. Lenny Bernstein conducted gorgeously the world premiere of the Third Symphony with his Philharmonic in April. It was the best performance of anything I've ever had anywhere: from that score of two million flytracks Lenny brought forth sounds I'd not known I'd placed there. Jay Harrison later wrote that the piece was all about being young and loving it; actually it was composed as a five-movement lament for Claude. The juxtaposition of interpretations is less ironic than the fact that the first rehearsal (which for a performance of such importance is a composer's most precious moment) coincided precisely with my appointment for an interview with Unemployment Insurance renewal. When I explained this incomprehensible situation to the interviewer (couldn't we hurry a little?) his answer was

Huh! Of such is the stuff of our nation. So I left, met Shirley, and we rushed through the afternoon to Carnegie Hall where some two hundred of what I took to be Girl Scouts were assembled with special passes to attend the rehearsal. For their delectation Lenny, upon reaching the silent 2/4 measure on page 27, let loose a Cossack-type shriek which impelled the whole orchestra into their jazzy quadruple-fortissimo entrance. The Girl Scouts were thrilled, as was I, and though the yell was not repeated in performance, it shall of course be incorporated into the final publication. As to the content of the music, so much had altered my outer and inner selves since it was written that I hardly recognized it, much less recalled the conditions under which it was made. On the same program, though, was Bill Russo's new piece whose attractive last movement featured Maynard Ferguson's trumpet which, like Truman Capote's opinions, sometimes reached pitches only dogs can hear, sticking out like a sore thumb and rather sounding like one. . . . In early May the Second Symphony received its local premiere in Town Hall under Arthur Lief. And, oh yes, last February Bill Flanagan and I (with Patricia Neway) inaugurated to Standing Room Only the first in what we hope will be a series called *Music for the Voice by Americans.* So my winter's not been completely sour and profitless. Especially since Buffalo University's invited me to be a professor there for a year, and I guess I've accepted despite the fact that they don't know that I don't know anything about music.

I believe when I leave that — being gone — nothing will change: but everything does. I believe when I leave that (being gone) all will change. Nothing does.

I think as a plant, want to *be* a plant, *am* a plant.

Gold cake filled with ants is your lover left for the whorehouse. But one of these ants is someone else's gold cake, nor can we all think similar to what we see.

It is no accident that density's an anagram of destiny and rhymes with intensity.

During these five months Frank Etherton, the trial of us all, finally committed suicide in Cuba.

Drunkenness (for me) offers a necessary contrast to the body the way apparently wars do to a massive soul.

The year (the "season" from October to May) has for me stood still. It's closed now — with The Dresden Amen. Have I chosen my own condition?

Art *is* a camp, let us face it (*let's* face it). So's suicide . . . (comment on elision).

The most feminine of the masculine is still infinitely more masculine than the most masculine of the feminine. (Or: queens in drag are still butcher than bulldikes.) Ah! the humorless camp, the campless humor of it all! "Oh, he's a real she-devil! She was a real man: much muscles, much hair! (much feathers!)." So Jake and Tony then removed the pins from their silver hair which fell to the shoulders. Little Mrs. Pearl Fisher just laughed to see such sport, and so did Miss Joyce Twelve. They filled out the application blanks as follows:

Sex: male   Sex: housewife
Occupation: housewife   Occupation: male
                    Sex: Italian
                    Sex: *U*

There are games for which I no longer have the patience, and no one ever does the unexpected anymore.

Now I want to say it, *Now!* And by the time it's printed it won't make any difference anymore. . . .

Not Venice, but memories of Venice.

I don't like cripples (including especially the blind), or the aged, or children (their self-conscious vanity), or the Chinese, or the irritating and noisy confusion of women's purses, and elbows and voices.

And I don't like people who say Cleo*pah*tra (instead of Cleo*pay*tra), or H*igh*awatha (instead of H*ee*awatha), or seerup (instead of surup), or *cairamell* (instead of carmel).

But time passes and once again I can admire the greatness of Rachmaninoff, of Sibelius.

NED ROREM
Will commit suicide
next Tuesday the 24th at 9:30 P.M.
in his New York apartment — 247 West 13 Street
You are cordially invited to attend.
R.S.V.P.

(He used to be as handsome as he is today.)

Till now I've not conceded nor taken the world on any but my own terms. As for the Beat Generation—we learn only what we wish to learn. How are these parties different from those I've been attending all my life? Ginsberg lacks the dignity of Sartre because he practices which he *thinks* he preaches! The followers, almost by definition, can never really grasp their leaders' thoughts; but they have more "fun." They preach what they practice.

Unfortunately I can't get it up for people with money. I'm as ashamed of using the key of C as of biting my fingernails or liking cake. For this is self-indulgence and the easiest way out. I am vaguely hysterical and frightfully calm; I have kissed my own lips. (No: my own lips have kissed me.)

I never mean what I say. If that statement is true, it is therefore false. Ad infinitum. I never say what I mean, nor do the French who converse on simultaneous levels and take any side so long as the speech may glitter and rebound like a tennis racket or (as in the case of Cocteau) a silver handball. But Americans take things at face value, which makes them so boring in the parlor and terrifying in bed. "Hope I'll be as pretty as you when I'm your age," said the elderly gentleman to the blind nymphet. Lana Turner backward becomes Anal Renrut.

While watching carp in the lake of Yaddo:

If all life—or more generally, all creation—results from the union of male with female, then couldn't our galaxy be such an offspring, a birth bang? Couldn't the answer be found in searching with telescopes those parents, and theirs and theirs, and their extending like a V forever? In the beginning were two words: father and mother. . . . Do we inhabit a masculine or feminine universe? Will it eventually divide like the amoeba or mate like a man?

Tomorrow I return to Manhattan where (since my apartment's sublet) Libby [Holman] will let me use her top floor and piano for a couple of weeks. And thank God! because I've got all these *speeches* to write about music from inside out. From there I'll go to Philly for a month, then to Maggy Magerstadt's in Fish Creek for another month, and then—O Lord—to Buffalo! Libby, meanwhile, has become a loyal and hospitable friend—just at a time when I was convinced I'd never allow more people into my life. Naturally, like anyone not born rich she's unclear about that money beyond cultivating the widest variety of daffodil in America and sponsoring her own recitals which are more stimulating than anyone's in this dead day of the voice. Eventually she'll turn away from the crippled, the lost, the vain, and get solidly married. Then I shall lose her, as one loses most of one's men friends and all of one's women friends with weddings.

Order is the acceptance of incompatibility. Or: marriage is chaos accepted.

> *I've often thought that I would like*
> *To be the saddle of a bike.*
>
> AUDEN

Zeus and Hera quarreled, each claiming the other's sex was more capable of gratification. To prove the point they called in the hermaphrodite Teresias.

"Who has more fun in bed, Teresias, man or woman?"

"Woman."

In fury Hera struck Teresias blind. In compassion Zeus bestowed foresight upon him.

For so hard I think on man the thought crumbles into absolute un-nature. . . .

PAUL GOODMAN

The bachelor, simply because he's used to it, will confront oncoming solitude with more felicity and circumspection than the widower. Now the confirmed bachelor is probably pederastical, since the sexuality of 99 out of 100 unmarried men over forty is suspect, and the 100th is no Casanova but a hermit. Of course it doesn't follow that a homosexual is more circumspect and felicitous than a hetero (we know better), but then again it's not sure he's *less* so. But he *is* more versed in loneliness, thanks to his dubious talent for promiscuity.

I speak of it as a thing with a future as yet badly done by amateurs neglecting the opportunity to be discriminating.

KAY BOYLE

A Turkish bath, like the Quaker service, is a place of silent meeting. The silence is shared solely by men, men who come uniquely together not to speak but to act. More even than the army, the bath is by definition a male, if not a masculine, domain. (Though in Paris, whimsically, it's a lady who presents you your *billet d'entrée*, robe and towel.) There are as many varieties of bath as of motel, from the scorpion-ridden hammams of Marrakech, where like Rimbaud in a boxcar you'll be systematically violated by a regiment, to the carpeted saunas of Frisco, where like a corpse in a glossy morgue you'll be a slab of flab on marble with Musak. There is no variety, however, in the purpose served: anonymous carnality. As in a whorehouse, you check interpersonal responsibility at the door; but unlike the whorehouse, here a *ménage* might accidentally meet in mutual infidelity. The ethical value too is like prostitution's: the consolation that no one can prove you are not more fulfilled by a stranger (precisely because there's no responsibility to deflect your fantasies—fantasies which now are real) than by the mate you dearly love, and the realization that Good Sex is not in performing as the other person wants but as you want. You will reconfirm this as you retreat into time through every bath of history.

For decades there has existed in central Manhattan one such establishment, notorious throughout the planet but never written about. Certainly this one seeks no publicity: word of mouth seems sufficient to promote its million-dollar business. Located in the heart of a wholesale floral district, there's small chance that an unsuspecting salesman might happen in for a simple rubdown, the nearest hotel

being the Martha Washington—for women only. The customers do
constitute as heterogeneou; a cross section as you'll ever find. (There
are only two uncategorizable phenomena: the care and feeding of
so-called creative artists, and the nature of a Turkish bath's clientele.)
Minors and majors, beatniks and bartenders, all ages and proclivi-
ties of the married and single, the famous and tough, so *many* from
Jersey! but curiously few mad queens because it's hard to maintain
a style stark naked. To run across your friends is less embarrassing
than cumbersome: who wants gossip now?

You enter at any age, in any condition, any time of night or week,
pay dearly for a fetid cubicle, and are given a torn gown and a pair of
mismated slippers (insufficient against the grime that remains in your
toes for days). You penetrate an obscure world, disrobe in private
while reading graffiti, emerge rerobed into the public of gray wan-
derers so often compared to the lost souls of Dante, although this
geography is not built of seven circles but of four square stories each
capable of housing some eighty mortals. Once, you are told, this was
a synagogue; today it's a brothel lit like *Guernica* by one nude bulb.
The top floor is a suite of squalid rooms giving onto a corrodor from
The Blood of a Poet with background music of a constant pitty-pat,
whips and whispers, slurps and groans. The second floor, more of
same, plus massive dormitory. On the ground floor are cubicles, a
television room, a monastic refectory. The basement contains fringe
benefits: a dryer, a massage room, a large dirty pool, and the famous
steam-room wherein *partouzes* are not discouraged.

The personnel, working in shifts, comprises at any given time
some ten people, including two masseurs and a uniformed policeman.
Each of these appears dull-witted due to years of inhaling the gloomy
disinfectant of locker room and hamburger grease.

There are feast and fast days, rough Spanish mornings and sneaky
afternoons, even Embryo Night at the Baths. Eternal motion, never
action (meaning production): despite a daily ocean of orgasm the
ceaseless efforts at cross-breeding could hardly make a mule. Not from
want of trying: at any time you may witness couplings of white with
black, beauty with horror, aardvark with dinosaur, panda with pachy-
derm, skinny-old-slate-gray-potbelly-bald with chubby-old-slate-gray-
potbelly-bald, heartbreakingly gentle with stimulatingly rugged—
but always, paradoxically, like with like. Your pupils widen as a faun
mounts that stevedore, or when a mountain descends on Mohammed.

Some cluster forever together in a throbbing Medusa's head; others disentangle themselves to squat in foggy corners, immobile as carnivorous orchids, waiting to "go up" on whatever passes. There's one! on his knees, praying with tongue more active than a windmill in a hurricane, neck thrown back like Mata Hari's and smeared with tears nobody notices mingling with steam. All are centered on the spasm that in a fraction switches from sublime to ridiculous, the sickening spasm sought by poets and peasants, and which, like great love, makes the great seem silly. . . . Yet if at those suburban wife-swapping gangbangs there's risk of pregnancy, these mirthless matings stay sterile — not because the sexes aren't mixed but because the species *are*.

If you don't believe me, says Maldoror, go see for yourself. You won't believe it *of* yourself, the money and months you've passed, a cultured person lurking in shadows governed by groin! Did you *honestly* spend the night? Can you, with your splitting head, manage it down the hall to pee, through shafts of black sunlight and idiot eyes and churning mouths that never say die, and crunched on the floor those tropical roaches you hadn't noticed last evening? Don't slip in the sperm while retching at the fact that it's 8 A.M. and there's still a dull moan and a sound of belts (they've really no sense of proportion). So leave, descend while cackling still rends the ear, reclaim that responsibility checked with your wallet. Hate all those bad people; or, if you will, feel lightened and purged. Allow the sounds to dim — the anticlimactic puffing and shooting and slippery striving, the friendless hasty jerkings that could fertilize a universe in the dirty dark (*quel embarras de richesses!*). Quit the baths to go home and bathe, but make clear to yourself that such uncommitted hilarity doesn't necessarily preclude a throbbing heart. For three times there you found eternal love.

With "Oedipal types" it's not mothers but fathers that are loved and sought.

Buffalo, November 1959
Again, five months later.

I write less and less in this book. Instead of daily, weekly, it's now semi-annually, and even then without length or drive. Journals, of course, are a European preoccupation; and here in America, after more than two years, my interests are centered elsewhere than auto-biography (though certainly — alas! perhaps — not in love affairs). So there is not an urge to explain how I've come to Buffalo as professor in the 37th year, but only to notate the accumulated store of anecdotes, now devoid of spontaneity.

Why must every day be an exceptional day for me? killing myself in order to live? The pretense of caring. Literally. Not a week passes but I consider suicide — the vanity of bars, of people, of liquor, of work. Locked in the cage of veins, the constricting net that still (at thirty-six) Christianly inhibits adventure. Then abandon myself to it (only, though, with wine), finding always what I most abhor yet most perceive: mediocrity. Thoughts gain order today in talking of music (not writing it), and scant need of diaries.

How recite the death toll so long later? Billie Holiday went in July with more tears from me than for Landowska in August. She reigned undiminishing and ever-glamorous over my generation.

Excessive moderation. My dying words will be: "When I grow up — !"

I am now a professor at Buffalo University. This diary will therefore by definition become "A Self-Portrait of an Artist as a Middle-Aged Man." But *Self-Portrait* implies a certain objective knowledge I no longer have: today I understand less about me than ever: I may know what I am, but not who. *Artist* once implied a man of superior, or at least special, qualities set apart either by himself or by society; in that sense the word is now completely out of fashion. And *middle-aged* suggests precisely that, and is a state which, though I may be facing it, I don't wish to focus on.

As for Art with a Capital A, it no longer means anything — at least to the young who now make the laws, set the tone, dictate the future. For them art is where they find it, not necessarily framed in museums or formally presented from concert stages by genteel con-ductors or ladies in long dresses. It is no longer in the sacrosanct crea-tion of one ego who signs his name big, but rather in the thawing snow out there, or happening among us here (*happening* is specifically the word), in the environment, the popular, the communal. For the first time ever there is a new definition, the only restrictions being time and space—and then not always. The nineteenth-century of worshipful romantic ostracism is over, and we have retreated—or rather advanced again—into a period of group communication, although the subject matter is usually "lack of communication," at least in the movies, which are today's healthiest expression.

Today's *un*healthiest expression is music, which, inasmuch as it has serious intentions, has become, for elite and commoner alike, a great big bore. Throughout the planet there has been disseminated a disgust for sound. Accomplished musicians and sophisticated laymen alike no longer find listening to concert music very attractive. This is partly due to the oversaturation of music through Muzak (you can look away from paintings, but you can't listen away from pieces), partly to the standardization of subscription concerts which play only Beethoven, and partly (so far as the avant-garde is concerned) to the intellectualization of music which paradoxically alienates the intellectuals. The "In" audiences today (as usual, a Mutual Admiration Society) may cheer loud, but the cheering is mirthless. As to ecstatic swooning, perish the thought! The language, having become academically accepted internationally, is now a sort of neutralized Esperanto devoid of character; everyone's writing the same piece somewhat as Action Painters all paint one picture. It's not facetiously that I esteem jazz (or folk, or rock, or whatever it's called) more highly than I do most of my so-called serious colleagues. These new young performers at their best make tunes equal to Schubert—better, so far as I'm concerned—harmonies more satisfying than the most ingenious Frenchman, and perform with the nuance of our greatest vocalists against orchestrations that have at once more ingenuity and simplicity than anyone else's. Their real power for the young though of course comes through their words, their poems.

For it's the vocal or visual, not the abstract-auditory, which are the preemptive arts today: they echo most coherently the incoherence of our time. Which is why movies are now the healthiest expression. (Though for me they always were.) Young artists, what's more, seem less and less involved with easel painting, and more and more with the movable. They turn to movies or to choreography.

Whereas for over a decade American music — *all* music — has been treading water in the four currents of serial, jazz, chance, and (for want of a better term) conservative, which flowed from different directions toward an ultimate point without merging or broadening or bursting into a geyser. The composers, floundering in an *embarras de richesses* and unsure about which way to turn, ended by turning away from music and toward prose. Their prose was an explication of their work, since it was no longer possible, as the saying goes, to let the music speak for itself. Whatever the future holds by way of purely musical vitality, the American composer as a verbally articulate phenomenon (contrary to the painter or movie-maker who practice trades which, for the moment, are more vigorous than music and so don't need explaining) has come to be the accepted thing today.

The art of music (or the craft of sound, or whatever you now choose to call it) is. . . .

My discipline avoids the actual. Whenever I pick up a newspaper my mind wanders. On purpose?

I count things, everything, why? Count and recount the pendants on Ellen Adler's chandelier, recount and recount the spots on Bill Flanagan's wall, the strands in his rug; count and count again the notes on a staff in my brain. A mania, phobia of counting. Why? Could it be I'm a 12-toner *manqué*?

The young today, it seems, all smoke pot. How *démodé* my drinking seems to them. And yet to me how *démodé* already is their psychoanalysis which gears them to accept rather than to examine bourgeois standards.

Anecdotes are a diary's heart's blood. Yet their annotation requires more skill and patience than philosophic musings (not to mention love affairs, which are immobile). Comedy, as everyone knows, is tougher than tragedy.

I make lists. To remind myself of everything, even to shit. The lists are iron rules—what was written must be performed. To remind myself even to make a list. Existence is a list. This book, in a sense, is a mere reminder that I have lived. . . . Oh words, words, why? Is there not intelligent silence? Does anyone care, finally, that the musician has *expressed* himself? Could he not sit merely on a park bench considering how he doesn't wish to notate, to notate forever, but let his posterity be absorbed and—so to speak—disseminated by the fabulous clouds?

And if this book, these books, are ever published in hard print, how much will be even myself of the past?

What if I now were to say (to confess!) that this whole diary's been a hoax, a red herring, a fiction to make myself interesting! Would (could) it, for that, *be* a hoax? Are my lies lies, and therefore the truth? Could even I know the answer? Do I? You'll never know.

I've never let myself go all the way—in loving, suffering, drinking, composing. Each is reined to prevent its infringing on the others. So they all diminish.

To feel, one must think. Yet to think—at least for me—precludes feeling. Seldom have I loved for the "sake" of loving, to have loved and lost, that is, been lost in love—in the *act* of love. Though surely I've been lost in the *thought* of love. I think I feel.

An artist's duty is not to present solutions, but to clarify dilemmas so that the public will seek solutions. For an artist is concerned with all, and "all" has no one solution. If a man is capable of resolving satisfactorily his exposed dilemma, the dilemma is by definition limited; so such a man is not an artist but a scientist or craftsman. I'm not sure I believe this—at least insofar as it relates to music.

Another gorgeous torture: lack of privacy. To be forever naked and alone within an illuminated plate-glass cell surrounded by an audience rotating twenty-four hours a day. But (not unironically) you are permitted any behavior.

Must there be a point to every story? Do you like killing two birds with one stone? . . . Rich Chinese, it's told, once feasted on the raw gray matter of living monkeys. After fixing the animal's head in a vise, the gourmet took a jade instrument which, in one whack, scalped the creature like a soft-boiled egg, exposing alive the delicacy of its steaming brains. Like the eggs and meat provided by today's factory-poultry which are, so to speak, born in their coffins, the skull of a monkey (as he expired) once provided both soup dish and soup.

  — *Et pourtant vous serez semblable à cette ordure.* . . .

The girl with the bat in her hair screams so loudly she can't hear the screams of the bat.

Inconvenience of coincidence. Two lovers (desperately, intimately in love), on saying good-bye in the morning make a date for that evening. But during the day they unexpectedly meet on the street. What can they say to each other now? What, out in the busy world where both are pressed for time?

After a labyrinthine correspondence with Theodore Roethke, letters of practical suspicion and mutual praise, the settings of his eight poems are finally completed for Alice Esty. Because — and not despite the fact that — my heart wasn't in them, they've turned out to be great songs. (For musicians the heart is a dangerous vulgarian.) To celebrate, I took a long weekend away from the strenuous Buffalo blizzards and flew to New York for the usual pastimes.

  Edward [Albee] took me to his *Zoo Story* which plays even better than it reads, and which he himself observed as for the first time with that damn inscrutable Cheshire smile. He's clearly quite pleased with himself, as I too am with him; and now, never really having had him, I shall lose him forever since, in a manner of speaking, he too's had a wedding.

Jay Harrison, housed with not only Jane and their two infant daughters but now with his stepmother, the maid, the nurse, and a female English sheepdog named Oboe, declares in distraction: "Do you realize I'm living surrounded by twenty-two tits!" (The dog has five pair.)

Nice ladies sit with their legs together, virile gents with theirs apart, contrary to the positions they'll probably assume in sexual intercourse. And now I'm back in the snows of the north.

A student contralto asks: "Before I sing this song of yours, Mr. Rorem, could you explain what the words mean?" "The words mean what my music tells you they mean." What more do I know about poetry?

On the bus I sit next to a girl engrossed in *The Buffalo Evening News*. Her bovine eyes are caressing an image of myself printed there in advertisement of next week's concert. I lean over to see more clearly. She turns on me with a snarl.

Well, yes I did go back to Chicago for three days last August — to hear Wallenstein do my symphony at Ravinia — and then on to visit dear Maggy in Wisconsin. The return, and mescaline, were the *important* events of my thirties. How not to cry when nothing changes but one's self? When for the first time in thirteen years one visits the scene of childhood crimes? Nothing, *nothing* was different, except there were no parents to call out to. Sunlit vines on our building were no thicker than memory; smells, wind, the time of day, converged to make the past the present. The recall of roller skates, easy on the tarred street, less pleasant on the rough cement, that cement which still contained a clean N.R. scrawled there a quarter-century back when it was soft. The bright Chekhovian parlor where first I wrote music, and thought of (and practiced) the sexual privileges (stigmas at least have benefits).

Bruce Phemister rescued me from brooding as we covered all Hyde Park at sunset, past the Oriental Institute and "Juliet's Garden" of the Theological Seminary, past Jackman Field, where our high school ghosts playing goalies gave a lackadaisical kick at the soccer ball — preferring to discuss Debussy or Dietrich, past his mother's lilac garden which so many thousand midnights ago intoxicated our poems. Lake Michigan, and her saxophones of the Palm Grove Inn wailing into the summer watered lights purpler than the cake frosting we swam in. Was it us? Or was that all I can really write now for another five months?

PART 11
1960–61

Saratoga, New York,
Buffalo, New York

"How wonderful to be alive," he thought.
"But why does it always hurt? God exists, of course.
But if He exists, then it's me."

Doctor Zhivago

Mais, vrai, j'ai trop pleuré.

RIMBAUD

Yaddo (Saratoga Springs) June 1960
Not five, but more than seven. And only a few pages back I was in
Yaddo a year ago.

The odor of orange on my fingertips retrieved Morocco today in
a flashing dream of the whole decade, doubtless because I'm engaged
in reading (with a certain enjoyable boredom) the Durrell tetralogy.

The diary, recording, somehow removes the bloom from memory.
The scrapbook is a morgue. But anonymity still scares; and if now I
see that old photographs prevent new life, I know too I'll really die.
Which is why I don't tell tales here (or even *write* any longer) — but
eat, like a child and monkey, my own pubic lice, crabs, *quoi de plus
naturel?* The world (my own) of that stranger, the heart of the crotch —
complete and complacent — goes off and ignores me into other worlds.
We go nowhere. So I write in the air (have you tried it?). Write in the
air and attempt to separate the words. You can't. The invisible ink
retreats oozing into the clenched fist more maddening than the weary
slapstick of vaudevillians with Scotch tape.

Sailor. Sailors. Feeling almost assured the café was empty, I nevertheless had to see for myself. It was. But no sooner home than I felt
it filling up. On returning, to my horror, I found it overrun.

Women argue that they've never been given a chance. Chances are
taken, not given.

Poets, why do they complete their public readings: "And now, to end
on a cheerful note"! Would they say this if their chief preoccupation
were *not* cheerful? To leave behind the truest ectoplasm they'd do
better to end on a somber note.

A painter with his variety of styles through the years retains a
same signature. No, not even his handwriting alters.

Inscription, latrine wall, men's room of Deco's, Washington
Street, Buffalo: "Tom I was here again please come back."

Glad you're glad I'm glad you're. . . . Do not compare yourself to me though both admire the smell of man. Yet I am disinterested in anyone who is disinterested in me. I'm ever more disinterested!

Bobby Cone's drowning: most shocking is that the intellectual cannot die a shepherd's death. (Exposure.) Yet he did. At best the intellectual dies of suicide, old age, or heart attacks; at worst in auto wrecks or of drink. But as victim to the elements? Words speak louder than actions.

"Si j'étais un homme," she said to me, "j'aimerais te baiser." . . . The panic of cities. In Buffalo starlings annoyed me at 5 A.M. There, even *after* the auto wreck, I remained drunk.

Death toll (at the new year): Camus, Margaret Sullavan, Ankey Larrabee.

Some people still do care. (I *think!*) Awfully.

I've met and experienced everyone and thing I've desired. Now to compose that which I must. Or rather to come to life. Come to Death? END is an anagram of NED. Oh.

July (Yaddo)

Boredom springs eternal in the human breast. Not to speak of the suffocating shock of sterility now that I'm *supposed* to create. Yaddo's a luxurious concentration camp where I can neither camp nor concentrate, hence the luxury's guilt-making. While everyone else is busy doing poems and pieces and pictures (as though it made a difference) I stay reading, wondering why I have to be a composer — still, still dictated by terms of alcohol and unoriginal sin. Their outside impression is of my gross generalities, when really I'm (not so much aggressively shy as) bored, bored, the mind miles off. But off where?

Fourteen years ago Klaus Mann stung my thigh with morphine and killed himself. Yes, the diary, the scrapbook stunts, sucks, and gluts, allows experience only for the sake of altered memories. So I fly with voluptuous gluttony out into a night of the park to see about living. Grand illusion of love, of even sex. Flinging mucous or fingernails about, or sperm, or hairs in a comb, sections of Ned scattered in earth. An impotent three weeks — and in three months or more I'm thirty-seven.

But there are tantalizing contemplative consolations. For instance the dolphins. We now learn of their intelligence, their undersea language. They've glided far past logic not caring that they don't know that they know that they just like happily *to be*. Aren't we finally wise enough for migration into water? We'll walk upside-down on the undersurface of the lake (mirroring Jesus) as though gravity were in the sky. Swim *down* to the surface. Conspire with the porpoise. Smart purpose.

Well, at least Nature (as they say) is all around, notably in the form of baby swallows (I could use a grown-up swallow), daily hurricanes, and (when I walk into Saratoga for the laundry or something) massive mosquito flocks holding on like pilot fish. Do I indeed stand in my own way, fashion my own impediments? Or suffer, like others here, from a terrible handicap (!): no talent. It's not talent but enthusiastic patience, a missing ingredient. I'd rather go deaf than blind. But I'm not *visual! Mais justement!* In Europe, not being a "success" doesn't mean you're a flop.

I said to Joe LeSueur: "I've decided to become charitable." His answer: "Really? How do you intend to go about it?" And he quotes Maugham: "It's not enough that I succeed, my friends must fail." Then adds: "It's not enough that I fail, my friends must fail."

The difference between that eternal aggravation: "What do you like?" "Everything," and: "What do you like?" "Anything."

Communication. How I hate the word. Communication indeed! Tonight we saw northern lights. Green.

Am I also really going to die? *La vie s'arrête pile.* The breath is caught. Can't believe it.

My Flute Trio is finished and never have I written a work with less enthusiasm. The drunken spontaneity is, for me, today gone from *all* music. On the other hand I'm obsessed with my theater. Yet, seated before the famous blank sheet, about to type the first phrases of a drama, I write: Who am I to think of making a play? And even those words look pretentious. What? Humility! But it's not for nothing I've been fifteen years diaryzing.... Working title: *The Pastry Shop* (a monologue for Judith Malina).

Haven't had a drink in about eight weeks. Beginning to feel the need. I *must* sometimes, to allow the other "me" (more schizoid than Joanne Woodward's Eve) to get some air. And I *must* recall the hangover, the lovely hangover with a head like a sizzling watermelon when I sit on the toilet, scarcely human, reading praiseworthy clippings about myself, and thinking thickly: is that me? By accident two weeks ago I was offered a glass of tonic containing a *soupçon* of gin; my reaction disturbed for days; all or nothing is how it is since I was released from high school twenty summers back. Salt, salt in tangerine tones.

"Sometimes it rains on Thursday," he lied. He always lied. And the dyke who announced: "Be back later, kids. Gotta go home and take a shit, a shave and a shower."

For myself I have, in principle, stopped swearing.

Because of always falling in love with puzzling women I've solved the riddle through simple men. What a solution! Great emotions I put off till next week: " . . . he shrank from every connection with the actual because he saw therein a threat to the possible. The potential was his kingdom. . . . " —*Dr. Faustus*

Povla Frijsh died last month. So did Ellie Kassman. "Death is the mother of beauty," said Wallace Stevens. Idyll, Idle, Idol, Ideal.

August. In Philadelphia to visit Rosemary and her five children as antidote to a frenzied New York week of lust, liquor and laziness which in turn was antidote to two months of Yaddo where I painfully ejected a flute trio and easily produced a little play: *The Pastry Shop.* Yaddo is for me (have I said it?) *the concentration camp de luxe* — but purposed: starting today and tomorrow the days and tomorrows start to blend indistinguishably! But in New York days blend with *nights* — and each separate pair is jagged — not smooth; where all I do is drink, walk the streets, and when people say aren't you a composer? how can I stay home when other people don't — or if they do, how do they dare when I don't? Tonight I went with Rosemary to see Brigitte Bardot.

Back in New York now. And more drinking, more and more, interlaced with movies and the Turkish bath, hay fever and procrastination, dental devastating work and huge bills. Heat wave, and the day's a smear.

Write children's piano pieces with as titles Colors & Days, Numbers & Months: Blue, Tuesday, Four, October, Yellow, Saturday, Seven, February. Some for right-hand alone, some for left.

Write a nonvocal piece on words, like Beethoven's *Muss es sein? Es muss sein!* Then eliminate the words. Or — going farther than Berio — set a poem, then sing it backwards, first by words, then syllables, finally letters. Symmetry. Or: song for two voices with overlapping of syllables: one voice continues where the other leaves off, in midstream. Also simultaneous crescendo and decrescendo on same note. . . . The word *gold* has six sounds, a double tripthong: guh-ah-oh-oo-ll-d.

Write a piece containing as much as possible of the hate I have for the world, for you, all you, of how alone I feel, how alone, yet how the aloneness will not be reduced by being less hateful.

September, chez Morris, Water Island
No I'm not particularly happy, yes I am particularly sad, and for reasons more concrete than fifteen years ago, namely, I'm fifteen years older, and do they stop dead in the street anymore? Of course no love. Depressed for this country we inhabit, which belongs to me as well as you, which we've destined for chaos soon. Thrill at visions of the young (who'd have thought it would come to that?), and Youth is Beauty, Beauty Youth. Requiem for the West. Our work, if we like it, is the *compensation* which remains the most faithful friend. Such

vivid bromides are in keeping with the lonesome fawn décor of this isle. "Well," they ask, "what is more terrible than unhappiness?" Oh, I don't know. Boredom, I suppose. Because unhappiness is at least active, whereas boredom has never, I think, made adrenalin flow. And time won't tell. Yet as Bill F. pointed out the other day: for the likes of *us* the future lies in a latrine.

October

Back in Buffalo. Cool already. Smell of bonfires and pencil shavings: going-back-to-school weather. Tom Prentiss in South Wales is a boon.

The Pastry Shop. Suddenly everyone's shocked at what I've written there. As though for twenty years I hadn't been composing obscenities in music! But what *is* obscene in the elusive "meanings" of nonvocal music? Light as black, heavy as white. Compose a hateful quarrel, all done softly.

The other night without explanation I waited at home. The more I waited the more love grew. Three hours late the person arrived: love wilted on the spot.

An equality permitting dislike of certain Negroes as much as certain whites, a freedom to choose enemies as we choose friends. And that, without the scrutiny of "progressives" with inverted prejudice (everyone, provided he is an underdog, is good!) or the I-told-you-so attitude of "reactionaries" with more direct resentment (everyone, provided he is an underdog, is bad).

No white American can—under any circumstances nor by whatever transference—know what it is to be a Negro, because he does not of necessity think of himself as white, whereas the Negro of necessity always thinks of himself as black.

Well, in those Manhattan weeks, the dentist revamped my bite to the tune of nearly $900. And I gave two parties. After the second one, while drinking a sixteenth gin-and-tonic at a bar *mal-famé* near the Cherry Lane Theater (the last of the disreputable taverns to tolerate my presence: in the Village now I'm permitted only in respectable bars!) a nondescript person engaged me in an *entretien* the upshot of which was that his envy of my person provoked a desire not for rape but for strangulation. I, being drunk, was intrigued, but understood (why explain) that he meant this, and that he had committed such "crimes" in the past. But when my friends approached he vanished, and I only recalled his words and nervous hands in my hungover sheets next day. Now I ask you, is this the proper company for America's tenth most-played composer?

Yesterday I was thirty-seven. Ah. Today already it's snowing. That's Buffalo. Title: *The Disgusting Birthday.*

I am staying home from school (as when a child) with aches and sore throat, canceling appointments and just let the wind howl outside. Small wonder: overdrinking and overworking both with mediocre people. Drinking to get laid (and don't) and working on my speech and Weill's *Jasager* with a conscientiousness unfocused. Nobody knows what most people are talking about most of the time, but most of the time it makes no difference. A difference that's important is the (subtle) one between articulation and communication.

Yes, feeling sick, staying home, day and night drenched in soggy odoriferous naps—you know. Not sick enough to sleep—too sick to work—just think and resent. About the shock of the famous. The shocks of growing up to see that great poets are not only personally as petty and vicious as "real people," but can also be fascist nigger-hating fairy-baiters. What's more they fucked and despised me—those Chicago intellectuals of my childhood. Am I fair?—being fair? Of course not: artists aren't fair. They just build better mousetraps. To tell them don't complain is more irrational than saying don't squeeze that pimple white-ripe and plangent.

Religion is through. Religion is really through. I realized this most clearly the other morning on awakening (too soon) from a hangover when all is not confused but—on the contrary—electrically delineated. Religion as such is a farce in America and no one can fail to feel this on some level.

Oh I'm ill and reeling. Today Mitropoulos died. Elliott Carter's 2nd Quartet: four madmen yell in a language I can't understand but I know their words are wonderful. Or do I understand without knowing the tongue—like birds heard through mescaline, or angels through dreams? The world ends here: that's our art speech—and not *sans humour.*

Am not now interested in writing more music. That's no way for venting current spleen. Why don't they give me time to start and finish "The Voyeuse With Poor Vision"?

Theater means: the artificial concentration of an event. All art is theater. The most tangible versions are staged.

In musical theater the broadest event is Opera, wherein a singer for several hours becomes someone else. The narrowest event is Song, wherein a singer for a brief moment becomes someone else. As to which projection is more difficult depends on training, and the emphasis of training depends on location in history.

Today we all seem more equipped for the Great Lie—the huge single schizoid split of opera, than for the White Lie, the small multiple-personality segments of the song recital. For singers this equipment is an economic necessity: there is simply no living except in opera. The young ones now are vocally oriented to decibels, psychologically to long-range transference. If ever they do sing songs they approach those songs as the obsolete is always approached—without a point of view—and usually mistreat them as arias, meaning as events bigger than life. A song is an intimate experience having less to do with mammoth scope than with miniature intensity. This last quality has become, at least in America, like a needle in a haystack. The needle is still occasionally sought and found by a rare few, such as Phyllis Curtin, who rub off the rust and try to make it serve again.

Phyllis last week braved northern New York's worst blizzard since 1902 and a fee one-fourth the size of her usual one, to fly here and prepare a Rorem-Poulenc recital (some twenty odd songs she'd never sung) simply from fondness for a dying medium and friendship for me. I love her. I love her voice even more. But I love mostly her way with a song, a way that makes her constantly a new person with each song sung, rather than the same person with each new song.

And last Thursday. My squalid evening with the young J. It is not so much his shock as my own which disturbs. For how long is it now (fifteen years? twenty?) that I've been pulling the same fiasco,

demolishing expressly my possibilities, destroying my angel by showing the whining devil—in short, killing the "thing I love"? And Friday I awoke to write this sort of hungover reflection: It hurts to look
at you, you force abjection, abjection thank God, I can still be it, it:
drunk—the only *proof* is suicide. Proof to whom?

Well, Beauty *does* hurt. Since then I've been torturing myself
with hope. Wrong numbers sound. Phenobarbital doesn't work on
me. For while it numbs my sick body, my sick brain burns and won't
be undone.

(And Friday I found I'd written also this: Cloisters and sequences
are my haven. Hot marble thoughts. Pink wasn't warm. Warm wasn't
pink. Hot marble asses. Sequences and cloisters—my haven.)

And Esther Berger now has died. So told me Sylvia Marlowe
whose fatal harpsichord case is coffin for a cyclops.

January 1961
Over the holidays in Pittsburgh there was a forum on my music (very
successful, of course) although Ormandy because of illness had to
cancel *Eagles*. Parties for me in Pennsylvania: it's quite respectable
to take the parents because they live there, while in Buffalo where
I'm professor "composers don't have fathers"—though in a pinch I
can take Mother.

This volume of the diary covers a larger span (already three and
a half years) than the others—lately because of the plays and lec-
tures and essays and teaching, plus now scant interest in love and
name-dropping and recipes and blood.

Nevertheless I passed twenty Christmas days in Manhattan slush
where for the new year I took Joe LeSueur to Ruth Ford's and there
was Garbo. (Annually the Scotts receive what are called "celebrities,"
all very on-stage. When Garbo, uninvited, walked in, they were all
suddenly off-stage. For who can do better? Joe whispered, "Is that
who I *think* it is? Promise, that whether or not we meet her, we must
say we did! Her eyes *are* larger than anyone's have a right to be.")
Later Joe took *me* to 42nd Street where—I mean it!—I'd never been,
and two days before I brought home at 5 A.M. a maniac who tore
open my hand with a broken candlestick and I was stitched at Saint
Vincent's, then next evening played good piano at Phyllis Curtin's.

See, see, even such recent looking back makes you turn salty.

I am not interested when a student explains: "But I *felt* it that way."
Justification through emotion is worthless, in music as in law. Of *course*
a composer has feelings or he wouldn't be composing. But those feelings can take care of themselves and will always show through. So I
am interested in how they can be controlled. Now a verbal explication of such control is not so easy for the "inspired" type of composer
who uses sheer sound as his guide, as for the "objective" type whose
intellectual procedures are themselves the music. This second type
is as exasperating as the first in that he categorically denies feelings
as impetus. As a teacher, then, I get it both ways.

Taste, touch and smell are for sex (i.e., survival) while the eyes, the
ears, are reserved for art.

Defiantly looking as *louche* as possible — because really we're waiting for Mother. Defiantly looking as innocent as possible — because
really we're cruising.

A writer needn't go out and live, but stay home and invent, crying
himself to sleep occasionally.
  "Do you know the *Missa Solemnis?*"
  "No, who is she?"

  Beethoven to his wife: "But you can't leave me! You're my
inspiration!"
  "Me your inspiration? That's a laugh!
                                            ha ha ha ha

Who am I to be deferred to by students? I've only myself begun to be
a composer.

This evening, to the accompaniment of Fizdale & Gold, I made my debut as actor by reciting the Pierre Loüys texts to Debussy's *Cinq Epigraphes Antiques* on my final lecture-recital in Buffalo. During the question-and-answer period, when asked my opinion of the symphony here, I replied that though it was excellent it did not—like most American orchestras do not—perform enough new music. At which point Josef Krips (who has beautifully played three works of mine, who had been my host earlier in the evening, and who was now in the audience) got up and walked out. This misunderstanding will eventually be resolved, for both Mitzi and Josef have been my good friends, and real friends just don't nurse quarrels. But it's sad that we will have to make up by mail, because tomorrow I leave permanently for New York. . . . Meanwhile I only hope the students will have gained half as much from me as I have from them: the best thing about teaching is that you learn so much.

Ides of March in the evening. The Buffalo stint is over. Back in New York.

If I never write here anymore it's because I write nothing nowhere. Haven't put down a note of music in six months—the longest ever. Been six weeks back from Buffalo, a city that never existed, harboring some unknown Ned Rorem who for a year and a half did his job in a trance brilliantly, then vanished. As indeed I have. Waiting, waiting immobile again for something (what?) while others scurry ambitiously to money and love. It's ambition here that breaks the spirit, sterilizing all endeavor: can no longer work for pleasure. These New York weeks have been blurred in frantic socializing, indiscriminate fucking, even more indiscriminate drinking. An old story. Who am I trying to fool? In less than three years I'll be forty. And next month I finally return to France seeking the insane, the grey-haired, the dead and dying, those caught in their own problems, and my not-forgotten yet vanished boyhood. Still, this is no mistake. (I wrote Virgil in Paris: "Have you seen my lost youth around?" He answered: "There's plenty of lost youth around but I don't know if any of it's yours.") It's not Paris but myself in Paris that I miss: those infinitesimal hotel rooms near Cluny with hot Algerians eleven years ago smelling of urine, novelty, despair, and *gros rouge* with radishes at noon.

Like torture, only worse. To parody Poe: Manhattan's sadomasochistic alcoholism is *"S. and M. found in a Bottle."* All nature is immune to human fleas. Witness: *People in the Snow.* Their awful, their ridiculous vulnerability. Drunk, G.L. spent the night—left his watch. A week later, drunk, some *inconnu* spent the night, stole the watch—which watch had not left its place on my mantel. I'm impervious to the inanimate ("possessions"), but that whole week a blizzard was moving, moving, killing us who are corpses on leave of absence.

April Fool's Night. In three weeks I leave for Europe.

Lovers fade from these pages like Anna from *L'Avventura*. And how I like those new movies of Antonioni seen lately with frightening Ruth Yorck! They and she know how to put one in one's place. How much more agreeably troubling to watch the rich suffer than the poor (as with De Sica): their boredom and stupidity is the same, but they are *bored in ermine*. Anyway, why are the poor, by virtue of being poor, more virtuous and intelligent than the rich? As father likes to say: "Born of poor but dishonest parents."

Opera scene: twelve minutes of music *without* singing. She waits. She wonders—as in *L'Avventura*. But she never opens her mouth. Obviously a movie opera and for Antonioni, the only great man around these days, beyond definition, like a great beached whale.

Antonioni's star is the scenery. That's not just an aphorism: what we grow closest to and come to love is not the mobile name but the inanimate place which, framed by his camera, takes on a life of its own.

The child says: when I grow up the important part will begin. As a grown-up he says: those first lost years were the important part.

When will I learn about getting older? Well, look in the mirror! Yes, but it only lies concerning right and left (meaning right and wrong). The Late Late Show informs us better of our lives' lengths: those landmarks of yesternight, that close focus on each Una Merkel pimple which looks the same though our eyes have opened and shut—how many times since 1933?

What remains between this moment and my death? How will I grow old? — as though that question were not being answered every minute! Time for a few tears now: it has, after all been so long. While writing, the lamp shines across these icky ball-point smears transparent as infant wrists, and this transparency *in itself* saddens me — inexplicable as the menopause depression. Did *high* and *low* musically to old Greeks mean any more to them on our terms than current western male & female attitudes do to, say, Hindus? That sentence is unclear: Does high in music everywhere signify up? Is the man always on top? Can a man's wish for dominance exclude the brain? and does dominance necessarily mean top? (In choruses the woman is on top, the bass sustains. A ground bass — beneath, by definition — is the essence of maleness.) Could our perversions happily invert and intermesh? Will I cease courtesanship and become The Musician With Problems? If I died today it would not really be — well, *incorrect.* Now in the shadow of late thirties looking back I've obtained the best of that sought and produced of myself (through fever, shame, dignity): an artist and a person, not perhaps to other eyes, which see shreds, but to myself at least. To announce that my advancement prefers the urgencies of pure nature to urban ambitions would be to lie. Yet where and what can I go and do that I've not gone and done better? Henceforth I foresee only declining flesh inanely coupling with reason, sputtering, a dimming of commitment, a pointless ending, a silence which is not even a silence. Yet to kill myself now would be less from not caring as from a certain wistfullness which, after all, I suppose *is* caring. . . . Already I am becoming The Musician With Problems, for many minutes have passed since I wrote Time for a few tears now: yet the gift for self-dramatization does not make nights less sleepless. Sleep isn't death. Staying awake is.

Sexual intercourse: think of it, obsessing the heart, dominating logic, teasing nights, wasting whole days! Isn't it really — well — rather silly, or at least senseless: two clumsy positions rubbing like washboards with ugly grunts and an ultimate thump that rhymes with nothing, except maybe "Go away!" — when two minutes earlier, for some wild reason, it was almost "I love you"? For that we walk the streets fifty-two weeks a year!

The horror of the carnal hunt, as though the cultural hunt weren't sufficiently atrocious.

*I am in love again for the first time. Need to giggle, to jump up and
down. Our planet, bulging with joy, seems too small,* etc.

Did I write that? Are nearly two thousand days gone since the
fall of 1956 when I met Claude? How utterly remote, the agonies
of love when they're over, while those of work remain as irksome
(to put it mildly) as Damocles' sword! The comings and goings, ris-
ings and fallings, the *breathings* of this diary appear, with the overall scope of hindsight, more steady than a sleeper's. Yet tonight,
snared by details of other years, pausing at past landmarks, I retrieve lost episodes with the identical instability of their first occurrence.

These poor journals have never been those of a musician: musically I express myself elsewhere and otherwise. Today of course they
have become (perhaps alas!) the jottings only of someone rapidly
advancing, maybe decaying, who may feel a need for the fatal backward glance. But a glance at what? Because those things which are
daily concerns are hardly discussed: family and close friends, compositions in progress, low points of the high life (as in the Paris diaries).
Not even my state of mind, just a state of body. These journals then
will provide only that backward glance toward a state of body denied or indulged. As to whether I had any life, or even lived, that
may (or may not) be seen when I'm dead—if I die.

If, after dying, I discover there's no Life After Death, will I be furious?

Not to believe in love anymore means to believe in love. One must
believe in the existence of something in order to disbelieve it.

Weary of myself. So perhaps are my friends. So perhaps is nature,
who will kill me off. But not all that soon—she doesn't love me enough.
France will rejuvenate.

If our year 1961 is the same upside-down and backward, and not until 6009 A.D. will the phenomenon recur, then we have five thousand and forty-eight years of waiting to sober up.

Sitting in one denuded Manhattan room whose center contains a mountain of packing cases to be removed tomorrow by Robert Phelps. Without paying last month's rent I fly Friday for London, meanwhile have already left, can only sit, wondering, in this denuded room for five days more.

Wondering about those three things (and there are only three) we all desire: success in love, success in society, success in our work. Any two of these may be achieved and possessed simultaneously, but not all three — there isn't time. If you think you have the three — beware! You're teetering on an abyss. You can't, with everyone's equalized happiness, have a lover *and* friends *and* career. And even just career and love, despite what they tell you, are, in the long run, mutually exclusive.

Ignorance of the future is all that can save us. We need less the time to think than the time to think about what we think. Before finding the solution we must find the problem. Love, profession, society. Now I feel less than a flop in the first two. Assuming European doors will open as before, are love or acclaim also lurking? In my glib quick wit with smiles lighting, when others say: What! you sad? that's a laugh! Yet who ever shows his "real" side — assuming there is a real side? O God, when a whole life's spent wishing we could or had, then finding ourselves *in the fact* (as though suddenly) and wondering: well, this is it, and is this all? There must be something more! People keep wondering: where does the man leave off and the artist begin? This is where.

Other titles of interest

ALVIN AILEY
A Life in Dance
Jennifer Dunning
496 pp., 27 illus.
80825-0 $16.95

CONTEMPORARY
COMPOSERS ON
CONTEMPORARY MUSIC
Expanded Edition
Edited by Elliott Schwartz and
Barney Childs, with Jim Fox
512 pp., 95 music exam., 9 illus.
80819-6 $18.95

HEAD TO TOE: A Novel
& UP AGAINST IT:
A Screenplay for the Beatles
Joe Orton
Introduction to *Up Against It*
by John Lahr
275 pp.
80836-6 $14.95

ALL AMERICAN MUSIC
Composition in the Late
Twentieth Century
John Rockwell
New preface by the author
294 pp.
80750-5 $14.95

CHARLES IVES REMEMBERED
An Oral History
Vivian Perlis
256 pp., 80 illus.
80576-6 $13.95

THE COMPANION TO
20th-CENTURY MUSIC
Norman Lebrecht
440 pp., 151 illus.
80734-3 $16.95

IMPROVISATION
Its Nature and Practice in Music
Derek Bailey
172 pp., 12 photos
80528-6 $13.95

JOHN CAGE
An Anthology
Edited by Richard Kostelanetz
237 pp., 64 illus.
80435-2 $14.95

MUSIC BY PHILIP GLASS
Updated Edition
Philip Glass
Edited by Robert T. Jones
264 pp., 50 photos
80636-3 $13.95

THE ORTON DIARIES
Edited by John Lahr
332 pp., 51 photos
80733-5 $14.95

THE COMPLETE LYRICS
OF LORENZ HART
Expanded Edition
Edited by Dorothy Hart and
Robert Kimball
367 pp., 47 illus.
80667-3 $25.00

THE COMPLETE LYRICS
OF COLE PORTER
Edited by Robert Kimball
535 pp., 13 illus.
80483-2 $22.50

THE DIFFICULTY OF BEING
Jean Cocteau
Introd. by Ned Rorem
174 pp.
80633-9 $13.95

LIBERATION WAS
FOR OTHERS
Memoirs of a Gay Survivor
of the Nazi Holocaust
Pierre Seel
translated from the French by
Joachim Neugroschel
200 pp.
80756-4 $13.95

THE DA CAPO CATALOG OF
CLASSICAL MUSIC
COMPOSITIONS
Jerzy Chwialkowski
1,412 pp.
80701-7 paperback $29.50
79666-X hardcover $85.00

THE DA CAPO OPERA
MANUAL
Nicholas Ivor Martin
752 pp.
80807-2 $24.50

SCREENING THE SEXES
Homosexuality in the Movies
Parker Tyler
New foreword by Andrew Sarris
New afterword by
Charles Boultenhouse
419 pp., 71 photos
80543-X $15.95

WARHOL
The Biography
Victor Bockris
570 pp., 53 photos
80795-5 $17.95